ON CHRISTIAN BELIEFS

Tenore presentium nos Johannes permissione divina Oxon Episcopus Notum facimus universis quod nos Episcopus antedictus die Dominica ... Animo nunc die mensis Septembris Anno Domini Millesimo Septingentesimo vicesimo quinto in Ecclesia Cathedrali Christi Oxon, Sacros Ordines Dei Omnipotentis gratia die celebratus Dilectum nobis in Christo Johannem Westley Art: Bacc ... Oxon de vita sua laudabili & morum & virtutum suarum, nobis plurimum commendatum Necnon in Sacraru Literarum doctrina & scientia sufficienter eruditum, prastito primitus per eum Juramento de Supremitate Regia potestatis in causis & negotiis quibuscunq Ecclesiasticis & temporalibus agnoscenda ad Sancta Dei Evangelia in debita Juris forma juratum: Atq insuper tribus istis Articulis in Canone Tricesimo Sexto contentis per eum sponte ac voluntarie subscriptis ad Sacrum Diaconatus Ordinem juxta morem & ritus Ecclesiæ Anglicana admisimus ipsumq in Diaconum tunc & ibidem rite & Canonice Ordinavimus Datum sub Sigillo nostro Episcopali in premissorum fidem ac testimonium die mensis Annoq Domini supra extressis & nostrae Consecrationis Anno Undecimo.

Jo. Oxon

The Bishop of Oxford, John Potter, ordained John Wesley a deacon in the Church of England on Sunday, September 19, 1725. Three years later, on September 22, 1728 Bishop Potter ordained Wesley a priest. In 1737 Bishop Potter became Archbishop of Canterbury. Always, he remained on good terms with John Wesley.

Wesley later ordained Methodist ministers for British and American Methodism. He also consecrated Thomas Coke the first superintendent (bishop) of American Methodism. Thus, all ordinations in Methodism's family of churches are based on John Wesley's being ordained deacon and Presbyter. Note on the ordination certificate that at a later date someone added a "t" to the name of Wesley. The translation of this Latin text of John Wesley's certificate of ordination as deacon follows below.

Both of Wesley's certificates of ordination are in the archives of Wesley College in Bristol, England, by whose permission this certification of his ordination as deacon appears on the facing page.

In the course of present affairs, I, John, the Bishop of Oxford, with divine permission make known to all that on the Lord's Day, the 19th of September, Seventeen Hundred Twenty-Five (1725) in the Church of Christ Cathedral at Oxford, I, the aforementioned Bishop, celebrated Sacred Orders with the help of God Almighty. John Wesley, B.A., my beloved in Christ, a student in Christ's sanctuary at Oxford, was recommended for his praiseworthy life of both character and virtue. I especially commend him for his gifts although he is not yet sufficiently learned in the Doctrine and Science of Sacred Literature. When he took the oath for the first time concerning the supremacy of royal authority in matters and affairs, which both church and state must acknowledge, he swore the oath to God's Holy Gospel in due manner of law. And moreover, when he agreed to these articles contained in the 36th canon for the Sacred Order of the Diaconate both willingly and voluntarily, as is usual, I admitted him into the rank and rite of the Anglican Church. This very man, presented to me, then and there, ritually and canonically, I ordained as Deacon under my episcopal seal in trust and testimony of the things sent me, on the day and month and in the year of our Lord noted above, and in the eleventh year of my consecration as Bishop.

—Bishop John Potter

John Wesley

ON CHRISTIAN BELIEFS

THE

STANDARD

SERMONS

IN

MODERN

ENGLISH

VOLUME 1, SERMONS 1-20

KENNETH CAIN KINGHORN

ABINGDON PRESS / Nashville

JOHN WESLEY ON CHRISTIAN BELIEFS
THE STANDARD SERMONS IN MODERN ENGLISH, VOL. 1

Library of Congress Cataloging-in-Publication Data

Wesley, John, 1703-1791.
  [Sermons on several occasions. Selections]
  John Wesley on Christian beliefs : the standard sermons in modern English, 1-20 / [edited by] Kenneth Cain Kinghorn.
    p. cm.
  Includes sermons 1-20 of John Wesley's standard sermons.
  Includes bibliographical references and index.
  ISBN 0-687-05296-3 (alk. paper)
  1. methodist Church—Sermons. 2. Sermons, English. I. Kinghorn, Kenneth C. II. Title.
  BX8217.W54 K56 2002
  252'.07—dc21

2001055256

02 03 04 05 06 07 08 09 10 11—10 9 8 7 6 5 4 3 2 1

MANUFACTURED IN THE UNITED STATES OF AMERICA

Contents

Introduction

John Wesley's life and work have earned him a place of permanent distinction in the Christian community. As the founder of Methodism, he is the spiritual father of a number of denominations and the principal creator of the Wesleyan tradition. Many stained glass windows honor his memory, innumerable books and articles detail his life, and a myriad of colleges and churches bear his name. Westminster Abby has memorialized him as a distinguished figure of extraordinary merit. Artists have produced more portraits and engravings of John Wesley than any other person in English history, with the exception of Queen Victoria.

The renowned historian Lord John Acton concluded in his survey of the eighteenth century that "in universality of influence and in range of achievement, he [John Wesley] was more important than any."[1] Even Wesley's enemies conceded that he was an unusually gifted and effective leader. Bishop William Warburton objected to his "enthusiasm," but admitted, "He was formed of the best stuff Nature ever put into a fanatic." William Edward Lecky's study of eighteenth-century England concluded, "John Wesley has wielded a wider constructive influence in the sphere of practical Christianity than any other man who has appeared since the sixteenth century."[2] The Oxford Dictionary of the Christian Church states simply, "John Wesley was one of the greatest Christians of his age."[3] His enduring renown was due in part to his ability to articulate the Christian message in plain words.

I. The Sermon as a Means of Theological Communication

Although Wesley was active in many roles, he defined himself chiefly as a preacher. His superior skills as an Oxford don, linguist, logician, historian, patristic scholar, author, and ecclesiastical administrator were

9

undisputed. He believed, however, that his main mission was to preach. As a young man, he wrote, "As my tongue is a devoted thing, I hope . . . to use it only as such, that all who hear me may know of a truth, the words I speak are not mine, but His that sent me."[4] Indeed, both his tongue and pen were "devoted things."

Wesley derived his belief in the importance of preaching in part from reading the book of Acts and the history of the early church. Commenting on the leaders of the New Testament Christian community, he observed, "In the first Church, the primary business of apostles, evangelists, and bishops was to preach the word of God."[5] Wesley made that business his own. We find in his journal frequent references to God's anointing his proclamation of the Bible. He wrote, "Preaching we have always found to be accompanied with power, and to have the blessing of God following it."[6] Often, we read in his journal, "God himself made the application,"[7] "God was speaking to their hearts,"[8] and "God spoke to the hearts of many."[9] He wrote, "I do indeed *live* by preaching!"[10]

Although Wesley wrote in a variety of literary forms, his sermons provide the best means for understanding his mind and spirit. He intended it that way. Wesley poured his best efforts into his preaching, and his published sermons constitute the best expression of his theology. At least three motivations lay behind his sermon-publishing ventures.

1. John Wesley chose to articulate his message principally through the medium of the sermon. Wesley elected not to produce a systematic theology that could be described as a *Summa*. He did not write a dogmatic theology, as did Origin, John of Damascus, Thomas Aquinas, Philip Melanchthon, John Calvin, and the Lutheran divines. Nor did he lead in drafting a new creed or Confession of Faith, as did the sixteenth-century Reformers, Anabaptists, and Anglicans. He did not write as a philosopher or a systematic theologian.[11] By design, he wrote sermons containing "plain truth for plain people."[12]

To be sure, Wesley wrote theological tracts for the times, which addressed the crucial concerns of the day. Furthermore, he was entirely familiar with the major theological works, creeds, and confessions. He conceived his main mission, however, as bringing others to faith by the ministry of preaching. Wesley echoed St. Paul: "Faith, indeed ordinarily cometh by hearing; even by hearing the word of God."[13]

2. John Wesley's published sermons help clear up mistaken ideas about Methodism. In Wesley's day, numerous people denounced, reviled, and falsely represented his teaching. Several of his detractors published their own interpretations of his beliefs, and these accounts were often seriously inaccurate. For example, Bishop William Warburton attacked Wesley with callous invective. Because Wesley took pains to write "plainly," he was perplexed that Warburton consistently misrepresented his message.[11] He commented that Bishop Warburton was "a person not very prone to commend,"[15] noting that Warburton's accounts of his theology were "caricaturas."[16] Wesley believed that the best means of correcting these errors was to clarify his views through his printed sermons, which for over sixty years he preached throughout Great Britain.

John Wesley left a total of 151 published sermons. From these discourses, he selected a collection of 53 messages, commonly referred to as his Standard Sermons. The first edition of these discourses was published serially in four volumes, in 1746, 1748, 1750, and 1760, as *Sermons on Several Occasions*. Later, in 1771 (at the age of 68) he began the publication of what he considered his most significant writings. He titled these 32 volumes *The Works of the Rev. John Wesley, M.A., Late Fellow of Lincoln College, Oxford*.[17] Volumes I through IV of the 1771 edition of his works contain his 53 Standard Sermons, which he arranged in his preferred order.[18] Finally, in 1787–1788 he published his final collection of sermons, which consisted of 100 discourses in eight volumes.[19]

The preface of Wesley's Standard Sermons states, "Every serious man who peruses these will therefore see in the clearest manner what those doctrines are which I embrace and teach as the essentials of true religion."[20] He insisted, "To the best of my knowledge . . . the doctrines we preach are the doctrines of the Church of England; indeed, the fundamental doctrines of the Church, clearly laid down, both in her Prayers, Articles, and Homilies."[21]

Wesley did not see himself as an innovator, but as a transmitter.[22] His position paralleled that of Vincent of Lérins (c. 450), who stated only that orthodoxy consists of "what has been believed everywhere, always, and by all."[23] Wesley said to his followers, "I, and all who follow my judgment, do vehemently refuse to be distinguished from other men, by any but the common principles of Christianity—the plain, old Christianity that I teach, renouncing and detesting all other marks of distinction."[24] Those who desire to understand John Wesley must read his Standard Sermons.

3. The printed versions of John Wesley's sermons contain the essence of his theological legacy. In Wesley's preface to the different editions of his sermons, he described them as containing the "substance" of his preaching. Many of the reports of Wesley's preaching tell that he used illustrations and anecdotes, which are mostly lacking in his published sermons. His printed sermons contain the core of what he taught, and he prepared them for his and subsequent generations. These sermons constitute the marrow of Methodism.

Eighteenth-century travel in Great Britain was unpredictable, due to changing weather conditions, bad roads, and the uncertain schedules of coaches and ferries. Inexpensive sheets of Wesley's sermons (which usually sold for a pence or two-pence) proved invaluable for the increase, oversight, and coherence of the Methodist movement. Henry Moore, one of Wesley's early biographers, noted that Wesley published his sermons "as a concise, but clear and full body of divinity in keeping of which [the Methodists] could not greatly err [so that] if they should continue one body [they would] hear the same truths and mind the same things."[25]

Wesley's sermons address the entire range of the human condition. In simple language, they speak both to educated and uneducated people. They communicate with people of position and privilege, as well as to the neglected and powerless. These messages contain biblical exposition, theological essentials, spiritual wisdom, and practical counsel. Wesley scholar Maldwyn Edwards stated, "Like all the truly great, John Wesley makes a fresh appeal to each new age: still he can stir the mind and still can move the heart. The world has not ceased to be his parish."[26]

II. Reading Wesley's Sermons Today

Almost forty years ago, Oxford University Press's LIBRARY OF PROTESTANT THEOLOGY series issued Albert Outler's volume titled *John Wesley*. This book contained representative selections from Wesley's writings, illustrating the major lines of his thought. In his Preface, Dr. Outler said, "[Wesley] was always striving to clarify his message and to communicate it to the people of his day and age. [His] distinctive theological perspective merits serious consideration . . . in another age and atmosphere."[27] The aim of this transcription of John Wesley's *Standard Sermons* is to make them understandable to modern ears, by bringing them into "another age and atmosphere." This volume seeks to communicate the precise meaning of what he wrote, and the guiding principle is *clarity without compromise*.

Although Wesley had the training and temperament of a scholar, he had a passion to communicate with ordinary people. In the preface to his Sermons he wrote,

> I labour to avoid all words which are not easy to be understood, all which are not used in common life; and in particular those kinds of technical terms that so frequently occur in bodies of divinity, those modes of speaking which men of reading are intimately acquainted with, but which to common people are an unknown tongue [28]

According to contemporary accounts, Wesley's eighteenth-century hearers and readers readily comprehended his speaking and writing. Indeed, in his generation he surpassed every other religious writer in communicating serious theological content to the masses.

Despite Wesley's clarity in his own time, many people today do not find it easy to comprehend his sermons. The problem does not lie in their content, but in the changes that have occurred in the English language during the past three hundred years. Furthermore, Wesley's sermons contain numerous Hebrew, Greek, and Latin phrases.[29] For many modern readers, these factors combine to make Wesley's sermons difficult to follow.

Language is fluid and dynamic. *Encyclopædia Britannica* states, "Changes are constantly taking place in the course of the learned transmission of a language from one generation to another. . . . Languages change in all their aspects, in their pronunciation, word forms, syntax, and word meanings."[30] And few, if any, languages have evolved more than the English language. We can liken English to a river that continually overflows its banks and carves out new directions.

The stated mission of Samuel Johnson's (1709–84) eighteenth-century *Dictionary of the English Language* was "to refine our language to grammatical purity, and to clear it from colloquial barbarisms, licentious idioms, and irregular combinations." Yet Johnson himself observed that no one could "embalm" language or "secure it from corruption." He averred, "No dictionary of a living tongue can ever be perfect, since while it is hastening to publication, some words are budding, and some falling away."

Since Johnson's (and Wesley's) eighteenth-century era, the changes in English have been significant. Indeed, as Professor Albert Outler reminded us, "The general styles of orthography, punctuation, and emphasis were undergoing a major mutation during Wesley's lifetime."[31] Wesley wrote and published many of his sermons more than 265 years ago, and if he were publishing today he doubtless would write differently.

Wesley scholar Kenneth Collins said, "Although it is a commonplace in Wesley Studies that the father of Methodism spoke 'plain truth for plain people,' his sermons [are] not so plain to my students. Indeed, they

[are] often discouraged by the eighteenth-century style of the writings . . . and by their own inability to grasp the interrelationships of the various pieces."[32] My experience confirms that of Professor Collins. A number of my seminary students whose academic backgrounds are in technology, engineering, and the sciences find that the eighteenth-century language of Wesley's sermons slows them down—sometimes to a stop. Those for whom English is a second language have a particularly difficult time comprehending Wesley's eighteenth-century prose. Specifically, why is the eighteenth-century text of Wesley's sermons difficult for today's readers to understand?

1. Vocabulary. In part, modern readers may stumble while reading Wesley's original sermons because the meanings of many eighteenth-century words have changed. For instance, Wesley states in one of his sermons, "Do not be straitened in thy bowels." Not all modern readers immediately comprehend his meaning. I changed this phrase to "Do not limit your affections." In Sermon #52 Wesley wrote about some good people whom a mob *dragged through the kennels*. In the eighteenth century, *kennels* did not always refer to a facility for dogs. At that time, Wesley's listeners (or readers) would have understood the phrase *through the kennels* to mean "through the street gutters."

In Wesley's day, a *rude* person was an uncultured or uneducated person. To *rate* others did not mean to "evaluate" them. Rather, the term meant to "scold," as an angry person would rebuke a stubborn mule. The eighteenth-century phrase *I was with two persons who I doubt are properly enthusiasts*, in today's English means "I was with two persons who I *believe* are real enthusiasts." This transcription casts such words and phrases into their modern equivalents.

The following list illustrates how the meanings of some words have changed since Wesley's day.

WESLEY'S WORDS	TODAY'S MEANING
analogy of faith	evangelical system of belief
to be careful	to worry
conversation	manner of life (often)
disinterested	impartial
ejaculation	exclamation
end	goal or purpose
experimentally	experientially

an increase of	more
meet	fit or proper (often)
peculiar	particular or distinct
prove	know by personal experience
several	different or various
temper	disposition, attitude, temperament
to own	to acknowledge
vulgar	common or popular
want	need or lack

This transcription also modernizes such words as *hath, art, thy, worketh, knoweth*, and *hast*. Where it is appropriate, this volume replaces the generic word *man* with the use of appropriate substitutes.

2. **The use of scripture.** Consciously and unconsciously, Wesley used biblical imagery in everything he said and wrote. One who is not thoroughly familiar with the Bible can sometimes miss Wesley's meaning. For instance, in Sermon #30 Wesley says, "This approach is the best possible way to make Felix tremble." Those who do not recall the account in Acts 24:25 of St. Paul's defense before Governor Felix might fail to understand Wesley's meaning. His mind was so steeped in scriptural images and vocabulary that often he unconsciously blended several biblical quotations, images, and paraphrases into a single sentence. For example, in Sermon #28 Wesley wrote, "The delight of your eyes, the desire of your eyes, the wife of your youth, your only child, or your most intimate friend may be taken away in a single stroke." In this sentence one finds references to Ezek. 24:16, 21; Prov. 5:18; Mal. 2:14; Deut. 13:6; and 1 Sam. 18:3.

Wesley used a great number of biblical, as well as apocryphal, allusions. He read the apocryphal books, but drew no doctrine from them. Principally, he borrowed from these books certain striking phrases and moral maxims. Wesley agreed with his church regarding these non-canonical writings: "The church doth read [these books] for example of life and instruction of manners: but yet doth it not apply to them to establish any doctrine."[33] In most instances, this transcription substitutes the NRSV translation for Wesley's use of King James and earlier English translations. This volume transcribes Wesley's Hebrew and Greek biblical citations into modern English. I also translated Wesley's Greek and Latin quotations from classical authors.

3. Grammar and syntax. This transcription modernizes Wesley's grammar, while seeking to preserve his meaning. The following sentence illustrates these kinds of grammatical changes.

WESLEY: "But do not you put faith in the room of Christ, or of his righteousness?"

TRANSCRIPTION: "Do you not substitute faith for Christ or his righteousness?"

Often, Wesley separates pronouns from their subjects by one or more sentences, and sometimes by a paragraph. Words such as *this, that, these, those, it,* and *them* often dangle without an immediately clear reference. Reading Wesley's text, one must often pause to search for the noun to which these pronouns refer (especially in sentences that are up to ten lines long!). In hundreds of instances, it has been necessary to supply the appropriate subject or object of a pronoun. For instance:

WESLEY: "He less openly but no less effectually works in dissemblers."

Looking back several sentences, one sees that the pronoun "he" refers to the devil.

TRANSCRIPTION: "Less openly, but no less effectively, the devil works in hypocrites."

Wesley frequently omitted verbs, because he assumed that their appearance in an earlier sentence was sufficient for a later sentence. From the context, I add missing verbs where they are needed. Wesley sometimes uses a comma instead of a verb, which I supply.

4. Spelling, punctuation, and style. Wesley's sermons (especially the earlier ones) contain a variety of spellings. Words such as *aromatick* and *batchelor* become "aromatic" and "bachelor." I rendered Wesley's *ye, thou,* and *thee* as "you." *Offence* becomes *offense; inlarge* becomes *enlarge; pretence* becomes *pretense.*

Because Wesley punctuated his sermons with a view to their being read in public, he used an overabundance of commas, semicolons, parentheses, and dashes. To accord with modern English usage, this transcription removes confusing and unnecessary punctuation marks. Wesley habitually used commas to replace the word "that."[34] I have repaired these kinds of awkward constructions.

As was common with other eighteenth-century authors, Wesley tended frequently and inconsistently to use *italics* and CAPITAL LETTERS. Where these forms are unnecessary, I removed them. At the same time, this transcription occasionally *adds* italics to indicate Wesley's contextual emphases. The present transcription normalizes the use of capitals.

Style is, of course, a matter of preference and taste. Wesley's paragraphs often contain long sentences—*very* long sentences. This transcription breaks up long sentences into shorter ones in order to clarify Wesley's meaning and speed readers along their way. When Wesley introduces a new thought or subject, this transcription begins a new paragraph. By the use of Roman numerals and boldface type, this transcription marks the several "heads" of each of the sermons.

Throughout his life span, John Wesley read and absorbed the works of the best classical, theological, philosophical, and devotional writers. In his ministry, he put to practical use this lifetime of constant reading, thought, and experience. Because he usually quoted from memory, his quotations were seldom letter perfect.[35] This transcription adjusts some of Wesley's quotations (which he cited from memory) to conform more accurately to their authors' exact words.

III. The Lasting Legacy of Wesley's Sermons

1. Fixed focus. Wesley lived and worked with a paramount purpose—the glory of God and the full redemption of humankind. Late in life, he reflected on his early decision to make God his sole aim in life: "In 1739, my brother and I published a volume of 'Hymns and Sacred Poems.' In many of these we declared our sentiments strongly and explicitly. . . .

> *Turn the full stream of nature's tide;*
> *Let all our actions tend*
> *To thee, their source, thy love the guide,*
> *Thy glory be the end.*
> *Earth then a scale to heaven shall be;*
> *Sense shall point out the road;*
> *The creatures all shall lead to thee,*
> *And all we taste be God."*[36]

Because Wesley's sermons reflect this single-minded purpose, they radiate an undeniable moral authority. And to an amazing degree, these sermons continue to transform human lives.

After hearing Wesley speak, an eighteenth-century listener said, "When he spoke I thought his whole discourse was aimed at me." Numerous other people reported the same effect. The following entry in Wesley's journal is typical of many. "At six in the evening, I began preaching on a tombstone, close to the south side of the church. The multitude roared on every side; but my voice soon prevailed, and more and more of the people were melted down."[37] This power continues in Wesley's printed sermons.

2. Biblical balance. To Wesley's commitment to personal spiritual growth, he added purpose-driven scholarship. He continued, therefore, to develop. Because of his lifelong growth, when preparing his sermons he was able to draw upon an impressive store of knowledge and wisdom.

The poet and hymnwriter William Cowper gave tribute to Mr. Wesley as one

> *Who, when occasion justified its use,*
> *Had wit as bright as ready to produce;*
> *Could fetch from records of an earlier age,*
> *Or from philosophy's enlightened page,*
> *His rich materials, and regale your ear*
> *With strains it was a privilege to hear.*
> *Yet above all his luxury supreme,*
> *And his chief glory, was the gospel theme;*
> *There he was copious as old Greece or Rome,*
> *His happy eloquence seem'd there at home,*
> *Ambitious not to shine or to excel,*
> *But to treat justly what he loved so well.*[38]

Cowper's poem underscored Wesley's intellectual depth and scholarly breadth. Yet, his sermons contain no unnecessary displays of erudition. Their main mission is to speak plain truth to plain people.

The Bible was Wesley's final source of authority. To the end of his life, he avoided falling into the theological fads and fashions that came and went with the seasons. Again and again, throughout his more than sixty years of public ministry, he brought balance to the theological climate of England. At the age of 87, a year prior to his death, he wrote to a friend, "I have been uniform both in doctrine and discipline for above these fifty years; and it is a little too late for me to turn into a new path now I am grey-headed. . . . If you and I should be called hence this year [to heaven], we may bless God that we have not lived in vain. Come, let us have a few more strokes at Satan's kingdom, and then we shall depart in peace!"[39]

3. Apostolic love. One wonders how this Oxford don, who read Latin and Greek classical authors as he rode on horseback, could captivate large audiences and inspire them to devote their lives to the worship of God and the service of neighbors. While the theological content of these sermons is compelling, there was, and is, an additional element that imparts authority to his words. This ingredient is *love*.

Matthew Lelièvre, one of Wesley's biographers, stated, "Love for souls, that pure and noble passion enkindled in the heart by the love of God, alone accounts for this otherwise incomprehensible phenomenon. This alone can explain, also, the indefatigable perseverance which pro longed such an apostleship beyond the bounds of half a century."[40] In a typical journal entry, at the age of 86 Wesley wrote,

> About one I preached at Oxford, to a very quiet, deeply serious congrega-
> tion. . . . I dearly love this people; they are so simple of heart, and so much
> alive to God. After dinner we returned to Oxford. . . . I found great liber-
> ty of speech in enforcing the first and great commandment [on love]; and
> could not but hope there will be a great work of God here, notwithstand-
> ing all the wisdom of the world.[41]

As the pilot of a ship on a stormy sea, Wesley stayed his course with fixed focus, biblical balance, and apostolic love.

IV. The Enduring Value of Wesley's Sermons

John Wesley used his profound knowledge of the Bible, his classical education, and his intuitive theological ability to write sermons that open our minds and spirits to God's truth. He said, "It is no part of my design to save either learned or unlearned men from the trouble of thinking . . . On the contrary, my intention is to make them think, and assist them in thinking."[42] Through sermons that clarify the biblical revelation, Wesley's messages continue their ministry into our time. A combi-
nation of factors underlies the uniqueness of these enduring sermonic discourses.

1. **Wesley's sermons focus on fundamental subjects.** These discourses contain no secondary matters of transitory concern or fleeting interest. Rather, Wesley deals with the most basic and profound themes of the Bible, developing them with frankness, clarity, and authenticity. As early as 1727, he came to see that it was important for him to restrict his time to religion's most essential elements. That year he wrote his mother:

I am perfectly come over to your opinion, that there are many truths it is not worthwhile to know. Curiosity, indeed, might be a sufficient plea for our laying out some time upon them, if we had half a dozen centuries of life to come; but methinks it is great ill-husbandry to spend a considerable part of the small pittance now allowed us, in what makes us neither a quick nor a sure return.[43]

Later, he reinforced this commitment to Christian fundamentals by warning against "a zeal for things which [comprise] no part of religion, as though they [are] essential branches of it." He complained that "many have laid as great, if not greater, stress on trifles, as on the weightier matters of the law."[44]

Wesley was careful to distinguish between religious opinions and "essential doctrines." He opposed spending time on inconsequential issues, insisting that "mere opinions" are at best only a small part of religion. [45] At the same time, he believed that a person must be as "fixed as the sun in his judgment concerning the main branches of Christian doctrine." These "main branches" are original sin, the atonement of Christ, justification by faith, the Holy Spirit, the new birth, Christian assurance, and holiness.[46] Wesley warned, "How many of those who profess to believe the whole, yet, in effect, preach another gospel; so disguising the essential doctrines thereof, by their new interpretations, as to retain the words only, but nothing of 'the faith once delivered to the saints!'"[47] To this day, Wesley's writings are a reliable exponent of biblical basics.

2. Wesley's sermons contain sound logic and clear thinking. Wesley was a direct preacher. His printed sermons move straight to the point and lead readers immediately to the heart of the subject at hand. Benjamin Kennicott, the celebrated Old Testament scholar and a contemporary of Wesley, disliked Wesley's "enthusiasm," but admired his intelligence and precision. After Wesley's most controversial sermon at Oxford, Kennicott declared that his preaching had "agreeable emphasis" and that "he is allowed to be a man of great parts" and "sound sense."[48]

Wesley had an exceptional gift for accurate reasoning. His natural ability to think clearly was sharpened by his study of logic at the University of Oxford, where his intellectual gifts gained him an appointment as a Fellow of Oxford's Lincoln College. Luke Tyerman summarized the academic achievements that Wesley had attained while he was yet in his early twenties: "All parties acknowledged him to be a man of talents and of learning; while his skill in logic was known to be remarkable."[49]

In 1766 Wesley recalled:

For several years I was Moderator in the disputations which were held six times a week at Lincoln College, in Oxford. I could not avoid acquiring hereby some degree of expertness in arguing; and especially in discerning and pointing out well-covered [well-concealed] and plausible fallacies. I have since found abundant reason to praise God for giving me this honest art. By this, when men have hedged me in by what they called demonstrations, I have been many times able to dash them in pieces; in spite of all its covers, to touch the very point where the fallacy lay; and it flew open in a moment.[50]

Wesley's logic was especially effective because he was rooted in scripture and classical Christian doctrine, which the best religious minds of the centuries had consistently articulated. He was familiar with the piety, theology, and wisdom of the early Church Fathers. He knew and appreciated the Protestant Reformers and the finest Roman Catholic writers. This theological breadth combined with his keen logic to make his sermons a continuing source of sound instruction, helpful illumination, and practical application.

3. Wesley's sermons speak both to the head and the heart. For Wesley, the mind and the affections are not antithetical human endowments that are at odds with each other. His sermons speak to head and heart, mind and body, reason and emotion. Wesley believed that God intended for all aspects of human nature to function as a harmonious whole. Professor Theodore Runyon reminds us, "Unlike the rationalists who saw the mind operating quite independently from the body, Wesley insisted that the mind and the body work together."[51] Wesley contended, "An embodied spirit cannot form one thought but by the mediation of its bodily organs."[52]

In Sermon # 1, Wesley wrote, "Saving faith differs from the faith of a devil. Saving faith is not merely a speculative, rational thing, a cold, lifeless assent, or a train of ideas in the head. It is primarily a disposition of the heart."[53] Wesley reacted to a letter that claimed, "A clergyman ought to be all intellect; [and] no passion." He replied, "By this means we might avoid much pain: But we should also lose much happiness. Therefore this is a state which I cannot desire. Rather give me the pleasure and pain too."[54]

Wesley wrote in his journal, "If you read all your life, this [information] will only be in your head, and that head will perish: So that, if you have not the love of God in your heart, you will go to hell."[55] Because Wesley's sermons addressed the whole person, they have the power to move us to repentance, faith, holiness, self-denial, and service. To borrow Wesley's own phrase, his sermons "cut to the quick and search the heart to the bottom."[56] They mediate his favorite message: "The kingdom of God is righteousness, peace, and joy in the Holy Spirit."

4. Wesley's sermons link theory and practice. At all times, Wesley evaluated doctrine and polity in the light of their relevance to daily life. Almost all his sermons conclude with a call to action. He contended, "For what avails the clearest knowledge, even of the most excellent things, even of the things of God, if it go no farther than speculation, if it be not reduced to practice? He that hath ears to hear, let him hear! And what he hears, let him instantly put in practice."[57]

Wesley wrote, "I have one point in view, — to promote, so far as I am able, vital, practical religion; and by the grace of God to beget, preserve, and increase the life of God in the souls of men. On this single principle I have hitherto proceeded, and taken no step but in subserviency to it."[58] Wesley's sermons develop a practical religion that unites theory and action. Wesley avoided works without faith as well as faith without works.

5. Wesley's sermons are easy to comprehend. In a letter to a young preacher, Wesley emphasized his concern for "plain" communication:

> Clearness in particular is necessary for you and me; because we are to instruct people of the lowest understanding. Therefore . . . if we think with the wise, yet [we] must speak with the vulgar [ordinary people]. We should constantly use the most common, little, easy words . . . which our language affords. When I had been a member of the University about ten years, I wrote and talked much as you do now. But when I talked to plain people in the castle, or the town, I observed they gaped and stared. This quickly obliged me to alter my style, and adopt the language of those I spoke to. And yet there is a dignity in this simplicity, which is not disagreeable to those of the highest rank.[59]

Wesley was one of the best-educated people in England, and he gained the intellectual respect of the educated scholars. At the same time, through his clear communication he earned the esteem and affection of the unlearned. John Hampson, one of Wesley's early biographers, wrote that his sermons were "simple, perspicuous, and admirably adapted to the capacity of his hearers."[60]

Even if Wesley's eighteenth-century language is now dated, his timeless ideas are straightforward and easy to grasp. He framed his thoughts simply and without pretentiousness. Wesley contended, "Stiffness, apparent exactness, artificialness of style [is] the main defect to be avoided, next to solecism [bad grammar] and impropriety. . . . Dr. [Conyers] Middleton is no standard for a preacher. . . . His diction is stiff, formal, affected, unnatural. The art glares, and therefore shocks a man of true taste. Always to talk or write like him would be as absurd as always to walk in minuet step."[61]

The reader is never left in doubt as to the point that Wesley makes and what he thinks God expects as a response to the matter at hand. In the preface to his sermons, he stated:

> Nothing here appears in an elaborate, elegant, or oratorical dress. If it had been my desire or design to write thus, my leisure would not permit. But, in truth, I, at present, designed nothing less; for I now write, as I generally speak, *ad populum* [to ordinary people], —to the bulk of mankind, to those who neither relish nor understand the art of speaking; but who, notwithstanding, are competent judges of those truths which are necessary to present and future happiness.[62]

Adapting the words of Francis Bacon, John Wesley's reading made him a full man, his conferencing with others made him a ready man, and his writing made him an exact man.[63] Ease of comprehension is a mark of Wesley's sermons.

6. **Wesley's sermons champion relational religion.** These sermons are not mere doctrinal discourses. They communicate a religion of the heart, which connects one with God personally in a vital relationship. Wesley wrote, "In every work of our hands, we 'pursue nothing but in relation to him.'"[64] Wesley insists that intellectual assent to biblical truth, faithful participation in the Lord's Supper, winning others to Christ, and serving one's neighbor are important, but they do not constitute the essence of real religion. Rather, genuine Christianity consists of one's union with Christ in a relationship of love. In *The Principles of a Methodist Farther Explained*, Wesley defined "religion itself" as "loving God with all our heart, and our neighbour as ourselves. . . . This love we believe to be the medicine of life, the never-failing remedy for all the evils of a disordered world, for all the miseries and vices of men. Wherever this is, there are virtue and happiness going hand in hand."[65]

In calling us to relational religion, Wesley's sermons use the biblical images of bridegroom and bride,[66] vine and branches,[67] parent and child.[68] Union with Christ is not based on predetermined decrees or a one-time legal transaction. For Wesley, the Christian life is living in an ongoing and loving union with the Beloved. Wesley's sermonic discourses lead his readers into a personal and interactive union with Christ.

7. Wesley's sermons underscore the centrality of holiness. Wesley's sermons show that holiness is the most distinguishing feature of Christianity. These discourses develop the scriptural directive to "be holy, as God is holy." The longing for heart purity invariably emerges when Christ comes into our lives. This universal Christian hunger for holiness appears throughout the prayers, liturgy, and hymns of the church. For instance, the Prayer of Humble Access contains these words:

> Almighty God, unto whom all hearts are open, all desires known, and from whom no secrets are hid: Cleanse the thoughts of our hearts by the inspiration of thy Holy Spirit, that we may perfectly love thee, and worthily magnify thy holy name, through Christ our Lord.

Wesley's sermons emphasize that the work of God's grace in human life leads to freedom from both sin's *guilt* and sin's *power*. After preaching at Macclesfield, Wesley wrote, "I hope none of them will hereafter dream of going to heaven by any faith which does not produce holiness."[69]

John Wesley's sermons explain that holiness does not begin when Christians enter heaven. Holiness begins in the present life. Wesley grounds his call to holiness in scripture. For instance, in the Old Testament God promised, "A new heart I will give you, and a new spirit I will put within you; and I will remove from your body the heart of stone and give you a heart of flesh. I will put my spirit within you, and make you follow my statutes and be careful to observe my ordinances."[70] In the New Testament, Paul wrote,

> God did not call us to impurity but in holiness. Therefore, whoever rejects this rejects not human authority but God. . . . May the God of peace himself sanctify you entirely; and may your spirit and soul and body be kept sound and blameless at the coming of our Lord Jesus Christ. The one who calls you is faithful, and he will do this.[71]

According to Wesley, we cannot be happy unless we are holy, and God gives both blessings in the present life.

Wesley insisted that God both *accounts* believers righteous and *makes* them righteous. In justification and adoption, God gives us a new *standing*; in regeneration and sanctification, God gives us a new *state*. Real religion transforms believers' religious affections, enabling them to conform to the pattern of Jesus Christ himself. Wesley said that sanctification "is a renewal of the heart in the whole image of God, the full likeness of Him that created it."[72] This description of holiness is not eccentric, but rather the central message of Christianity through the centuries.

John Wesley wrote an informative account of his early decision to become an earnest Christian: "In the year 1725, being in the twenty-third year of my age. . . I resolved to dedicate all my life to God, all my thoughts, and words, and actions; being thoroughly convinced, there was no medium; but that every part of my life (not some only) must either be a sacrifice to God, or myself, that is, in effect, to the devil. Can any serious person doubt of this, or find a medium between serving God and serving the devil?"[73] The sermons of John Wesley reflect this concept of Christianity, and their enduring value lies in their power to articulate this plain truth for plain people.

Notes

1. John E. E. D. Acton, *The Cambridge Modern History, vol. VI, The Eighteenth Century* (New York: Macmillan Company, 1918), p. 77.

2. William Edward Lecky, *A History of England in the Eighteenth Century*, 8 vols. (London: Longmans, Green and Co.), 2:558.

3. F. L. Cross and E. A. Livingstone, *The Oxford Dictionary of the Christian Church*, 2nd ed. (Oxford: Oxford University Press, 1989), p. 1467.

4. Frank Baker, ed., *The Works of John Wesley*, Bicentennial ed., *Letters*, October 10, 1735 (Nashville; Abingdon Press, 1980), 25:441.

5. *Explanatory Notes upon the New Testament*, Acts 6:2.

6. Thomas Jackson, ed., *The Works of John Wesley*, 14 vols. (London: Wesleyan Conference Office, 1872), 1:127.

7. W. Reginald Ward and Richard P. Heitzenrater, eds., *The Works of John Wesley*, Bicentennial ed. (Nashville: Abingdon Press, 1995), *Journals and Diaries*, Journal, August 16, 1776, 23:28.

8. Ibid., 1991, *Journal*, March 25, 1750, 20:326.

9. Ibid., 1992, *Journal*, Sept 14, 1735, 21:29.

10. Ibid., *Journal*, July 28, 1757, 21:118.

11. George Eayrs, *John Wesley, Christian Philosopher and Church Founder* (London: The Epworth Press, 1926), pp. 72, 73.

12. Alongside Wesley's sermons are his *Explanatory Notes upon the New Testament*, and these two sources traditionally serve as doctrinal standards for world wide Methodism.

13. *Explanatory Notes upon the New Testament*.

14. In a letter to his brother Charles (Jan. 5, 1762) Wesley wrote, "I was a little surprised to find Bishop Warburton so entirely unacquainted with the New Testament: And, notwith-

standing all his parade of learning, I believe he is no critic in Greek" (Jackson, *Wesley's Works*, 12:122).

15. Albert C. Outler, ed., *The Works of John Wesley*, Bicentennial ed. (Nashville: Abingdon Press, 1984), *Sermons*, 4 vols., *On Dissipation*, §18, 3:123.

16. Ward and Heitzenrater, *Journal and Diaries*, August 27, 1770, 22:246.

17. This edition of Wesley's Works was published by William Pine in Bristol from 1771–74.

18. Some editions of Wesley's *Standard Sermons* contain 44 sermons, following the British tradition. Other editions contain 52 *Standard Sermons*, omitting Sermon #53, "The Death of George Whitefield."

19. Published by George Paramore in London.

20. Outler, *Wesley's Sermons*, 1:103.

21. Ward and Heitzenrater, *Wesley's Journal and Diaries*, September 13, 1739, 19:96.

22. Frank Baker, *John Wesley and the Church of England* (Nashville: Abingdon Press, 1970), p. 109.

23. For instance, see Wesley's sermon, *On Sin in Believers*, III, §9. Vincent of Lerins's formula was *Quod ubique, quod semper, quod ab omnibus creditum est [what has been believed everywhere, always, and by all]*. See Philip Schaff and Henry Wace, eds., *Nicene and Post-Nicene Fathers*, Second Series (Peabody, Mass.: Hendrickson Publishers, 1994, 11:132-33). See also Wesley's *Works*, Bicentennial ed., 2:341.

24. Rupert E. Davies, ed., *The Works of John Wesley*, Bicentennial ed., *The Methodist Societies: History, Nature, and Design* (Nashville: Abingdon Press, 1989), *The Character of a Methodist*, 9:41.

25. Henry Moore, *The Life of the Rev. John Wesley*, 2 vols. (London: Printed for John Kershaw, 1825), 2:403.

26. Maldwyn Edwards, "John Wesley," *A History of the Methodist Church in Great Britain*, ed. Rupert Davies & Gordon Rupp, 4 vols. (London: Epworth Press, 1965), 1:79.

27. Albert C. Outler, *John Wesley* (New York: Oxford University Press, 1964), A Library of Protestant Thought, p. ix.

28. Outler, *Wesley's Sermons*, 1:104.

29. James Downey, *The Eighteenth Century Pulpit: A Study of the Sermons of Butler, Berkeley, Secker, Sterne, Whitefield, and Wesley* (Oxford: Clarendon Press, 1969), pp. 217-18. Wesley's written sermons contain numerous Latin and Greek quotes from ancient writers such as Cicero, Homer, Horace, Juvenal, Ovid, Plato, Quintilian, Seneca, Suetonius, Terence, and Virgil. He also quotes from more recent English authors such as Joseph Addison, Abraham Cowley, John Davies, James Hervey, John Milton, Alexander Pope, Matthew Prior, William Shakespeare, and Edward Young.

30. "Language," *Encyclopædia Britannica*, 15th ed., *Macropædia*, 10:660.

31. Albert Outler, *John Wesley*, p. x.

32. Kenneth Collins, *Wesley on Salvation: A Study in the Standard Sermons* (Grand Rapids: Francis Asbury Press, 1989), p. 11.

33. Thirty-nine Articles, §6.

34. See Frank Baker, "Wesley's Text: Editions, Transmission, Presentation, and Variant Readings," Outler, *Wesley's Sermons*, 4:423.

35. Writing as he did, while traveling, Wesley often had no access to his library.

36. Jackson, *Wesley's Works*, 11:370.

37. Ward and Heitzenrater, *Wesley's Journals and Diaries*, August 13, 1746, 20:129.

38. T. S. Grimshawe, *The Works of William Cowper: His Life, Letters, and Poems* (New York: Robert Carter & Brothers, 1849), p. 555.

39. John Telford, ed., *The Letters of the Rev. John Wesley*, 8 vols. (London: Epworth Press, 1931), January 13, 1790, 8:196-97.

40. Matthew Lelièvre, "Wesley as a Popular Preacher," *The Wesley Memorial Volume: Wesley and the Methodist Movement* (New York: Phillips & Hunt; Cincinnati: Walden & Stowe, 1880), p. 294.

41. Nehemiah Curnock, ed., *The Journal of the Rev. John Wesley*, 8 vols. (London: Epworth Press, 1909–19), October 14, 1787, 7:334.

42. Jackson, *Wesley's Works*, 14:252.

43. Baker, *Wesley's Letters*, Jan. 24, 1727, 25:208.

44. Gerald R. Cragg, ed., *The Works of John Wesley*, Bicentennial ed. (Nashville: Abingdon Press, 1989), *The Appeals to Men of Reason and Religion and Certain Related Open Letters, A Farther Appeal to Men of Reason and Religion*, Part III, 1, §9, 11:277.

45. Telford, *Wesley's Letters*, May 14, 1765, 4:297.

46. Ibid., Letter to Thomas Church, June 17, 1746, 2:267-68.

47. Outler, *Wesley's Sermons*, 3:536.

48. *Methodist Magazine*, 1866, p. 44.

49. Luke Tyerman, *The Life and Times of the Rev. John Wesley, M.A.*, 3 vols. (London: Hodder and Stoughton, 1870), 1:48.

50. Jackson, *Wesley's Works*, 10:353.

51. Theodore Runyon, *The New Creation: John Wesley's Theology Today* (Nashville: Abingdon Press, 1998), p. 156.

52. Outler, *Wesley's Sermons*, 2:405-06.

53. *Salvation by Faith*, I, §4.

54. Telford, *Wesley's Letters*, February 11, 1775, 6:139.

55. Ward and Heitzenrater, *Wesley's Journals and Diaries*, March 21, 1770, 22:221.

56. Jackson, *Wesley's Works*, 8:273.

57. Outler, *Wesley's Sermons*, 3:236.

58. Telford, *Wesley's Letters*, September 3, 1756, 3:192.

59. Ibid., July 15, 1764, 4:258.

60. John Hampson, *Memoirs of the late Rev. John Wesley, A.M., with a review of his life writings: and a History of Methodism from it's commencement in 1729 to the present time*, 3 vols. (Sunderland, England: Printed for the author by James Graham, 1791), 3:168.

61. Telford, *Wesley's Letters*, March 6, 1764, 4:232.

62. Outler, *Wesley's Sermons*, 1:103-04.

63. Cf. Francis Bacon, *Essays*, 50, "On Studies."

64. *A Plain Account of Christian Perfection*, §6.

65. Jackson, *Wesley's Works*, 8:474.

66. Ibid., 11:330.

67. Ibid., 10:246.

68. Ibid., 8:234.

69. Ward and Heitzenrater, *Wesley's Journal and Diaries*, April 30, 1777, 23:46.

70. Ezek. 36:26, 27.

71. 1 Thess. 4:7, 8; 5:23.

72. Jackson, *Wesley's Works*, 11:444.

73. Ibid., 11:366.

John Wesley's Preface

Written in 1746

1 The following sermons contain the substance of what I have been preaching for the past eight or nine years. During that time I have frequently spoken in public on every subject in this collection of sermons. I am not conscious that there is any point of doctrine which I regularly preach, in passing or at the center of the sermon, that is not offered here to every Christian reader. All serious persons who examine these sermons will clearly see what are the doctrines that I embrace and teach as the essentials of true religion.

2. I am certainly aware that these doctrinal essentials are not presented in the way that some people might expect. Nothing appears here in an elaborate, ornate, or overblown style. Even if it had been my wish or plan to write this way, the pressures of time would not have permitted it. Truly, I want nothing more than to write as I usually speak. I preach to ordinary people, who neither enjoy nor understand artful oratory. Even so, they are competent judges of those truths that are necessary for present and future happiness. I mention this point, so that interested readers may spare themselves the labor of looking for what they will not find.

3. I intend to speak plain truth for plain people. Therefore, I intentionally forgo all subtle and philosophical speculations, as well as all complicated and complex thoughts. As far as possible I refrain from a display of scholarship, except I do sometimes refer to the original language of the scriptures. I strive to avoid all difficult words that people do not commonly use in daily life. Particularly, I do not use the technical terms that so frequently occur in religious discourses. People of learning are well acquainted with such words, but to ordinary folk they seem like an unknown tongue. Still, I am not confident that I never unintentionally

slip into using difficult words. It is quite easy to think that a word that is familiar to oneself is also familiar to everyone else.

4. To some extent, my plan is to forget everything that ever I have read. I intend to speak in common language, as if I had never read a single author, ancient or modern. (Of course I do not mean that I plan to ignore the inspired scriptures.) On the one hand, I am persuaded that this way of writing will be a means of enabling me more clearly to express the deliberations of my heart. I simply follow the chain of my own thoughts without entangling myself with those of other writers. On the other hand, I will come to my task with fewer hindrances in my mind and with less bias and prejudice when seeking the simple truths of the gospel for myself or when preaching them to others.

5. To sincere and reasonable people I do not hesitate to share openly what have been the innermost thoughts of my heart. I am aware that I am a creature of a day, passing through life as an arrow through the sky. I am a spirit come from God and returning to God. I am just hovering over a great gulf for a few moments until I will no more be seen. Then, I drop into an unchangeable eternity! I want to know one thing—the way to heaven. I want to know how to land safely on that happy shore. God himself has descended to teach the way; it is for this very purpose that Christ came from heaven. He has written the way in a book. O, give me that book! At any price give me the Book of God! I have it, and it contains knowledge enough for me. Let me be *homo unius libri—a man of one book*. Here I am, far from the busy ways of life. I sit down alone, and only God is with me. In his presence I open and read his Book for the purpose of finding the way to heaven. Is there any doubt about the meaning of what I read? Does anything appear mysterious or complicated? If so, I lift up my heart to the Father of lights. Lord, does your word not say, "If any of you is lacking in wisdom, ask God?" Does your word not say, "God gives to all generously and ungrudgingly?" You have said, "Anyone who resolves to do the will of God will know it." I am willing to do your will, and I pray that you will reveal it to me. So I search and ponder parallel passages of Scripture, comparing spiritual things with spiritual things. I meditate on them with all the attention and seriousness of which my mind is capable. If any doubt still remains, I consult others who are experienced in the things of God. Next, I look to the writings of those who although they are dead, yet still they speak. And what I learn in this way, I teach.

6. Accordingly, in the following sermons I have set down what I find in the Bible concerning the way to heaven. I am concerned to distinguish God's way from all human inventions. I have tried to describe true, scrip-

tural, experiential religion so as to omit nothing that is a genuine part of it. I add not one thing to it that is not a vital component.

In this task, it is especially my desire, first, to protect those that are just setting their faces toward heaven, but who have little familiarity with the things of God. These people are more prone to be turned aside from God's way. My desire is to safeguard them from the kind of religious ceremonies that are only outward forms. Such substitutes for genuine religion have almost driven heart-religion out of the world.

Secondly, I want to warn those who know the religion of the heart, which is faith working by love. I want to keep them at any time from undermining the moral law by claiming that all they need is faith. To claim faith without its leading to good works is to fall back into the snare of the devil.

7. Heeding the advice and request of some of my friends, at the beginning of these sermons I have added three of my sermons and one of my brother's that we preached before the University of Oxford. My plan for this volume required some discourses on the subjects contained in these sermons, and I preferred them above any others. They provide a stronger answer than any other to those who have frequently asserted that we have recently changed our doctrine and no longer preach what we preached several years ago. All intelligent persons can now judge for themselves, when they compare the sermons we now preach with those that we preached at an earlier date.

8. Some may say, however, that I have misunderstood the way myself, although I presume to teach it to others. It is likely that many people will think this way, and it is quite possible that I may have misunderstood at some points. I trust, though, that where I am in the wrong, my mind is open to being changed. I sincerely desire to be better informed. I say to God and others, "What I do not know, teach me."

9. Are you convinced that you see more clearly than I do? It is not improbable that you may. If so, treat me as you would want to be treated yourself under the same circumstances. Lead me to a better way than I have yet known. Show me my mistake by plain proof of Scripture. And if I delay on the path I have been accustomed to taking and if I seem unwilling to leave it, work with me. Take me by the hand and lead me as I am able to accept it. Do not be angry if I beg you not to beat me down in order to quicken my pace. I can move forward only feebly and slowly at best. If you belittle me, I might not be able to move forward at all. Also, may I ask you not to call me cruel names in order to bring me into the right way? Suppose I was ever so much in the wrong, I doubt that scolding would set me straight. Rather, it would make me run so

much the farther from you. In that case, I would move out of the path of truth still more and more.

10. Indeed, if you are angry I will become angry also, and then there would be little hope of my finding the truth. Once anger arises ("like a puff of smoke," as Homer somewhere expressed it), the smoke will so cloud the eyes of my soul that I will not be able to see anything clearly. For God's sake, if it is possible to avoid it, let us not provoke one another to anger. Let us not ignite this fire of hell in each other, much less fan it into a flame. If we could discern truth by the dreadful light of anger's fires, would it not be a loss instead of a gain? Even with many wrong opinions, how much more is love to be preferred before truth without love? We may die without the knowledge of many truths and yet be carried into Abraham's bosom. But if we die without love, what good would knowledge be to us? It would do us no more good than it does for the devil and his angels!

May the God of love keep us from anger. May he prepare us for the knowledge of all truth, by filling our hearts with the fullness of his love and with all joy and peace in believing.

John Wesley, 1746

SALVATION BY FAITH

On June 11, 1738, just eighteen days after John Wesley's famed heart-warming religious experience at Aldersgate, he preached this sermon at the University of Oxford in the Church of the Blessed Virgin Mary. This church has a rich tradition due to the many important sermons that have been preached from its historic pulpit. For instance, in 1556 Thomas Cranmer delivered a sermon here just prior to sealing his confession of faith by being burned at the stake at Oxford, as ordered by the Roman Catholic Queen Mary. Later, in this church John Henry Newman and Edward Bouverie Pusey preached sermons that led to the nineteenth-century Tractarian Movement and the Anglo-Catholic revival.

In Wesley's day, university sermons at Oxford were preached at 2:00 P.M. on Sundays and at 10:00 A.M. on Saints' Days. The university required all Doctors, Masters, graduates, and scholars to attend the sermons, except in instances of being justifiably prevented. Prior to his missionary trip to Georgia, Wesley preached at least nine university sermons here, evidence that the university had asked him to preach more often than his normal preaching rotation would require. This fact suggests that his colleagues held him in high esteem. The university asked Wesley to preach this sermon soon after his return from his term as a missionary in Georgia. The university community was eager to hear Wesley, who had now resumed his place as an Oxford don.

In all, five of Wesley's *Standard Sermons* were preached at St. Mary's Church: this present sermon, *Salvation by Faith* (1738); #17, "*The*

33

Circumcision of the Heart (1733); #2, *The Almost Christian* (1741); #3, *Awake, Thou That Sleepest* (preached by Charles Wesley in 1742); and #4, *Scriptural Christianity* (1744).

In this sermon, Wesley does not distinguish between justification and sanctification, as he later does. Here, he states that believers are without sin, a view he subsequently revised, especially in sermon #13, *On Sin in Believers* and sermon #43, *The Scripture Way of Salvation*. The later revision reflects his mature understanding of the order of salvation.

Nevertheless, this sermon articulates Wesley's new awareness that we cannot be saved either by good works or human merit. This sermon's development parallels his own personal struggle to find saving faith. In his journal he wrote that a group of true Christians had convinced him that saving faith was the free gift of God, who would bestow salvation upon all who earnestly and perseveringly sought it. Wesley recorded in his journal, "I was now thoroughly convinced; and, by the grace of God, I resolved to seek it unto the end, 1. By absolutely renouncing all dependence, in whole or in part, upon my own works or righteousness; on which I had really grounded my hope of salvation, though I knew it not, from my youth up. 2. By adding to the constant use of all the other means of grace, continual prayer for this very thing, justifying, saving faith, a full reliance on the blood of Christ shed for me; a trust in Him, as my Christ, as my sole justification, sanctification, and redemption."[1]

Prior to preaching this sermon at Oxford, Wesley had already preached *Salvation by Faith* in several churches in London. This doctrine of salvation by faith sounded strange to Wesley's hearers, and some objected to this "new kind of preaching." In an earlier sermon at St. Mary's Church, preached on New Year's Day, 1733, Wesley had said, "It is the melancholy remark of an excellent man, that he who now preaches the most essential duties of Christianity, runs the hazard of being esteemed, by a great part of his hearers, 'a setter forth of new doctrines.' Most men have so lived away the substance of that religion, the profession whereof they still retain, that no sooner are any of those truths proposed which difference the Spirit of Christ from the spirit of the world, than they cry out, 'Thou bringest strange things to our ears; we would know what these things mean.'"[2]

In this sermon, Wesley did not entirely escape a common tendency of young Christians to speak with presumptive zeal. The sermon contains hints of self-righteousness and a tendency sweepingly to condemn his hearers, some of whom were without doubt genuine Christians. Nonetheless, this sermon marks the first public occasion at Oxford following his Aldersgate experience at which John Wesley publicly proclaimed the drastic difference between nominal religion and authentic Christianity. The sermon contrasts a human centered religion of good works and a Christ centered religion of salvation by grace through faith. The sermon also prefigures Wesley's lifetime interest in holiness of heart and life. These important themes became the thrust of what was to unfold as England's famous eighteenth-century evangelical awakening and the birth of Methodism

SALVATION BY FAITH

By grace you have been saved, through faith. (Eph. 2:8)

1 All the blessings that God has bestowed upon humankind come entirely from his grace. These blessings flow from his generous, undeserved favor, and we have no rightful claim to the least of his mercies. God in his grace "formed man from the dust of the ground, and breathed into his nostrils the breath of life; and the man became a living being." It was God who stamped on our souls his own image, and "put all things under our feet." God's free grace continues with us and gives us "life and breath and all things." There is nothing that we are, or have, or do, that deserves God's smallest blessings. As Isaiah declares, "All that we have done, you have done for us." All the things we are and have come as gifts of God's free mercy, and any righteousness we may have is likewise the gift of God.

2. By what means can we sinful people atone for even the least of our sins? With good works? No. Even if we have performed numerous good works, none of them are our own; they are God's, who made them possible. In truth, even our so-called good works are unholy and sinful. They need atonement because a corrupt tree can produce only corrupt fruit. Our hearts are altogether corrupt and reprehensible because "all have sinned and fall short of the glory of God." We have failed to retain the glorious righteousness originally impressed on the soul, patterned after the image of the great Creator. Therefore, because we cannot claim our own righteousness or good works, we have nothing with which to

37

atone for our sins. Let "every mouth be silenced, and the whole world be held accountable to God."

3. If we sinful people find favor with God, it is only from the fullness of his grace that we receive blessing after blessing. If God favors us by pouring fresh blessings upon us—yes, the greatest of all blessings, which is salvation—we can only say, "Thanks be unto God for his indescribable gift!" And so it is that "God demonstrated his love for us in this: While we were still sinners, Christ died for us." For by grace you have been saved through faith, and this is not your own doing; it is the gift of God. Grace is the source and faith the condition of our salvation.

If we are to benefit from the grace of God, we need carefully to inquire into (1) the nature of the faith by which we are saved, (2) the nature of the salvation that comes through faith, and (3) the answers to some objections.

I. The faith by which we are saved

1. Saving faith is not the same as the faith of heathen (those who do not worship the God of the Bible). God requires all people to believe that "without faith it is impossible to please God, for whoever would approach him must believe that he exists and that he rewards those who seek him." God expects us all to give him thanks for everything and to practice moral virtue, justice, mercy, and truth toward our fellow human beings. Spiritually unenlightened Greeks, Romans, Scythians, and Indians were without excuse if their faith did not lead them at least this far. God expected even them to believe in the being and attributes of God, a future state of rewards or punishments, and the necessity of moral virtue. Those completely outside the knowledge of God are expected to have this minimum level of faith.

2. Saving faith is not merely the intellectual knowledge held by demons. The faith of demons is only a mental belief in God—although a demon's faith exceeds the faith of those that do not know God. The devil himself believes that there is a wise and powerful God who is gracious to reward and just to punish. In addition, the devil knows that Jesus is the Son of God, the Christ, and the Savior of the world. Thus, in the Gospel of Luke we find a demon expressly declaring to Jesus, "I know who you are, the Holy One of God." Moreover, we do not doubt that this demon acknowledged the truth of all the words that Jesus spoke. It believed even those things that were written by God's righteous people. It was an evil spirit who confessed that Paul and Silas were "slaves of the Most High God, who proclaim the way of salvation." All the demons, those archenemies of God, believe these things and they tremble in the presence

of Jesus Christ. They know that God "was revealed in the flesh," that he will "put all his enemies under his feet," and that "All scripture is inspired by God." The faith of a demon acknowledges all these truths.

3. Saving faith is not the faith that the apostles had prior to the resurrection of Christ. The apostles had faith in Christ while he was still on earth. They trusted him to such an extent that Peter said, "We have left everything and followed you!" The apostles even had faith to work miracles, to "heal every disease and sickness." Indeed, they had "power and authority over all demons." Furthermore, their Master even "sent them out to proclaim the kingdom of God."

4. What, then, is saving faith? To begin with, we may answer this question in general by saying that saving faith is trust in Christ. Christ and God the Father through Christ are the proper objects of saving faith. This faith is properly and completely distinguished from the faith of ancient or modern persons who do not know the true God. Saving faith differs from the faith of a devil. Saving faith is not merely a speculative, rational thing, a cold, lifeless assent, or a train of ideas in the head. It is primarily a disposition of the heart. Scripture declares, "If you confess with your lips that Jesus is Lord and believe in your heart that God raised him from the dead, you will be saved."

5. By confessing Christ in this way, saving faith differs from the kind of faith that the Apostles had while our Lord was on earth. Saving faith understands the necessity of Christ's death, its merit, and the power of his Resurrection. This faith acknowledges the death of Jesus as the only satisfactory means of redeeming humankind from everlasting death. It confesses Christ's resurrection as the restoration of us all to life and immortality. For Christ "was handed over to death for our trespasses and was raised for our justification."

Thus, Christian faith is more than an intellectual assent to the entire gospel of Christ. It also means a complete reliance on the blood of Christ; it is full trust in the merits of his life, death, and Resurrection. Saving faith is a resting upon Christ as our atonement and our life—a savior who gave himself for us and lives in us. The result of saving faith is uniting with Christ, and adhering firmly to him "who became for us wisdom from God, and righteousness and sanctification and redemption." In a word, Christ is our salvation.

II. The salvation that comes through faith

1. First, redemption is something that we can obtain in the present—indeed, now while we are on the earth. Paul said to the Christian

believers at Ephesus, and through them to the believers of all ages, not that we will be saved (although that also is true). Paul said, "You *have been* saved, through faith."

2. In sum, Christ saves us from sin. The salvation that comes through faith is that great salvation predicted by the angel, before God brought his first-begotten son, Jesus, into the world. An angel said to Joseph in a dream, "You are to name him Jesus, for he will save his people from their sins." Neither here nor elsewhere in scripture are there limitations on, or restrictions to, the extent of Christ's redeeming work. Every trusting person "who believes in him receives forgiveness of sins through his name." Jesus Christ is willing to save all the people from all their sins—original and actual, past and present, sins of the flesh and sins of the spirit. Through faith in him, those who believe are saved both from the guilt and from the power of sin.

3. To begin with, Christ saves us from the guilt of all past sin. The entire world is guilty before God. As the psalmist wrote, "If you, O LORD, should mark iniquities, Lord, who could stand?" The law brings the knowledge of sin, but the law cannot bring deliverance from sin. Paul concluded, "No human being will be justified in his sight by deeds prescribed by the law, for through the law comes the knowledge of sin." "The righteousness of God comes through faith in Jesus Christ for all who believe." According to Paul, people "are now justified by his grace as a gift, through the redemption that is in Christ Jesus, whom God put forward as a sacrifice of atonement by his blood." "Christ redeemed us from the curse of the law by becoming a curse for us." God "erased the record that stood against us with its legal demands. He set this aside, nailing it to the cross." "There is therefore now no condemnation for those who are in Christ Jesus."

4. Because those who trust in Christ are saved from guilt, they are saved from fear. They are not freed from a son or daughter's dread of displeasing a parent, but they are freed from all slavish fear. Christian believers are free from tormenting fear, from dread of punishment, and from anxiety about the wrath of God. They no longer regard God as an oppressive master, but as a kind parent. In the words of Paul, "You did not receive a spirit of slavery to fall back into fear, but you have received a spirit of adoption. When we cry, 'Abba! Father!' it is that very Spirit bearing witness with our spirit that we are children of God." Christian believers are also saved from the dread, though not from the possibility, of falling away from the grace of God and of coming short of his precious and very great promises. As a consequence, they have "peace with God through our Lord Jesus Christ." They rejoice in the hope of the glory of God because "God's love has been poured into our hearts

through the Holy Spirit who has been given to us." Consequently, those who believe are convinced (although perhaps not at all times, nor with the same strength of conviction) that "neither death, nor life, neither the present or the future will be able to separate them from the love of God that is in Christ Jesus our Lord."

5. Through this faith, Christian believers are saved from the power and guilt of sin. Therefore, the Apostle John declares, "You know that he was revealed to take away sins, and in him there is no sin. No one who abides in him keeps on sinning." John continues, "Dear children, do not let anyone lead you astray. . . . He who does what is sinful is of the devil." "Those who have been born of God do not sin, because God's seed abides in them; they cannot continue to sin, because they have been born of God." Once more, "We know that those who are born of God do not continue to sin, but the one who was born of God protects them, and the evil one does not touch them."

6. Those who by faith are born of God do not continue in sin. (1) They are no longer in bondage to besetting sins that stem from the reign of sin in the heart. Sin no longer rules the lives of Christian believers. (2) Believers are no longer captives to willful sin. So long as they continue in faith, sin is as abhorrent to them as a deadly poison. (3) Christians lose their lust for sin because they now desire the holy and perfect will of God. By God's grace, tendencies toward unholy desires can be resisted as soon as they arise. (4) Those human infirmities that are neither deliberate nor intentional may cause us to fall short. But if they are neither deliberate nor intentional, they are not properly considered as sins. Therefore, "No one who is born of God will continue to sin." Although Christian believers cannot claim that they have never sinned, they no longer need be subject to sin's power.

7. We have been considering the present day salvation that comes through faith. This salvation delivers us from sin and its consequences. We often refer to this work of God as justification. Understood in its largest sense, justification means deliverance from guilt and punishment through the atonement of Christ, which is applied to the soul of the sinner who trusts in him. This trust leads to deliverance from the power of sin, through Christ who lives in the heart. Those who are justified in this way—that is, saved by faith—are truly born again of the Spirit into a new life. These believers are "now hidden with Christ in God." These newly born children of God gladly receive the "pure spiritual milk, so that by it they may grow in their salvation." New Christians continue in the strength of the Lord, from faith to faith, from grace to grace, until they come to "maturity, to the measure of the full stature of Christ."

41

3. Answers to some objections to salvation by faith

1. Some might charge, "To preach salvation, or justification by faith alone, is to preach against holiness and good works." There is a short answer to this criticism: The preaching of faith could imply the neglect of or the disparagement of good works if one means, as some do, a faith that is separated from works. However, we are speaking of a faith that is the foundation of all good works and of all holiness.

2. We need to consider in greater depth the alleged conflict between faith and works. This supposed conflict is not a new issue. It is as old as the time of St. Paul. Even then, some asked, "Do we then overthrow the law by this faith?" We answer, first, that those who incorrectly preach faith *do* undermine the law. Directly and ignorantly, through their disclaimers and commentaries they wear away the entire force of the text. In addition, any failure to preach both faith and works can indirectly weaken the need for good works. It is only by faith that we are able to do good works.

Secondly, "we establish the law" only by understanding its full extent and spiritual meaning. We promote good works only by calling people to faith, through which "the just requirement of the law might be fulfilled in us." Those who trust in the blood of Christ alone use all the ordinances that he has instituted. They do all the "good works, which God prepared beforehand to be our way of life." They enjoy and manifest all holy and heavenly affections—having the same mind in them that was in Christ Jesus.

3. Some may ask, "But does not preaching salvation by faith lead people into pride?" We answer that possibly such could be the case. Therefore, we should earnestly caution every believer with the words of Paul who said that the Jews were broken off because of unbelief, but the Gentiles remain only through faith. "So do not become proud, but stand in awe. For if God did not spare the natural branches, perhaps he will not spare you. Note then the kindness and the severity of God: severity toward those who have fallen, but God's kindness toward you, provided you continue in his kindness; otherwise, you also will be cut off." And as believers continue in faith, they should remember those words of St. Paul, words that anticipate and answer the objection that preaching faith leads people into pride: "Then what becomes of boasting? It is excluded. By what principle? By that of works? No, but by the law of faith."

If works justify us, we would have a basis for pride. However, there is no basis for pride in the one who "without works trusts him who justifies the ungodly. Such faith is reckoned to him as righteousness." But there is no boasting for him. The same meaning is found in these verses: "But God, who is rich in mercy, made us alive together with Christ. By grace you have been saved. God raised us up with Christ and seated us with him in the heavenly places in Christ Jesus, so that in the ages to come he might show the immeasurable riches of his grace in kindness toward us in Christ Jesus. For by grace you have been saved through faith, and this is not your own doing."

We ourselves cannot produce either faith or salvation. God freely gives these gifts to us, as undeserving as we are. It is because of God's good pleasure and pure grace that he adds to us the faith that brings us to salvation. The fact that you believe is one of the works of his grace. That believing, you are saved is another of God's works. Salvation is "not the result of works, so that no one may boast." Our good works and "righteousness" prior to our believing gained us no merit. We remained under God's condemnation. Human efforts to earn God's favor are antithetical to faith. For that matter, even good works done by Christian believers cannot earn salvation. It is God who enables us to do good works. Any rewards we receive for good works are for the deeds that *God* enables. This fact magnifies the riches of his mercy and leaves us without any basis for pride.

4. Some may object by saying, "Might speaking about the mercy of God as justifying us freely by faith alone (that is, saving us) invite us to sin?" Indeed it might, and it will do so if we join with those who say that we can "continue in sin in order that grace may abound." However, such people are responsible for their own destruction. The goodness of God should lead them to repentance. And it will do so for those who have sincere hearts. When they know that God will still forgive them through faith in Jesus, they will see aright that he would blot out their sins. And if they earnestly and steadfastly repent, if they seek God through the means he has provided, and if they refuse to be satisfied until the Lord comes to them, "the one who is coming will come and will not delay."

Furthermore, God can do much work in a short time. In the book of Acts, there are many examples of God's imparting faith to human hearts as swiftly as lightning from heaven. In the same hour that Paul and Silas began to preach, the jailer repented, believed, and was baptized. When St. Peter preached on the day of Pentecost, three thousand souls repented and believed when they heard his first sermon. Blessed be God, there are now many living proofs that he is still "mighty to save."

5. On the other hand, when the truth of salvation by grace through faith is considered from another perspective, an opposite objection is made. Some will claim, "If we cannot be saved by what we can do, we

will plunge into despair." It is true that people will despair of being saved by their own good works, merits, or their own righteousness. And so they should. In truth, we cannot trust in the merits of Christ until we have utterly renounced our worthiness. Those who seek to establish their own righteousness have not submitted to God's righteousness. They cannot receive the righteousness of God. The righteousness that comes through faith cannot be given to us so long as we trust in our completing the works of the law.

6. Some say that denying that our good works can save us is an "uncomfortable doctrine." So said the devil himself, lying without truth or shame. Salvation through human effort is "very full of comfort" only to all self-destroyed, self-condemned sinners. Scripture states that "whoever believes in him will not be put to shame." "The same Lord is Lord of all and is generous to all who call on him." This doctrine is true, bringing comfort as high as heaven, and stronger than death!

Will God give mercy to all? To Zacchaeus, a tax collector? To Mary Magdalene, a common prostitute? It seems to me that I can hear someone say, "Then, even I can hope for mercy!" And, afflicted one whom no one has comforted, so you can! God will not turn away your prayer. No, indeed. Perhaps he may say even now, "Take heart, child; your sins are forgiven." You are so completely forgiven that your sins will control you no longer. Surely, "God's Spirit bears witness with our spirit that we are children of God." O, good news of great joy for all the people (Luke 2:10). "Everyone who thirsts, come to the waters; and you that have no money, come, buy and eat!" Whatever your sins may be, though red as crimson, though more than the hairs of your head, "return to the LORD, that he may have mercy on you, and to our God, for he will abundantly pardon."

7. After objections have been answered, some may say, "Salvation by faith only ought not to be preached as the first doctrine nor preached to everyone." But what does the Holy Spirit say? "No one can lay any foundation other than the one that has been laid; that foundation is Jesus Christ." Therefore, the truth remains constant: "Everyone who believes in him may not perish but may have eternal life." This truth is the foundation of all our preaching, and it must be preached first and foremost.

Some may say, "Well enough, but not to everyone." To whom, then, are we *not* to preach it? Who shall we except? The poor? No; they have a distinctive right to have the gospel preached to them. Shall we omit the unlearned? No. From the beginning, God has revealed these mysteries to unlearned and ignorant people. Shall we ignore the young? By no means. Jesus said, "Let the little children come to me; do not stop them; for it is to such as these that the kingdom of God belongs." Shall we exclude the sinners? Least of all, should we exclude sinners. "Christ came not to call the righteous, but sinners to repentance."

If any, we might exclude the rich, the learned, the reputable, the moral. It is true, they too often exclude themselves from hearing. Even so, we must speak the words of our Lord to everyone. This is the substance of our commission: "Go into all the world and proclaim the good news to the whole creation." If any one twist or explain away any part of it, to his destruction, he must carry his own load. Always, "as the Lord lives, whatever the Lord says to me, that I will speak."

8. Now, more especially we are determined to proclaim, "By grace you have been saved through faith." We take this position because never more than now has it been more important to uphold the doctrine of salvation by faith. Nothing other than this gospel can with greater effect prevent the increase of the Romish delusion among us. It is ever necessary to strike out, one by one, against all the errors of that church. And salvation by faith strikes at the root of untruth, and all false doctrines crumble when we establish this doctrine. It was the doctrine of salvation by faith that our church justly calls the strong rock and foundation of the Christian religion that first drove Popery out of these kingdoms. It is this doctrine alone that can keep it out. Nothing but this truth can stop the immorality that has flooded the land.

Can you empty the great ocean drop by drop? If so, you could reform the nation by turning us away from particular vices. But let the "righteousness that comes from God and is by faith" come forth, and then will the proud waves of evil be held back. Nothing but this divine truth can stop the mouths of those whose glory is in their shame, who openly deny the sovereign Lord who bought them.

These people can talk sublimely of the law, acting as though God wrote it on their hearts. To hear them speak on this subject might lead one to think that they were not far from the kingdom of God. But to bring them out of the law into the gospel, we must begin by preaching the righteousness that comes by faith. Begin with Christ, who is "the end of the law" so that there may be righteousness for everyone who believes. Then, those who appeared as almost, but not completely, Christians will see themselves as the sons and daughters of perdition. God be merciful to them! They are as far from life and salvation as the depth of hell is from the height of heaven.

9. Because the gospel brings light, the devil rages intensely whenever salvation by faith is proclaimed to the world. For this reason, he stirred up earth and hell in order to destroy those who first preached the gospel

45

of grace. And because he knew that faith alone could overturn the foundations of his kingdom, he called forth all his forces and employed all his artful lies and false accusations, seeking to frighten Martin Luther from reviving this truth.

We should not be surprised at Satan's strategy. As Luther himself observed, "How it would enrage a proud strong man well armed, to be stopped and overcome by a little child standing against him with a reed in his hand!" So much more is this true, when the strong man knew that the little child would surely overthrow him, and tread him under foot. Amen, Lord Jesus! Child of faith, your strength is always "made perfect in weakness!" Go forth, then, little child who trusts in Christ, and his "right hand will display awesome deeds!" Although you are as helpless and weak as is a newborn infant, the devil will not be able to stand before you. You shall prevail over him, and subdue him, and overthrow him, and trample him under your feet. You shall march on, under the great Captain of your salvation, conquering and to conquer until all your enemies are destroyed, and "death has been swallowed up in victory."

Thanks be to God, who gives us the victory through our Lord Jesus Christ, to whom, with the Father and the Holy Spirit blessing and glory and wisdom and thanksgiving and honor and power and might be to our God forever and ever! Amen.

Notes

1. Nehemiah Curnock, ed., *The Journal of the Rev. John Wesley*, 8 vols. (London: Epworth Press, 1909–16), 1:472.
2. Albert C. Outler, ed., *The Works of John Wesley*, Bicentennial Ed., Vols. 1–4, *Sermons* (Nashville: Abingdon Press, 1984–87), 1:401.

THE ALMOST CHRISTIAN

On July 25, 1741, John Wesley preached *The Almost Christian* as a university sermon in St. Mary's Church, Oxford. That day, he wrote in his journal, "It being my turn . . . I preached . . . before the University. The harvest truly is plenteous. So numerous a congregation (from whatever motives they come) I have seldom seen at Oxford. My text was the confession of poor Agrippa, 'Almost thou persuadest me to be a Christian.' I have 'cast my bread upon the waters.' Let me 'find it again after many days!'"[1] On the day that John Wesley preached this sermon, Charles Wesley's journal has this entry: "We met at ten to pray for a blessing on my brother's sermon, which he is preaching at this hour before the University."[2]

This sermon attracted wide attention, and it was rushed into print and sold for two pence, allowing many people to read and discuss it. The fact that Wesley placed *The Almost Christian* as #2 in the Standard Sermons indicates that he regarded it as a foundational message.

In the time that had passed since Wesley's previous sermon at Oxford, he had attracted national attention. Indeed, he had become one of the most recognized persons in England. People either ridiculed him or praised him. Part of the opposition to Wesley was due to his open-air preaching, a practice that offended "proper" churchmen. George Whitefield, a member of the Oxford Holy Club, had pioneered outdoor preaching, and his bishop had threatened to excommunicate him if he continued this "scandalous" practice. Despite ecclesiastical disapproval, Wesley saw open-air preaching as an opportunity to reach the unchurched masses. So he set aside convention and followed Whitefield's example.

Wesley's critics also derided him for teaching that Christians can have the assurance of their salvation. The philosopher John Locke disapprovingly charged that people only claim personal "revelations" when they cannot account for their views by reason.[3] Wesley disagreed with Locke and insisted that one could be entirely rational and at the same time communicate directly with God. Also, opposition came to Wesley because on some occasions certain physical manifestations took place when sinners were converted to Christ under Methodist preaching. Heated discussions swirled around the appearance of these "embarrassing" phenomena.

During the three years prior to delivering this sermon, Wesley had drawn additional criticism because he had organized numerous Methodist societies and permitted lay speakers to preach. Adding fuel to the fires of criticism, Wesley had purchased and opened the Foundery (a renovated iron foundery) in London as a place for Methodist worship. This facility had a chapel seating 1,500 people. The Methodists who attended services at the Foundery supported controversial social ministries such as a free school, almshouse, book room, and dispensary. Wesley had also revived the practice of Love Feasts and Watch Night Services. Although the Anglican ritual provided for these kinds of services, they had long been neglected. The Methodists received criticism for reinstating them.

Thus, numerous church leaders and secular critics condemned Methodist ministries, innovations, and successes. At this time, most of the members of London's clergy would not permit Wesley to preach in their pulpits. (There were four exceptions.) It is not surprising that the occasion of this sermon attracted a large congregation of curious people to hear the controversial evangelist. Those in the congregation riveted their eyes on John Wesley, the much-discussed Oxford don.

In this sermon, Wesley describes the religion of the Almost Christian, as what he saw in many members of the Oxford university community who were present in the congregation. He declared that Almost Christians have a form of godliness, but lack the power of those who are Altogether Christians. This sermon presses home Wesley's message that good works are not saving. He insists that only a personal conversion can transform one from an Almost Christian into an Altogether Christian.

Many years later, in 1787, Wesley contrasted unfaithful and faithful clergymen, explaining the difference between Almost and Altogether Christians:

They would have their parishioners moral men; that is, in plain terms, honest Heathens; but they would not have them pious men, men devoted to God, Bible Christians. If, therefore, the Methodist Preachers would stop here, would preach outward religion and no more, many Clergymen would not only encourage them therein, but likewise cordially join them. But when they persuade men, not to be almost, but altogether, Christians; to maintain a constant "fellowship with the Father, and his Son Jesus Christ" to be transformed into that "image of God wherein they were created," and thenceforth to live that "life which is hid with Christ in God;"let them not expect that any will give them the right hand of fellowship, but those God hath "chosen out of the world."[4]

The divisions of "the form of godliness" outlined in this sermon shaped the General Rules of the United Societies (of Methodists) that John and Charles Wesley published in 1743. This sermon explains Wesley's distinction between the Almost Christian and the Altogether Christian, while underscoring his belief in the necessity of demonstrating both the form and the power of godliness.

Sermon 2

THE ALMOST CHRISTIAN

Preached at St. Mary's, Oxford, before the university on July 25, 1741.

Are you so quickly persuading me to become a Christian?
(Acts 26:28)

Ever since the Christian religion came into the world, there have been many people in every age and nation who have been *almost* persuaded to become Christians. However, because we gain no advantage before God to go only that far, it is highly important for us to consider (1) what is an Almost Christian and (2) what is an Altogether Christian.

I. The Almost Christian

1. Being an Almost Christian includes the common virtue that can be found even in those who do not worship the God of the Bible. No one, I think, will dispute this claim. I do not refer only to those things that heathen philosophers recommend in their writings. I am also referring to those things that ordinary unbelievers expected from one another, and what many of them actually practiced. They gained the knowledge that they ought not to be unjust in their dealings with their neighbors by robbing, thieving, oppressing the friendless, extorting, cheating, or defraud-

ing either the poor or the rich. Heathen writers taught against taking away the rights of others or owing them unpaid debts.

2. Even ordinary people without spiritual enlightenment have recognized that we have obligations to truth and justice. Accordingly, they have looked with disgust toward those who perjure themselves, give false testimony in God's name, slander, or falsely accuse others. Heathens held liars of any kind in contempt, considering them disgraceful examples and blights on society.

3. Even people who have been ignorant of the religion of the Bible have demonstrated a willingness to love and help others. Heathen people expected everyone to give mutual assistance, without putting self in first place. They applied this principle not only to small services of courtesy that required little expense or effort. As they were able, out of their abundance, they fed the hungry and clothed the naked. Overall, heathen people gave the things they could spare to those in need. Thus, this code of ethics, held by those without the full knowledge of God, is the first mark of an Almost Christian.

4. A second mark of an Almost Christian is holding to the outward form of godliness, that is, the outer life of reverence and conduct that scripture requires of the real Christian. Hence, the Almost Christian does nothing that the gospel forbids. He or she does not make wrongful use of the name of God, but blesses others and refrains from judging them. Almost Christians do not swear oaths. Instead, they speak a simple Yes or No. They do not desecrate the Lord's Day or even permit it to be defiled by their guests. The Almost Christian avoids adultery, fornication, and unchaste behavior—even the slightest word or glance that tends toward these things. The Almost Christian avoids useless and vain conversation, slander, speaking evil of others, gossip, foul language, and obscene, silly, and "vulgar talk." (The original word means "uncouth jesting," or "buffoonery," which is a type of virtue in some cultures.) In a word, the Almost Christian does not engage in social interchange that is not useful or constructive. Such conduct grieves the Holy Spirit of God, by whom Christians are marked with a seal for the day of redemption.

5. The Almost Christian abstains from wine, which leads to debauchery, and from carousing and gluttony. As much as possible, Almost Christians avoid strife and altercations, always seeking to live peaceably with everyone. If forced to endure wrong, they do not avenge themselves or return evil for evil. With regard to the faults or weaknesses of neighbors, Almost Christians are not scoffers, brawlers, or mocking scorners. They do not willingly harm, hurt, or grieve any one. In every situation,

Almost Christians act and speak by the simple rule, "In everything do to others as you would have them do to you."

6. Seeking to live virtuously, Almost Christians do not limit themselves to light and easy acts of kindness. Rather, their attitude is to work and persevere for the benefit of many, serving others in every way possible. Despite toil and discomfort, the Almost Christian lives by the precept, "Whatever your hand finds to do, do with your might." Almost Christians help friend and foe, assisting evil folk and good folk. Not lagging in zeal, whenever they have an opportunity they work for the good of all, for their souls and bodies. Almost Christians correct evil people, instruct uninformed people, strengthen those of unsettled opinion, encourage good people, and comfort those in distress. They work to rouse those that are asleep and to guide those whom God has awakened to the fountain opened for sin and impurity. The Almost Christian will encourage unconverted people to become pure in God's cleansing fountain, while encouraging Christians, through faith, to live out Christ's gospel in every circumstance.

7. Those that have a form of godliness (but not yet its power) use the means of grace in all circumstances. They faithfully attend the house of God, seeking to worship in truth, not as those who strut into God's presence with a show of riches, fine clothing, and pretentious fashions. Such people, by their insincere flatteries and irreverent behavior, renounce any claims to the form and power of godliness. God forbid that there are any among us that fall under such condemnation! I hope that none come into this place of worship, perhaps with vacant stares, signs of indifference, or careless apathy—even while appearing to pray for God's blessing on their lives. Even during an awe-inspiring service of worship, these people are either asleep or slouched in a comfortable posture, as though they assumed that God were asleep. They talk with each other or look around, being entirely uninterested in genuine worship.

You could never accuse these people of having even the form of godliness. No, not at all. Those who have the form of godliness behave in a serious manner and give attention to every part of the worship service. They are especially reverent in approaching the Lord's Table, never with a frivolous or careless attitude. Instead, by disposition and action they are clearly saying, "God be merciful to me, a sinner."

8. To sincere attitudes and actions, we must add the regular use of family prayer, conducted by those in charge of households. As well, the Almost Christian also sets aside dedicated times for private conversations with God. To have the form of godliness, one gives daily attention

to one's behavior, applying religion to one's public life. One thing more is needed to be an Almost Christian—sincerity.

9. By sincerity I mean a genuine inner principle of religion, which is the true source of outward actions. Definitely, if we are not sincere we do not have even the virtues of spiritually unenlightened people—not even enough integrity to meet the requirements of a heathen Epicurean poet. Truly, in their serious reflections such pitiable persons are moved solemnly to declare,

> Good men avoid sin from the love of virtue;
> Wicked men avoid sin from the fear of punishment.[5]

Thus, if one abstains from doing evil only to avoid punishment, as the heathen proverb declares, "He shall not be hanged on the cross to feed the crows." This escape from retribution is one's only reward. Even the heathen author would not grant such a person the status of a good heathen. If, then, one should abstain from evil deeds only to avoid punishment, the loss of friends, reduced profits, or the loss of reputation, and perform good works and use every means of grace—we still cannot properly call him an Almost Christian. Unless he has a higher motive in his heart, he is a complete hypocrite.

10. Sincerity, therefore, is necessary for one to become an Almost Christian. One needs to have a genuine commitment to serve God, and also a zealous desire to do his will. In everything one does or avoids, it is necessary to have a sincere intention completely to please God in all conduct and manner of living. If one is to be even an Almost Christian, this purpose runs through the whole tenor of his or her life. Serving God must be the moving principle in good works, avoiding evil, and taking the sacraments.

11. Now, someone might ask, "Is it possible that any living person could live this way and yet remain only an Almost Christian? What greater standard is involved in being a Christian altogether?" To begin with, I answer that it is possible to go this far, and still be only an Almost Christian. I gain this understanding from the Bible and also from the unfailing evidence of experience.

12. St. Paul said, "Brothers, I have great pride in you." "Forgive me this wrong, if I declare my own foolish ignorance from the housetop for your and the gospel's sake." "Permit me to speak freely about my conviction, even as I might speak as a third person. I am content to lower myself in order to elevate you and to be of small account for the glory of my Lord."

13. For many years, I have abided by the outward forms, as many here can witness. I have been diligent to shun all evil, and to keep my conscience clear, making the most of every opportunity to do good toward everyone. I have steadfastly and carefully used every public and private means of grace. Always and everywhere, I have striven for a consistent seriousness in my conduct. God, before whom I stand, is my witness that I have sincerely maintained a genuine purpose to serve him. I have had a zealous craving to do his will in everything. I have desired only to please him who called me to "fight the good fight," and to "take hold of eternal life." Even so, by the Holy spirit, my own conscience bears witness to me that all this time I was only an Almost Christian.

II. The Altogether Christian

If someone asks, "What more than this is involved in being an Altogether Christian?" I answer,

1. First, the Altogether Christian has a love for God. As Jesus said, "Love the Lord your God with all your heart, and all your soul, and with all your mind and with all your strength." This kind of love completely lays hold of the entire self. It claims every affection, fills the entire capacity of the soul, and engages the full range of its abilities. In those that so love the Lord their God, their spirits continuously "rejoice in God their Savior." They take great pleasure in the Lord as master and as their complete sufficiency, to whom they give thanks in all circumstances. Altogether Christians desire only God and repeatedly call upon his name. Their hearts continuously cry out, "Whom have I in heaven but you? There is nothing on earth that I desire other than you." Indeed, what better object can we desire than God? Certainly, not the world or the things of the world.

Altogether Christians have been "crucified to the world, and the world crucified to them." They are dead to the cravings of sinful humanity, "the desire of the flesh, the desire of the eyes, the pride in riches." Indeed, Altogether Christians are crucified to every kind of conceit, for love is not proud. Those who abide in love, God abides in them. These people regard themselves as completely insufficient without God.

2. The second component of an Altogether Christian is love for others. Our Lord plainly said, "You shall love your neighbor as yourself." If any one asks, "Who is my neighbor?" we reply plainly. Your neighbor is every person in the world, every human being created by God, the maker of us all. We must not exclude loving our enemies, the enemies of

God, or those who are their own enemies. We are to live lives of love for others, just as Christ loved us.

Those that want to understand this kind of love may consider St. Paul's description: "Love is patient; love is kind; love is not envious or boastful or arrogant." Love causes us to serve neighbors. "Love is not rude;" it becomes "all things to all people." The love that Paul describes does not seek its own interests. Rather, it seeks only the welfare and salvation of all people. "Love is not easily angered." It turns away from animosity, an attitude that reveals the lack of love. "Love keeps no record of wrongs. Love does not delight in evil but rejoices in the truth. It always protects, always trusts, always hopes, always perseveres."

3. There is still one more characteristic of the Altogether Christian. We may consider it separately, although it cannot properly be separated from loving God and neighbor. I am speaking of that which is the ground of all the rest—faith.

Scripture speaks an abundance of good things about this spiritual virtue. John said, "Everyone who believes that Jesus is the Christ has been born of God." "To all who received him, who believed in his name, he gave power to become children of God." "This is the victory that conquers the world—our faith." Indeed, our Lord himself declared, "Very truly, I tell you, anyone who hears my word and believes him who sent me has eternal life, and does not come under judgment, but has passed from death to life."

4. With these truths before us, let no one be self-deceived. It is crucial to keep in mind that the kind of faith which fails to produce repentance, love, and good works is not genuine living faith. Instead, it is dead and entirely deficient. Remember, even the demons believe that Christ was born of a virgin, that he wrought all kinds of miracles, and that he declared himself fully God. Demons understand that, for our sakes, Christ suffered a most painful death to redeem us from everlasting destruction. They know that he arose on the third day, that he ascended into heaven, that he sits at the right hand of the Father, and that at the end of the age he shall come again to judge both the living and the dead. The demons believe these articles of our faith. They also believe everything that is written in the Old and New Testaments. Still, for all this belief, they continue to remain in their damnable condition, devoid of authentic Christian faith.

5. In the words of our Anglican Church, true and genuine Christian faith is "not only to believe that holy Scripture and the Articles of our faith are true, but also to have a steadfast faith and confidence in Christ to save us from everlasting condemnation. It is a certain faith and

confidence that one places in God, trusting in the merits of Christ that one's sins are forgiven and one is reconciled to God. From this faith proceeds a heart that loves him and obeys his commandments."[6]

6. On the basis of unwavering faith, whoever believes in the full sufficiency of Christ is an Altogether Christian. This faith, resulting from God's power within us, cleanses our hearts from pride, anger, lusts, all unrighteousness, and "every defilement of body and spirit." God's inner presence is stronger than death, filling our hearts with love for him and for all people. The heart obeys God and is happy to spend and to be spent for others. With joy, this kind of trust patiently bears the world's censure against Christ. It endures being mocked, disdained, and hated. It accepts whatever God's providence permits, whether from malicious people or from demons. Those who have this faith that works by love are more than Almost Christians. They are Altogether Christians.

7. Now, are there any living examples of these truths? I urgently entreat you, brothers and sisters who stand in the presence of the God before whom death and destruction cannot be concealed, understand even how much more known to God are human hearts! Let all people examine their hearts and ask themselves, "Am I a living testimony of what it means to be an Altogether Christian?

"Do I practice justice, mercy, and truth, even to the standards that heathen virtue requires? If so, do I actually have the outward characteristics of a Christian? Do I have the form of godliness? Do I abstain from evil and those things the written word of God forbids? With a full will and with all my might, do I do everything my hand finds to do? At every opportunity, do I earnestly attend to all the ordinances of God? Furthermore, do I do these things with a sincere intention and earnest desire to please God in all things?"

8. Are many of you conscious that you have not come this far? Is it true that you are not even an Almost Christian and that you do not even arrive at the standard of heathen virtue? Can you say that you have a form of Christian godliness? Does God see in you sincerity and a genuine intention to please him in everything? Do you aim at dedicating all your words, deeds, pursuits, studies, and diversions to God's glory? Perhaps you have never planned or desired to do everything "in the name of the Lord Jesus" and to become "a spiritual sacrifice, acceptable to God through Jesus Christ."

9. Let us suppose, however, that you do have such good intentions. Do good plans and good wishes make one a Christian? By no means, unless your plans result in actions that achieve your aspirations. Someone has said, "Hell is paved with good intentions."[7] The supreme question,

therefore, still remains: Has God's love been poured into your heart? Can you say to him, "My God, and my all"? Do you desire nothing but him? Are you happy in God? Is he your glory, your delight, your crown of rejoicing?

Furthermore, is the following commandment written in your heart: "Whoever loves God must also love his brother?" Do you love your neighbor as yourself and as Christ loved you? Do you love even your enemies and the enemies of God? Can you say that you believe Christ loves you and gave himself for you? Do you have faith in his blood? Do you believe that the Lamb of God has taken away your sins and cast them as a stone into the depth of the sea? Do you believe that God has expunged the record against you, removing it and nailing it to his cross? Do you truly have redemption through his blood, even the remission of your sins? And does God's Spirit bear witness with your spirit that you are a child of God?

10. The God and Father of our Lord Jesus Christ now stands in our midst. If any one should die without faith in, and love for, him, it would have been better for that person if he had not been born. Awake, therefore, you that sleep, and call upon your God. Call upon him just now, while he may be found. Do not cease praying until he causes all his goodness to pass before you, and he will proclaim the name of the Lord before you. "The Lord, who is the compassionate and gracious God, slow to anger, abounding in love and faithfulness, maintaining love to thousands, will forgive wickedness, rebellion, and sin." Let no one turn you aside by empty words and cause you to stop short of the goal of winning the prize to which God has called you. Rather, keep on seeking him until you know him in whom you place your faith and can say, "My Lord, and my God!" Remember, "Always pray and do not lose heart." Never lose faith, until you can lift your hand to heaven, and proclaim to the eternal God, "Lord, you know all things; you know that I love you."

11. May we all move beyond being merely Almost Christians. We can become Altogether Christians. Then, we will be justified through faith by the redemption that is in Jesus, knowing that we have peace with God through our Lord Jesus Christ. Rejoicing in anticipation of the glory of God, we experience God's love poured out into our hearts by the Holy Spirit whom he has given us.

Notes

1. W. Reginald Ward and Richard Heitzenrater, eds., *The Works of John Wesley,* Bicentennial Ed., Vols. 18-23, Journals and Diaries (Nashville: Abingdon Press, 1988–1995), 19:205-06.

2. Charles Wesley, *The Journal of Charles Wesley,* 2 vols. (London: Robert Cully, 1910; reprinted by Beacon Hill Press, 1980), July 25, 1741, 1:200.

3. John Locke, An Essay *Concerning Human Understanding: To Which are Now Added, I. An Analysis of Mr. Locke's Doctrine of Ideas, on a Large Sheet. II. A Defence of Mr. Locke's Opinion Concerning Personal Identity, With an Appendix Essay Concerning Human Understanding, "Of Enthusiasm,"* 3 vols., 1st American from the 20th London ed. (Boston : Printed by David Carlisle, for Thomas & Andrews, Joseph Nancrede, 1803).

4. Thomas Jackson, *The Works of the Rev. John Wesley,* 14 vols. (London: Wesleyan Methodist Book Room, 1829–31), "An Answer to an Important Question," 13:263.

5. Horace, *Epistles,* 1.xvi, 52, 53.

6. *Homilies,* On the Salvation of Man, part III.

7. Attributed to Samuel Johnson. See James Boswell, *Life of Dr. Johnson,* 1:555.

Introduction to Sermon 8

"AWAKE, THOU THAT SLEEPEST"

Of the standard printed sermons published by John Wesley, this discourse is the only one preached by Charles Wesley. He delivered it before the University of Oxford in St. Mary's Church on Sunday, April 4, 1742. It is one of two sermons of Charles Wesley published during his lifetime.

As in the case of the sermons that John Wesley preached at Oxford, Charles forthrightly told his listeners that without faith in Christ they were lost forever and bound for perdition. Charles's blunt message upset many members of the university community and created much discussion. Matthew Simon, who was present at the service that day, reflected the views of those who took offense at Charles Wesley's message: "Having insulted and abused all degrees [students and those with bachelors, masters, and doctoral degrees], from the highest to the lowest, he was in a manner hissed out of the pulpit by the lads."

After delivering this message, Charles Wesley met with the vice-chancellor of the university and the Dean of Christ Church. Charles summarized the conversation:

I waited upon the Dean, who spoke with unusual severity against field-preaching, and Mr Whitefield. He explained away all inward religion, and union with God. That the world, and their god, abhor our manner of acting, I have too sensible proof. . . . He denied justification by faith only; and all vital religion: promised me, however to read [William] Law and [Blaise] Pascal.[1]

59

Despite the criticisms of many who first heard this sermon, history has judged it to be a Christian classic. Thomas Jackson, one of Charles Wesley's biographers, later reviewed the positive aspects of this sermon:

> It is plain, simple, and unadorned; but withal energetic and earnest almost beyond example. . . . The discourse is addressed with great fidelity and power to the consciences of unconverted men. The accomplished Collegian is lost in the Christian Minister, whose heart is all on fire to turn the people from sin, worldliness, and misery, to Christ, and holiness, and heaven. It is doubtful whether any sermon in the English language, or in any language upon earth, has passed through so many editions, or has been a means of so much spiritual good.[2]

This sermon represents the agreement that John and Charles Wesley had regarding matters of essential doctrine. On the day that Charles preached this sermon, John Wesley wrote in his journal, "About two in the afternoon, being the time my brother was preaching at Oxford, before the University, I desired a few persons to meet with me, and join in prayer. We continued herein much longer than we first designed, and believed we had the petition we asked of God."[3]

John was a master of logic; Charles excelled in flights of emotion and powers of description. Each brother's preaching style was effective because it fit his personality and ability. Concerning their manner of public speaking, in 1766 John wrote Charles, "In connexion I beat you; but in strong, pointed sentences you beat me. Go on, in your own way, what God has peculiarly called you to."[4] Charles Wesley's poetic imagery and flaming zeal are apparent in this sermon. Edward Sugden evaluated the preaching of Charles Wesley: "The bewildering swiftness of his rapier-play beats down his opponent's guard and does not allow him an instant to recover himself. He gains his point, not by dint of argument, but by the irresistible rush of the torrent of his emotion."[5]

An observer of one of Charles's outdoor sermons wrote, "He preached about an hour in such a manner as I scarce ever heard any man preach. . . . I never heard any man discover such evident signs of a vehement desire, or labour so earnestly, to convince his hearers that they were all by nature in a sinful, lost, undone state. He showed how great a change a faith in Christ would produce in the whole man; and that every man who is in Christ—that is, who believe in him unto salvation—is a new creature."[6]

At the end of the sermon, Charles Wesley modulates into prayer: "Help us, O God our Savior, for the glory of your name; deliver us and atone for our sins for your name's sake. And then we will not turn away from you. Revive us, and we will call on your name. Restore us, O Lord God almighty; make your face shine upon us, that we may be saved."

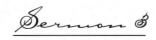

"AWAKE, THOU THAT SLEEPEST"

Sleeper, awake! Rise from the dead, and Christ will shine on you. *(Ephesians 5:14)*

In preaching on these words, with the help of God, (1) I will describe the sleepers, to whom this text is spoken, (2) I will give a summons: "Wake up! O sleeper, rise from the dead, and Christ will shine on you," and (3) I will expound upon the promise, "Christ will shine on you."

I. The sleepers: those to whom the promise is given

1. The natural state of humankind is to be spiritually asleep. This sleep follows from the fall of Adam, and it blankets all his descendants. Moral lethargy, laziness, and dullness of understanding characterize this spiritual slumber. Ignorance of one's true spiritual condition characterizes everyone, and this state continues until the voice of God awakens us from our sleep.

2. "Those who sleep, sleep at night." Our natural state of slumber is one of utter darkness. This sleep is a state in which "darkness covers the earth and thick darkness is over the peoples." Regardless of how much understanding people may have of other things, impoverished, unawakened sinners have no understanding of their own spiritual state. "The man who thinks he knows something does not yet know as he ought to know." People do not understand that they are unregenerate. They are

fallen spirits whose only task in the present world is to recover from their fallen state and regain the image of God in which they were created. Those who are spiritually asleep see no necessity for the one thing needful—a total inward change, the "birth from above." This new birth is represented by baptism, which is the beginning of a complete restoration to life. This work of God is the sanctification of spirit, soul, and body, "without which no one shall see the Lord."

3. Unawakened sleepers, despite being full of all spiritual diseases, imagine themselves to be in perfect health. Shackled by misery and chains, the sleepers dream that they are free. They say, "Peace! Peace!" while the devil, as "a strong man, fully armed," has full possession of their souls. The unawakened continue to sleep, although hell yawns from beneath to receive them. Death, from whence there is no return, has opened its mouth to swallow them up. A fire has ignited around them, although they do not know it. Indeed, it already burns them, but they pay no attention.

4. Would to God that we all might understand that those who sleep are sinners who are contented in their lost condition. They are satisfied to remain in their fallen state and to live and die without being renewed in the image of God. Sleepers are ignorant both of their disease and of its only remedy. Some were never warned, others ignore the warning voice of God "to flee from the wrath to come," and still others never comprehend "the danger of hell fire." These sleepers never cry out in earnestness of soul, "What must I do to be saved?"

5. If those who sleep are not outwardly addicted to immorality, as a rule their sleep is the deepest of all. These persons may be of the Laodicean spirit, "neither cold nor hot." They are quiet, rational, inoffensive, good-natured people who profess the religion of their parents. Perhaps they are zealous and orthodox, "according to the strictest sect of our religion," and live as a Pharisee. According to scripture, a Pharisee is one who pronounces himself righteous and works to establish his own holiness as the basis of God's acceptance.

6. Those who sleep "have a form of godliness but deny its power." In truth, they very likely revile holiness in whatever form it appears, regarding it as sheer excess or mere delusion. All the while, these woeful self-deceivers thank God that they are "not like other men—robbers, evildoers, adulterers, unjust, or extortioners." They claim that they never harm others, fast twice a week, tithe their income, and do all the good they can. As for legalistic righteousness, they are faultless (Phil. 3:6). They lack nothing of outward godliness, except its inner power. They are not without "religion," but they lack its true spirit. They have the forms of Christianity, but they do not possess its reality and life.

7. Do you not know that however highly esteemed such people may be, they are an abomination in the sight of God? They inherit every calamity that the Son of God has proclaimed and continues to proclaim against "Scribes, Pharisees, and hypocrites." They clean the outside of the cup and dish, but inside they are full of every uncleanness. A vile disease besets them and their hearts are filled with destruction. Our Lord appropriately compares them to "whitewashed tombs" which "appear beautiful on the outside," but nevertheless are "full of dead men's bones and everything unclean." In Ezekiel's words, the dry bones had tendons and flesh and skin covering them, but there was no breath in them. That is, they had no Spirit of the living God. Now, "if anyone does not have the Spirit of Christ, he does not belong to Christ." However, you are of Christ, if the Spirit of God lives in you. If the Holy Spirit does not abide within you, God knows that even now you continue in death.

8. There is an additional characteristic of sleepers, about which I will speak. They remain in death, although they do not know it. They are lifeless toward God—"dead in transgressions and sins," because "the sinful mind is death." St. Paul wrote, "Sin entered the world through one man, and death through sin, and in this way death came to all." This death is not only temporal, but also spiritual and eternal. God said to Adam "You will surely die." Adam did not die physically (of course he did become mortal). He died spiritually. He lost the life of his soul. He died to God, became separated from him, and lost God's gifts of life and happiness.

9. First of all, sin deprives us of the vital union of our souls with God. Now, in the midst of natural life, we exist in spiritual death. And we remain in this state until the Second Adam, Jesus Christ, becomes a life-giving Spirit within us, and awakens us who are spiritually dead in sin, pleasure, riches, or fame. However, before any dead soul can come to life it "hears" (responds to) "the voice of the Son of God." The soul is made aware of its lost condition, and accepts God's sentence of death. The slumbering ones come to know that they are "dead even while they live." They are dead to God and the things of God, having no more power to perform the deeds of a vital Christian than a dead body can perform the functions of one who is alive.

10. Furthermore, it is most certain that those who are dead in sin do not have the capacity to distinguish good from evil. Having eyes, they fail to see; having ears they fail to hear. They do not "taste and see that the Lord is good." They "have never seen God" nor "heard his voice," nor "touched Christ, the living word." The name of Jesus remains meaningless to them; it is "like perfume poured out," "whose robes are fra-

grant with myrrh and aloes and cassia." The soul that sleeps in death has no knowledge of any matters of this sort. The heart has lost all sensitivity and cannot understand these realities.

11. Consequently, sleepers have no spiritual perception, no capacity for sacred knowledge. Those without God's Spirit do not accept the things that come from him, for they are foolishness to them, and they cannot understand them. Those who sleep are not content with being completely unaware of spiritual things, but they deny their actual existence. To them, spiritual impressions are the pure foolishness of a weak mind. They ask, "How can these things be? How can any one know that he is alive to God in the same way that one knows that his body is alive?" All the sleeper needs is the "proof of things"—that divine witness of the Spirit, that testimony of God which is larger and stronger than ten thousand human witnesses.

12. If God's Spirit does not presently bear witness with your spirit that you are a child of God, I pray that by his manifestation and power he would convince you, a destitute, sleeping sinner, that you are a child of the devil! I pray, as I preach, that just now there might be "a noise, a rattling sound" and may "the bones come together, bone to bone." "Come from the four winds, O breath, and breathe into these slain, that they may live." Do not harden your hearts and resist the Holy Spirit, who even now is here to show you your sin "because you have not believed in the name of God's one and only Son."

II. The summons: Wake up, O sleeper, rise from the dead, and Christ will shine on you.

1. With these matters in view, "Wake up, O sleeper, rise from the dead." God calls you now through my message. You bankrupt spirit, he invites you personally to know what is your condition and your only concern here on earth. "How can you sleep? Get up and call upon your God! Maybe he will take notice of you and you will not perish." A mighty storm rages around you, and you are sinking into the depth of damnation, the abyss of God's final condemnation. If you want to escape God's judgments, leap into them and judge yourself so that God will not judge you.

2. Wake up, wake up! Arise this instant, so that you do not "drink from the hand of the Lord the cup of his wrath." Arouse yourself. "Cling to the Lord, the Lord your Righteousness, who is mighty to save!" "Shake off your dust." At the least, let the earthquake of God's fore-

warnings dislodge you. Wake up and call out with the terrified jailer, "What must I do to be saved?" Never rest until you put your faith in the Lord Jesus. Even your faith, which is God's gift, operates by the Holy Spirit.

3. If I am speaking to any of you more than to others, it is to you who think that this exhortation does not concern you. "I have a message from God for you." In his name, I warn you to "flee from the coming wrath." You profane soul, compare yourself with condemned Peter, lying in the dark dungeon, chained between the soldiers, while the jailers guarded the prison door. The night is nearly over; the day is almost here. Then, you are to be ushered out to your execution. In this dreadful state of being, you are sound asleep. You are slumbering in the devil's arms, on the precipice of the pit, in the jaws of everlasting destruction!

4. I pray that the Angel of the Lord will come to you and that light will shine into your prison! May you feel the touch of an all-powerful hand, awakening you with the words, "Quick, get up! Put on your clothes and sandals. Wrap your cloak around you and follow me."

5. Wake up, you eternal spirit! Come out of your slumber of earthly contentment! Do you not know that God created you for himself? You cannot rest until you rest in him. Return, you wanderer! Fly back to the ark of your safety. This world is not your home. Do not consider building transient tents here on earth. You are only an alien and stranger upon the earth. You are only a created being, a temporary resident, just ready to slide into an unchangeable state of being. Act quickly. Eternity draws near, and infinite happiness or infinite misery hinges on what you do now.

6. What is the state of your soul? Even as I speak, were God to require a reckoning, are you prepared to meet death and judgment? Are you able to stand in his sight, "whose eyes are too pure to look on evil?" Are you qualified "to share in the inheritance of the saints in the kingdom of light?" Have you "fought the good fight, and kept the faith?" Have you laid hold of the one thing that is needed? Have you regained the image of God which consists of true righteousness and holiness? Have you put off your old self and put on the new self? Are you invested with the garments of Christ?

7. Do you have oil in your lamp? Grace in your heart? Do you "Love the Lord your God with all your heart and with all your soul and with all your mind and with all your strength?" Do you have the mind in you which was also in Christ Jesus? Are you a Christian in reality, that is, a new creation? Is the old life gone, and have all things become new?

8. Are you a "partaker of the divine nature"? Do you not realize that until Christ Jesus is in you, you live in condemnation? Do you have the practical knowledge that, through the Holy Spirit God has given you, he lives in you and you live in him? Do you not know that "your body is a temple of the Holy Spirit, whom you have received from God"? Do you have the testimony of the Holy Spirit within you, a deposit guaranteeing your inheritance? Have you "received the Holy Spirit"? Are you shocked at this question, not even having heard that there is a Holy Spirit?

9. If the question offends you, you can be assured that you are not a Christian, nor do you want to become one. No, not at all. Even your prayer becomes sinful and you have mocked God this very day. You do so by praying for "the inspiration of his Holy Spirit," when you did not believe there was any such thing to be received.

10. Nevertheless, on the authority of God's word and that of our own Church, I must repeat the question, "Have you received the Holy Spirit?" If you have not, you are not yet a Christian. A Christian is one who is "anointed with the Holy Spirit and power." Without this experience, you have not yet been made a partaker of a religion that is pure and faultless. Do you know what religion is? It is a participation in the divine nature—the life of God in the soul of man.

Religion is Christ formed in the heart—Christ in you, the hope of glory. It is holiness and happiness, heaven begun upon the earth. Religion is not an outward thing; it is "the kingdom of God within you." "The kingdom of God is not a matter of eating and drinking, but of righteousness, peace and joy in the Holy Spirit." It is an everlasting kingdom brought into your soul, "the peace of God which transcends all understanding," "an inexpressible and glorious joy."

11. Do you know that "in Christ Jesus neither circumcision nor uncircumcision has any value"? The only thing that counts is faith expressing itself through love. The important thing is becoming "a new creation" in Christ. Do you see the necessity of inward change, spiritual birth, life from the dead, and holiness? And are you thoroughly convinced that without these things no one will see the Lord? Are you striving after God, being all the more eager to make your calling and election sure? Are you "working out your salvation with reverence and trembling" and are you making every effort to enter through the narrow door? Are you in earnest about your soul? And can you say to the searcher of hearts, "You, O God, are what I long for"? Do you pray, "Lord, you know all things; you know that I love you"?

12. You hope to be saved, but what reason do you have for this hope? Are you resting your hope on having done no harm to others? Or do you rely on having done much good? Do you expect to be saved because, in contrast to others, you are wise, learned, honest, morally good, respected by others, and possess a desirable reputation? I am sorry! All these attributes will never bring you to God. In his reckoning, these things count for nothing. Do you know Jesus Christ, whom God has sent? Has he taught you that "by grace we are saved through faith— and this not from yourselves, it is the gift of God—not by works, so that no one can boast?" As the entire foundation of your hope, have you accepted this true saying: "Christ Jesus came into the world to save sinners?" Do you understand the meaning of Christ's declarations, "I have not come to call the righteous, but sinners" and "I was sent only to the lost sheep?"

Those that hear, let them understand. Are you aware that even now you are lost, dead, and damned? Do you know what you really deserve? Do you sense your destitution? Are you "poor in spirit," anguishing for God and refusing to be comforted? Has the prodigal "come to his senses" and therefore become willing to confess the degradation of feeding on the husks that the pigs eat? Are you willing to live a godly life and ready to suffer the consequent persecution? Do people insult you, persecute you and falsely say all kinds of evil against you because of your love for Christ?

13. I pray that in all these questions you will hear the voice that awakens the dead, and feel the hammer of God's word that breaks a rock in pieces! "Today, if you hear his voice, do not harden your hearts." Now, "Wake up, O sleeper," you who slumber in spiritual death, so that you will not sleep in eternal death! Sense your lost condition and "arise from the dead." Leave your former companions who live in sin and death. Follow Jesus, and let the dead bury their dead. "Save yourselves from this corrupt generation." "Come out from them and be separate. Touch no unclean thing, and the Lord will receive you," and "Christ will shine on you."

III. The promise: Christ will shine upon you

1. Finally, I will explain Christ's promise to shine upon those who believe. How encouraging a concept is the promise, "Christ will give you light." Whoever responds to Christ's call will never seek his face in vain! Even now, if you wake up and rise from spiritual death, Christ has

pledged to give you light. "The Lord will give you favor and honor"—the light of his favor here on earth, and the light of his honor when you receive "the crown of glory that will never fade away." "Your light will break forth like the dawn and your night will become like the noonday." "God who said, 'Let light shine out of darkness,' make his light shine in our hearts to give us the light of the knowledge of the glory of God in the face of Christ. For you who revere his name, the sun of righteousness will rise with healing in his wings." And in the day of reckoning the Lord will say to you, "Arise, shine, for your light has come, and the glory of the Lord rises upon you." Christ will reveal himself in you—and he is the true Light.

2. God is light. And God will give himself to every awakened sinner who waits for him. In Christ, you shall become a temple of the living God, and Christ will dwell in your hearts through faith. Being rooted and established in love, you will have power, together with all the saints, to grasp how wide and long and high and deep is the love of Christ which surpasses knowledge.

3. Understand your calling, brothers. God invites us to become "a dwelling in which God lives by his Spirit." And through his Spirit dwelling in us, here on earth we become saints and we share in the inheritance of the saints in the kingdom of light. How very great and precious are the promises that are truly given to us who believe. By faith "we do not receive the spirit of the world but the Spirit who is from God." This blessing is the sum of all the promises, "that we may understand what God has freely given us."

4. The Spirit of Christ is the supreme gift of God, which, at various times and in different ways, he for so long promised us. Now, after Christ was glorified, God has fully given this gift. God has fulfilled those promises he previously made to the Old Testament fathers: "I will put my Spirit in you and move you to follow my decrees." "I will pour water on the thirsty land, and streams on the dry ground; I will pour out my Spirit on your offspring."

5. Every one of you may become living witnesses of these realities—the forgiveness of sins and the seal of the Holy Spirit. "Everything is possible for him who believes." "Who among you reveres the Lord and yet continues to walk in the dark without light?" In the name of Jesus, I ask you, "Do you believe that his arm is too short, that he is still mighty to save, that he is the same yesterday and today and forever, and that he has authority on earth to forgive sins?" If so, "Take heart, son; your sins are forgiven." God, for Christ's sake, has forgiven you. Accept this word,

"not as the word of men, but as it actually is, the word of God." Then, you are justified freely through faith. Also, you shall be sanctified through the faith that is in Jesus. You will personally attest that "God has given us eternal life, and this life is in his Son."

6. All who hear me, let me freely speak to you; I urge you to accept my word of exhortation, although I am the least regarded in the church. Your conscience confirms it in the Holy Spirit that these things are true, if you have tasted that the Lord is good. "This is eternal life: that we may know him, the only true God, and Jesus Christ, whom he has sent."

Only the knowledge that comes from personal experience constitutes true Christianity. The only genuine Christians are those who have received the Spirit of Christ. Those that have not received him are not Christians. Furthermore, it is not possible to have received the Holy Spirit and not know it. Concerning the reception of the Holy Spirit, the Lord said, "On that day you will realize that I am in my Father, and you are in me, and I am in you." He declared, "The world cannot accept the Spirit of truth, because it neither sees him nor knows him. But you know him, for he lives with you and will be in you."

7. Those who are rooted in this world cannot receive the Holy Spirit. They utterly reject the promise of the Father, speaking against him and reviling him. Everyone who does not acknowledge the Holy Spirit is not of God. Indeed, "This is the spirit of the antichrist, which you have heard is coming and even now is already in the world." Whoever denies the inspiration of the Holy Spirit, or that the indwelling Spirit of God is the common privilege of all believers, is against Christ. The test of a true Christian is belief in the Holy Spirit—the blessing of the gospel and God's inexpressible gift and universal promise.

8. It does not help people to say, "We do not deny the assistance of God's Spirit. We only deny his inspiration, receiving him within, and being able to perceive his presence." Some say, "It is only perceiving the Spirit, being impressed by the spirit or being filled with the Spirit that we deny to have a place in proper religion." I answer, however, that in denying this work of the Holy Spirit, you deny the entire Bible, the whole truth, as well as the promise and testimony of God.

9. Our own excellent church makes no such diabolical distinction. Rather, it speaks plainly about "feeling the Spirit of Christ;" being "moved by the Holy Spirit," and knowing and feeling there is no other name than that of Jesus by which we can receive life and salvation. The church teaches us all to pray for the "inspiration of the Holy Spirit," indeed that we may be "filled with the Holy Spirit." Furthermore, every

presbyter in the church professes to receive the Holy Spirit by the laying on of hands in ordination. Therefore, to deny any of these church teachings is, in effect, to renounce the Church of England as well as the entire Christian Revelation.

10. The wisdom of God has always been "foolishness" in the eyes of unbelievers. It is no wonder, then, that today the great mystery of the gospel would also be "hidden from the wise and learned" as it was in former times. It need not surprise you that the gospel should be almost everywhere denied, ridiculed, and driven from the stage as mere delirium. All who dare openly declare the gospel still are marked as madmen and fanatics! This turn of events is that "falling away" which Paul foretold—that general apostasy among persons of rank and station that has spread over the world. "Go up and down the streets of Jerusalem, look around, consider, and search for only one person who loves the Lord his God with all his heart, and serves him with all his strength." We need to look no further than our own nation to consider the extent to which ungodliness inundates our land! Day by day, people are committing deep depravities of every kind, all too often with impunity. They sin flagrantly and boast in their shame! Who can calculate the instances of the swearing, cursing, irreverence, blasphemy, lying, slandering, gossip, Sabbath desecration, gluttony, drunkenness, revenge, harlotry, adultery, obscenities, fraud, injustice, oppression, and extortion? As a flood, these evils spread over our land.

11. Even among those who have kept themselves pure from the most obscene abominations, how much we see in them anger, sloth, blandness, effeminacy, luxury, self-indulgence, covetousness, lust for preferment, thirst for flattery, materialism, and cowardice! Meanwhile, how little we see of true religion! Where are those that love either God or neighbor, as the Lord has commanded?

On the one hand, we see those who do not even have the form of godliness. On the other hand, we see those who have only the form. Before us on the one hand there stands the open sepulcher; on the other hand we see the whitewashed sepulcher. In actual fact, whoever carefully examines any public gathering of people (I fear, even church gatherings), might easily see that one group consists of Sadducees and the other of Pharisees. The first party has no more concern about religion than if there were no resurrection, angels, or spirits. The other party turns religion into nothing less than a lifeless form, a dull routine of external exercises lacking true faith, love for God, or joy in the Holy Spirit!

71

12. How I wish I could exempt us here in this place! "Brethren, my heart's desire and prayer to God for you is that you will be saved"— saved from this flood of ungodliness. May its torrents of destruction be turned back. But is this the case? Only God knows. Indeed, our own moral sense cannot discern the matter. We have not kept ourselves pure. We are corrupt and detestable. Today, there are only a few that comprehend our plight, few that worship God in spirit and in truth. "We are a stubborn and rebellious generation, whose hearts are not loyal to God, whose spirits are not faithful to him." The Lord appointed us to be "the salt of the earth." "But if the salt loses its saltiness, how can it be made salty again? It is no longer good for anything except to be thrown out and trampled by humankind."

13. The Lord declares, "Should I not punish them for this? Should I not avenge myself on such a nation as this?" Indeed, we do not know how soon God may say to the sword, "Let the sword pass throughout the land." He has given us a long period in which to repent. God is staying his hand of judgment now, as in the past. He warns us, however, and awakens us by thunder. His judgments are before us on the earth. We have every reason to expect the severest judgments of all—that he will come to us and remove our lampstand from its place, unless we repent and do the things we did at first. Judgment will come if we do not return to the principles of the Reformation, the truth and simplicity of the gospel. It is possible that we are now resisting the last effort of God's divine grace to save us. Perhaps we have almost filled up the measure of our iniquities, by rejecting the counsel of God against ourselves, while rejecting his messengers

14. O God, "in wrath remember mercy!" Be glorified in our acts of reformation, not in our deeds of destruction! Let us "heed the rod and the One who appointed it." Now that "his judgments are in all the earth," "let the people of the world learn righteousness."

15. My brethren, it is high time for us to awaken out of sleep, before the "great trumpet of the Lord will sound," and our land becomes a field of blood. May we quickly comprehend the things that make for our peace, before they are hidden from our eyes! "Restore us again, O God our Savior, and put away your displeasure toward us." O Lord, look down from heaven and see! Watch over this vine and cause us to know the time of your visitation. "Help us, O God our Savior, for the glory of your name; deliver us and atone for our sins for your name's sake." And then we will not turn away from you. "Revive us, and we will call on your name. Restore us, O Lord God almighty; make your face shine upon us, that we may be saved."

"Now to him who is able to do immeasurably more than all we ask or imagine, according to his power that is at work within us, to him be glory in the church and in Christ Jesus throughout all generations, for ever and ever! Amen."

Notes

1. Thomas Jackson, *The Life of the Rev. Charles Wesley*, 1:181-82.
2. Ibid., I, 309-10.
3. Ward and Heitzenrater, *Wesley's Journals and Diaries*, April 4, 1742, 19:258.
4. John Telford, *The Letters of the Rev. John Wesley, A.M.*, 8 vols. (London: Epworth Press, 1931), June 27, 1766, 5:16.
5. Edward Sugden, *Wesley's Standard Sermons*, 2 vols. (London: Epworth Press, 1921), 1:69.
6. *Life and Times of Selina Countess of Huntingdon*, by a member of the houses of Shirley and Hastings, 2 vols. (London: William Edward Painter, Strand, 1844), 2:365.
7. 1 Pet. 1:4. Note the phrase from Henry Scougal's book, *The Life of God in the Soul of Man*, which John Wesley abridged in 1744.

SCRIPTURAL CHRISTIANITY

John Wesley delivered this sermon at the University of Oxford at St. Mary's Church on August 24, 1744. It proved to be the last discourse that he ever preached at the university. By this time, the growing Methodist movement had been rejected by many within the church and the university. Today, ironically, Wesley's portraits and statuary are prominently displayed in several of Oxford's halls and courtyards.

When Wesley delivered this sermon, the Methodist revival had spread widely and gained many converts. Much of the movement's growth had occurred outside the established church, a development that generated much hostility against the Methodists. Only weeks prior to Wesley's scheduled preaching rotation at Oxford, the Methodists had conducted their first conference, a development that was not lost on Wesley's ecclesiastical critics at Oxford.

The first three divisions of this sermon constitute an outline of the order of salvation, and *theologically* there is nothing in this sermon that would have aroused significant disagreement among most of Wesley's Oxford hearers. The first part of the sermon is a glowing account of the mighty work of God that was so evident in apostolic times. Although Wesley does not say so, his descriptions of first and second century Christianity were being duplicated throughout England in the Methodist revivals. It is not possible to know how many of his hearers made that connection. In any case, the objections to this sermon did not stem from doctrinal differences.

It was the fourth division of this sermon that ignited sharp controversy within the Oxford academic community assembled in St. Mary's Church. In this last section of the sermon Wesley made what he called a "plain and practical application." After describing Apostolic Christianity, Wesley asks, "Where in Oxford can one now find this kind of religion? In whom at Oxford is this religion found today?" It was Wesley's uncompromising application to his hearers' lives that brought down their fury upon him.

Evaluations of this sermon vary greatly. Thomas Jackson, a Methodist historian, gave the following summary of the last section of this discourse: "The concluding application to the Heads of Colleges and Halls, to the Fellows and Tutors, and to the body of the undergraduates, assumes their general and wide departure from the true Christian character, and abandonment to formality, worldliness, levity, and sloth. . . . [The conclusion is] marked throughout by seriousness, fidelity, and tender affection."[1] Concerning this sermon, Luke Tyerman, one of Wesley's biographers, wrote, "Who can find fault with it? Rather, who will not commend the bold preacher, who, in such yearning accents, gave utterance to truths of the highest consequence, but which perhaps no one but himself, in such a congregation, durst have uttered?"[2]

However, other reports contrast with those of Jackson and Tyerman. Present in the congregation was William Blackstone, later the author of Commentaries on the Laws of England. Four days after Wesley's sermon, Blackstone reacted in a letter, "Among other equally modest particulars, he informed us, first, that there was not one Christian among all the Heads of Houses; secondly, that pride, gluttony, avarice, luxury, sensuality and drunkenness were general characteristics of all Fellows of Colleges. . . ."

Benjamin Kennicott, an undergraduate who later became a renowned Hebrew scholar and Canon of Christ Church at Oxford, sat in the undergraduate gallery. He listened intently, and subsequently wrote a lengthy assessment of the sermon. Kennicott concluded:

> When he mounted the pulpit, I fixed my eyes on him and his behaviour. He is neither tall nor fat, for the latter would ill become a Methodist. His black hair quite smooth, and parted very exactly, added to a peculiar composure in his countenance, showed him to be an uncommon man. . . . I liked some of his freedom; such as calling the generality of young gownsmen "a generation of triflers," and many other just invectives. But considering how many shining lights are here that are the glory of the Christian cause, his sacred censure was much too flaming and strong, and his char-

ity much too weak in not making large allowances. . . . Had these things been omitted, and his censures moderated, I think his discourse, as to style and delivery, would have been uncommonly pleasing to others as well as to myself. He is allowed to be a man of great parts.[3]

To be sure, Wesley's sermon is strongly worded and plainly judgmental. Of greater importance, however, is the truth that many people within the university were not yet ready to receive Wesley's assessment of their state of grace. They simply were not willing to accept his boldness in calling them to repentance. They intensely disliked the "enthusiasm" of the Methodist revival that was spreading across England, and they wanted no representative of this religious excitement to lower the dignity of Oxford's hallowed halls.

Charles Wesley was present in the congregation, and he recorded the following observation in his journal: "Never have I seen a more attentive congregation. They did not let a word slip them. Some of the Heads stood up the whole time, and fixed their eyes on him. . . . We walked back in form, the little band of us four, for of the rest durst [dared] none join himself to us."[4]

John Wesley preached this sermon because of his love for Oxford and its community of scholars. Although there were good and godly people at Oxford in that time, it must be remembered that numerous sources confirm that the academic and moral climate of the university was at a low point.[5] Wesley brought home this reality in the strongest words— and most of the Oxford community resented the message. After preaching, Wesley wrote the following passage in his journal: "The Beadle came to me afterwards, and told me the Vice-Chancellor had sent him for my notes. I sent them without delay, not without admiring the wise providence of God. Perhaps few men of note would have given a sermon of mine the reading, if I had put it into their hands; but by this means it came to be read, probably more than once, by every man of eminence in the University."[6]

Later, John Wesley summarized the occasion of his delivering this sermon in his little book *A Short History of the People Called Methodists:*

Friday, August 24, St. Bartholomew's day, I preached for the last time before the University of Oxford. I am now clear of the blood of these men: I have fully delivered my own soul. And I am well pleased that it should be the very day on which, in the last century, near two thousand burning and shining lights were put out at one stroke [a reference to the St. Bartholomew's Day Massacre in France during August 23-24, 1572]. Yet what a wide difference is there between their case and mine! They were turned out of house and home, and all that they had; whereas I am only hindered from preaching, without any other loss; and that in a kind of honourable manner; it being determined, that, when my next turn to preach came, they would pay another person to preach for me. And so they did twice or thrice, even to the time that I resigned my fellowship.[7]

In this sermon Wesley said to the faculty, "You respected men, you are especially called to form the tender minds of young people, dispelling from them the darkness of ignorance and error, and informing them about salvation. Are you filled with the Holy Spirit?" Are you filled with the 'fruits of the Spirit' that your important office so absolutely requires? Is your heart perfect with God and full of love and zeal for establishing his kingdom on the earth? Do you constantly remind those under your care that the one intelligent goal of all our studies is to know, love, and serve 'the only true God and Jesus Christ whom God has sent?'"

Wesley charged the students with being "a generation of triflers—triflers with God, with one another and with your own souls." He closes this sermon with this prayer: "Lord, save us! We are perishing! Take us out of the morass, so that we do not sink. Help us overcome our enemies! Human help is useless. But for God all things are possible. According to the greatness of your power, safeguard us who are all headed for eternity."

Thereafter, when the rotation of preachers brought up John Wesley's name, the university secured and paid for a substitute preacher to take his place. As stated above, he never spoke at the university again. Finally, in June 1751 in a one-sentence letter, written in Latin, Wesley resigned his fellowship in Lincoln College, Oxford. The closing phrase is translated, ". . . wishing to all and each . . . perpetual peace and every species of felicity in Christ."[8]

SCRIPTURAL CHRISTIANITY

Preached at St. Mary's, Oxford before the University,
August 24, 1744.

It was not my design when I wrote ever to print the latter
part of the following sermon. But the false and scurrilous
accounts of it which have been published almost in every
corner of the nation constrain me to publish the whole,
just as it was preached, that men of reason may judge for
themselves.

—John Wesley

I f any who hear the sound of the trumpet do not take warning, and
the sword comes and takes them away, their blood shall be upon their
own heads (Ezek. 33:4).

And they were all filled with the Holy Spirit (Acts 4:31).

1. The words of our text also appear in the second chapter of Acts:
"When the day of Pentecost had come, they were all together in one
place (the Apostles, the women, the mother of Jesus, and his brethren).
Divided tongues, as of fire, appeared among them, and a tongue rested

on each of them. All of them were filled with the Holy Spirit." An immediate result of this event was that "they began to speak in other languages," so that the Parthians, Medes, Elamites, and the other strangers heard them in their own languages "speaking about God's deeds of power."

2. In the fourth chapter of Acts, we read that as the Apostles and the others were praying and praising God, "the place in which they were gathered together was shaken; and they were all filled with the Holy Spirit." On this occasion, we do not discover any visible phenomena, such as had appeared in the preceding instance. Moreover, the text does not report that any of those that were present received extraordinary gifts of the Holy Spirit—such as gifts of healing, working of miracles, prophecy, the discernment of spirits, various kinds of tongues, and the interpretation of tongues.

3. It is not necessary here to decide whether these gifts of the Holy Spirit were meant to remain in the Church throughout all ages or whether they will be restored at the imminent approach of "the time of universal restitution." However, it is necessary to observe that even in the infancy of the church God sparingly distributed these extraordinary gifts. Even then, were all prophets? Did all work miracles? Did all have healing gifts? Did all speak with tongues? No, not at all. Perhaps God gave miraculous gifts to only one in a thousand. Probably, he imparted these special abilities to none but the teachers in the Church—and only to some of them. Therefore, it was for a superior reason that those in the early church were filled with the Holy Spirit.

4. No one can deny that God sent the Holy Spirit for a purpose that is undeniably essential to all Christians in all ages. The Holy Spirit imparts to us "the same mind that was in Christ Jesus." Those that do not have the holy fruit of the Spirit which was in Christ do not belong to Christ. God sent the Spirit to fill his people with "love, joy, peace, patience, kindness, generosity, faithfulness, gentleness, and self-control." Because of an inward change, God enabled those Christians to crucify the flesh with its passions and desires and to manifest outer righteousness. God's purpose is to enable us to "walk just as Jesus walked" in our "work of faith, labor of love, and steadfastness of hope."

5. Without occupying ourselves, therefore, with tedious and unnecessary inquiries about those extraordinary gifts of the Spirit, let us take a closer look at the fruit of the Spirit that God intends for all people. Scripture tells us that these virtues continue throughout all ages of God's working among humankind. Once, we used only one word to express this work of God—Christianity. I mean Christianity not as a set of

opinions or a system of doctrines, but as it refers to transformed human hearts and lives. It may be useful to consider Christianity in four ways: (1) Christianity as it begins to exist in individuals. (2) Christianity as it extended from one person to another. (3) Christianity as it spread across the world. (4) And I propose to close these deliberations with a clear and practical application.

I. Christianity as it begins to exist in individuals

1. First, let us consider Christianity as it begins in the lives of individuals. Suppose one of those who heard the Apostle Peter preaching repentance and remission of sins was pierced to the heart, convicted of sin, and then repented and believed in Jesus. This faith in the work of God is based on the "assurance of things hoped for and the conviction of things not seen." Through this faith, believers immediately receive "a spirit of adoption," by which they cry "*Abba*! Father!" For the first time, by the Holy Spirit, the new believer is enabled to call Jesus "Lord." "That very Spirit bears witness with our spirit that we are children of God." It is now possible for the one who trusts Christ truly to say, "It is no longer I who live, but it is Christ who lives in me. And the life I now live in the flesh I live by faith in the Son of God, who loved me and gave himself for me."

2. This reality is the very essence of faith—a divine evidence or conviction of the love of God the Father, through the Son of his love, to a sinner, now accepted in the Beloved One. "Since we are justified by faith, we have peace with God." Yes, we have "the peace of Christ ruling in the heart." This peace, which transcends all understanding, guards our hearts and minds from all doubt and fear through the knowledge of him in whom we have believed. As a consequence of trusting in Christ, the New Testament believers did not have any fear of bad news because they "stood firm in the Lord." They had no fear of what others could do to them, because they knew that God numbered the very hairs of their heads. They no longer feared the powers of darkness which God daily crushed under their feet. Certainly, they were not afraid to die. St. Paul desired "to depart and be with Christ." Christ, through his death, had "destroyed the one who has the power of death, that is, the devil, and freed those who all their lives were held in slavery by the fear of death."

3. Consequently, the new believers' souls "rejoiced in God their savior." With an inexpressible and glorious joy, they rejoiced in the one who had reconciled them to God the Father. In Christ, they had redemption

through his blood, the forgiveness of their trespasses. They rejoiced that "the very Spirit bears witness with our spirits that we are children of God." Even more abundantly, they rejoiced "in the hope of the glory of God," anticipating the glorious likeness of God—the complete renewal of their souls in "true righteousness and holiness." They found there the hope of that crown of glory—"an inheritance that is imperishable, undefiled, and unfading."

4. God's love was poured into the believers' hearts through the Holy Spirit that was given to them. Because they were God's children, God sent the Spirit of his Son into their hearts, crying, "Abba! Father!" Furthermore, the believers' filial love for God grew continually, due to the testimony of God's pardoning love now within them. Their love also grew by realizing how great is the love the Father had lavished on them, that they should be called children of God! God was now their desire, the strength of their hearts and their portion forever.

5. Those who loved God in this way could not refrain from also loving their sisters and brothers, "not in word or speech only, but in truth and action." They believed, "Since God so loved us, we also ought to love one another," yes, every living soul, because "the Lord is good to all, and his compassion is over all that he has made." Consistent with this outlook, the affection of these lovers of God embraced all people for Christ's sake. Such love did not exclude those whom they had never seen, or those about whom they knew nothing more than that they were "God's offspring." They understood that God's son had died for all, including the evil, the unthankful, and those enemies who hated, persecuted, or despitefully used them for their Master's sake. Persecutors occupied a special place in their hearts and prayers. They loved even their enemies, "as Christ loved them."

6. Christian love "is not proud." Love humbles to the dust every soul in whom it dwells. Accordingly, the early Christian believers were gentle, and they held a humble opinion of themselves. They neither sought nor received the praise of others; they wanted only the approval of God. They were mild tempered, patient, considerate, and submissive. Constancy and truth typified those Christian believers; these qualities were bound around their necks and written on the tablets of their hearts Leading them as small children, the Holy Spirit enabled them to be self-controlled. The world was crucified to them, and they to the world. They had overcome "the cravings of sinful men, the lust of the eyes and the boasting of what they had and did." God's omnipotent love saved these early believers from uncontrolled emotions, lust, conceit, craving for preferment, covetousness, and every disposition that was not of Christ.

7. It is easy to believe that those who had God's love in their hearts would do no wrong to their neighbors. It was impossible for them, knowingly and intentionally, to harm any person. They were completely disengaged from cruelty, wrongdoing, and any unjust or unkind behavior. Alertly, they set guards over their mouths and kept watch over the door of their lips. They carefully avoided words that hindered justice, mercy, or truth. They discarded lying, deception, and fraud. No deceit was found in their mouths, and no unkind words ever came from their lips.

8. These New Testament believers were deeply aware of the truth of Christ's word, "Apart from me you can do nothing." Because they knew that they needed God continuously to water their vineyard, daily they made use of the ordinances of God. That is, they used Christ's stated means of grace. Those early Christian believers remained "in the apostles' teaching and fellowship." Eagerly receiving nourishment for the soul, they participated in the "breaking of bread," which they experienced as the communion of the body of Christ. As well, they took part in the prayers and praises which the worshiping Christian community offered up to God. By these means, daily they "grew in grace," increasing in strength and in the knowledge and love of God.

9. They were not content merely to abstain from doing evil—their souls thirsted to do good. The continuous assertion of their hearts was: "My Father is always at his work to this very day, and I, too, am working." Therefore, at the very least, the New Testament believers took every opportunity to feed the hungry, clothe the naked, relieve the orphan and stranger, and visit and assist the ill and imprisoned. They gave their resources to feed the poor, and they delighted to labor for them. If in any way they could benefit another, they denied their own needs in order to do so. They remembered the word of the Lord: "Whatever you did for one of the least of these brothers of mine, you did for me." They considered nothing too valuable to part with in order to help the poor.

10. Thus, these attitudes and actions characterized New Testament Christianity as it took root in individual lives. I have described the Christians in the early days of Christianity. Every one of those that heard the threatenings of the chief priests and elders, "raised their voices together to God, and they were all filled with the Holy Spirit." "The whole group of those who believed were of one heart and soul." The love of Christ, in whom they trusted, energized them to love each other. "No one claimed private ownership of any possessions, but everything they owned was held in common." They were completely crucified to the

world, and the world crucified to them! Without wavering, in one heart and mind they continued steadfastly together in the Apostles' teaching and in the breaking of bread and in prayer. "Great grace was upon them all. There was not a needy person among them, for as many as owned lands or houses sold them and brought the proceeds of what was sold. They laid it at the apostles' feet, and it was distributed to each as any had need."

II. Christianity as it spread from one person to another

1. In the second place, let us observe Christianity as it spread from person to person and gradually expanded into the world. Growth was the will of God concerning the church, which did not "light a lamp and put it under a bushel basket." Instead, Christians put a lamp on its lampstand, so that it could give light to all in the house. Our Lord said to his first disciples, "You are the salt of the earth, the light of the world." He also gave the general command, "Let your light shine before others, so that they may see your good works and give glory to your Father in heaven."

2. Suppose a few of these Christians who loved humankind saw clearly that "the whole world lies under the power of the evil one." Can we believe that they would remain unconcerned when seeing the wretched circumstances of those for whom their Lord died? Would not their compassion cause their hearts to melt at the sight of this calamity? Even if the Christ they loved did not give them a specific command, could they stand idle all day? No! Would they not work in every possible way to pluck some of these burning brands from the fire? Without doubt, they would. They spared no pains to rescue as many as they could of those poor "sheep going astray to return them to the shepherd and overseer of their souls."

3. This is the way that the early Christians lived: When they had opportunity, they labored "to do good to all people," warning them "to flee from the coming wrath" and immediately to "escape being condemned to hell." Those Christians preached this message: "In the past God overlooked the times of human ignorance, but now he commands all people everywhere to repent." They cried out, "Turn back, turn back from your evil ways! Then sin will not be your ruin." They conversed with others about "justice, self-control, and the coming judgment"—of virtues contrary to their besetting sins. They talked about the wrath of God, which will surely be administered to evildoers on that day when he will judge the world.

83

4. In these important matters, the early Christians attempted to speak to everyone individually according to his or her needs. To the careless and unconcerned people who lived in darkness and deepest gloom, the Christians thundered, "Sleeper, awake! Rise from the dead, and Christ will shine on you." To those who were already awakened out of spiritual sleep and oppressed under a sense of the wrath of God, the Christians preached, "We have an advocate with the Father, Jesus Christ the righteous; and he is the atoning sacrifice for our sins." At the same time, they considered how to spur fellow believers on toward love and good deeds, to persistence in doing good, abounding more and more in the holiness without which no one will see the Lord.

5. In the Lord, their labor was not in vain. His word spread rapidly and was glorified. The word of God extended widely and grew in power. At the same time, resentment against Christians became common. The world system became angry because the church "testified against it that its works were evil." Pleasure-seekers became outraged because the Christians felt compelled to criticize their values. Worldly people charged, "Those who profess a knowledge of God have a manner of life that is unlike that of others; their ways are strange; they avoid our ways as unclean; they boast that God is their father." Those that opposed Christianity became increasingly furious because so many of their comrades were taken away and would "no longer join them in the same excesses of dissipation." Those that enjoyed public esteem took offense because the spread of the gospel caused them to lose their flattering titles and the sort of homage that is due only to God.

Businessmen would call a meeting and declare, "Comrades, you know that we get our wealth from this business. You also see and hear that these Christians have persuaded and drawn away a considerable number of people, and there is danger that this trade of ours may come into disrepute." The so-called "religious people" (they were in fact devoid of true religion), these "saints of the present world," took every opportunity to complain, "Men of Israel, help us! We have found these men to be troublemakers who stir up riots throughout the world." These Christians "teach everyone everywhere against our people, our law, and this place."

6. Due to the church's clash with culture, the heavens grew black with clouds and the storm gathered with full speed. Those who rejected Christ believed that the further Christianity spread, the greater harm it caused. More and more, the numbers of angry people grew, and they charged Christians with "turning the world upside down." Increasingly, they raged, "Away with these people; they should not be allowed to live." The

enemies of the church were completely convinced that whoever killed Christians would be serving God.

7. All the while, those that opposed the Christians renounced them as evil to such an extent that "people everywhere talked against them." Critics charged them with all kinds of evil things, in the same way that others had persecuted the prophets who came before them. Whatever charges were asserted, others would believe. Thus, onslaughts against Christians grew as numerous as the stars of the skies. As foreseen by God the Father, all forms of persecution arose at that time. For a period, some Christians suffered only shame and reproach; others endured "the plundering of their possessions" and "mocking and flogging," while still others "resisted to the point of shedding their blood."

8. At this time, the pillars of hell were shaken—and still the kingdom of God spread more and more. Everywhere, sinners "turned from darkness to light, and from the power of Satan to God." The Lord gave his children "words and wisdom that none of their opponents were able to resist," and their lives were as powerful as their words. Above everything else, however, the sufferings of the Christians spoke to the entire world. As God's servants, they "commended themselves in afflictions, hardships, calamities, beatings, incarcerations, riots, labors, danger at sea, danger in the wilderness, weariness, pain, hunger and thirst, and cold and nakedness." And after having fought the good fight, they were taken as sheep to the slaughter. They became as sacrificial offerings for their faith in God. Afterward, the blood of each martyr gained the attention of ungodly people, who admitted, "They died, but through their faith they still speak."

9. In this way, Christianity spread across the earth. All too soon, however, weeds appeared among the wheat. The mystery of iniquity began to grow along side the mystery of godliness. Satan even "set himself up in God's temple," "forcing the woman to flee into the wilderness." The faithful were again ostracized from their environment. Here, we travel down a familiar road. From time to time, God has raised up witnesses to recount the ever-growing corruptions of succeeding generations. These witnesses have demonstrated that Christ built his church upon a rock, and the gates of Hades will not prevail against it.

III. Christianity as it spread across the world

1. Shall we expect to see greater developments than those of the past—even greater than those that have already occurred since the beginning of

the world? Can Satan stop the advance of God's truth or cause his promises to come to nothing? If not, then the time will come when Christianity will prevail over everything and cover the earth. In line with this third division of the sermon, let us pause to survey an amazing vista—the coming Christian world.

The ancient prophets gazed intently, carefully searched, and inquired diligently into this prospect. Concerning this coming salvation, God's Spirit testified through them:

In days to come the mountain of the Lord's house shall be established as the highest of the mountains, and shall be raised above the hills; all the nations shall stream to it. They shall beat their swords into plowshares, and their spears into pruning hooks; nation shall not lift up sword against nation, neither shall they learn war any more.

On that day the root of Jesse shall stand as a signal to the peoples; the nations shall inquire of him, and his dwelling shall be glorious. On that day, the Lord will extend his hand yet a second time to recover the remnant that is left of his people. He will raise a signal for the nations, and will assemble the outcasts of Israel, and gather the dispersed of Judah from the four corners of the earth. He will raise a banner for the nations and gather the exiles of Israel; he will assemble the scattered people of Judah from the four quarters of the earth.

The wolf shall live with the lamb, the leopard shall lie down with the kid, the calf and the lion and the fatling together, and a little child shall lead them. They will not hurt or destroy on all my holy mountain; for the earth will be full of the knowledge of the Lord as the waters cover the sea.

2. Pointing to the same end are the words of the great Apostle Paul, although his prophecy is yet to be fulfilled: "I ask, then, has God rejected his people? By no means! Rather, through their stumbling salvation has come to the Gentiles, so as to make Israel jealous. Now if their stumbling means riches for the world, and if their defeat means riches for Gentiles, how much more will their full inclusion mean! I want you to understand this mystery: a hardening has come upon part of Israel, until the full number of the Gentiles has come in. And so all Israel will be saved."

3. Assume that the fullness of time has now arrived and that the prophecies have been fulfilled. What a great prospect is this coming reality! The effect of righteousness will be peace, and "the result of righteousness, quietness and trust forever." There will be no clamor of weapons, no "garments soaked in blood." "The very memory of enemies will have perished." Wars will cease from the earth. Neither are there any internal feuds, no brother attacking brother, no nation or city divided

against itself and destroying itself. Civil discord will have come to an end forever, and there will be no one left to destroy or harm others. In that day, there is no cruelty "to make the wise foolish," no illegal seizures "to grind the face of the poor." There will be no robbery or wrongdoing, no plundering or injustice, and all people will be content with what they have. In that time, "righteousness and peace will kiss each other." These blessings will "take deep root and fill the land; righteousness will spring forth out of the earth and peace will look down from heaven."

4. Along with righteousness and justice, there will also be mercy. The earth will no longer be full of violent haunts. The Lord will have destroyed the bloodthirsty and deceitful, the envious and revengeful. Even if there were any provocation, there will be nobody who pays back wrong for wrong. Indeed, there is no one that does evil, not a single person—for all will be as innocent as doves. Being filled with peace and joy in believing, and united in one body by one Spirit, people will all love each other as sisters and brothers. They will all be of one heart and soul. "Everything they own will be held in common." There will be no one among the redeemed company that will have any need, for all will love their neighbors as themselves. Furthermore, all people will walk by one rule—"In everything, do to others as you would have them do to you."

5. Consequently, no unkind word can ever be heard among the redeemed—no accusing tongues, controversy, abusive language, or slander. Rather, all will "open their mouths with wisdom, and the teaching of kindness will be on their tongues." The redeemed are equally incapable of deception or dishonest cunning. Their love is genuine. Always, their words will truthfully express their thoughts, opening a window into the inner self, so that whoever wishes may look into their hearts and see that only love and God are there.

6. Wherever the Lord God Almighty assumes his mighty power and begins to rule, he will "make all things subject to himself," causing every heart to overflow with love, and filling every mouth with praise. "Happy are the people to whom such blessings fall; happy are the people whose God is the Lord." The Lord has said, "Arise, shine; for your light has come, and the glory of the Lord has risen upon you. You shall know that I, the Lord, am your Savior and your Redeemer, the Mighty One of Jacob. I will appoint Peace as your overseer and Righteousness as your taskmaster. Violence shall no more be heard in your land, devastation or destruction within your borders; you shall call your walls Salvation, and your gates Praise. Your people shall all be righteous; they shall possess the land forever. They are the shoot that I planted, the work of my hands, so that I might be glorified." "The sun shall no longer be your light by

day, nor for brightness shall the moon give light to you by night; but the Lord will be your everlasting light, and your God will be your glory."

IV. A practical application

Having briefly considered Christianity as beginning, spreading, and covering the earth, it only remains that I should close this sermon with a clear and practical application.

1. First, I will ask the question, "Where does this Christianity now exist? Where do the Christians live? Where can we find a place in which the inhabitants are all filled with the Holy Spirit? Where are those who have one heart and mind, and see that no one lacks anything, and continuously give to any one in need? Is there a place where all the people have God's love filling their hearts and causing them to love their neighbors as themselves? Where are those who have "clothed themselves with compassion, kindness, humility, meekness, and patience?" Who are those that do not in any way violate justice, mercy, or truth, either by word or deed? Rather, at every point they do to others as they would have them do in return. Can we properly term any territory a Christian country, if it does not conform to this description? In that case, let us confess that we have never yet seen a Christian country upon the earth.

2. I entreat you, sisters and brothers, by the mercies of God. Even if you consider me a fool, hear me out. It is absolutely necessary for someone to speak to you in very clear terms. It is all the more important at this time, for who knows whether this assembly will be our last one? Who knows how soon the righteous Judge may say, "I will not hear any more prayers for these people"? "Even if Noah, Daniel, and Job were in it, as I live, says the Lord God, they would save neither son nor daughter; they would save only their own lives by their righteousness."

If I do not speak to you in this direct way, then who will? Accordingly, I will deliver my message to you. I earnestly entreat you, by the living God, that you do not harden your hearts against receiving a blessing even from me. Do not say in your hearts, "You cannot persuade me, even though you have been convincing." Do not say, "Lord, you shall not send the messenger of your choosing; I would rather perish in my own blood than be saved by this man."

3. Brothers, "even though I speak in this way, I am confident of better things of you." So then, in tender love and in the spirit of humility, let me ask you, "Is this a Christian city?" Is genuine, scriptural Christianity found here? Taken as a community of people, are we filled

88

with the Holy Spirit, so that we enjoy in our hearts and exemplify in our lives the authentic fruits of the Spirit? Are the Magistrates, Principals, Governors of Colleges and Halls, and their respective Societies, (not to mention the inhabitants of the town) "of one heart and mind?" Is "the love of God poured out into our souls?" Are our inclinations the same as those of Christ? In all our conduct, are we "holy, as the one who calls us is holy?"

4. I plead with you to notice that we are not considering different kinds of strange theories. The point under discussion is not one of debatable opinions. Instead, we are considering undeniable aspects of our common faith. And as for evaluating what I say, I appeal to your own consciences, guided by the word of God. The one whose own heart does not condemn him, let that one be free from judgment.

5. In seriousness and the fear of God (before whom you and I will shortly appear), let us consider a question. I implore you that are in authority over us, whom I respect because of your office, to consider (and not like impostors before God) this important question: "Are you filled with the Holy Spirit?" Are you living portrayals of him whom you are appointed to represent among the people? We read in the Psalms, "You are gods, children of the Most High." You magistrates and governors, by your office you are quite closely linked with the God of heaven! In your individual posts and ranks, God calls you to portray for us a pattern of "the Lord our Sovereign." Are all your inner thoughts, affections, and desires suited to your high calling? Are all your words like those that come from the mouth of God? Do dignity and love characterize all your actions? Is there in your life a nobleness that words cannot describe, but which can flow only from a heart full of God? Of course, we allow that every mortal is "but a maggot, and a human being, who is a worm!"

6. You respected teachers, you are especially called to shape the tender minds of young people, dispelling from them the darkness of ignorance and error, and informing them about salvation. Are you "filled with the Holy Spirit?" Are you filled with the "fruits of the Spirit" that your important office so absolutely requires? Is your heart perfect with God and full of love and zeal for establishing his kingdom on the earth? Do you constantly remind those under your care that the one intelligent goal of all our studies is to know, love, and serve "the only true God and Jesus Christ whom God has sent?"

Do you daily impress upon others the fact that love never fails, whereas tongues will fail and philosophical knowledge will pass away? Do you press home the truth that without love all learning is only showy

89

ignorance, self-important foolishness, and empty distress of spirit? Does everything that you teach have a genuine tendency to lead to the love of God and, for his sake, to the love of others? Do you have this goal in view in everything that you prescribe pertaining to the subjects, procedure, and quantity of your students' studies? Is it your wish and work that, wherever these young soldiers of Christ may go, they may become burning and shining lights, in every way making attractive the teaching of the gospel of Christ? And permit me to ask if you spend all your strength in the immense work you have undertaken? Do you exert yourself in this work with all your powers? Do you exercise every capacity of your being, put to use all the gifts that God has loaned you, and do you do so to the utmost of your ability?

7. Let it not be said that I am speaking as if all under your care intend to become clergymen. That is not the case. I only speak as if they all are intending to be Christians. What example do we set for them—those of us who enjoy the generous gifts of our predecessors? What example is set by fellows, students, scholars, and especially by those who hold rank and prominent positions? Brothers, do you abound in spiritual fruit, humility, self-denial, and self-discipline? Do you demonstrate earnestness, calmness, patience, humility, moderation, and self-control? Do you, in tireless, active endeavors, do every kind of good to all people to relieve their outward needs and to bring their souls to the true knowledge and love of God? Do these things characterize the general character of the fellows of our colleges?

I fear they do not. Instead, have we not been charged with pride, haughtiness, impatience, ill temper, laziness, indolence, gluttony, sensuality, and a proverbial irrelevance? Perhaps these charges have not always come from our enemies, nor been made without good cause. O that God would remove this reproach from us, so that the very memory of it might perish forever!

8. Many of us are more strictly consecrated to God, because we are called to minister holy things. Are we examples to others, "in speech and conduct, in love, in faith, in purity"? Is there written on our foreheads and hearts, "Holy to the Lord"?

From what motives did we enter this ministerial office? Was it indeed with a solitary view "to serve God, trusting that we were inwardly moved by the Holy Spirit, to take upon us this ministry for promoting God's glory and edifying his people"? Have we "clearly determined, by God's grace, to give ourselves wholly to this office"?[9] As much as is possible, do we forsake and set aside all worldly cares and studies? Do we apply ourselves completely to this one thing and bring all our concerns and studies toward this end? Are we competent to teach? Does God teach us so that we are able to teach others? Do we know God? Do we know Jesus Christ? Has "God revealed his Son to us?" And has God "made us competent to be ministers of a new covenant."

Where, then, are the "seals of our apostleship?" Who that were dead in transgressions and sins have been brought to life by our word? Do we have a burning zeal to save souls from death, so that for their sakes we often even forget to eat our food? Do we "set forth truth plainly, commending ourselves to every man's conscience in the sight of God"? Are we dead to the world, and the things of the world, "storing up our treasures in heaven?" Do we lord it over those entrusted to us?

Or, have we become the very least of all and servants of everyone? When we bear disgrace for the sake of Christ, does it weigh us down, or do we rejoice? When we are struck on the cheek, do we resent it? Are we impatient over indignities, or do we turn the other cheek? Do we overcome evil by overcoming evil with good? Do we have harsh enthusiasm that causes us to strive fervently and passionately with those that are ignorant and going astray. Or, is our enthusiasm a flame of love that leads us to speak with gentleness, modesty, and humility?

9. Once again, what shall we say about the young people of this place? Do you have either the form or the power of Christian godliness? Are you humble, teachable, and prudent? Or are you stubborn, obstinate, rash, and arrogant? Are you as obedient to those over you as to your parents, or do you scorn those to whom you owe the most patient respect? Are you diligent in your simple work, pursuing your studies with all your strength? Do you make the most of every opportunity to redeem the time, squeezing as much work into each day as you are able?

Or, are you unaware that day after day you squander your opportunities, either by reading what has no tendency toward Christianity or in playing at one thing or another. Are you better managers of your treasures than of your time? Do you, out of principle, let no debt remain outstanding? Do you "remember the Sabbath day by keeping it holy," using the day for a more intimate worship of God? When you are in the Lord's house, do you ponder the fact that God is there? Do you conduct yourself as "seeing him who is invisible?" Do you know how to "control your own body in holiness and honor"?

Is it not true that drunkenness and immorality exist among you? Indeed, are there not some of you whose "glory is in your shame?" Is it not true that many of you "misuse the name of the Lord your God," perhaps regularly and without contrition or fright? Indeed, are there not many of you who have abandoned your faith? I fear that there is a fast growing company for which this is true. Brothers, do not be shocked at what I say.

Before God and this congregation, I confess that I, too, have been among the number of those who solemnly vowed to observe all those canons, which at the time I did not understand. I agreed to abide by those statutes that I did not so much as read, either then or for years afterward. If this is not perjury, then what is? O what a weight of sin— yes, sin of no ordinary kind—rests on us! And does not the Most High have full knowledge of these things?

10. Can it be that one of the consequences of this sin is that many of you belong to a generation of triflers—triflers with God, with one another and with your own souls. From week to week, how few of you spend a single hour in private prayer! How few of you give any thought to God during the general course of your life! Do you give any thought to God in your manner of life? Who among you is in any way familiar with the work of God's Spirit and his supernatural work in human life? Can you tolerate (unless occasionally in a church) any discussion about the Holy Spirit? Would you not take it for granted that if someone brought up this subject, his motivation was either hypocrisy or fanaticism? In the name of the Lord God Almighty, I ask, "What religion do you embrace?" You cannot and will not tolerate even discussions about Christianity. Brothers, what sort of a Christian city is this! "It is time for the Lord to act, for his law has been broken!"

11. Indeed, from a merely human standpoint, what probability— rather, what possibility—is there that true scriptural Christianity will again become the religion of this place? Only when it does will we speak and live as those "filled with the Holy Spirit." Who will restore vital Christianity? Are you willing to devote your fortune, freedom, and very lives to restoring it? Suppose you have a desire to restore authentic Christianity. Who has power equal to the task?

Perhaps some of you have made a few faint attempts, but how little success we see! Will Christianity, then, be restored by young, unknown, insignificant people? I do not know whether you are willing to allow it. Would not some of you cry out, "Young man, your ministry is a reproach to us?" But there is no danger of your being put to that test, because sin has engulfed us like a flood. Who or what will God send to restore genuine Christianity? Will he send famine and the plague (God's final messengers to a blameworthy land) or war? Will he send an army of proselytizing zealots to restore us to our first love? God forbid. "Let us fall into the hand of the Lord, for his mercy is great; but let us not fall into human hands."

Lord, save us! We are perishing! Take us out of the morass, so that we do not sink. Help us overcome our enemies! Human help is useless. But for God all things are possible. According to the greatness of your power, safeguard us who are all headed for eternity. Protect us in the way that you choose. Lord, not what we want but what you want!

Notes

1. Jackson, *The Life of The Rev. Charles Wesley, M. A.,* 1:403.

2. Luke Tyerman, *The Life and Times of the Rev. John Wesley, M.A.,* 3 vols. (London: Hodder and Stoughton, 1870), 1:452-53.

3. Printed in the *Methodist Magazine,* January, 1866, pp. 44-48.

4. Charles Wesley, *Journal,* August 24, 1744, 1:380.

5. Alfred Denis Godley, *Oxford in the Eighteenth Century* (London: Methuen & Co., 1908).

6. Curnock, *Wesley's Journal,* August 24, 1744, 3:147-48.

7. Rupert E. Davies, *The Works of John Wesley,* Bicentennial ed., *The Methodist Societies: History, Nature, and Design* (Nashville: Abingdon Press, 1989), 9:440.

8. Ward and Heitzenrater, *Wesley's Journal and Diaries,* June 1, 1751, 20:389.

9. *Book of Common Prayer,* "The Form and Manner of Making Deacons."

JUSTIFICATION BY FAITH

In this sermon, John Wesley outlines the New Testament teaching concerning the means by which we partake of the salvation provided through Jesus Christ. It was the rediscovery of justification by faith that had launched the Protestant Reformation during the second decade of the sixteenth century. In the eighteenth century, John Wesley was probably the most articulate champion of this central New Testament doctrine.

The previous four Standard Sermons marked a new direction for John and Charles Wesley. *Salvation by Faith; The Almost Christian; Awake, Thou that Sleepest;* and *Scriptural Christianity* forthrightly declared the tragedy of sin, the lost estate of humankind, and the necessity of repentance and the new birth. With these sermons, the two brothers moved from comfortable and relatively noncontroversial lives into conflict-ridden evangelistic and prophetic ministries.

This discourse begins a series of eight sermons which explain and apply foundational biblical doctrines, concerning which Wesley said "the Church stands or falls." Here, Wesley describes justification as resulting in pardon and a right relationship with God. It marks one's transition from darkness to light, and from estrangement from God to reconciliation to God through Jesus Christ. This experience brings humankind from spiritual death to spiritual life. This blessing is not the consequence of human striving or merit. It comes by grace through faith in Christ, whose death on the cross secured salvation for all who believe. Here, Wesley contends that this truth shaped the doctrine of the ancient church, the Church of England, and all churches that are faithful to the teaching of the Bible.

Wesley first preached about justification by faith on May 28, 1738, four days after his Aldersgate experience. His preaching this message provoked immediate opposition. He wrote, "I was roughly attacked in a large company as an enthusiast, a seducer, and a setter-forth of new doctrines. By the blessing of God, I was not moved to anger, but after a calm and short reply went away; though not with so tender a concern as was due to those who were seeking death in the error of their life."[1]

In 1742, John Wesley visited the parish church at Epworth, where his father had once been the rector. The incumbent rector refused to allow Wesley to preach in the sanctuary. Standing on his father's tomb outside the church, he preached from the text of this sermon.[2] Wesley remained in Epworth for eight days and preached to appreciative crowds. Concerning his ministry there, he wrote to John Smith, "Among my parishioners in Lincolnshire I tried for some years; but I am well assured I did far more good to them by preaching three days on my father's tomb, than I did by preaching three years in his pulpit."[3]

Before John Wesley's heart-warming experience of May 24, 1738, he had labored to earn God's favor through his good works. Countless times he had participated in the liturgy of Holy Communion and recited the confession that Jesus Christ is "our only Mediator and Advocate." Yet, a preoccupation with his personal religious performance tended to cloud his understanding of the liturgy. As yet, he had not personally experienced justification by faith. Following his Aldersgate religious experience, he came to understand the following statement in his church's Thirty-nine Articles of Religion:

> We are accounted righteous before God, only for the merit of our Lord and Saviour Jesus Christ by Faith, and not for our own works or deservings. Wherefore, that we are justified by Faith only, is a most wholesome Doctrine, and very full of comfort, as more largely is expressed in the Homily of Justification.[4]

The words of the liturgy came alive after he experienced their meaning. He later wrote in another sermon, "I hold all the doctrines of the Church of England. I love her liturgy. I approve her plan of discipline, and only wish it could be put in execution."[5]

Wesley insisted that justification by faith is one of Christianity's most fundamental doctrines. In the Preface to his 1740 *Hymns and Sacred Poems*, he wrote:

"By grace," saith St. Paul, "ye are saved through faith." And it is indeed a great salvation which they have received, who truly "believe on the name of the Son of God." It is such as "eye hath not seen, nor ear heard, nor hath it entered into the heart of man to conceive," until God "hath revealed it by his Spirit," which alone showeth these "deep things of God." This great gift of God, the salvation of our souls, which is begun on earth, but perfected in heaven, is no other than the image of God fresh stamped upon our hearts. It is a renewal in the spirit of our minds after the likeness of Him that created us. It is a salvation from sin, and doubt, and fear: From fear; for, "being justified freely," they who believe "have peace with God through Jesus Christ our Lord, and rejoice in hope of the glory of God:" From doubt; for "the Spirit of God beareth witness with their spirit, that they are the children of God:" And from sin; for being now "made free from sin, they are become the servants of righteousness."

Justification by Faith corrects a widespread and pervasive error that appeared in many pulpits in Wesley's day. The error that Wesley sought to remedy was that good works and sanctification must *precede* justification. Wesley agreed with his church's official position on this matter, and he championed it—even if many of his contemporaries ignored or rejected it. This sermon stands as a classic expression of justification by faith, and continues as one of Wesley's best expositions of the subject.

JUSTIFICATION BY FAITH

*To one who without works trusts him who justifies
the ungodly, such faith is reckoned as righteousness.*
(Romans 4:5)

1 The question of how we can be justified before God, the Lord and
Judge of all, is one of supreme importance to every one of us. The
foundation of all our hope is a right relationship with God. And as
long as this relationship is lacking, we cannot have true peace or real joy,
either in time or in eternity. How can we have peace, so long as our own
hearts find us guilty? Even more to the point, St. John wrote, "God is
greater than our hearts, and he knows everything." We cannot have real
joy, either in this world or the world to come, so long as God's wrath
remains on us.

2. Yet, how insufficiently we understand the crucial issue of being in
a right relationship with God. Many people hold confused notions about
it! Indeed, their notions are not only confused, but often are completely
false, and they may be as contrary to the truth as light is to darkness.
Our confused notions are totally inconsistent with the general and true
sense of scripture. Therefore, because people err concerning the very
foundation of a right relationship with God, they cannot do works that
count as "gold, silver, or precious stones"—works that will endure when
tested by fire. Instead, they can only produce works that, when judged,
will be reckoned as "wood, hay, or straw." Their works are neither
acceptable to God nor beneficial to others.

97

3. So far as I am able, in this sermon I hope to do justice to this vastly important subject. I hope to save those who sincerely seek the truth from "meaningless talk" and "disputes about words." I will try to clear up the confused thinking into which so many have already been led. I want to give them true and accurate conceptions of the great mystery of our religion. To this end, I will endeavor to show (1) the foundation of the doctrine of justification, (2) the nature of justification, (3) who are the justified, and (4) how we can be justified.

I. The foundation of the doctrine of justification

1. God made Adam in his own image. He made the original man holy as God is holy and merciful. God made Adam and Eve perfect as the Father in heaven is perfect. As God is love, so Adam and Eve also lived in love, and dwelled in God, and God in them. God made them to be an "image of his own eternity," an untainted reflection of his glory. Adam and Eve were correspondingly pure as God is pure, and they were free from every taint of sin. They knew no evil of any kind or degree. Inwardly and outwardly, they were sinless and undefiled. They loved the Lord their God with all their hearts, and with all their souls, and with their entire minds, and with all their strength.

2. To this upright and perfect pair, God gave a perfect law, to which he required full and total compliance. From the moment the man and the woman became living souls until their probation would end, they were to continue their detailed and full obedience without interruption. God did not make provision for partial obedience. Indeed, there was no need to excuse the original man and woman from doing the tasks God assigned to them, because they were "proficient and equipped for every good work."

3. God's complete law of love was written on their hearts. Perhaps Adam and Eve were not able to sin against it directly. In God's wisdom, it seemed good to him to add a direct command: "You shall not eat of the fruit of the tree that is in the middle of the garden." God added the penalty, "Nor shall you touch it, or you shall die."

4. Such was the state of Adam and Eve in Paradise. Having the free, unmerited love of God, they were holy and happy. They knew, loved, and enjoyed God, which is the essence of eternal life. The man and the woman were forever to live in this life of love. If they continued to obey God in every way, they would remain in this state of being. However, if

they disobeyed God in any, they would forfeit everything. God said, "In the day that you eat of it you shall die."

5. They *did* disobey God. They "ate from the tree about which God commanded, 'You must not eat of it.'" And that very day they were condemned by the righteous judgment of God. The consequence of what God had warned against began to fall upon the man and the woman. The moment they tasted the forbidden fruit, they died spiritually and became separated from God. Estranged from the Creator, the soul has no more life in it than the body has when separated from the soul. Adam's and Eve's bodies became mortal and liable to corruption. The sentence of death descended upon them. Being already dead in spirit and dead to God, they became dead in sin, and they plunged into everlasting death. Their end would be the destruction of both body and soul in the fire that never goes out.

6. "Therefore, just as sin came into the world through one man, and death came through sin, so death spread to all." Adam and Eve are the common parents and representatives of us all. Thus, by the trespass of the one man and woman all are dead. We are all dead to God, dead in sin, dwelling in a corruptible, mortal body. We soon will die, and we are under the sentence of eternal death. For just as by the one man's disobedience the many were made sinners, by that transgression everyone came under condemnation.

7. While we were all in this lost condition, "God so loved the world that he gave his only Son, so that everyone who believes in him may not perish but may have eternal life." In the fullness of time, God assumed human form and became another common head of humankind—a second general parent and representative of the entire human race. And as our representative he "bore our infirmities," and "the LORD has laid on him the iniquity of us all." He was "wounded for our transgressions and crushed for our iniquities." Christ "made his life an offering for sin." He shed his blood for the transgressors. He "bore our sins in his body on the cross" that "by his bruises we are healed." And by that one sacrifice of himself, once offered, he has redeemed me and all humankind, having thereby "made a full, perfect, and sufficient sacrifice and satisfaction for the sins of the whole world."

8. Because the Son of God has "tasted death for everyone," God has "reconciled the world to himself, not counting our sins against us." "Therefore just as one man's trespass led to condemnation for all, so one man's act of righteousness leads to justification and life for all." Now, for the sake of his well-beloved son, God takes into account what he has done and suffered for us. On only one condition, which God enables us

to meet, God guarantees to remit the punishment due our sins and to bring us back into his favor. As the pledge of eternal life, God restores our dead souls to spiritual life.

9. This work of Christ, therefore, is the foundation of the entire doctrine of justification. By the sin of the first Adam, who was the father and representative of us all, we all fell short of the glory of God; by nature we all became children of wrath. As the Apostle Paul expressed it, the result was "condemnation for all." However, the Second Adam, Jesus Christ, as representative of us all, made a sacrifice for our sin. God is now reconciled to the entire world, and he has given us a new covenant. Because Christ fulfilled the conditions for this covenant, "there is now no condemnation" for us, but we "are justified freely by his grace through the redemption that is in Christ Jesus."

II. The nature of justification

1. What does it mean to be justified? What, in fact, is justification? This subject is the second point that I propose to explain. From what has already been stated, it is evident that justification does not mean not being *made* actually upright and righteous. Our becoming upright and righteous is the work of *sanctification*. To be sure, in some degree, sanctification is the immediate fruit of justification. Still, sanctification is a separate gift of God and of a completely different nature. Justification pertains to what God does *for* us through his Son; sanctification pertains to what God works *in* us by his Spirit. We may find some rare instances where the terms *justified* or *justification* are used in a broad sense so as to include sanctification. In general use, however, justification and sanctification are clearly distinguished from each other, both by St. Paul and by the other inspired biblical writers.

2. It is not far-fetched arrogance to claim that justification frees us from the accusations of Satan. This assertion is easy to prove from clear texts in the Bible. Given what has already been stated, none of the biblical accounts of justification appear to discuss the accuser, Satan, or his accusations. We cannot deny that he is the "accuser" of us all. He is deliberately given that name. But in no way does it appear that the great Apostle Paul even mentions Satan's accusations in what he wrote to the Romans or Galatians about justification.

3. Furthermore, it is much easier to assume than to prove from any clear scriptural passage that justification frees us from the indictment brought against us by the law. At the very least, we can say that even

though we have transgressed God's law and in so doing deserve the condemnation of hell, God does not inflict on justified persons the punishments they deserve.

4. Most certainly, justification does not imply that God is deceived about those he justifies. He does not regard them to be what in fact they are not. Nor does God account justified persons to be something different than they are. Justification by no means implies that God regards us contrary to the actual nature of things, that he accounts us better than we really are, or believes us to be righteous when we are unrighteous. Surely, that is not the case. The discernment of the all-wise God is always according to truth. With unerring wisdom, God's evaluations do not account me to be innocent, righteous, or holy if the facts are otherwise. God can no more confuse me with Christ than with David or Abraham. Let anyone to whom God has given understanding weigh this matter without prejudice. Then one cannot help but conclude that such a notion about justification is not reconcilable with either reason or Scripture.

5. The clear scriptural conception of justification is *pardon*. It is the forgiveness of sins. Justification is that act of God the Father, based on the atonement made by the blood of his Son, in which God "showed his righteousness (or mercy) by passing over the sins previously committed." This concept of justification is the familiar, straightforward account that St. Paul gives throughout Romans. In the fourth and fifth chapters of Romans he explains justification in this way: "Blessed are those whose iniquities are forgiven, and whose sins are covered; blessed is the one against whom the Lord will not reckon sin." To those who are justified, or forgiven, God will never count their sins against them toward their condemnation. God will not condemn them for their sins, either in this world or in the world to come.

He covers and blots out all past sins of thought, word, and deed. They will not be remembered or mentioned. It is as though the sins of justified sinners had never existed. God will not inflict on them what they deserve to suffer, because the Son of his love has suffered for us. And from the time we are "accepted in the Beloved One," having "redemption through his blood," God loves, blesses, and watches over us for our welfare, even as if we had never sinned.

Indeed, in one place Paul seems to extend the meaning of justification farther. He wrote, "It is not the hearers of the law who are righteous in God's sight, but the doers of the law who will be justified." Here, Paul appears to be referring to justification at the final judgment. Without question, the Lord himself also speaks about final justification: "By your words you will be justified." This statement proves that "you will have to give an account for every careless word you utter." We can scarcely find another instance of Paul's using justification in that future sense. In the general course of his writings, especially in our present text, it is evident that Paul does not refer to a future justification. The text before us does not speak of those who have "finished the race." It speaks of those who are just setting out, those just beginning to "run the race that is set before them."

III. Identifying those who are justified

1. The third thing which we are to consider is the question, "Who are the justified?" Paul the Apostle tells us explicitly that God justifies the unrighteous. God "justifies the ungodly"—the wicked of every sort and degree, and none but the ungodly. Those who think that they are righteous do not see any need for repentance. It is only those who know that they are sinners who have any reason to seek pardon. Only sin requires forgiveness. Forgiveness, therefore, has a direct reference to sin, and to nothing else. The pardoning God is merciful toward our unrighteousness, remembering no more our iniquity.

2. Those who zealously contend that we must be sanctified, that is, become holy, *before* we can be justified do not understand that God justifies *sinners*. They mistakenly contend that universal holiness, or obedience, must precede justification. (They do talk about final justification at the last day, but that is a matter which we are not discussing here.) Those who say that we must be holy before God forgives us completely ignore justification in the present. They contend that such a possibility does not remotely exist. They fail to see that there can be no holiness without love for God and that we can love God only because he first loves us. Those who hold that we must be sanctified prior to justification believe that it is absurd and self-contradicting for God to justify sinners in the present.

We have seen, however, that God does not justify the godly, but the ungodly. He does not justify those that are already holy—he justifies the *unholy*. Later, I will consider on what condition God justifies sinners. But whatever the condition, it cannot be our holiness. To assert human worthiness as a condition for justification is to say that the Lamb of God takes away only those sins that have already been taken away.

3. In that case, does the good Shepherd seek and save only those who are already found? No. He came to seek out and save the lost. Christ pardons those who need his pardoning mercy. He saves us from the guilt of sin (and at the same time, from the power of sin). Christ saves sinners of

every kind and degree. He saves those who, until their salvation, are altogether ungodly. The love of the Father is not in them; therefore, there is nothing good in them—not a single good or truly Christian disposition. Rather, within them are such evil traits as pride, anger, and love of the world, the actual harvest of the mind that is set on the flesh, which is "hostile to God."

4. Those who are sick, whose burden of sin is unbearable, are the ones that need a physician. The ones who need God's pardon are those who are guilty and who moan under a sense of God's condemnation. They are already condemned by God and by their own consciences, as if a thousand witnesses cry out against all their ungodliness in thought, word, and deed. They call upon him who "justifies the ungodly, through the redemption that is in Christ Jesus." God justifies the ungodly and "those who are without works"—that is, those who are without good deeds or anything truly virtuous or holy. They are in fact only evil, and continuously so. Until God pours his love into their hearts, they are inescapably and fundamentally evil. So long as the tree is corrupt, so are its fruits. "A bad tree cannot bear good fruit."

5. Someone might challenge my point by saying, "No, before one is justified he may feed the hungry or clothe the naked, and these are good works." The answer to this objection is easy. One *may* do these good things, even before he is justified. In one sense, they are "excellent works" and "profitable to everyone." Strictly speaking, however, it does not follow that they are good in themselves or good in God's sight. All truly good works (to use the words of our church) follow after justification. They are good and "acceptable to God in Christ," because they "spring out of a true and living faith."[7] For a parallel reason, *no* works done before justification are good in the Christian sense. They do not spring from faith in Jesus Christ (although they may spring from some kind of belief in God). Because these works are not performed according to God's guidance, I do not doubt that "they have the nature of sin," regardless of how strange it may seem to some.[8]

6. Perhaps those who doubt the saving merit of good works prior to justification have not considered the convincing reason for my assertion. Here is the argument:

- No works are good that are not done as God has willed and commanded.
- None of the works before justification are done as God has willed and commanded.
- Therefore, no works done prior to justification are good works.

The first proposition is self-evident. The second proposition, that no works done before justification are done as God has willed and commanded them to be done, appears equally plain and undeniable. Only consider the following logic: God has willed and commanded that all our works should be done in a spirit of love—a love for God that results in love for others. However, we cannot do good works in God's love so long as love of God the Father is not in us. And this love cannot be in us until we receive "a spirit of adoption that cries out in our hearts, 'Abba, Father.'" If God does not justify the unrighteous and those who have no good works, then Christ died in vain. In that case, even though Christ died, no one could be justified.

IV. How we can be justified

1. On what terms, then, can unrighteous people who are without good works be justified? There is only one basis for justification—*faith*. Saving faith "trusts in him that justifies the unrighteous." "Those who believe in him are not condemned;" yes, they have "passed from death to life." For all who believe, "the righteousness of God comes through faith in Jesus Christ." For them, "God put forward a sacrifice of atonement by his blood, effective through faith" to demonstrate that "he himself is righteous and that he justifies the one who has faith in Jesus." Therefore, "we hold that a person is justified by faith apart from works prescribed by the law."

Justification comes without previous obedience to the moral law, which, indeed, we cannot fulfill until *after* justification. It is clear that St. Paul is talking only about the moral law, and the following words verify this understanding: "Do we then overthrow the law by this faith? By no means! On the contrary, we uphold the law." What law is it that we establish by faith? Faith does not establish the ritualistic or ceremonial laws of Moses. In no manner! Paul is speaking of the momentous, changeless law of love—the holy love of God and neighbor.

2. In general, faith is a divine, supernatural certainty. It is an evidence or conviction "of things not seen." These things cannot be discovered by our physical senses, as belonging to the past, future, or intuitional realms. Justifying faith involves a divine evidence or conviction that "in Christ, God was reconciling the world to himself." Faith also includes a sure trust and confidence that Christ died for my sins, that he loved me, and gave himself for me. Whenever sinners believe in this way—whether in early childhood, in their mature years, or when they are old and gray—God justifies those unrighteous ones.

For the sake of his son, God pardons and absolves those who as yet have done no good works in Christ's name. Of course, God enables repentance, which is nothing other than a deep sense of the absence of good and the presence of evil. Then, after people trust in God through Christ, whatever good they do is done by faith. These good works are the fruit of faith. First the tree is good, and then the fruit is good also

3. I can best describe the nature of justifying faith in the words of a homily of our own church:

> The only instrument of salvation, of which justification is one aspect, is faith. Faith is a certain trust and confidence that God has and will forgive our sins, that he has accepted us again into his favor, for the merits of Christ's death and passion. . . . But here we must take care not to cease making progress with God through a fluctuating, wavering faith. Peter, walking on the water toward Christ, was in danger of drowning because his faith diminished. If our faith in Christ begins to waver or doubt, the possibility exists that we will sink as Peter did. We will not sink into the water, however, but into the bottomless pit of hell fire.[9]

Therefore, maintain a certain and constant faith that the death of Christ is available for the entire world and that he has made a full and sufficient sacrifice for you. He offers perfect cleansing for your sins. With the Apostle, you can say that he loved you and gave himself for you. Your faith makes Christ your own and applies his merits personally to you.[10]

4. By affirming that faith is the condition of justification, I mean several things. First, there is no justification without faith. "Those who do not have faith are condemned already." As long as one does not believe, one cannot be free from condemnation. The person without faith must endure God's wrath. For our salvation, "there is no other name under heaven" other than the name of Jesus of Nazareth. Outside Jesus Christ, there is no other merit by which a condemned sinner can ever be saved from the guilt of sin; there is no other way of obtaining a share in his merit than by faith in his name. For as long as we are without this faith, we are "aliens from the covenants of promise;" "we are strangers from the commonwealth of Israel, having no hope and without God in the world."

Now, I will speak about those to whom the gospel is preached; for "what have I to do with judging those outside?" Whatever so-called "virtues and good works" one may have, they are of no advantage as means of salvation. Until we trust in Jesus, we are still children of wrath and under the curse.

5. Faith is the necessary condition for justification—indeed, faith is its *only* necessary condition. And this truth is my second point pertaining to how we are justified. Faith is the gift of God. And at the very moment that God gives faith to the "ungodly who are without works," that faith "is reckoned to them as righteousness." Prior to this gift of faith, we have no righteousness at all, not even negative righteousness or innocence. The very moment that we trust in Christ, "faith is reckoned to us as righteousness."

As I have already stated, God does not account us to be what we are not. God "made Christ to be sin for us," regarding him as a sinner and punishing him for our transgressions. From the moment that we trust in Christ, God accounts us righteous. He does not punish us for our sins; indeed, he treats us as though we were blameless and righteous.

6. Any difficulty of assenting to the proposition that "faith is the only condition of justification" must arise from a failure to understand it. By this proposition we mean that faith is the one thing without which no one can be justified. Faith is the only requirement that is directly, necessarily, and absolutely imperative to receive God's pardon.

On one hand, even though one might have everything else, without faith we cannot be justified. On the other hand, even if one lacks everything else, yet has faith, that person will most certainly be justified.

Suppose a sinner is thoroughly ungodly and cannot think, speak or do any good whatsoever, and he or she absolutely deserves the fire of hell. If helpless and hopeless sinners throw themselves entirely on God's mercy in Christ (which they can do only by the grace of God), in an instant God will forgive them. Who can doubt it? Who dares to say that sinners need anything more to be justified? Even if there has been only one such instance from the beginning of the world (and there have been and there are even now ten thousand times ten thousand such instances), it clearly follows that faith is the sole condition for justification.

7. It is not proper for poor, guilty, sinful wretches who receive whatever blessings of God's grace they enjoy (from the smallest drop of water that cools the tongue to the immense riches of glory in eternity) to ask God the reasons for his method of salvation. It is not fitting for us to call God into question. He "will answer none of our words." How dare we demand, "Why did you make faith the only condition of justification? Why did you decree, 'Only the one who believes will be saved?'"

Salvation by faith is the very point that St. Paul so strongly insists on in the ninth chapter of Romans. The terms of pardon and acceptance do not depend on us, but on him who calls us. St. Paul insisted that there is no injustice on God's part in his setting his own terms, which are not according to human ideas, but according to his own good pleasure. With justice, God declares, "I have mercy on whomever I choose," namely, on him who believes in Jesus. So, it depends not on human will or exertion to accept the condition on which one will find acceptance with God. It depends on God who shows mercy. God accepts no one at all, other than through his own sovereign love and unmerited grace. God has mercy on whomever he chooses. That is, he justifies all those who believe in his beloved Son. God has mercy on whomever he chooses, and he hardens the heart of whomever he chooses.

8. Humbly, we may conceive of one reason why God has established faith as the only condition of justification. The prescription "Believe in the Lord Jesus, and you will be saved" removes human pride. Pride had already destroyed the very angels of God and "swept down a third of the stars of heaven." Likewise, in large measure it was pride that caused Adam to respond to the tempter who said, "You will be like God." Yielding to pride, Adam fell from his own secure place and brought sin and death into the world. It was therefore a demonstration of wisdom worthy of God to designate faith as the condition of reconciliation for Adam and Eve and for those in all future generations. The condition of faith might effectively humble all of us to the dust.

The very nature of faith is remarkably fitted to beget humility. For those that come to God by faith must focus their eyes on their own sinfulness, guilt, and helplessness. They cannot have the least regard for any supposed good in themselves. We cannot in any way rely on personal virtue or righteousness. Faith requires us to come to God as sheer sinners, both inwardly and outwardly. Faith obligates us to be self-devastated and self-condemned; we can bring nothing to God but ungodliness. We can claim nothing of our own except sin and misery. Only when sinners' mouths are stopped and they stand utterly guilty before God can they look to Jesus as the complete and only atonement for their sins. Faith alone enables us to be found in Christ and to receive the "righteousness of God through faith."

9. You ungodly one, who hear or read these words, you are a vile, helpless, miserable sinner! I earnestly urge you before God, who is the Judge of everyone, to turn straight to him with all your ungodliness. Take caution that you do not destroy your own soul by pleading your righteousness, whether great or small. Turn to God, as one who is entirely ungodly, guilty, lost, destroyed, deserving hell and dropping into its abyss. Then you will find favor in his sight and understand that he justifies the ungodly. Coming to God in this way, you will be brought to the sprinkled blood as a condemned, helpless, doomed sinner.

Look to Jesus! Here is the Lamb of God who takes away your sins! Plead for yourself no works or righteousness of your own! Do not in any way appeal to your own humility, contrition, or sincerity. To do so would be to deny the Lord that bought you. Instead, rely entirely on the blood of the covenant and the ransom paid for your proud, stubborn, and sinful soul. Who among you now see and feel your inward and outward ungodliness? You are the man! I covet you for my Lord. I claim you as a child of God by faith! The Lord wants you. Those of you who feel that you rightfully deserve hell can be fit to advance the glory of God, whose free grace justifies the ungodly apart from good works. O, turn to him quickly! Believe in the Lord Jesus, and you can personally be reconciled to God.

Notes

1. Curnock, *Wesley's Journal*, May 28, 1738, 1:479-80.
2. Ward and Heitzenrater, *Wesley's Journal and Diaries*, June 8, 1742, 19:274-75.
3. Jackson, *Wesley's Works*, Letters, March 3, 1747, 12:90.
4. Thirty-nine Articles of Religion, Art. 11.
5. Outler, *Wesley's Sermons*, "Prophets and Priests," ¶15, 4:80-81.
6. *Book of Common Prayer*, "The Order for the Administration of the Lord's Supper."
7. Thirty-nine Articles, Art. 12.
8. Thirty-nine Articles, Art. 13.
9. *Homilies*, "Second Sermon on the Passion."
10. *Homilies*, "Sermon on the Sacrament."

THE RIGHTEOUSNESS OF FAITH

The initial years of Methodism occasionally saw extraordinary manifestations of religious fervor. In those early years, John Wesley's preaching sometimes resulted in physical demonstrations. For instance, once while Wesley was preaching at Epworth, numerous people cried aloud, "God be merciful to me a sinner."[1] During the delivery of another sermon, several people dropped as though they were dead.[2] Now and then, during a sermon, cries of penitents drowned out Wesley's voice. He reported that following these emotional displays many people found peace with God and broke forth in shouts of thanksgiving.[3]

On one occasion, Wesley wrote:

> While I was earnestly inviting all sinners to "enter into the holiest" by this "new and living way," many of those that heard began to call upon God with strong cries and tears. Some sunk down, and there remained no strength in them; others exceedingly trembled and quaked: Some were torn with a kind of convulsive motion in every part of their bodies, and that so violently, that often four or five persons could not hold one of them. I have seen many hysterical and many epileptic fits; but none of them were like these, in many respects. I immediately prayed, that God would not suffer those who were weak to be offended.[4]

Robert Southey, one of Wesley's biographers, suggested that emotional displays were due to Wesley's passionate oratory and his encouraging his congregations to "throw off all restraint, and abandon themselves before the congregation to these mixed sensations of mind and body."[5] The evidence, however, does not support Southey's supposition. Wesley was an exceptionally effective preacher, but he was not an especially emotional speaker. In sermons, he used controlled and measured prose; he never "ranted." Furthermore, he never encouraged his listeners to fall into ecstatic experiences. Both George Whitefield and Charles Wesley preached with greater emotional passion, physical vehemence, and fiery zeal than John Wesley did. Yet, they did not see the degree of emotional displays which sometimes attended John's preaching during the early years of the Methodist revival.

Probably, the occasions when John Wesley's early sermons produced emotional displays can be explained on grounds other than those suggested by Robert Southey. A possible theory is that emotional and physical displays sometimes appeared when Wesley preached because, at one time he stressed that people were utterly damned unless they felt a conscious awareness of God's pardoning grace. Thus, people's anxieties about their lack of assurance of salvation may have been responsible for their emotional responses.[6] Wesley's early preaching left some unconverted people in total despair, even if they were earnestly seeking God.

In contrast to John Wesley's early preaching, George Whitefield and Charles Wesley tended to give comfort to those who were seeking after justifying faith. Even though they preached with great emotion, they encouraged their hearers that if they earnestly sought salvation they would surely find it.

Indeed, by the early 1740s, John Wesley himself moderated his message to give hope and encouragement to those who had not yet received the witness of the Spirit. He encouraged the "seekers" to expect that eventually God would give them an assurance of the salvation for which they longed. When Wesley adjusted his message in this way, the emotional demonstrations subsided.

The 1746 Conference of Wesley's preachers dealt with the question, "Can it be conceived that God has any regard to the sincerity of an unbeliever?" The answer formulated was, "Yes, so much, that, if he perseveres therein, God will infallibly give him faith." Methodist preaching took on this optimistic cast, and soon the physical and emotional displays virtually ceased.

It was within the context of debates about religious emotion that Wesley preached the present sermon, which articulates the fundamental distinction between the righteousness of the law and the righteousness of faith. This sermon explains the contrast between the covenant of works and the covenant of faith. The covenant of works given to Adam and Eve demanded perfect performance. In our fallen state of sin we cannot live up to the covenant that God gave to the first man and woman. Wesley contends that all attempts to achieve salvation by good works are completely unavailing.

In this sermon Wesley proclaims the good news of God's covenant of faith. This covenant (in contrast to the covenant of works) rests on the righteousness of Christ and his atonement for our sins. We have strong reasons to rejoice in the goodness of God, because he graciously gives justifying grace to all those who repent and trust Christ as their personal savior. The righteousness of faith comes by God's grace, and he always gives this grace to those who repent and believe.

Sermon 6

THE RIGHTEOUSNESS OF FAITH

Moses writes concerning the righteousness that comes from the law, that "the person who does these things will live by them." But the righteousness that comes from faith says, "Do not say in your heart, 'Who will ascend into heaven?'" (that is, to bring Christ down) "or 'Who will descend into the abyss?'" (that is, to bring Christ up from the dead). But what does it say? "The word is near you, on your lips and in your heart." (that is, the word of faith that we proclaim). (Romans 10:5-8)

1 In this passage of scripture the Apostle Paul does not set the covenant given by Moses against the covenant given by Christ. If we ever imagined this to be the case, it was because we failed to observe that within the context of his time Moses spoke to the people of Israel about both covenants.

On the one hand, St. Paul speaks in our text about the covenant of grace that God through Christ has established with people in every age (with the ancient Hebrews and with those after the coming of Christ). On the other hand, St. Paul speaks of the covenant of works that God made with Adam in Paradise. It is commonly supposed (particularly by the Jews about whom Paul writes) that the covenant of works is the only covenant that God ever made with humankind.

2. At the beginning of Romans 10, Paul affectionately spoke about the Jews: "Brothers and sisters, my heart's desire and prayer to God for them is that they may be saved. I can testify that they have a zeal for God, but it is not an informed zeal. They are ignorant of the righteousness that comes from God. That is, they do not understand the justification that comes entirely from the grace and mercy of God, who freely forgives our sins because of his beloved Son and the redemption that he secured for us. As a result of this ignorance, they are seeking to establish their own righteousness, prior to faith in God who justifies the ungodly." They have not "submitted to God's righteousness." Consequently, in their misdirected error they are actually inviting death.

3. The Jews were ignorant that "Christ is the end of the law for everyone who believes." By the one offering of himself, Christ put an end to the first covenant (which God did not give to Moses, but to Adam in his state of innocence). The exacting and continuing tone of this covenant was, "Do this, and live." God has also provided us with a better covenant, "Believe, and live; believe, and you will be saved." Believe, and you will be rescued from the guilt and power of sin. In your believing, God will save you from the wages of sin.

4. How many today are as equally ignorant of the new covenant as the Jews were, even some of those who bear the name of Christ! How many there are who have a "zeal for God," yet their zeal "is not enlightened." They continue to seek "to establish their own righteousness" as the basis for their pardon and acceptance before God. They emphatically refuse to "submit to the righteousness of God." Certainly, my heart's desire and prayer to God for you, brothers, is that you may be saved. In order to remove this great stumbling block out of your way, (1) I will endeavor to distinguish between the righteousness of the law and the righteousness that comes by faith, (2) I will speak about the absurdity of trusting in the righteousness of the law, and (3) I will explain the wisdom of submitting to the righteousness that comes from faith.

I. The righteousness of the law and the righteousness of faith

1. First, the righteousness that comes through the law claims that those who do the works of the law will find life through the law. It is claimed that if we constantly and perfectly observe the entire law, we will live forever. God gave the law, or covenant (usually called the Covenant of Works) to Adam in Paradise. It required a perfect and absolute obedience; it was an obedience that lacked nothing. This kind of obedience

was the condition of Adam's permanent continuation in the holiness and happiness in which God created him.

2. The righteousness that comes by the law requires one to fulfill all righteousness. Perfect fulfillment must be inward and outward, negative and positive. One must abstain from every careless word and avoid every evil venture. One has to keep every natural impulse, desire, and thought in obedience to the will of God. One is required to remain holy in heart and life, even as God the creator is holy. One must be pure in heart, just as God is pure; one is obligated to be perfect, even as the Father in heaven is perfect. The righteousness of the law demanded that Adam and Eve love the Lord their God with all their hearts, with all their souls, with all their minds, and with all their strength. It means that they must love every soul that God has made, just as God loves us. The covenant of works obligates us to dwell in God (who is love), and God will live in us. The law requires people to serve the Lord their God with all their strength and in everything sincerely to seek his glory.

3. The law required these things so that one might live. The law further obligated one to a perfect degree of obedience. The law permitted no compromise. There was no possible allowance for falling short of outward or inward obedience in any way—not in a single detail. Even if everyone obeyed all commandments relating to outward things, it would not be adequate unless one did so with all one's strength—to the fullest extent and in the most perfect manner. Furthermore, the demand of the law to love God with every ability and capacity is not satisfied unless one does these things to the fullest measure.

4. Still, the righteousness that comes by the law required one more thing—uninterrupted and entire obedience and perfect holiness both of heart and life. From the moment that God created Adam by breathing into him the breath of life, there could be no lapses in obedience until the days of his testing would end and he would be confirmed in life everlasting.

5. The righteousness that comes by the law speaks to us this way: "Man of God, stand firm in love, remain in the image of God in which you are created. If you are to remain in life, keep the commandments, which are written on your heart. Love the Lord your God with all your heart. As you love yourself, love every soul that God has made. Desire nothing else but God. Aim at God in your every thought, word, and deed. In body or soul do not veer from him in a single gesture if you would reach your goal for the prize of the heavenly call. With every ability and capacity of your soul, in every way, in every degree, and at every moment of your existence, let everything in you bless his holy name "Do

this, and you shall live." Your light will shine, your love will blaze more and more until God receives you into his house in the heavens to reign with him forever and ever.

6. By contrast, the righteousness that comes from faith speaks in a different way: "Do not say in your heart, 'Who will ascend into heaven?' (that is, to bring Christ down)" as though it were some impossible task which God required you first to perform before gaining his acceptance. "Do not say, 'Who will descend into the abyss?' (that is, to bring Christ up from the dead, as though that were still remaining to be done), and if you accomplish this task God will accept you."

Then, what message *does* the righteousness that comes by faith have for us? "The word is near you, on your lips and in your heart." This new covenant is the word of faith that I preach. It has even now been established with sinful people through Jesus Christ.

7. By "the righteousness that comes from faith," I mean the state of justification that brings present and final salvation, so long as we hold fast to the end. Justification is God's gift to fallen humankind, given through the merits and mediation of his only begotten Son. The promise was partially revealed to Adam soon after his fall; it was even contained in the original promise that God made to him and his progeny. The promise was that the offspring of the woman would strike the serpent's head.

The promise was still more clearly revealed to Abraham by God's angel from heaven. The angel said, "By myself I have sworn, says the Lord, all the nations of the earth shall gain blessing for themselves." The promise was made even more fully known to Moses, David, and to the prophets that followed. Through them, the promise was transmitted to many of the people of God in their respective generations. Even so, the majority of them remained ignorant of the promise, and very few understood it clearly. "Life and immortality" were not "brought to light" to the ancient Jews to the extent that these blessings have now come to us "through the gospel."

8. Today, the new covenant does not say to sinful people, "Render sin less obedience, and you will live." If this requirement were in effect, we could not benefit by everything that Christ has done and suffered for us. If the old covenant were required in order for us to have life we would need to "ascend into heaven to bring Christ down," or "descend into the abyss to bring Christ up from the dead." The new covenant does not require us to do impossible things. (To ordinary people, the requirements of the old covenant would be impossible; but not impossible to those assisted by the Spirit of God.) The demands of the old covenant only

mock human weakness, whereas, legally speaking, the covenant of grace does not require us to do anything at all as a complete and necessary requirement in order to receive justification.

We need only to trust in God who justifies us for the sake of his Son and the atonement that he has made. God "justifies the ungodly without works" and imputes their faith to them for righteousness. It was in this way that Abraham trusted the Lord, and the Lord "reckoned it to him as righteousness." "He received the sign of circumcision as a seal of the righteousness that he had gained by faith, that he might become the ancestor of all who believe, so that righteousness might be reckoned to them also."

The words, "It was reckoned to him," were not written for Abraham's sake alone. They were written also for us. To those who believe, faith will be accounted for righteousness, and faith will stand in the place of perfect obedience. We have acceptance with God if we "believe in him who raised Jesus our Lord from the dead, who was handed over to death for our trespasses and was raised for our justification." Those who trust in Christ have the assurance of the remission of sins and of a new life to follow.

9. What does the covenant of forgiveness, unmerited love, and pardoning mercy say to us? This new covenant says, "Believe on the Lord Jesus, and you will be saved." In the day that you believe, you will surely live. You will be restored to God's favor, and in finding delight in him you find life. You will be saved from the condemnation and wrath of God. You will be brought from death to life and enabled to partake of a life of righteousness. And if, trusting in Jesus, you endure to the end, you will never taste the second death. Having suffered with your Lord, you will also live and reign with him for eternity.

10. Now, "the word is near you." The provision for finding life is clear, easy, and always available. Through the operation of the Spirit of God, the word is "in your mouth and your heart." The instant you "confess with your lips that Jesus is Lord and believe in your heart that God raised him from the dead, you will be saved." You will be saved from condemnation, guilt, and punishment for your former sins. You will receive power to serve God in true holiness all the remaining days of your life.

11. What then is the distinction between the "righteousness which comes from the law" and the "righteousness which comes from faith"? What distinguishes the first covenant, which is of works, and the second covenant, which is of grace?

Here is the essential, unchangeable difference: The covenant of works assumes one to be already holy and happy, having been created in the image of God and enjoying his favor. This covenant prescribes the condition by which one may *continue* in God's favor and have love, joy, life, and immortality. The second covenant assumes one to be unholy and unhappy, having fallen short of the glorious image of God and having deserved God's wrath. In this state of sin and spiritual death, one is hastening toward physical and eternal death. It is to such a person that the second covenant prescribes the condition by which he may regain the pearl he has lost, recover the favor and image of God, retrieve the life of God in his soul, and be *restored* to the knowledge and the love of God. This benefit marks the beginning of everlasting life.

12. I will summarize the covenant of works: In order to *remain* in God's favor and in his knowledge, love, holiness, and happiness, one who was created perfect was required to demonstrate perfect and uninterrupted obedience to every point of the law of God. By contrast, under the covenant of grace, in order for one to recover the favor and life of God, one needs only faith. This faith is a living trust in God, who through Christ justifies those that have not fully obeyed him.

13. Once again, the covenant of works required Adam and all his children to pay the entire price themselves. This condition was necessary if they were to receive all the future blessings of God. However, in the covenant of grace we must recognize that we have nothing with which to pay our debt. God "freely cancels all our debts." His condition is that we trust in the One who has paid the price for us. "He is the atoning sacrifice for our sins, and not for ours only but also for the sins of the whole world."

14. Therefore, the first covenant required what is now out of range for every human being—namely, sinless obedience. Such compliance with God's law is not possible for those who are "conceived and born in sin." By contrast, the second covenant requires what is easily accessible to us. It is as if the second covenant says, "You are sinful, but God is love!" By your sin you have fallen short of the glory of God. Yet, there is mercy with the Lord. Therefore, bring all your sins to the pardoning God, and they will vanish away like smoke.

If you were not ungodly, there would be no reason for him to justify you as an ungodly being. Now, draw near in full assurance of faith. God speaks, and it is done. Fear not, and only believe. The just God "justifies everyone who trusts in Jesus."

II. The absurdity of trusting in the righteousness of the law

1. Having considered the covenant of law and the covenant of grace, it is easy to show, as I propose to do in my second point, the absurdity of trusting in the "righteousness which is of the law." It is also simple to show the wisdom of submitting to "the righteousness which is of faith."

Let us consider the foolishness of continuing to trust in the "righteousness which is of the law." The conditions of this kind of righteousness are "Do this, and live." The fundamental mistake of those who try to live by the law is to begin with a basic error. First, before they can ever think of claiming any blessing based on the covenant of the law they must assume that they are in the same state as those with whom God made this covenant. But how vainglorious is this supposition. The covenant of works was made with Adam who was created in a state of innocence! How weak, therefore, must the entire building be which rests on such a false foundation. How foolish are those who build their house on the sand!

They seem not to have considered that the covenant of works was never given to those who are "dead in trespasses and sins." When Adam knew no sin, he was alive to God. He was holy, as God is holy. The covenant of works was not designed for the *recovery* of the favor and life of God after it had been lost. It was designed only for Adam and Eve. They were to continue and grow in God's favor and life until they would be complete in everlasting life.

2. In addition, those who seek to live by their good works fail to consider that they are seeking to establish their "own righteousness, which is of the law." Consider the exacting standards of obedience and righteousness that the law inescapably requires. These virtues must be perfect and entire in every point if they are to fulfill the law's demand. Which one of you is able to perform the standard of obedience required by the law? Who among you fulfills every detail of even the outward commandments of God?

Do you avoid everything, great or small, that God forbids? Do you leave nothing undone that he requires? Do you speak no trivial word? Is your conversation always "useful for ministering grace to others?" Whether you eat or drink or whatever you do, do you do everything for the glory of God? How much less are you able to fulfill all the *inward* commandments of God! He requires that every disposition and stirring of your soul be holy to the Lord. Are you able to "love God with all your heart"? Do you love all humankind as your own soul? Do you pray without ceasing, give thanks in all circumstances, keep God always before you? Do you keep your every affection, desire, and thought in obedience to God's law?

3. Furthermore, you should consider that the righteousness of the law requires obedience to *every* command of God, negative and positive, internal and external. And this obedience must be perfect to the fullest degree. In every possible circumstance, the command of the law says, "You shall love the Lord your God with all your heart, and with all your strength." This requirement permits no slackening of any kind. It pardons no defect. It condemns every falling short of the full measure of obedience and immediately pronounces a curse on the offender. The law requires nothing less than the unchanging rules of justice. It says, "I know of no way to show mercy."

4. Who then can appear before such a Judge? "If he should mark iniquities, who could stand?" How fragile are those who wish to be tried at the bar of judgment where "no human being will be justified!" Not a single offspring of Adam is able. Suppose that we did keep every commandment with all our strength. A single transgression completely destroys our entire claim to life. If we have ever transgressed at only one point, the righteousness that comes from the law is at an end. The law condemns everyone who does not perform perpetual and perfect obedience. For the one that has once sinned in any way, according to the sentence of the law, "there remains a fearful prospect of judgment, and a fury of fire that will consume the adversaries."

5. Is it not, therefore, the very absurdity of stupidity for fallen humankind to seek life by the righteousness that comes by the law? For we were "born guilty, sinners when our mothers conceived us." We are by nature "earthly, unspiritual, devilish," "corrupt and abominable." Until we find grace, "nothing good dwells in us." Of ourselves, we cannot think a single good thought. We are indeed completely sinful, plain lumps of ungodliness that commit sin in every breath we draw. Our actual transgressions in word and deed are more numerous than the hairs of our heads. What stupidity and senselessness it is for such unclean, guilty, and helpless worms to dream of seeking God's acceptance through their own righteousness that comes from the law!

6. Now, the same facts that prove the absurdity of trusting in the "righteousness of our own that comes from the law" also prove the wisdom of submitting to "the righteousness from God based on faith." Each of the preceding considerations demonstrates my message. The wisdom of the first step, which is to disclaim our own righteousness, plainly rests upon the real nature of things. What better agrees with reality than, with our heart and lips, to acknowledge our true spiritual state? Is it not obvi-

ous that we bring with us into the world a corrupt and sinful nature that is more depraved than we can easily conceive or express?

As a consequence of our sinful nature, are we not prone to everything that is evil and opposed to everything that is good? Are we not full of pride, self-will, unruly passions, foolish desires, and vile and immoderate affections? Are we not lovers of the world and lovers of pleasure more than lovers of God? Is it not true that our deeds have been no better than our hearts and that they are ungodly and unholy in many ways? Have not our actual sins in word and deed been as numerous as the stars of heaven? Does it not accord with reality to say that on all these points we are displeasing to him who is of purer eyes than to behold iniquity?

Is it not true that we deserve nothing from God but indignation, wrath, and death, which are the wages of sin? Is it not the case that none of our own righteousness (indeed, we have none at all) or works (our works grow from an evil tree) can appease the wrath of God? How can we avert the punishment we justly deserve? If left to ourselves, we will only grow worse and worse, sink deeper and deeper into sin, and offend God more and more. We sin with our evil deeds and with the inclinations of our carnal minds.

Finally, we will fill up the measure of our iniquities and bring upon ourselves swift destruction. In truth, is this not the condition in which we find ourselves? It is true wisdom to acknowledge our unrighteousness with heart and lips. If we are to act according to the true nature of things, we must renounce our own righteousness, "the righteousness which is of the law." To do so is a display of true wisdom.

7. There is a further consideration pertaining to the wisdom of submitting to "the righteousness of faith." To do so is to receive the righteousness of God. Faith as a means of being reconciled with God is the method that God himself has established. He is both the God of perfect wisdom and the sovereign Lord of heaven, earth, and every living thing he created. In view of this fact, it is never fitting for us to say to God, "What are you doing?"

No one, except those who are completely devoid of understanding, will dispute with the One who is mightier than we are. God's kingdom rules over everything. Thus, it is a mark of true wisdom and sound understanding to concur with whatever he has ordained. In the matter of salvation, as in everything else, it is wise to say "It is the Lord; let him do what seems good to him."

8. We may also contemplate that out of pure grace, sovereign love, and undeserved mercy, God has bestowed upon sinful humanity a means of being reconciled with him. God does not cut us off from his working

or completely blot us out of his thoughts. We are wise to accept with gratitude whatever method of salvation he has been pleased to designate. Out of his compassionate mercy and unmerited goodness, he designed a way to reconcile his enemies that have so strongly revolted and so obstinately rebelled against him for such a long time. Because his way brings us into his favor, it is undoubtedly wise to accept it with total gratitude.

9. I mention one more consideration: It is wisdom to aim at the best end by the best means. Now the best goal that anyone can pursue is happiness in God. And the best goal that fallen humanity can pursue is the recovery of the favor and image of God. The best and only means under heaven given to us by which we may regain the favor of God is to accept the "righteousness that comes by faith." This gift, better than life itself, is the image of God, which is the true life of the soul. It is "believing in the only Son of God."

III. The wisdom of submitting to the righteousness that comes from faith

1. Whoever you are that desire to be forgiven and reconciled to the favor of God, do not say in your heart, "First, I must conquer every sin; break off every evil word and work, and do every good to everyone." Do not say, "I must first go to church, receive the Lord's Supper, hear more sermons, and say more prayers." What a pity, my brother or sister! You have entirely missed the way. You remain "ignorant of the righteousness that comes from God." You are "seeking to establish your own righteousness" as the ground of your reconciliation.

Do you not know that, until you are reconciled to God, you can do nothing but sin? For what reason, then, do you say, "I must first do this and that, and then I will believe"? No. Believe first! Trust in the Lord Jesus Christ who is the atonement for your sins. First, allow this good foundation to be laid. Then, you can do everything well.

2. Neither should you say in your heart, "I cannot be accepted yet, because I am not good enough." Who is good enough, or ever was good enough, to merit God's acceptance? Has any child of Adam ever been righteous enough to earn God's favor? Will there be any such person until the culmination of all things? As for you, you are not good at all. Indeed, "Nothing good dwells within you." And you never will be good, until you believe in Jesus. Until you do trust Christ, you will find yourself becoming worse and worse.

Is there any need of becoming worse than you are, in order to be accepted by God? Are you not bad enough already? Indeed, you are already sufficiently evil. God knows it, and you know it. So, do not delay. Everything is ready. "Arise, and have your sins washed away." Now, the fountain is open. It is the time to be washed white in the blood of the Lamb. God will "purge you with hyssop, and you shall be clean."

3. Do not say, "But wait, I am sure that I am not sufficiently repentant, I am not adequately aware of my sins." I pray to God that you *were* more aware of your sins and a thousand times more repentant than you are. However, do not wait for this deeper sense of sin and repentance. It may be that God will make you so—but not *before* you believe, but *through* believing. It may be that you will not weep much until you love much, in gratitude that much has been forgiven. In the meantime, look to Jesus. Behold, how he loves you! What more could he have done for you than what he has already done?

> O Lamb of God, was ever pain,
> Was ever love like thine?[7]

Look steadfastly upon the Lord, until he looks on you and breaks your hard heart. Then, your "head will become a spring of water and your eyes a fountain of tears."

4. Do not say, "I must do something more before I come to Christ." If the Lord were to delay his coming, I agree that it would be fitting and right for you to wait for his appearance by doing good works, to the best of your ability in whatever he has commanded. There is no need, however, to posit such a theory. How can you know that he will delay his coming? Perhaps before the morning light, he will appear as the dawn from on high. O, do not appoint him the time to return! Expect the Lord every moment. God is near! Even at the door!

5. For what purpose would you wait until you have more earnestness before your sins are blotted out? Would you wait until you become more worthy of the grace of God? Pitiably, you would be seeking to "establish your own righteousness." The Lord will have mercy, not because you are worthy of it, but because "his mercies never come to an end." God shows mercy, not because you are righteous, but because Jesus Christ has atoned for your sins. Once again, if there is any merit in sincerity why do you expect its fruits before believing? *Faith* is the only root of anything that is really good and holy.

Above all, how long will you continue to forget that nothing that you do or have can ever count in your favor toward gaining God's forgiveness? Indeed, you must cast behind your back and trample under foot all your good works and your position. You must consider these things of no account, or you will never find favor in God's sight. Until you abandon self-effort, you cannot come to God. Seek him as the absolute sinner you are—guilty, lost, and condemned. You have no merit to plead or anything to present to God. You can offer to God only the merits of his beloved Son, "who loved you and gave himself for you."

6. To conclude my message, I speak to those of you who *know* that you are living under the sentence of death. See yourself as condemned sinners who live under God's condemnation. The Lord does not say to you, "Perfectly obey all my commandments, and you shall live." Instead, God says to you, "Believe in the Lord Jesus Christ, and you will be saved." The word of faith has come near to you. Immediately, in the present moment, in your present condition as the sinner you are, come to him. Just as you are, believe the gospel. The Lord will say to you, "I will be merciful toward your iniquities, and I will remember your sins no more."

Notes

1. Ward and Heitzenrater, *Wesley's Journal and Diaries*, June 9, 1742, 19:275.
2. Curnock, *Wesley's Journal*, June 22, 1739, 2:226.
3. Tyerman, *The Life and Times of the Rev. John Wesley*, M. A., 1:388-89.
4. Ward and Heitzenrater, *Wesley's Journal and Diaries*, June 15, 1739, 19:70.
5. Robert Southey, *The Life of Wesley and the Rise and Progress of Methodism*, 2 vols. (London: Longman, Hurst, Rees, Orme, and Brown, 1820) 1:246-7.
6. See Bernard G. Holland, "A Species of Madness: The Effect of John Wesley's Early Preaching," *Proceedings of the Wesley Historical Society*, 39:77-85.
7. Written by John Wesley's father, Samuel Wesley, Sr.

THE WAY TO THE KINGDOM

On June 6, 1742 John Wesley visited his boyhood church in Epworth, where his father had served as rector from 1697 until his death in 1735. On that visit, Wesley offered his services to John Romley, the church's curate. Romley, however, refused Wesley's offer to assist him. Indeed, he used the occasion of Wesley's presence in Epworth to preach against the Methodists. Romley declared that their enthusiasm quenched the Holy Spirit, although he did not explain how Methodism harmed the work of God.

Wesley reflected on the disagreeable attitude of the rector and challenged his denunciation of Methodism:

> A little before the Service began, I went to Mr. Romley, the Curate, and offered to assist him either by preaching or reading Prayers. But he did not care to accept of my assistance. The church was exceeding full in the afternoon, a rumour being spread, that I was to preach. But the sermon on, "Quench not the Spirit," was not suitable to the expectation of many of the hearers. Mr. Romley told them, one of the most dangerous ways of quenching the Spirit was by enthusiasm; and enlarged on the character of an enthusiast, in a very florid and oratorical manner. After sermon John Taylor stood in the church-yard, and gave notice, as the people were coming out, "Mr. Wesley, not being permitted to preach in the church, designs to preach here at six o'clock." Accordingly at six I came, and found such a congregation as I believe Epworth never saw before. I stood near the east end of the church, upon my father's tomb-stone, and cried, "The kingdom of heaven is not meat and drink; but righteousness, and peace, and joy in the Holy Ghost."[1]

Although that sermon was never published, its substance appears in this present sermon—*The Way to the Kingdom.*

This discourse begins with a discussion of the nature of the kingdom of God, which is not primarily outward, but inward. The inward kingdom of God does not consist merely of orthodoxy or right opinions. It is holiness, which invariably results in happiness. Next, Wesley goes on to expound the text, "The kingdom of God is at hand: repent ye, and believe the gospel." In this sermon, Wesley's call to repentance is a classic expression of Christian evangelism.

This sermon does not so much explain the *nature* of the kingdom of God as it does the *way* into his kingdom. Wesley the evangelist declares that humankind's supreme desire should be to know the way to the kingdom of God. The sermon contends that society can be changed only when individuals have been transformed through the Holy Spirit. In the sermon's closing exhortation Wesley declares, "This repentance, faith, peace, joy, love, and transformation from one degree of glory to another is what the wisdom of the world has voted to be insanity, mere fanaticism, and utter confusion. But you, O child of God, do not heed the world's opinion. . . . Be in no way apprehensive about those who speak evil against the things about which they do not know. God will soon turn your faint spirit into joy."

This sermon contains one of Wesley's clearest statements about repentance. This instruction was needed because some in his day were teaching that the doctrine of salvation by faith alone canceled the need to repent. Wesley, however, was determined to balance faith with works, including the work of repentance. To be sure, repentance does not merit God's favor, but it does open us to justifying and sanctifying grace. Preaching repentance in this way, Wesley was in harmony with his church's Articles of Religion, which state:

> Albeit Good Works which are the fruits of Faith, and follow after Justification, cannot put away our sins . . . yet are they pleasing and acceptable to God in Christ, and do spring out necessarily of a true and lively Faith; insomuch that by them a lively Faith may be as evidently known as a tree may be known by its fruit.[2]

The sermon insists that before one repents one must come to the awareness of personal spiritual need and experience deep remorse for having offended God. Wesley declares, "Know what is the first step in repentance, prior to faith: it is conviction, or self-understanding. Sleeper, awake! Understand the corruption of your inner self, the depravity by which you are very distant from original righteousness." In this message Wesley underscores the teaching of Jesus: "Blessed are the poor in spirit: for theirs is the kingdom of heaven." He closes the sermon by declaring, "However many your sins may be, just now cast yourself upon the Lamb of God. Then, 'an entry into the eternal kingdom of our Lord and Savior Jesus Christ will be richly provided for you.'"

THE WAY TO THE KINGDOM

The kingdom of God has come near; repent, and believe in the good news.   (Mark 1:15)

The words of this text naturally lead us to consider: (1) the nature of true religion, which here our Lord calls "the kingdom of God." He said, "It has come near." (2) The way into the kingdom: "Repent, and believe in the good news."

I. The nature of true religion

1. First, we will consider the nature of true religion, which our Lord described as "the kingdom of God." The great Apostle Paul uses the same expression in Romans, where he expounds on the Lord's words: "The kingdom of God is not food and drink but righteousness and peace and joy in the Holy Spirit."

2. "The kingdom of God," or true religion, "is not food and drink." Despite this description, it is well known that the unconverted Jews and large numbers of those who had learned about the faith of Christ were "zealous for the law." Here, St. Paul is referring to the ceremonial law of Moses. In that law, they found prescriptions concerning food and drink offerings and distinctions between clean and unclean meats. They not only observed these laws themselves, but they zealously urged them on the "Gentiles who were turning to God." These legalists championed the

law to such an extent that everywhere they went some of them taught, "Unless you are circumcised according to the custom of Moses, you cannot be saved." In opposition to these zealots for the law, St. Paul declared in the book of Romans and in many other places that true religion does not consist of any outward thing at all. True religion resides in the heart. The entire essence of real religion is "righteousness, peace, and joy in the Holy Spirit."

4. True religion is not an outward thing that consists of forms and ceremonies—even those of the most commendable sort. Let us assume that outward ceremonies are ever so proper, as they reflect and express inward things. Assume as well that outward religious forms are ever so helpful to those unrefined people whose thought reaches little farther than their sight. Assume also that ceremonies are helpful to persons of understanding and greater endowments, as doubtless they may sometimes be. Indeed, let us assume that God himself established certain outer ceremonies, such as those he gave to the Jews.

Nevertheless, even during the period of time when outward ceremonies were in force, true religion never consisted primarily of rituals. No, not in any literal sense. How much more is this the case with rites and forms that have only human origins! The religion of Christ rises infinitely higher than mere ceremony; it reaches immensely deeper than all rites and forms.

Ceremonies are good in their place, so long as they remain subservient to true religion. Of course, it is irrational to object to rituals, so long as we use them only as occasional helps to human frailty. However, let no one carry them any farther. Let none imagine that ceremonies have any intrinsic worth or that religion cannot exist without them. To think this way would be abhorrent to the Lord.

5. The nature of real religion is far distant from worship forms, rites, and ceremonies; it does not correctly consist of any of these things at all. It is true that one cannot have any religion if one is guilty of degenerate and immoral actions. Genuinely religious people do not do to others what they would not want them to do in return if they were in the same circumstances.

It is also true that one can have no real religion if "he knows the right thing to do and fails to do it." Even so, one may abstain from outward evil and also do good, yet still have no genuine religion. Yes, two persons may do the same outward work—say, feeding the hungry or clothing the naked—while one of them may be truly religious and the other have no religion at all. One may act from the love of God and the other acts to be seen by people. It is obvious that while true religion naturally leads to every good word and work, the real nature of religion lies deeper still. It lies in "the hidden man of the heart."

6. Religion resides in the *heart*, not in mere orthodoxy or right opinions. Although orthodoxy and correct beliefs are not strictly outward things, still, they do not reside in the heart. They lie in the mind. One person may be orthodox in every point and espouse right opinions, which he or she zealously defends against all contenders. One may think rightly about the incarnation of our Lord, the ever-blessed Trinity, and every other doctrine contained in the Bible. People may assent to all the three Creeds the Apostles', the Nicene, and the Athanasian Creeds. Even so, it is possible that they would have no religion at all. They may have no more religion than a Jew, Moslem, or Pagan. Concerning the facts of Christianity, they may be almost as orthodox as the devil. Not completely orthodox, however, because everyone errs in some way. We cannot imagine, however, that the devil holds any erroneous views about Christ. Still, all the while, a person of orthodox views may be as great a stranger to the religion of the heart as the devil is.

7. In the sight of God, only a religion of the heart has great worth. Paul sums up heart religion in three points. It is "righteousness, and peace, and joy in the Holy Spirit."

First, true religion consists of righteousness. We cannot doubt this fact if we remember the words of our Lord describing the two grand branches of righteousness. On these hang all the law and the prophets. "You shall love the Lord your God with all your heart, and with all your soul, and with all your mind. This is the first and greatest commandment," the first and great branch of Christian righteousness. You shall delight yourself in the Lord your God, and you will seek and find all happiness in him. In time and eternity, the Lord will be "your shield, and your reward shall be very great." Your entire frame will cry out, "Whom have I in heaven but you? And there is nothing on earth that I desire other than you."

Then you will hear and fulfill the word of God who says, "My child, give me your heart." And, having given him your heart, your inmost self, in which he reigns without a rival, you may well cry out in the fullness of your soul, "The LORD is my rock, my fortress, and my deliverer, my God, my rock in whom I take refuge, my shield, and the horn of my salvation, my stronghold."

8. The second great branch of Christian righteousness is closely and inseparably connected with the first branch: "You shall love your neighbor as yourself." That is, you are to embrace others with the most kindhearted goodwill and the most sincere and gracious affection. With

regard to others, your most impassioned desires are to prevent or remove every evil from them and seek for them every possible good.

Your neighbors include more than the virtuous, the friendly, or those who love you. Your neighbors are also those who do not accept your kindness but rather return it back to you. Every child of Adam is our neighbor—every human being, every soul that God has made. We do not exclude those you have never seen in the flesh or those you do not know by face or name. You are not to exclude those you know to be evil and unthankful or those that continue hatefully to use and persecute you. You will love them as you love yourself. You must love them with a constant desire for their complete happiness and the same tireless care to defend them from whatever might grieve or hurt their souls or bodies.

9. Is not this kind of love "the fulfilling of the law" and the sum of all Christian righteousness? This righteousness is inward, because it necessarily implies "compassion and humility," because "love is not boastful." This righteousness also implies gentleness, meekness, and patience—because love "is not irritable or resentful, but believes all things, hopes all things, endures all things." This righteousness is also outward, because "love does no wrong to a neighbor" either by word or deed. Love cannot willingly hurt or grieve any one, and it is zealous of good deeds. All who truly love others, "whenever they have an opportunity, work for the good of all," because they love without partiality or hypocrisy. They are "full of mercy and good fruits."

10. In addition to holiness, real religion (a heart that is right toward God and others) also implies happiness. True religion is not only "righteousness," but also "peace, and joy in the Holy Spirit." What kind of peace is meant in this scripture? "The peace of God" which only God can impart and which the world cannot take away. It is the peace that "surpasses all understanding;" it transcends all narrowly rational comprehension. This peace is a supernatural comprehension, a divine taste of "the powers of the age to come."

The natural person cannot know this peace, however wise he or she may be in the things of this world. Indeed, in such a state one cannot know peace because it is "spiritually discerned." It is a peace that banishes all doubt and painful uncertainty. The Spirit of God bears witness with the spirits of Christians that they are "children of God." This peace banishes every tormenting fear of punishment, the fear of God's wrath, hell, the devil—and especially the fear of death. If it were God's will, those who know the peace of God desire "to depart and to be with Christ."

11. Wherever this peace is established in the soul there is also "joy in the Holy Spirit." It is the ever-blessed Spirit of God who imparts this joy to the heart. It is he who works in us that calm and humble rejoicing in God through Christ Jesus. By him, "we have now received reconciliation." This reconciliation with God enables us boldly to confirm the truth of the royal Psalmist's declaration, "Happy are those whose transgression is forgiven, whose sin is covered." It is the Lord who inspires the Christian soul with that steady, reliable joy which arises from the witness of the Holy Spirit to Christians that they are children of God. The Christian is able to "rejoice with an indescribable and glorious joy," "in hope of sharing the glory of God." This joy includes hope for the glorious image of God, which is now in part and shall be fully revealed to us. This crown of glory never fades away and it is kept in heaven for us.

12. Joined together, holiness and happiness are sometimes referred to in the Bible as "the kingdom of God" (as in the text for this sermon) and sometimes as "the kingdom of heaven." It is termed "the kingdom of God" because it is the immediate consequence of God's reigning in the soul. As soon as the Lord exercises his mighty power and sets up his throne in our hearts, they are immediately filled with "righteousness, and peace, and joy in the Holy Spirit." It is called "the kingdom of heaven" because, in a measure, it is heaven opened within us. Whoever experiences this kind of religion can declare before angels and men,

> Everlasting life is won,
> Glory is on earth begun.[3]

The constant tone of scripture is that everlasting life has been gained and glory has begun on earth.

The Bible consistently tells us that "God gave us eternal life, and this life is in his Son." Those who have the Son reigning in their hearts "have everlasting life." "This is eternal life, to know the only true God, and Jesus Christ whom he has sent." And those to whom this grace is given may confidently commune with God, even though they might be in the middle of a furnace of blazing fire.

> You, Lord, safe shielded by your power,
> You, Son of God, Jehovah we adore;
> In human form coming down to appear:
> To you be ceaseless hallelujahs given,
> Praise, as in heaven at your throne, we offer here;
> For where your presence is displayed, is heaven.[4]

13. Even now, the "kingdom of God (or of heaven) has come near." When these words were originally spoken, they meant that at that point "the time was fulfilled." God was being "revealed in flesh," and he would establish his kingdom among us and reign in the hearts of his people. Is it not true that the time is now fulfilled? Christ said to those who preach the remission of sins in his name, "Remember, I am with you always, to the end of the age." Therefore, wherever the gospel of Christ is preached, "the kingdom of God is near." It is not far from every one of you. You may enter in at this very hour. Just listen to his invitation, "Repent, and believe the gospel."

II. The way into the kingdom of God

1. Our text tells us the way into the kingdom of God. The first step is to *repent*. "This is the way; walk in it" (Isa. 30:21). All of you: know now the first step in repentance, prior to faith. It is conviction, or self-understanding. Sleeper, awake! Understand the corruption of your inner self, the depravity by which you are very distant from original righteousness. Because of your condition, "what your flesh desires is opposed to the Spirit." "The flesh is hostile to God; it does not submit to God's law—indeed it cannot." Know that you are corrupted in every capacity, in every faculty of your soul. You are totally depraved throughout your being; all the foundations of your life are misaligned. The eyes of your heart are darkened, so that they cannot comprehend God or the things of God. The clouds of ignorance and error surround you and cover you with the shadow of death.

As yet, you do not know anything as you ought to know it. You do not understand God, or the world, or yourself. Your will does not conform to God's will; instead, it is completely perverse and distorted. Your will opposes all good and everything that God loves. It is inclined to every evil that God despises. Your affections are alienated from God and scattered across the earth. Your passions, desires, aversions, joys, sorrows, hopes, and fears are crooked. They are either excessive in their measure or fixed on forbidden things. There is no health in your soul. To use the strong expression of Isaiah, "From the sole of the foot even to the head, there is no soundness in it, but bruises and sores and bleeding wounds."

2. This condition, then, is the inbred corruption of your heart, your inmost being. What kind of branches can you expect to grow from such an evil root? From this evil source springs unbelief, which always moves

away from the living God. It says, "Who is the Almighty, that I should serve him?" Unbelief says, "Nonsense! God does not even see or care." This attitude leads to self-sufficiency, the imagining that we can be like God. Out of your evil heart flows pride in all its forms, prompting you to say, "I am rich, I have prospered, and I need nothing."

From this evil fountain flow the bitter streams of vanity, lust for praise, ambition, covetousness, the desire of the flesh, the desire of the eyes, and pride in riches. From this depravity arise anger, hatred, malice, revenge, envy, quarrels, slander, and base suspicions. This wickedness leads to all the "senseless and harmful desires that plunge people into ruin and destruction." If these things are not promptly taken away, they will eventually plunge your soul into everlasting perdition.

3. What fruits can grow on such evil branches as these? Only fruits that are bitter and incessantly evil. Out of pride comes strife, foolish boasting, seeking and accepting the flattery of others. Pride robs God of the glory that he cannot give to another. From the lust of the flesh come gluttony, drunkenness, indulgence, carnal appetites, fornication, and immorality. In different ways, these sins defile your very body, which God designed as a temple of the Holy Spirit.

Unbelief is the source of every evil word and work. Time will not allow you to add up all the careless words you have spoken. These words provoked the Most High and grieved the Holy One of Israel. All the wicked works you have done are either wholly evil in themselves, or else they were not done for the glory of God. Your actual sins are more than you are able to say; they exceed the number of the hairs on your head. Who can count the sands of the sea or the drops of rain—or your iniquities?

4. Do you not know that "the wages of sin is death?" This death is not only temporal, but also eternal. The mouth of the Lord has spoken: "The person who sins shall die." This person will die the second death. And this sentence is to "suffer the punishment of eternal destruction, separated from the presence of the Lord and from the glory of his might."

Do you not know that every sinner is under the sentence of hell fire? This phrase is not properly translated *in danger of hell fire*. That expression is far too weak. Sinners are doomed *already*, and they are moving toward execution. You are condemned to everlasting death. This punishment is the just reward for your inner and outer wickedness. It is only justice that the sentence should now take place.

Do you understand? Do you sense your condemnation? Are you completely convinced that you deserve God's wrath and everlasting damnation? God would do you no injustice if he now commanded the earth to open, and swallow you up. Would God be unjust if you were now to go down suddenly into the pit, into the unquenchable fire? If God has given you a heart truly to repent, you have a deep sense that these things are so. You understand that it is of his mere mercy that you are not immediately consumed and swept off the face of the earth.

5. What will you do to appease the wrath of God, atone for all your sins, and escape the punishment that you so justly deserve? You cannot do anything. There is nothing you can do that will in any way make amends to God for even one evil work, word, or thought. Not even if you could at this time do everything perfectly. If, from this very hour until your soul returns to God, you could perform complete and uninterrupted obedience, you could never atone for what is past. Not increasing your debt will not discharge it. It would still remain as large as ever.

Indeed, the present and future obedience of all the people on the earth and all the angels in heaven would never atone for a single sin. How futile, then, is the notion of atoning for your own sins by anything you could do! It costs far more to redeem one soul than all humankind is able to pay. Because there is no other help for guilty sinners, beyond question they must perish everlastingly.

6. Assume, though, that perfect obedience from this time forward could atone for the sins that are past. This compliance would profit you nothing. You are not able to obey perfectly. No, not in a single point. Just try to begin to shake off that outward sin that so easily besets you. You cannot do it. How can you change your life from all evil to all good? Indeed, it is impossible to do, unless first your heart is changed. So long as the tree remains evil, it cannot produce good fruit. Are you able to change your own heart from all sin to all holiness? Can you give life to a soul that is dead in sin, one that is dead to God and alive only to the world?

You can no more do so than you can give life to a dead body. You can do no more or less in this matter; you are completely devoid of strength. To be deeply aware of how helpless, guilty, and sinful you are, is the "repentance not to be repented of." Conviction of sin is the prologue to the kingdom of God.

7. If you add one more thing to your strong conviction of your inner and outer sins, you are not far from the kingdom. To your conviction of your unqualified guilt and helplessness, you must add a proper attitude. You need to have heart-felt sorrow for having shunned the mercy offered to you. You are not far from the kingdom of God if you feel remorse and

self-condemnation, having your mouth stopped, being ashamed even to look up to heaven.

Conviction means to fear the wrath of God that rests on you, sense his condemnation hanging over your head, and dread the flaming fire inflicting vengeance on those who do not know God and obey our Lord Jesus Christ. Conviction for sin includes an earnest desire to escape from God's indignation, to cease from evil, and to learn to do good. Then, I say to you in the name of the Lord, "You are not far from the kingdom of God," Take one more step and you will enter in. Repent now and "believe the gospel."

8. The gospel (that is, glad tidings of good news for guilty, helpless sinners) in the largest sense of the word means the entire revelation made to humankind by Jesus Christ. Sometimes the gospel means the complete account of what our Lord did and suffered while he lived among us. The substance of the gospel is, "Christ Jesus came into the world to save sinners." The Gospel is that "God so loved the world that he gave his only Son, so that everyone who believes in him may not perish but may have eternal life." Again, "He was wounded for our transgressions, crushed for our iniquities; upon him was the punishment that made us whole, and by his bruises we are healed."

9. Believe the gospel, and the kingdom of God is yours. You can attain this promise by faith. Christ pardons and absolves all who truly repent and sincerely believe his holy gospel. His kingdom comes as soon as God has spoken to your heart the words, "Take heart, son; your sins are forgiven." You then have "righteousness and peace and joy in the Holy Spirit."

10. Concerning the nature of this faith, beware that you do not deceive yourself. Faith is not, as some have understood, a mere assent to the truth of the Bible, the articles of our Creed, or everything that is contained in the Old and New Testaments. Demons believe these things as well as you or I! Yet, they still remain demons. Over and above intellectual assent, faith is a certain trust in the mercy of God through Christ Jesus. Faith is confidence in a pardoning God. It is a divine evidence or conviction that God was in Christ reconciling the world to himself, not counting our trespasses against us." Faith is a personal trust in the Son of God, who loved me and gave himself for me and that even I am now reconciled to God by the blood of his cross.

11. Do you believe in this way? If so, the peace of God is in your heart, and sorrow and sighing will flee away. You no longer doubt the love of God because it becomes as clear as the noonday sun. You cry out, "I will sing of your steadfast love, O Lord, forever; with my mouth I will

135

proclaim your faithfulness to all generations." You are no longer afraid of hell, or death, or the devil who once had the power of death. No, you are no longer agonizingly afraid of God himself; you have only a sensitive, filial dread of grieving him. Do you believe in Christ? If so, your "soul magnifies the Lord, and your spirit rejoices in God your Savior." You rejoice that you have "redemption through his blood, the forgiveness of sins." You rejoice in the "Spirit of adoption," who witnesses in your heart, "Abba, Father!" You rejoice in a "hope full of immortality," while pressing toward "the prize of the heavenly call." You wait with earnest expectation for all the good things that God has prepared for those who love him.

12. Do you now believe? If so, "God's love has been poured into your heart." You love him because he first loved you. And because you love God, you also love your brothers and sisters. Being filled with "love, joy, and peace," you are also filled with "patience, kindness, generosity, faithfulness, gentleness, and self-control," and all the other fruits of the Holy Spirit. In a word, you are filled with holy, heavenly, and divine affections. You see with an unveiled face (the veil is now taken away) the glory of the Lord (in whose image you are created). And you are being transformed into the same image from one degree of glory to another; for this comes from the Lord, the Spirit."

13. This repentance, faith, peace, joy, love, and transformation from one degree of glory to another is what the wisdom of the world has voted to be insanity, mere fanaticism, and utter confusion. But you, O child of God, do not heed the world's opinion. Do not be swayed by any of these criticisms. You know in whom you have believed. See that no one steals your crown. Hold fast to what you have already attained, and continue until you obtain all of God's great and precious promises.

And you who do not yet know the Lord, do not allow foolish people to make you ashamed of the gospel of Christ. Be in no way apprehensive about those who speak evil against the things of which they are ignorant. God will soon turn your faint spirit into joy. O, do not allow your hands to hang down! In only a short time, God will remove your fears, and give you the spirit of a healthy mind. He who vindicates you is near. Who is to condemn? It is Christ Jesus, who died and was raised. He is at the right hand of God and most certainly intercedes for you. However many your sins may be, just now cast yourself upon the Lamb of God. Then, "an entry into the eternal kingdom of our Lord and Savior Jesus Christ will be richly provided for you."

Notes

1. Ward and Heitzenrater, Wesley's *Journal and Diaries*, June 6, 1742, 19:273-74.
2. Thirty-nine Articles of Religion, Art. 12.
3. Charles Wesley, "Hymn After the Sacrament," stanza 6, *Poet. Wks.*, I, 170.
4. Mark Le Pla, *A Paraphrase on the Song of the Three Children*, 1724.

THE FIRST-FRUITS
OF THE SPIRIT

Three of John Wesley's previous sermons—*Justification by Faith*, *The Righteousness of Faith*, and *The Way to the Kingdom*—articulated the gospel of grace and laid down the foundation for the Christian life. The present sermon deals with an inevitable problem facing Christians who have been justified by God's grace: they must deal with the reality that after conversion sin remains in their lives. So, in this sermon Wesley speaks not as an evangelist but as a pastor. The present discourse is not primarily addressed to the unconverted. Rather, it instructs believers on how to face the presence of sin within them and how to experience a conscious freedom from its condemnation and power.

Wesley explains that there are two extremes into which Christians can move. On the one hand, some Christians may ignore their sin and minimize or overlook their moral transgressions. These Christians neglect repentance and personal discipline, while claiming the atonement of Christ as a covering for their ongoing acts of deliberate and willful disobedience. This self-deceiving attitude leads to sins of presumption.

On the other hand, some Christians become overwhelmed and crushed by their sins. A sense of guilt and condemnation so envelops them that they have no peace, joy, or victory. They even fret about past sins that they have already confessed and for which they have received pardon. These Christians, consequently, plunge into depression and despair.

This sermon provides balance for both tendencies—the propensity to ignore one's sins and the inclination to become defeated by one's sins. Wesley clarifies what sin *is* and what sin *is not*. Here Wesley distinguishes between willful transgressions and involuntary human weaknesses. Elsewhere, in his *Plain Account of Christian Perfection*, Wesley explained the difference between sin "properly so called and sin improperly so called." The first kind of sin is "a voluntary transgression of a known law." The second kind of sin is "an involuntary transgression of a divine law, known or unknown."[1] Both kinds of sin, of course, need Christ's atoning blood. Wesley believed that in this life we cannot be freed from involuntary transgressions and the limitations of our finite humanity. He did insist, however, that we can expect deliverance from willfully transgressing God's known laws. This discourse assures sincere Christians that "there is no condemnation for those who are in Christ Jesus, who walk not according to the flesh but according to the Spirit."

Finally, the sermon calls those who have fallen into sin to trust God for pardon and deliverance from sin's power. This sermon keeps in biblical balance the realities of original sin, justification by faith, and the power of grace to lift Christians above the grip of sin and enable them to live holy lives. Both justification (what God does *for* us) and sanctification (what God does *in* us) are essential aspects of the gospel. Salvation comes by grace apart from human merit, and yet faith finds its fullness when it works by love to sanctify us and make us holy.

The First-fruits of the Spirit issues a strong warning to Christians who carelessly fall into sin and fail to repent. The sermon also contains an especially encouraging message to Christians whose sins have defeated and depressed them. Wesley offers particularly helpful counsel and practical advice on how to deal with human infirmities and defects. The sermon concludes, "Love [God] who loves you, and it is enough. More love produces more strength. When you love him with all your heart, you will be 'mature and complete, lacking in nothing.'"

THE FIRST-FRUITS
OF THE SPIRIT

*There is therefore now no condemnation for those who
are in Christ Jesus, who walk not according to the flesh but
according to the Spirit.* (Romans 8:1)

1. By the phrase, "those who are in Christ Jesus," St. Paul is clearly referring to those who truly believe in the Lord. They "are justified by faith and have peace with God through our Lord Jesus Christ." All who believe in this way no longer "walk after the flesh," following the inclinations of their corrupt nature. Instead, they "walk according to the Spirit." Their thoughts, words, and deeds are under the direction of the blessed Spirit of God.

2. For these believers, "there is therefore now no condemnation." God does not condemn them because "they are now justified by his grace through the redemption that is in Christ Jesus." He has forgiven all their iniquities, and blotted out all their sins. Furthermore, there is no condemnation to them from within their hearts. They have received not the spirit of the world, but the Spirit that is from God, so that we may understand the gifts that he bestows on us. The Holy Spirit bears witness with our spirits that we are children of God." Added to the testimony of conscience, believers "have behaved in the world with frankness and godly sincerity, not by earthly wisdom but by the grace of God."

3. Regrettably, this scripture has been frequently and dangerously misunderstood. There are ignorant and unstable people who were not taught by God and therefore not established in "truth that is in accordance with godliness." They twist this verse to their own destruction. As clearly as I can, therefore, I propose first to explain who those are "who are in Christ Jesus" and "walk not according to the flesh but according to the Spirit." Secondly, I will explain that "there is no condemnation for those who are in Christ Jesus." Thirdly, I will conclude with some practical considerations.

I. Those in Christ Jesus who walk according to the Spirit

1. First I will explain who those are that "are in Christ Jesus." Are they not those who believe in his name? They are those who are "found in him, not having a righteousness of their own, but one that comes through faith in Christ." It is correct to say that all who are in Christ "have redemption through his blood." They "abide in Christ and Christ abides in them." They are "united to the Lord and have become one spirit with him." They are engrafted into him as branches into a vine. In a manner which words cannot express, they are united as members of a body to the head. Before their union with Christ, they could never have been able to conceive the wonder of this relationship.

2. Further, "whoever abides in Christ does not continue in sin;" they "do not walk according to the flesh." In the usual language of St. Paul, the *flesh* signifies corrupt human nature. The apostle used the term in this sense when he wrote to the Galatians that "the works of the flesh are obvious." Just ahead of this verse, he wrote, "Live by the Spirit, and do not gratify the desires of the flesh." To confirm the idea that those who live by the Spirit do not gratify the desires of the flesh, the apostle immediately adds, "For what the flesh desires is opposed to the Spirit, and what the Spirit desires is opposed to the flesh; for these are opposed to each other, to prevent you from doing what you want." The words "to prevent you from doing what you want" should not be translated, "so that you cannot do the things that you want." It is not that the flesh overcomes the Spirit. This translation has nothing to do with the original text of the Apostle, and it makes his whole argument invalid. Indeed, it asserts just the reverse of what he is proving.

3. Those who belong to Christ abide in him; they "have crucified the flesh with its passions and desires." They abstain from all the works of the flesh—"adultery, fornication, impurity, licentiousness, idolatry,

sorcery, enmities, strife, jealousy, anger, quarrels, factions, envy, drunkenness, carousing, and things like these." They avoid every proposal, word, and deed to which corrupt human nature leads. Although they feel the root of bitterness rising within themselves, they are endued with power from on high to trample it continually under foot so that it cannot "spring up and cause trouble." Every fresh attack that they experience only gives them a new opportunity to praise and cry out, "Thanks be to God, who gives us the victory through our Lord Jesus Christ."

4. Those who are in Christ Jesus "walk after the Spirit" in their hearts and lives. The Spirit teaches them to love God and neighbor with a love which is as "a spring of water gushing up to eternal life." The Spirit leads them into every sanctified desire and every divine and heavenly affection, until every thought that arises in their hearts is holy to the Lord.

5. Those who "walk after the Spirit" are also led by the Spirit into holy conduct. Their "speech is always gracious," "seasoned with salt" and with the love and fear of God. "No evil talk comes out of their mouths, but only what is good, that which builds up and gives grace to those who hear." Day and night, in all their outward behavior they employ themselves doing only those things that please Christ, who "left us an example, so that we should follow his steps." In all their interchanges with their neighbors, they walk in justice, mercy, and truth. And in every circumstance of life, "whatever they do, they do for the glory of God."

6. Those who "walk according to the Spirit" are "filled with faith and the Holy Spirit." In the whole course of their words and actions, they hold in their hearts and demonstrate in their lives the genuine fruit of the Spirit of God—"love, joy, peace, patience, kindness, generosity, faithfulness, gentleness, and self-control." As well, they have whatever else is beautiful and commendable. "In everything they are an ornament to the doctrine of God our Savior," and they give full proof to everyone that they are truly motivated by the same Spirit "who raised Christ from the dead."

II. There is no condemnation for those who are in Christ Jesus

1. In the second place, I propose to prove that "there is no condemnation for those who are in Christ Jesus and therefore walk not according to the flesh but according to the Spirit."

First, for believers in Christ who walk according to the Spirit there is no condemnation concerning their past sins. God no longer condemns them for any of their former transgressions. It is as though they had never sinned and God has "cast all their iniquities as a stone into the depths of the sea" and "remembers their sin no more." "God put forward Christ as a sacrifice of atonement by his blood, effective through faith. He did this to show his righteousness, because in his divine forbearance he had passed over the sins previously committed." God holds none of their past sins against them; "the very memory of them has perished."

2. Also, believers in Christ have no condemnation within themselves, no sense of guilt, or dread of God's wrath. "Those who believe in the Son of God have the testimony in their hearts." They are conscious of their participation in the sprinkled blood of Christ. "They have not received a spirit of slavery to fall back into fear (doubt and agonizing uncertainty) but they have received a spirit of adoption, crying 'Abba! Father!'" Therefore, since they are "justified by faith, they have the peace of God" ruling in their hearts. This peace flows from a constant sense of God's pardoning mercy and "the appeal of a good conscience."

3. Someone may object, "But sometimes believers in Christ may lose sight of the mercy of God. At times, such darkness might descend to prevent them from seeing him who is invisible. They might no longer feel the Spirit's witness to their share in Christ's atoning blood. They become inwardly condemned, having again 'the sentence of death' in themselves."

In reply to this objection, I answer in the following way. If a person does not know the mercy of God, then that one is not a believer. I say this because faith implies light, the light of God shining upon the soul. To the extent that one loses this light, for the time being, he loses his faith. There is no doubt that genuine believers in Christ may lose the light of faith, and to the degree that faith is lost, they may for a time fall again into condemnation. However, this experience is not the case with those who are now "in Christ Jesus" and who trust in him. For as long as they believe and walk after the Spirit, neither God nor their own hearts condemn them.

4. Secondly, present sins do not condemn those who trust in Christ because they do not continually transgress against God's commandments. They do not "walk according to the flesh, but according to the Spirit." The continuing proof of their love for God is their obedience to his commandments, as St. John bears witness: "Those who have been born of God do not continue in sin, because God's seed abides in them; they cannot continue in sin, because they have been born of God." The believer cannot continue sinning, as long as that seed of God, that

loving, holy faith, remains in him. So long as "he keeps himself" in Christ, "the evil one does not touch him." It is evident, of course, that one is not condemned for the sins that he does not commit.

Those, therefore, who are "led by the Spirit are not subject to the law." They are not under the curse or condemnation of the law, because it only condemns those who break it. The law of God, "You shall not steal," condemns only those who steal. The law, "Remember the Sabbath day, and keep it holy" condemns only those who do not keep it holy. There is no law that condemns the fruit of the Spirit! St. Paul even more strongly reinforced this truth in those important words of his first epistle to Timothy. "We know that the law is good, if one uses it legitimately. This means that the law is laid down not for the innocent, but for the lawless and disobedient, for the godless and sinful, for the unholy and profane."

5. Third, those who trust in Christ are not condemned for inward sin, although it does remain. The corruption of the children of Adam remains even in those who by faith are the children of God. They have in them the seeds of pride, anger, lust, and evil appetites. Yes, they have the seeds of every kind of sin. This reality is too obvious to be denied; daily experience confirms it. This fact is the reason that St. Paul addressed those he had just affirmed as being "in Christ Jesus." To those who were called into the fellowship of God's son, Jesus Christ, St. Paul nevertheless declares, "I could not speak to you as spiritual people, but rather as people of the flesh, as infants in Christ." Thus, we see they were "in Christ," and yet still weak believers. How much sin remained in them! How strong was the "mind that is set on the flesh" that "does not submit to God's law!"

6. Yet, for all their imperfections, God does not condemn them. They feel their sinful desires and depravity; day by day they are ever more aware that their "hearts are devious above all else." Still, God is pleased with them, so long as they do not yield to sin and do not make room for the devil, but maintain a continual war with all sin, pride, anger, and lust. God does not condemn them as long as the flesh does not have dominion over them and so long as they "walk according to the Spirit." "There is therefore now no condemnation for those who are in Christ Jesus." God is well pleased with their sincere, although imperfect, obedience. They "have boldness before God," knowing they belong to him "by the Spirit that he has given them."

7. Fourth, there is no condemnation to those who trust in Christ, although they are conscious of not perfectly fulfilling the law, either in their thoughts, words, or deeds. Believers in Christ know that they do

not love the Lord their God with all their heart, mind, soul, and strength. Furthermore, they feel greater or lesser degrees of pride and self-will creeping into, and mixing with, their best work. Even in their prescribed times of communion with God—when assembled in a large congregation and when pouring out their souls in secret to God who sees the thoughts and intents of their hearts, they are continually ashamed of their wandering thoughts and the deadness and dullness of their affections.

Still, they are under no condemnation, either from God or from their own hearts. Their contemplation of their many defects only gives them a deeper awareness that they constantly need that sprinkled blood of Christ that speaks to God in their behalf. Their "advocate with the Father" "always lives to make intercession for them." Their shortcomings do not drive them away from him in whom they have believed. Instead, their weaknesses drive them all the closer to Christ whose presence they need every moment. The deeper their awareness of this need, the more fervent desire they feel, and the more diligent they become. "As they have received the Lord Jesus, they continue to live their lives in him."

8. Fifth, those who trust in Christ are not condemned for their "sins of weakness," as they are commonly called. Perhaps it is best just to call these shortcomings *infirmities*, so that we do not seem to give any sanction to sin or to lessen it in any degree by linking it with human finitude. However, if we must retain this ambiguous and dangerous term, by sins of infirmity or weakness I mean such involuntary failings as saying something we believe is true, although, in fact, it turns out to be false. A sin of infirmity is harming our neighbor without being aware of it or planning it—perhaps even when we intended to do good.

Certainly, these failings deviate from the holy, acceptable, and perfect will of God. Yet, properly understood, they are not sins. Nor do they bring any guilt to the consciences of "those who are in Christ Jesus." These failings do not separate from God those who trust in Christ. These kinds of shortcomings do not cut off the light of God's countenance, because they are not inconsistent with "walking not according to the flesh, but according to the Spirit."

9. Lastly, for those who trust Christ "there is no condemnation" for anything that is beyond their ability to control. This fact is true whether it is something inward or outward, or whether it is doing something or leaving something undone. For instance, suppose the Lord's supper is to be administered; but you do not partake of it. Why not? You are confined by sickness, so you cannot avoid missing it. Because you had no choice in the matter, you are not counted guilty. If the right desire is

present, "your gift is acceptable according to what you have, not according to what you do not have."

10. Believers may indeed sometimes become depressed because they cannot do what their souls yearn to do. When they are detained from worshipping God at church, they may pray, "As a deer longs for flowing streams, so my soul longs for you, O God. My soul thirsts for God, for the living God. When shall I come and behold the face of God?" While saying in their hearts, "yet not what I want but what you want," they may earnestly desire to "go with the throng, and lead them in procession to the house of God." But if they cannot go to the church, they still feel no condemnation, guilt, or sense of God's displeasure. Rather, they can joyfully surrender those desires to God, saying, "O my soul, hope in God; for I shall again praise you, my help and my God."

11. It is more difficult to decide the nature of those failings that we usually call "sins of surprise." An example would be when one who is usually calm and patient succumbs to a sudden and furious temptation and speaks or behaves in a way that is inconsistent with God's royal law, "You shall love your neighbor as yourself." Perhaps it is not easy to formulate a universal rule that deals with transgressions of this sort. In general, we cannot say whether people are, or are not, judged for sins of surprise. However, it appears that whenever by surprise a believer is overtaken in a transgression, the degree of condemnation hinges on the degree that the will is involved. To the extent that sinful desires, words, or deeds are voluntary, we may believe that God is more or less displeased and that there is more or less guilt upon the soul.

12. If this assumption is true, then there may be some sins of surprise that bring much guilt and condemnation. Sometimes being surprised by temptation or sin is due to some willful and blameworthy neglect on our part. The occasion of the transgression might have been prevented or resisted before the temptation came. Either God or another person may warn us that trials and dangers are near. Yet we may say to ourselves, "A little sleep, a little slumber, a little folding of the hands to rest." If afterward, even unexpectedly, we fall into the snare that we could have avoided we have no excuse. We should have anticipated and avoided the danger. In such a case as this one, the transgression, even if it catches us by surprise, is essentially a willful sin. As such, the transgression necessarily makes the sinner liable to condemnation. The sinner is judged by God and by his or her own conscience.

13. On the other hand, there may be sudden attacks that we did not envision, nor hardly could have anticipated. These may come from the world, or Satan, or (frequently) from our own evil hearts. When these

temptations come to believers who are weak in faith, with scarcely any concurrence of the will, the enticement may overcome them.

For instance, anger may cause people to think evil things about another person. In such a case, out of concern, God would undoubtedly show the transgressors that they had done foolishly. Those who failed would be convicted of swerving from the perfect law and from the mind that was in Christ. Therefore, they grieve with a godly sorrow, and become lovingly contrite before God. Even so, they do not need to come under condemnation. God does not condemn them for their foolishness, but rather shows kindness to them as "a father has compassion for his children." The transgressors' hearts do not condemn them. In the midst of remorse and regret, they can still say, "I will trust, and will not be afraid, for the Lord God is my strength and my might; he has become my salvation."

III. Some practical considerations

1. Now it remains only to draw some practical inferences from the preceding considerations. First, "why are you afraid, you of little faith?" For those who have previously sinned, "there is no condemnation for those who are in Christ Jesus" and "walk not according to the flesh but according to the Spirit." Although your sins once numbered more than the sand, what is that to you, now that you are in Christ Jesus? "Who will bring any charge against God's elect? It is God who justifies. Who is to condemn?" All the sins that you have committed from your youth until the hour when "grace was freely bestowed on you in the Beloved One" are swept away as chaff. Your transgressions are gone, absent, swallowed up, remembered no more. You are now "born of the Spirit."

Will you continue to be distraught or fearful of what you did before you were born again by the Spirit? Away with your fears! God does not call you to fear; God has given you "a spirit of power and of love and of self-discipline." Understand your calling! Rejoice in God your savior, and give thanks to God your Father through Christ!

2. Do you say, "But I have again committed sin, since I had redemption through his blood. And therefore 'I despise myself, and repent in dust and ashes?'" I answer that it is fitting that you *should* feel sorrow, because it is God who brought you to your sense of shame. But do you *now* trust in him? Has God once again enabled you to say, "I know that my Redeemer lives" and "the life I now live in the flesh I live by faith in the Son of God?" If you trust in Christ, faith again cancels everything in

the past and you are not under condemnation. Whenever you truly trust in the name of the Son of God, all your previous sins vanish away as the morning dew. "For freedom Christ has set us free. Stand firm, therefore." Christ has again unchained you from the power of sin, as well as its guilt and punishment.

I say to you, "Do not submit again to a yoke of slavery." Do not submit to the evil, demonic slavery of sin, depraved desires, affections, words, or deeds—the most painful yoke on this side of hell. Do not accept the bondage of slavish, tormenting fear, guilt, and self-condemnation.

3. Second, is it not true that all who abide in Christ "walk not according to the flesh but according to the Spirit?" If that is so, then we must conclude that those who presently continue to sin have no part or lot in Christ. Their own hearts even now condemn them. "Whenever our hearts condemn us," our own consciences bearing witness that we are guilty, undeniably God also condemns us. "He is greater than our hearts, and he knows everything." If we cannot deceive ourselves, we cannot deceive God.

Do not think that you can say, "Once, I was justified and my sins were forgiven." I cannot know that with certitude. I will not dispute whether your sins were once forgiven. Perhaps at this distance of time, it is next to impossible to know with any tolerable degree of confidence if you experienced a true, genuine work of God or whether you only deceived yourself. However, I do know with the greatest degree of certainty that "Everyone who continues to commit sin is a child of the devil."

Therefore, if you are living in sin, you are from your father the devil. That fact cannot be denied, because you are doing the works of your father. Do not deceive yourself with empty hopes! Do not say to yourself, "Peace, peace," because there is no peace. Out of the depths cry to the Lord, and perhaps he will hear your voice. Approach him as one who is dejected, poor, sinful, miserable, blind, and naked! Guard yourself from taking any rest until he again reveals his pardoning love, "heals your faithlessness," and fills you once more with "faith working through love."

4. Third, even if inward sinful tendencies remain, there is no condemnation to them who "walk according to the Spirit," so long as they do not give way to sin. Do not fret about defilement remaining in your heart. Do not languish because you still come short of the glorious image of God, or because pride, self-will, or unbelief cling to all your words and deeds. Do not be afraid to acknowledge all this evil bent in your heart or to know yourself as also you are known. Yes, ask God that you will not think of yourself more highly than you ought to think. Let this be your constant prayer:

Show me, as my soul can bear,
The depth of inbred sin;
All the unbelief declare,
The pride that lurks within.[2]

When God hears your prayer, exposes your heart, and shows you in detail what sort of spirit you have, then beware. Be on your guard that your faith does not fail you and that you do not permit the Lord's protection to be torn away from you. Be humiliated. Be humbled in the dust. See yourself as accounted by God "as less than nothing and emptiness.

At the same time, "Do not let your heart be troubled, and do not let it be afraid." Continue to hold steady and say, "I have an advocate with the Father, Jesus Christ the righteous." Say to yourself, "As the heavens are high above the earth, so God's love is even higher than my sins." God is merciful to you, a sinner—and such a great sinner you are! But, God is love; and Christ has died! The Father himself loves you, and you are his child! Therefore, he will withhold nothing from you that is good.

Would it be a good thing for the entire body of sin, now crucified in you, to be destroyed? It will be done! You will be "cleansed from every defilement of body and of spirit." Is it a good thing that nothing would remain in your heart other than the pure love of God? Be of good cheer! "You shall love the Lord your God with all your heart, and with all your soul, and with all your mind, and with all your strength." "He who has promised is faithful, and he will do it."

Your part is patiently to continue in the work of faith and in the labor of love. Wait before God in happy peace and humble confidence. Wait calmly and peacefully, and with fervent expectation. Wait until the "zeal of the Lord of Hosts does this for you."

5. Fourth, if those in Christ who walk according to the spirit are not condemned for their sins of infirmity, involuntary failings, or anything that they are not able to prevent, then beware, you who trust in his blood. Be watchful that Satan gains no advantage over you. You are still foolish, weak, blind, and ignorant. You are weaker than words can express, more foolish than it can enter your heart to conceive, and you do not yet understand as you should. Do not allow your weakness and foolishness or any of their fruits that you are not yet able to escape to shake your faith. Do not permit your weaknesses to undermine your childlike trust in God or disturb your peace and joy in the Lord.

The standards that some dangerously apply to willful sins are undoubtedly wise and safe if applied only to sins of weakness or infirmities. Have you fallen away, O child of God? If so, do not remain as

149

you are, worrying and lamenting your weaknesses. Instead, pray humbly, "Lord, I shall continue to fall every minute, unless you uphold me with your hand." "Arise, shine; for your light has come!" Leap and walk! Go on your way! "Run with perseverance the race that is set before you."

6. Lastly, call upon the Lord if you fall into transgressions. We have seen that those who trust Christ need not come into condemnation, even if what their souls despise catch them by surprise. (I am assuming that the transgressions are not due to their own carelessness or willful neglect.) If you believe that you have been overtaken in such a way, then weep before the Lord. Your sorrow will be a precious balm. Pour out your heart before him, and tell him about your distress. With all your heart, pray to God who "sympathizes with your weaknesses" that he will himself restore, support, strengthen, and establish you so that you will not fall again. God will no longer condemn you.

Why should you fear? You have no need to have any "fear that has to do with punishment." Love him who loves you, and it is enough. More love produces more strength. When you love him with all your heart, you will be "mature and complete, lacking in nothing." Wait peacefully for that hour when "the God of peace himself will sanctify you entirely; and your spirit and soul and body will be kept sound and blameless at the coming of our Lord Jesus Christ."

Notes

1. Jackson, *Wesley's Works*, 11:396.
2. Charles Wesley, "Waiting for Christ the Prophet," stanza 5, *Poet. Wks.* II, 263.

THE SPIRIT OF BONDAGE
AND OF ADOPTION

This sermon introduces an important Methodist distinctive—the witness of the Spirit. In this discourse Wesley clarifies the differences among three kinds of people—the "natural man," the "awakened sinner," and the "believer." He categorizes these three spiritual conditions as *natural*, *legal*, and *evangelical* states.

Wesley explains that people in a natural state live without either the fear or the love of God. These unawakened people live in a condition of spiritual sleep because their moral senses cannot discern good or evil. Their spiritual eyes and ears cannot see or hear spiritual reality (Eph. 1:18). All the avenues into their souls are blocked, and they live in ignorance of those things which they most need to understand. Those that loiter in a natural, unawakened state live as complete strangers to God; they are ignorant of the true, inward and spiritual meaning of God's law. They feel no concern about their spiritual condition and they have little or no thought about God. Some of these people are educated and successful, and frequently they boast of their own uprightness and wisdom. Although they are content with their lack of concern about eternity, they are actually enslaved by sin and headed for everlasting destruction. All the while, they are entirely unaware of their spiritual condition.

The second group of people consists of awakened sinners. These people are conscious of their accountability to God, and they sense their extreme unworthiness in his sight. Awakened people have become aware of the inner and spiritual meaning of God's laws. They are convicted of their sins and they know that they deserve God's just judgment. Their false sense of peace has now evaporated, and their sins no longer give them pleasure. These awakened people yearn for God's pardon and freedom from the bondage of sin. However, the more they struggle against sin, the tighter it grips them. They feel a burden from which they cannot free themselves. In their despair they come to see that their only hope lies in the God of grace and mercy who alone can forgive them and deliver them from the law of sin and death.

The third category of people consists of believers living under grace. God has opened their spiritual eyes and ears, and they have received Jesus Christ as their Lord. They experience the inner witness of the Holy Spirit who imparts peace and joy to them. Their new life in Christ gives them freedom from both the guilt and power of sin. They no longer fear hell and they have full confidence that they are heirs of the kingdom of heaven. They are free from the spirit of bondage. Now, they live under the Spirit of adoption.

In sum, *unawakened* sinners neither fear nor love God. Awakened sinners fear God, and sense that they are under his rightful condemnation and just judgment. Christian believers experience the joyful light of heaven because they both love and reverence God and his commands. The first category of people sleeps in spiritual death; the second group is awakened but has no peace; the third group possesses God's peace, which fills the heart.

In this sermon, Wesley teaches that we can vacillate between an unawakened and awakened state. He also points out that we sometimes waver back and forth between an awakened state and a trusting state. Thus, our position before God is not static. Rather, it is dynamic and relational. Moreover, our spiritual state is not fixed by divine decrees that predetermine who will be saved or lost. God chooses all people to be saved, and Christ died for everyone. However, not all people respond to God's prevenient grace, which grace enables them to accept his gracious invitation to salvation. Instead, they remain fixed in their self-satisfied independence. Others make a start with God but fail to persevere. As illustrated by seeds planted in shallow or weed-choked soil, a promising start does not always lead to God's intended purpose. True believers, however, respond to God's grace, which enables them to repent. They trust in Christ and bear the fruit of everlasting life.

In the early days of the Methodist awakening, Wesley preached this sermon with mixed results. On one occasion, he wrote in his journal: "A few, I trust, out of two or three thousand were awakened by the explanation of those words: 'Ye have not received the spirit of bondage again to fear; but ye have received the Spirit of adoption, whereby we cry, Abba, Father.'"[1] On another occasion, Wesley recorded in his journal, "I preached . . . in the morning . . . on the spirit of fear and the spirit of adoption. It was now first I felt that God was here also. . . . Many were here melted down, and filled with love toward Him whom 'God hath exalted to be a Prince and a Saviour.'"[2]

Whatever response the sermon elicits, it clearly articulates the distinctions among the natural person, the awakened person, and the evangelical person. The gospel message contained in this sermon is that God offers humankind freedom both from the guilt and the power of sin.

THE SPIRIT OF BONDAGE AND OF ADOPTION

For you did not receive a spirit of slavery to fall back into fear, but you have received a spirit of adoption. When we cry, "Abba! Father it is that very spirit bearing witness with our spirit that we are children of God."   *(Romans 8:15)*

1 In this text, St. Paul speaks to those who have become the children of God by faith. These believers have all "partaken of God's Spirit." The apostle declared, "You did not receive a spirit of slavery to fall back into fear." St. Paul also said, "Because you are his children God has sent the Spirit of his Son into your hearts, you have received a spirit of adoption that enables you to cry, 'Abba! Father.'"

2. By contrast, the spirit of slavery, which is falling back into fear, is far distant from this loving Spirit of adoption. Those who are influenced only by slavish fear cannot be called "children of God." However, some of them may be called his servants, and they are "not far from the kingdom of God."

3. It is to be feared, however, that the majority of people, indeed, most of those who compose what is called "the Christian world," have not attained even this level of trust. They are still far from God's kingdom; "God is not in any of their thoughts." We may find a few that love God and a few more that fear him. However, the greater number have

154

neither the "fear of God before their eyes" nor the love of God in their hearts.

4. Perhaps, by the mercy of God, most of you now partake of a better spirit. You may remember when you were as those who do not love or serve God. You may recall when you were under the same condemnation as they are. At first, however, you did not know your condition. Until you received the spirit of the fear of God, daily you were wallowing in your sins and spiritual death. However, you received the fear of God, which is his gift to you. Afterward, your fear vanished away, and the Spirit of love filled your hearts.

5. Scripture uses the term "natural man" to describe those without either a fear of God or a love for God. Those who are under the spirit of slavery and fear are sometimes said to be "under the law." (That expression most frequently signifies one who is under the Jewish dispensation, or one who thinks that he or she is obligated to observe all the rites and ceremonies of the Jewish law.) However, one who has exchanged the spirit of fear for the Spirit of love, is correctly said to be "under grace."

Because it is very important for us to know of what spirit we are, I will attempt to point out clearly, (1) The state of a "natural man." (2) The state of one who is "under the law." (3) The state of one who is "under grace." (4) The inadequacy of merely being sincere.

I. The state of a natural man

1. First, I will explain the state of a natural man. Scripture designates the natural man as being in a state of sleep. The call of God to this person is "Sleeper, awake!" In this state, people's souls are in a deep slumber, and their spiritual senses are not awake. Spiritually, the sleepers' senses cannot discern good or evil. The eyes of their minds are closed, tightly locked shut, and unable to perceive spiritual reality. Clouds and darkness continually cover their eyes, and they lie in the darkest valley.

Therefore, the sleepers have no inlets by which the knowledge of spiritual things can enter. All the avenues into their souls are obstructed, and they exist in grievous and stupid ignorance of whatever they need most to understand. They are utterly unaware of God, knowing none of the things about him that they should know. These "natural" people are complete strangers to the true, inward, spiritual meaning of God's law. They have no conception of holiness, without which no one will see the Lord; they lack the happiness known only to those whose "life is hidden with Christ in God."

2. Because we are sound asleep in our natural state, in some sense we are at rest. Such people feel secure in their blindness. They say, "There is nothing to be concerned about! No harm will come to me." The darkness that covers them on every side lulls them into a kind of peace, in so far as peace can exist with the works of the devil and with a worldly and devilish mind. Because they do not see that they stand on the edge of the pit, they do not fear it. They are not able to tremble at the danger they do not know. They do not understand enough to fear.

Why is it that they have no fear of God? It is because they are completely ignorant of him. Perhaps they say in their hearts, "There is no God." Or they might say, "He that sits on the circle of the heavens does not lower himself to observe the things done on the earth." To all intents and purposes, those interested primarily in sensual pleasures pacify themselves by saying, "God is merciful."

When people hold this inaccurate concept of mercy, they necessarily confuse and distort the concepts of holiness, sin, justice, wisdom, and truth. Because they lack understanding, they have no dread of the vengeance pronounced against those who "do not know God and do not obey the gospel of our Lord Jesus." They assume that they need only to live an outwardly moral life, and they do not understand that true religion extends to every disposition, desire, thought, and impulse of the heart.

It may be that they assume they have no obligation to the moral law because Christ came to "destroy the law and the prophets." They imagine that Christ came to save his people *in* their sins, not *from* them. They think that Christ brings us to heaven without holiness. All the while, Christ has said, "Not one stroke of a letter will pass from the law until all is accomplished." He also said, "Not everyone who says to me, 'Lord, Lord,' will enter the kingdom of heaven, but only the one who does the will of my Father in heaven."

3. Those who are spiritually asleep feel secure because they are completely ignorant of their true condition. They may talk of "repenting by and by," but they certainly do not know exactly when. They think that they will repent sometime before they die, and they take it for granted that it lies completely in their own power to repent. They ask themselves, "What will stop me from repenting, if I decide to repent?" They think that once they resolve to repent, they are able to do so when they are ready!

4. This ignorance is never so strongly glaring as in those who are considered people of learning. In their natural state, these people can talk expansively about their powers of logic, the autonomy of their wills, and

the absolute necessity of free choice as an essential component of being a moral agent. They read, debate, and "prove" their conclusions that all people can do as they choose to do. They think that we can incline our own hearts to evil or good as it seems best in our own eyes. In this way, the god of this world spreads a double veil of blindness over the sleepers' spiritual eyes. In every possible way the devil prevents "the light of the gospel of the glory of Christ" from shining upon their hearts.

5. From the natural persons' ignorance of themselves and God, sometimes there may arise a sort of satisfaction that leads them to congratulate themselves for their own wisdom and goodness. Unconverted people possess what the world calls "joy." They may delight in various kinds of pleasure—gratifying the desires of their flesh, the desires of their eyes, and their pride in riches. Especially if they have great possessions and enjoy an abundant fortune, they may "dress in purple and fine linen and feast sumptuously every day." And so long as they prosper, others will doubtless speak well of them. People will say, "He is a happy man; she is a happy woman." Undeniably, to them the things that constitute the sum of worldly happiness are to dress well, visit with others, talk, eat, and play.

6. It is not surprising that people in such circumstances as these, soothed with the narcotics of flattery and sin, should suppose, along with their other daydreams, that they walk in great freedom. How easily people can persuade themselves that they are free from all common faults, such as intolerance, poor judgment, and extremes. In one's natural state, one may say, "I am unfettered by all the fanaticism of weak and narrow souls and from superstition, the affliction of fools and cowards. I am free from being sanctimonious and from the bigotry that is always attached to those who do not possess an open and tolerant way of thinking." It is perfectly clear that such people *do* have a species of freedom. They are free from "the wisdom from above," from holiness, from the religion of the heart, from "the mind that was in Christ Jesus."

7. All the while, they are not truly free at all. They are slaves of sin. Day by day, they commit greater or lesser sins. They are not troubled by them, however. Some people may say, "Nothing restricts us." They feel no condemnation. They excuse themselves by saying, "We are frail beings; we are all weak; everyone has his infirmity"—even though they should acknowledge that this truth is a part of the God-given Christian Revelation. They may even quote the scriptures out of context, by declaring, "Does not Solomon say, 'The righteous fall seven times a day!'" They go on to assert, "Of course, there are hypocrites or fanatics who pretend to be better than their neighbors."

Whenever a serious thought settles upon them, they stifle it as soon as possible. They rationalize, "Why should I fear, since God is merciful, and 'while we still were sinners Christ died for us.'" So it is, they remain willing slaves of sin, content with the bondage of depravity. Inwardly and outwardly, they remain unrighteous. These unconverted people are content with their spiritual state. They not only fail to conquer sin, but they do not even try to overcome it—especially the sins that cling so closely to them.

8. I have described the state of every natural man and woman, whether they are vulgar and scandalous transgressors or more reputable and decent sinners who have the form of godliness, but not its power. Now, how can such persons be convicted of their sin? How can they be brought to repentance? How can they be brought under the law and receive the spirit of bondage unto fear? This is the next point that I will consider.

II. The state of one who is under the law

1. Through some awesome providential event or by God's word applied to the heart by the power of the Holy Spirit, God touches those who sleep in spiritual darkness and in the shadow of death. The Holy Spirit severely disturbs them out of their sleep and awakens them to an awareness of their danger. In a moment or by degrees, the eyes of their hearts are opened. The veil is partially removed and they discern their true state. Terrifying light breaks in upon their souls. This light seems to shine from the bottomless pit, from the deepest abyss, from a fiery lake that burns with sulfur. At last, they see that the loving and merciful God is "a consuming fire."

They come to understand that God is just and terrifying, repaying all people according to their works. God judges the ungodly for every careless word—yes, even for the thoughts of the heart. Awakened sinners clearly perceive that the eyes of the great and holy God are "too pure to behold evil." They come to understand that God avenges those that rebel and "repays in their own person those who reject him." It becomes clear to awakened sinners that "it is a fearful thing to fall into the hands of the living God."

2. Sleepers who are awakened in this way begin to sense that the inner and spiritual meaning of the law of God is scowling upon them. They perceive that God's commandments are extremely far-reaching and that nothing is hidden from the light. They become convinced that every aspect of the law pertains to them.

The law is not merely concerned with outward sin or obedience. It is also concerned with what transpires in the secret corners of the soul, where only God's eye can see. Now, awakened sinners hear the commandment, "You shall not kill." God speaks to them as thunder: "All who hate a brother or sister are murderers. And if you say, 'You fool,' You will be liable to the hell of fire." If the law says, "You shall not commit adultery," the voice of the Lord speaks in their ears, "Everyone who looks at a woman with lust has already committed adultery with her in his heart." And so, at every point, awakened sinners feel the word of God as "living and active, sharper than any two-edged sword, piercing until it divides soul from spirit, and joints from marrow."

They feel this conviction all the more because they are aware within themselves that they have neglected "so great a salvation." They know that they have "spurned the Son of God," who would have saved them from their sins. They understand that they have "profaned the blood of the covenant;" they have regarded it as an unholy, common thing that has no value for them.

3. Once they understand that everything is "naked and laid bare to the eyes of the one to whom we must render an account," they see themselves uncovered, stripped of all the fig leaves that they have stitched together. Awakened sinners clearly perceive all their paltry pretexts for religion and virtue; they recognize their lame excuses for sinning against God. They now regard themselves as being like the ancient sacrifices ("drawn and quartered," as it were, from the neck downward so that everything within them is clearly exposed). Their hearts become fully exposed, and they see that they are utterly sinful, "devious above all else, desperately wicked."

More than it is possible for tongue to express, they see that their hearts are thoroughly corrupted and abhorrent. They understand that nothing good dwells within them, only unrighteousness and ungodliness. They realize that every inclination of their hearts and every disposition and thought are continuously evil.

4. With a passion of soul which they cannot describe they understand and feel within themselves that they deserve condemnation. Even if their lives are without blame (which they are not and cannot be, because "a bad tree cannot bear good fruit"), they realize that they deserve to go into "the unquenchable fire." Awakened sinners perceive that "the wages of sin is death," the just recompense of their own sins. This eternal judgment is the second death—an everlasting death that is the destruction of body and soul in hell.

5. This conviction of sin ends their pleasant dreams, delusive rest, false peace, and empty security. Now, their joy vanishes like a fog in the sunlight. The pleasures they once loved no longer delight them. Their former enjoyments become stale to their tastes; they detest their sickening sweetness, and they become burdensome. All hints of happiness disappear and fall into oblivion. Everything is taken away from them, and they wander about seeking rest, but finding none.

6. Now that the haze of those narcotics has dissipated, they feel the distress of a wounded spirit. They find that the sin which is rampant within their souls has become perfect misery—whether their sin is pride, anger, evil lusts, self-will, malice, envy, revenge, or any other failing. Awakened sinners feel heart sorrow for the blessings they have missed, and they sense the condemnation that rests upon them.

They feel remorse for having wasted their lives and for having spurned God's mercy. Due to a quickened awareness of God's anger, they now fear the consequences of his wrath and impending judgment. Awakened sinners know that they justly deserve God's sentence of condemnation that hangs over their heads. They are now afraid of death, which is for them the gateway to hell and eternal destruction. They tremble for fear of the devil who prods them toward the wrath and righteous vengeance of God. They are frightened of those who, if they were able to kill the body, would hurl both body and soul into hell. Fear sometimes reaches such intensity that the destitute, sinful, guilty sinner is terrified of everything—even of nothing at all, such as the dark, or a leaf quaking in the wind. Indeed, fear may even border upon insanity, making one "drunk, but not with wine."

This fear disturbs their memory, understanding, and all their natural endowments. Sometimes fear may lead to the very brink of despair, causing them to tremble at the mention of death. This agony may be so intense as to cause them to want to die in order to escape—to "choose strangling rather than life." Because of a troubled heart, the fearful may cry out, as the ancient psalmist, "I am utterly spent and crushed; I groan because of the tumult of my heart."

7. Awakened sinners sincerely long to break free from sin, and they begin to struggle against it. However, even though they strive with all their might against sin, they cannot conquer it. Their sin is stronger than they are. They would gladly break free from it, but they are so constrained in sin's prison that they cannot escape. They resolve not to sin, yet they continue to succumb to it. They see sin's trap, yet they run headlong into it.

Their once-flaunted reason now only intensifies guilt and increases misery. So much for their vaunted free will! In truth, the will is free only to do evil and "drink iniquity like water." Awakened sinners meander farther and farther from the living God, and do even more "outrage to the Spirit of grace."

8. The more they struggle, hope, and labor to get free, the more they feel the dreary chains of sin. Satan binds these awakened sinners and "holds them captive to do his will." They are Satan's servants, even though they grieve ever so much over their sins. They fight the enemy, but they cannot prevail. Due to their sin, they remain in bondage and fear. Ordinarily, they fall victim to some outward sin to which they are particularly inclined by nature, custom, or outward circumstances. Always, however, some inward sin, evil disposition, or unholy affection defeats them. The more they fight against their sin, the more it prevails.

Awakened sinners may bite at their chains, but they cannot break them. So, they labor endlessly—repenting and sinning, and repenting and sinning over and over. Finally, the inadequate, sinful strugglers come to their wit's end, and they can barely cry, "Wretched one that I am! Who will rescue me from this body of death?"

9. The exertions of those who are "under the law" and bound by "the spirit of fear and bondage" are superbly described by Paul in the book of Romans. Assuming the voice of an awakened sinner, Paul said, "I was once alive apart from the law. I thought that I had much life, wisdom, strength, and virtue. However, when the commandment came, sin revived and I died. When the commandment, in its spiritual meaning, came to my heart, by God's power, my inbred sin was stirred up, vexed, and inflamed. Then, all my virtue died away. The very commandment that promised life proved to be death to me. For sin, seizing an opportunity in the commandment, deceived me and through it killed me. It came upon me by surprise, killed all my hopes, and plainly revealed that in the midst of life that I was actually in death. So the law is holy, and the commandment is holy and just and good. I no longer lay the blame on the law, but on the corruption of my own heart. I acknowledge that the law is spiritual; but I am of the flesh, sold into slavery under sin. I now see both the spiritual nature of the law and my own carnal, devilish heart sold under sin, completely enslaved (like slaves bought with money who were absolutely at their master's disposal). I do not do what I want, but I do the very thing I hate. Such is the bondage under which I groan; such is the tyranny of my hard master. I can will what is right, but I cannot do it. For I do not do the good I want, but the evil I do not want is what I do. I find it to be a law that when I want to do what is good, evil lies close at hand. For I delight in (consent to) the law of God in my inmost self."[3]

161

In the words that follow, Paul continues speaking the thoughts of his mind: "I see in my members another law [another constraining power] at war with the law of my mind [inward man] making me captive to the law [power] of sin that dwells in my members. This power is dragging me, as it were, by my conqueror's chariot wheels into the very thing that my soul abhors. Wretched man that I am! Who will rescue me from this body of death? Who will deliver me from this helpless, dying life and from this bondage of sin and misery? Until this is done for me, inwardly I am a slave to the law of God. My mind and conscience are on God's side, but with my body I am a slave to the law of sin. I am carried away by a force that I cannot resist."

10. How accurate is this portrait of those who live "under the law!" They feel a burden that they cannot shake off. They yearn for liberty, power, and love—yet they still remain in fear, weakness, and bondage! They continue to live this way until God answers these forlorn folk who cry out, "Who shall deliver me from the body of this death?" Our only salvation comes through "the grace of God which is given to us by Jesus Christ."

III. The state of one who is under grace

1. Our miserable bondage ends when Christ delivers us and we are no longer "under law but under grace." Now, thirdly, we will consider the state of those who have found mercy and favor in the sight of God the Father and who have received the grace and power of the Holy Spirit, who reigns in their hearts. In the language of Paul, they have received the spirit of adoption, and they cry, "Abba! Father!"

2. These people "cried to the Lord in their trouble, and he delivered them from their distress." Their eyes are opened in quite a different way than before, so that now they see a loving, gracious God. While these awakened sinners are calling, "Show me your glory, I pray," they hear a voice in their inmost souls. The voice says, "I will make all my goodness pass before you, and will proclaim before you the name, 'The LORD,' and I will be gracious to whom I will be gracious, and will show mercy on whom I will show mercy." And it is not long before the LORD descends in the cloud and proclaims the name, "the LORD."

Then the seekers see (though not with physical eyes) that "the LORD is a God merciful and gracious, slow to anger, and abounding in steadfast love and faithfulness, keeping steadfast love for the thousandth generation, forgiving iniquity and transgression and sin."

3. Heavenly healing light now breaks in upon the souls of repentant sinners. They "look on the one whom they had pierced." And the "God who said, 'Let light shine out of darkness,' shines in their hearts." Those who are born anew now see "the light of the knowledge of the glory of God in the face of Jesus Christ." They have a divine "conviction of things not seen" by natural senses. They even see "the depths of God," most especially the grace of God and his pardoning love to all who believe in Jesus.

Overawed by this awareness, the entire soul cries out, "My Lord and my God." Those who have come into a state of grace now see all their iniquities laid on him who "bore our sins in his body on the cross." They look to the Lamb of God who takes away their sin. How clearly they see that God in Christ was reconciling the world to himself, making him to be sin who knew no sin, so that in him we might become the righteousness of God. They understand that they are now reconciled to God by the blood of the covenant!

4. This transaction brings an end to both the guilt and the power of sin. The redeemed sinner can now say, "I have been crucified with Christ; and it is no longer I who live, but it is Christ who lives in me. And the life I now live in the flesh (this mortal body) I live by faith in the Son of God, who loved me and gave himself for me." Now, one's remorse, heart sorrow, and the anguish of a broken spirit all come to an end. "God turns mourning into joy." "God wounds, but he binds up." God takes away bondage and fear, because the new believers' hearts are steadfast, trusting in the Lord.

They no longer fear the wrath of God, because they know that it is now turned away from them. They regard God no more as an angry judge, but as a loving parent. They no longer fear the devil, knowing that he has "no power unless it is given from above." They do not fear hell, because they know that they are now heirs of the kingdom of heaven. Therefore, they have no fear of death, the state in which they lived for so many years as "subject to bondage." Rather, they know that "if the earthly tent we live in is destroyed, we have a building from God, a house not made with hands, eternal in the heavens. Here (on earth) indeed we groan, and long to put on our heavenly dwelling." They pray to shake off this house of earth, so that "what is mortal may be swallowed up by life." They understand that God "has prepared us for this very thing" and has "given us the Spirit as a guarantee."

5. Furthermore, "where the Spirit of the Lord is, there is freedom"—freedom from guilt, fear, and sin, that heaviest of all yokes and lowest form of bondage. Believers' labors are no longer in vain. Their bondage

is broken, and they have "escaped the snare of the fowlers." They not only strive, but also prevail; they not only fight, but also conquer.

Henceforth, they "no longer serve sin." Now, they are "dead to sin and alive to God." "Sin therefore no longer reigns in their mortal bodies, to make them obey their passions." "They do not yield their members to sin as instruments of wickedness, but yield themselves as instruments of righteousness to God." "Now, being made free from sin, they have become servants of righteousness."

6. Thus, new believers have peace with God through our Lord Jesus Christ, and they rejoice in hope of sharing the glory of God. They now have power over all sin, evil desires, dispositions, words, and works. They have become living witnesses of "the glorious liberty of the children of God." All these new believers have acquired a faith of equal standing to that of the apostles, because they have received a faith as precious as theirs. All believers declare with one voice, "We have received a spirit of adoption, and we cry, 'Abba! Father!'"

7. It is this spirit that continually "is at work in us, both to will and to work for God's good pleasure." It is the Holy Spirit given to us that pours God's love into our hearts. God's Spirit gives love for all humankind, purifying our hearts from the love of the world, and from the desire of the flesh, the desire of the eyes, and the pride in riches. The Spirit delivers us from anger, pride, and all evil and immoderate affections. As a consequence, we are delivered from evil words and works and from all unholy conduct. We do no wrong to any other person and continue to be zealous for all good deeds.

8. To sum up what I have said, in our natural state we neither fear nor love God. Those who are under the law fear God, and in a sense they love him. People in the first category have no light about the things of God and they walk in complete darkness. People in the second category see the painful light of hell. People in the third category see the joyous light of heaven.

The one who sleeps in death has a *false* peace. The one who is awakened has *no* peace. The one who trusts Christ has *genuine* peace. It is God's peace filling and ruling the heart. Those who do not know God (whether or not they are baptized) have an imaginary freedom that is in fact only slavery. The Jew, or the one who lives under the Jewish dispensation, is in heavy, distressing bondage. The Christian, however, enjoys "the freedom of the glory of the children of God."

Unawakened children of the devil sin willingly. Those who are awakened sin unwillingly. The children of God "do not continue in sin." Christ protects them, and the evil one does not touch them. To conclude, those in the natural state neither conquer sin nor struggle against it. Those who are under the law struggle against sin, but cannot conquer it. Those under grace fight against sin and do conquer it. Indeed, those who trust in Christ are "more than conquerors through him who loved us."

IV. The inadequacy of just being sincere

1. From this plain account of the three-fold state of humankind—the natural man, the legal man, and the evangelical man—it appears that it is not sufficient to divide humanity into only two classes—sincere and insincere. One may be sincere in any of these states. We might be "sincere" not only when we have received the "Spirit of adoption," but also while we have the "spirit of slavery into fear." Indeed, we can be sincere while having neither the fear of, or love for, God. Doubtless, there may be sincere heathens, as well as sincere Jews, or sincere Christians. Being sincere, then, by no means proves that one is in a state of being accepted by God.

Therefore, "examine yourselves," not only whether you are sincere, but also "whether you are living in the faith." Examine yourselves closely—it is a matter of great importance to you. What is the ruling principle in your soul? Is it the love and fear of God? Or, is it neither one or the other? Instead, is it the love of the world? Is it the love of pleasure, or gain? Is it the love of ease or reputation? If this is the case, you have not advanced even as far as a Jew. You are still only a heathen.

Do you have heaven in your heart? Do you have the Spirit of adoption, ever crying, "Abba! Father?" Or, do you cry unto God, as "out of the belly of the grave," overwhelmed with sorrow and fear? Or, are you a stranger to this entire matter and cannot comprehend what I mean? Unawakened sinner, pull off your mask! You have not yet clothed yourself with Christ! Stand up without any disguises! Look up to heaven and acknowledge before him who lives forever and ever that you have no place among either the children or servants of God!

Whoever you are, do you, or do you not commit sin? If you commit sin, do you sin willingly or unwillingly? In either case, God has told you to whom you belong: "Everyone who commits sin is a child of the devil." If you sin willingly, you are the devil's faithful servant, and he will not fail to reward your labor. If you sin unwillingly, you are still the devil's servant. May God deliver you out of his hands!

Are you constantly fighting against all sin and are you daily more than a conqueror? If so, I acknowledge you as a child of God. O, stand fast in your glorious liberty! Are you struggling against sin, but not conquering it, striving for the mastery over sin, but not able to attain it? If so, you are not yet a believer in Christ. Follow after him, however, and you will come to know him. Are you not at all struggling against sin, living an easy, slothful, fashionable life? How have you dared to name the name of Christ, only to make it a "mockery among the nations?" Sleeper, awake. Call upon your God before the abyss swallows you up!

2. Perhaps one reason so many people think of themselves more highly than they ought to think and fail to discern their true state is because these different spiritual conditions are often mingled together in the same person. Experience reveals that the legal state (state of fear) is frequently mixed with the natural state (state of false security). Few people are so deeply asleep in sin that they are not in some degree awakened to their condition.

Because the Spirit of God does not "depend on people," sometimes he makes himself heard directly. The Holy Spirit leads people to a sense of fear, so that, for at least a season, the heathen "know that they are only mortal." They feel the burden of sin and earnestly desire to flee from the wrath to come. But their sense of sin does not last very long within them. The unconverted seldom allow the arrows of conviction to go deep into their souls. Rather, they quickly suppress the grace of God and return to their wallowing in the mud.

In a similar way, the evangelical state (or state of love) is frequently mixed with the legal state (state of striving under the law). Few of those who have the spirit of slavery and fear permanently remain without hope. The wise and gracious God rarely permits this bondage to continue, because "he remembers that we are dust," and he does not will that "we would grow faint before him, even the souls that he has made."

Therefore, when God sees a good intention within us, he gives a dawning of light to those that sit in darkness. He causes a part of his goodness to pass before the unconverted and demonstrates that he is a "God who hears prayer." The unconverted see the promise that comes through faith in Christ Jesus, even if it is yet far off; and they are encouraged to "run with perseverance the race that is set before them."

3. Another reason many people deceive themselves is that they do not consider how far one may go and still be in a natural state, or at best a legal state. One may have a compassionate and benevolent disposition, be pleasant, courteous, generous, and friendly, and have some degree of humility, patience, self-control, and many other moral virtues. People may feel many desires to shake off all immorality to attain greater levels of virtue. They may abstain from endless evil, perhaps from everything

that is flagrantly contrary to justice, mercy, or truth. They may do much good, feed the hungry, clothe the naked, and relieve the widow and orphan. They may attend public worship, pray in private, and read many devotional books. Yet, despite these good deeds, they may be only in a natural state and neither understand themselves or God. Because they have neither repented nor believed the gospel, they may be strangers both to the spirit of fear and to the spirit of love.

In addition to their good works, suppose they have a deep conviction of sin. Suppose they are fearful of the wrath of God, fervently desire to put away every sin, and want to fulfill all righteousness. Suppose they often rejoice in hope, and assume that there are traces of love that often touch their souls. Still, these things do not prove that they are under God's grace and have a genuine, living, Christian faith. Only when the Spirit of adoption abides in the heart can one continually cry, "Abba! Father!"

4. You who are called by the name of Christ, beware that you do not come short of the goal of your heavenly call. Beware that you do not rest in a natural state along with all too many who are considered to be "good Christians." Do not rest in a legal state of living under the law, in which those who are highly esteemed are generally content to live and die.

If you continue until you attain the goal, God will prepare better things for you. You are not called to fear and shudder like demons. You are called to rejoice and love like the angels of God. "You shall love the Lord your God with all your heart, and with all your soul, and with all your mind, and with all your strength." You shall "rejoice always." You shall "pray without ceasing" and "give thanks in all circumstances." You will do the will of God on earth as it is done in heaven. O, discern "what is the will of God—what is good and acceptable and perfect." Just now, present your bodies "as living sacrifices, holy and acceptable to God." "Hold fast to what you have attained" by "straining forward to what lies ahead." "Now, the God of peace make you complete in everything good so that you will do his will, working among you that which is pleasing in his sight, through Jesus Christ, to whom be glory for ever and ever! Amen."

Notes

1. Ward and Heitzenrater, *Wesley's Journal and Diaries*, October 7, 1739, 19:102.
2. Ibid., June 14, 1742, 19:278.
3. Wesley's discussion here is based on Romans 7:9-25.

THE WITNESS OF THE SPIRIT, DISCOURSE 1

John Wesley's early spiritual journey was similar to the journeys of the Apostle Paul, Augustine, Francis of Assisi, and Martin Luther. Like so many Christians, Wesley went through a prolonged personal struggle to come to the assurance of salvation. Prior to his evangelical conversion, Wesley's life had been a paradigm of discipline, good works, and self-denial. Still, he lacked the assurance of salvation. Writing about his spiritual exertions, he said,

> In 1730 I began visiting the prisons; assisting the poor and sick in town; and doing what other good I could, by my presence, or my little fortune, to the bodies and souls of all men. To this end I abridged myself of all superfluities, and many that are called necessaries of life. . . . I diligently strove against all sin. I omitted no sort of self-denial which I thought lawful: I carefully used, both in public and in private, all the means of grace at all opportunities. I omitted no occasion of doing good: I for that reason suffered evil. . . . Yet when, after continuing some years in this course, I apprehended myself to be near death, I could not find that all this gave me any comfort, or any assurance of acceptance with God.[1]

It was not until his evangelical experience on May 24, 1738 that he was able to write, "I felt I did trust in Christ, Christ alone for salvation: And an assurance was given me, that he had taken away my sins, even mine, and saved me from the law of sin and death."[2] Thereafter, Wesley taught, wrote, and preached about Christian assurance. In the course of events, this doctrine became one of Methodism's most distinguishing marks.

The doctrine of assurance, of course, is not unique to Methodism. It is found in the writings of St. Paul and other teachers throughout the history of the church. Wesley knew his church's teaching about Christian assurance, especially as it was articulated in the homilies of the Church of England.[3] By the eighteenth century, however, this doctrine was seldom taught. For one thing, formalism's stress on ritual had all but ignored the possibility of a personal inner witness of being in right relationship with God. Form had overshadowed faith. Also, the influence of Deism had intruded itself into the church. This brand of rationalism, which posited a distant and impersonal God, did not allow for personal religious experience. For the Deists, reason and religious reserve were paramount. And, finally, the extravagant claims of some mystics had so overemphasized inner "revelations" that they contributed to bringing the idea of assurance into disfavor. For many, the mystics' intense subjectivity and zealous claims to special disclosures from God discredited the doctrine of the witness of the Holy Spirit. In sum, the formalists put too much stock in outer religion, the rationalists disparaged personal religious experience, and the mystics focused almost entirely on inward and subjective religion. Balance suffered.

By the mid-1740s, Wesley was convinced that it was important to clarify the doctrines of assurance and the witness of the Spirit. At the time, a debated issue was whether one's confidence in a right relationship with God comes from Christians or from the Holy Spirit. Some in Wesley's day were willing to accept Christian assurance as a logical conclusion that we can draw from the presence of the fruit of the Spirit in our lives. However, they did not believe that the witness of the Spirit was a direct, immediate, or instantaneous communication of the Spirit of God. In this sermon, Wesley seeks to clarify the doctrine of the witness of the Spirit and restore it within the church, while allowing a place for both the human spirit and the Holy Spirit.

In addition to the Bible's and the church's teaching on the witness of the Spirit, Wesley found confirmation for this doctrine in his own experience and in the experiences of others. In a letter to Mr. John Smith, Wesley wrote, "I am acquainted with more than twelve or thirteen hundred persons, whom I believe to be truly pious, and not on slight grounds, and who have severally testified to me with their own mouths that they do know the day when the love of God was first shed abroad in their hearts, and when his Spirit first witnessed with their spirits, that they were the children of God. Now, if you are determined to think all these liars or fools, this is no evidence to you; but to me it is strong evidence, who have for some years known the men and their communication."[4]

Wesley did not teach that the witness of the Spirit was necessary for salvation. He did see this experience, however, as a privilege available to all that are born of God. In 1768 he wrote,

> I believe a consciousness of being in the favour of God . . . is the common privilege of Christians, fearing God and working righteousness. Yet I do not affirm there are no exceptions to this general rule. Possibly some may be in the favour of God, and yet go mourning all the day long. But I believe this is usually owing either to disorder of body, or ignorance of the Gospel promises.[5]

Wesley believed that many people were ignorant of this special blessing and that the assurance of salvation was important for Christian joy and spiritual growth. Indeed, saving faith in itself has the seeds of confidence which bring the assurance of salvation.

THE WITNESS OF THE SPIRIT,
DISCOURSE 1

It is that very Spirit bearing witness with our spirit that we are children of God. (Romans 8:16)

1 How great are the numbers of arrogant people who do not understand what they say or advocate. Many of them have twisted this scripture text to the enormous loss of their souls, or even to their soul's destruction! How many have mistaken the impressions of their own imagination for the witness of the Holy Spirit. In doing so, they have carelessly presumed that they were children of God, while they were actually doing the works of the devil! Truly and accurately, these teachers are fanatics, in the worst sense of the word.

It is only with great difficulty that they can be convinced of their fanaticism, especially if they have imbibed deeply of the demonic spirit of error. They regard all efforts of others to bring them to the knowledge of themselves to be "fighting against God." They call their own fanaticism and lack of restraint "contending earnestly for the faith." The extent of their zeal takes them far beyond all the usual methods of defending a conviction. To these people we may well apply the saying, "With mortals it is impossible to be saved."

2. Who then can be surprised if many reasonable people see the appalling effects of this delusion and determine to keep as far from it as

171

they can? This state of affairs could cause one to lean toward an opposite extreme. Because these zealots have erred so seriously, some may refuse to believe *anyone* who claims to have the witness of the Spirit. Some people are almost ready to regard everyone to be a fanatic who uses the expressions that others have so exceedingly abused. They may question whether the witness of the Holy Spirit is the privilege of any ordinary Christian. They may think that the Spirit's witness is an extraordinary gift that was limited to the apostolic age.

3. However, is it necessary to go to one extreme in order to avoid another? On the one hand, can we not steer a middle course by keeping a safe distance from error and fanaticism? And on the other hand, can we not steer a middle course by refusing to give up this important privilege of God's children? Surely we can.

In the presence and fear of God, in order to gain a proper perspective, let us consider the following points: (1) What is the witness of the Spirit and how does the Holy Spirit bear witness with our spirits that we are the children of God? (2) How does the witness of the Spirit differ from the presumption of a natural mind and from demonic delusion?

I. The witness of the Holy Spirit and how he bears witness with our spirits that we are the children of God

1. Let us consider the witness, or testimony, of our human spirits. First, I wish to speak to all those who want to equate the witness of the Holy Spirit with the rational work of the human mind. Observe that in this text the Apostle Paul is so very far from speaking only about the testimony of *our* spirits that we may question whether he is even speaking of this testimony at all. Is St. Paul not speaking of the witness of *God's* Spirit? It appears that the original text may be justly understood in this way. In the preceding verse, the apostle has just said, "You have received a spirit of adoption, and we cry, 'Abba! Father!'" He immediately adds, "The same Spirit bears witness with our spirit, that we are the children of God." (The preposition denotes that God's Spirit witnesses to us at the same time that he enables us to cry "Abba! Father!") But I do not wish to contend for this point. Numerous other texts and the experiences of all genuine Christians adequately document that the witness of God's Spirit and the witness of the human spirit *both* testify that one is a child of God.

2. With regard to the witness of the human spirit that one is a child of God, we find a supporting foundation in those many scripture texts that

describe the characteristics of the children of God. They are so clear that those who seek for them will find them. Many ancient and modern writers have collated them and made them very evident to us. If anyone needs additional light on the matter, he or she may receive it by paying attention to God's word, by meditating on it privately, and by speaking with those who understand God's ways

Also, we may use the intellect that God has given us, which Christianity was designed not to extinguish, but to perfect. St. Paul wrote, "Brothers and sisters, do not be children in your thinking, rather, be infants in evil, but in thinking be adults." Anyone can apply the scriptural marks of a genuine Christian to discern if he or she is a child of God. To begin with, we may know that we are children of God by the following scripture: "For all who are led by the Spirit of God" into holy affections and actions "are children of God" (for which, one has the infallible assurance of the Bible). Secondly, if one can say, "I am led by the Holy Spirit," he or she can easily conclude as a consequence, "I am a child of God."

3. The Apostle John agrees with St. Paul that we can know with certainty that we belong to God. In 1 John, that apostle wrote parallel statements that agreed with St. Paul. For instance, consider these verses:

Now by this we may be sure that we know him, if we obey his commandments.

Whoever obeys his word, truly in this person the love of God has reached perfection. By this we may be sure that we are in him.

If you know that he is righteous, you may be sure that everyone who does right has been born of him.

We know that we have passed from death to life because we love one another.

And by this we will know that we are from the truth and will reassure our hearts before him, namely, because we love one another not in word or speech, but in truth and action.

By this we know that we abide in him and he in us, because he has given us of his Spirit.

The Spirit that he has given us is proof that we are one with him.

4. From the beginning of the world until today, it is highly probable there never have been any Christians that were farther advanced in the grace of God and the knowledge of our Lord Jesus Christ than the Apostle John and those mature spiritual "fathers" to whom he wrote in his day. And it is evident that St. John and those "pillars in the temple of

God" did not hesitate to accept the proofs that they were children of God. They applied these proofs to their own lives as confirmation of their faith. The witness of our spirits that we are children of God is based on the practical signs that we are Christians. In sum, those that have these proofs are children of God. If we have these marks in our lives, we can conclude that we are his children.

5. But how is it made evident that we have these marks? This question requires an answer. How is it made evident that we love God and our neighbor, and that we keep his commandments? Take notice that the question is not how it is made evident to others, but how it is made evident to *ourselves*. I would ask the one who posed this question, "How does it appear to *you*, that you are alive, and that you are now comfortable and not in pain?" Are you not directly aware of it? By the same immediate consciousness you will know if your soul is alive to God. You will know within yourself if you are saved from the affliction of prideful anger and that you possess the contentment of a gentle and quiet spirit. In the same way, you will know whether or not you love, rejoice, and delight in God. By the same self-understanding, you must be directly assured whether you love your neighbor as yourself, whether you love one another, and whether you are full of meekness and patience.

The Apostle John says that the *outward mark* of God's children is their obedience to his commandments. You undoubtedly know in your own heart if, by the grace of God, this mark belongs to you. From day to day, your conscience informs you if you do not speak God's name except with seriousness, affection, reverence, and godly awe. You know if you remember the Sabbath day and keep it holy, if you honor your father and mother, and if you do to others as you would have them do to you. You know if you control your own body in holiness and honor. You know whether you eat or drink, or whatever you do, you do everything for the glory of God.

6. The knowledge of these things is properly the testimony of our own spirits, that is the testimony of our own consciences. God gave us a conscience to help us to become holy in heart and life. The witness of the Spirit is a consciousness, in and by the Spirit of adoption, of our having received the inner disposition that the word of God states as characteristic of his adopted children. A loving heart toward God and toward all others marks the truly Christian life. Genuine Christians cling with childlike confidence to God the Father, desiring nothing but him, and casting all their care upon him. They embrace every person with sincere and kind affection, being willing to lay down their lives for others as Christ laid down his life for us. This disposition brings a consciousness that the

Spirit of God inwardly conforms us to the image of his Son and that we walk before him in justice, mercy, and truth, doing the things that please him.

7. What, then, is the witness of God's Spirit that is added to, and joined with, the inner testimony of our spirits? How does the Holy Spirit bear witness with our spirits that we are the children of God? It is hard to find human words to explain "the depth of God." Indeed, there are no earthly languages that will adequately express what the children of God experience. (I desire any that have been taught by God to correct, soften, or strengthen my explanation which follows.) Perhaps one might say that the testimony of the Spirit is an inward impression on the soul whereby the Spirit of God directly witnesses to my spirit that I am a child of God—that Jesus Christ loves me and gave himself for me, that all my sins are blotted out, and that even I have been reconciled to God.

8. In the very nature of things, this witness of the Holy Spirit must precede the witness of our own spirits. A single consideration verifies this fact. We must be holy in heart and life before we can be conscious that we are. This change must take place before the Holy Spirit witnesses that we are inwardly and outwardly holy. Now, we must love God before we can be holy in any way, because the love of God is the root of all holiness. We cannot love God until we first know that he loves us. "We love because he first loved us." And we cannot become aware of his pardoning love until his Spirit witnesses to our spirit concerning that love. Therefore, because the witness of his Spirit must precede our love of God and all holiness, it necessarily follows that God's witness to us must precede our inward consciousness of his love. This inward consciousness is the witness of our spirit.

9. First, the Holy Spirit witnesses to our spirits that "God loved us, sent his Son to be the atoning sacrifice for our sins," and "freed us from our sins by his blood." Only then, after God works in us, do "we love God because he first loved us" and for his sake we also "love our brothers and sisters." We cannot help being conscious of the work of God's Spirit within us, and "we understand the gifts bestowed on us by God." We know that we love God and keep his commandments; consequently, "we know that we are God's children." This awareness, then, is the witness of our own spirit. And as long as we continue to love God and keep his commandments, this witness remains within us and it is joined with the witness of God's Spirit "that we are children of God."

10. By no means do I want anything that I have said to be understood to exclude the work of the Holy Spirit from the witness of our spirit that we are God's children. Never. It is the Holy Spirit who produces every

good thing within us, enlightens us to his own work, and clearly witnesses to us what he has done. Accordingly, St. Paul spoke of the one great end of our receiving the Holy Spirit—"that we may understand the gifts bestowed on us by God." Our receiving the Holy Spirit strengthens the witness of our consciences pertaining to our "holiness and godly sincerity," and helps us see in a fuller and stronger light that we are doing those things that please God.

11. Suppose someone would ask, "How does the Holy Spirit bear witness with our spirits that we are God's children in a way so as to exclude all doubt and make clear the reality of our filial relationship?" The answer to this question is clear from what we have seen above. Let us look, first, at the witness of our spirits. The soul just as intimately and clearly perceives when it loves, delights, and rejoices in God, as when it loves and delights in anything on earth. And the soul cannot any more doubt whether or not it loves, delights, and rejoices than whether or not it exists. Therefore, if this reasoning is logical, we logically can conclude:

- Whoever loves God, delights and rejoices in him with a humble joy, holy delight, and obedient love is a child of God;
- I love, delight in, and rejoice in God;
- Therefore, I am a child of God.

With this truth in mind, genuine Christians can have no doubt that they are God's children. We can have as certain a knowledge of this conclusion as we have that the scriptures come from God. We can have full assurance of our loving God and of the inner witness that we do. These things are nothing less than self-evident. Thus, the witness of our own spirit accords with the most intimate conviction manifested to our hearts in such a way as, beyond all reasonable doubt, to prove the reality of our being God's children.

12. I do not take it upon myself to explain how the divine witness of the Spirit is manifested to the heart. "Such knowledge is too wonderful for me; it is so high that I cannot attain it." "The wind blows where it chooses, and you hear the sound of it, but you do not know where it comes from or where it goes." "For what human being knows what is truly human except the human spirit that is within? So also no one comprehends what is truly God's except the Spirit of God." However, the fact is clear that we know that the Spirit of God gives believers such a witness of their adoption. While that witness is present within the soul, we can no more doubt the reality of being God's child than we can doubt that the sun shines while we stand in the full brilliance of its beams.

II. How the witness of the Holy Spirit differs from the presumption of a natural mind and from demonic delusion

1. Next, we will consider how the joint testimony of God's Spirit and our spirit may be clearly and firmly distinguished from the presumption of a natural mind and from the delusion of the devil. In order to avoid self-deception, it is highly important for all who desire salvation from God to consider this question with the deepest attention. Biblical commentators normally agree that an error in this matter leads to the most fatal consequences. This statement is true because the one who goes astray at this point seldom discovers the mistake until it is too late to remedy it.

2. First, how can we distinguish the witness of the Spirit from the presumption of a natural mind? It is indisputable that those who have never been convicted of sin are always ready to flatter themselves (especially in spiritual things) into thinking of themselves more highly than they ought to think. Therefore, it is not at all strange for those who are hopelessly conceited in their carnal minds to hear of this privilege of true Christians and place themselves among those who have the witness of the Holy Spirit. They quickly convince themselves that they already have this blessing. Today, such instances abound in the world, and they have flourished in every age. So then, how can we distinguish the genuine witness of the Holy Spirit with our spirits from this damning presumption of those who do not know God?

3. I answer that the holy scriptures abound with signs, or marks, by which we can distinguish the genuine from the false testimony of the Holy Spirit. In the clearest manner, scripture describes the circumstances that precede, accompany, and follow the true and authentic witness of the Spirit of God with the spirits of believers. Whoever carefully ponders and heeds the Bible can avoid substituting darkness for light. The student of scripture will easily recognize the difference between the real and the counterfeit witness of the Spirit. I can confidently say that there will be no danger or possibility of confusing the one with the other.

4. By the signs found in the Bible, those who vainly presume that they have the witness of the Spirit can surely know the truth, if they really want to know it. By scripture, those who falsely presume to have the witness of the Holy Spirit can know that they have previously been "given up to a powerful delusion" and allowed themselves "to believe what is false." The scriptures show the clear and obvious marks that precede, accompany, and follow the witness of the Holy Spirit. Only a little reflection will convince deluded people, beyond all doubt, that these marks

have never been found in their lives. For instance, scripture describes repentance, or the conviction of sin, as constantly preceding the witness of God's pardon. Therefore, we read:

> Repent, for the kingdom of God has come near.
> Repent, and believe in the good news.
> Repent, and be baptized every one of you in the name of Jesus Christ so that your sins may be forgiven.
> Repent therefore, and turn to God so that your sins may be wiped out.

In conformity to these scriptures, our Church also continually places repentance before pardon and the assurance that we have been pardoned. God "pardons and absolves all those that truly repent, and sincerely believe his holy gospel."[6] We also read: "Almighty God has promised forgiveness of sins to all those, who, with wholehearted repentance and true faith, turn to Christ."[7]

However, those who have false testimonies of the Spirit are strangers to this kind of repentance. They never had "a broken and a contrite heart." They do not say, "The remembrance of my sins is grievous to me" or "The burden of my sins is intolerable."[8] In repeating those words, they never meant what they said. They paid only lip service to God. And if it were only from the lack of this prior work of God, those that falsely profess to be religious have ample reason to understand that they have grasped only a mere shadow of the authentic witness of the Spirit. They have never yet known the genuine privileges of the children of God.

5. Also, the scriptures describe what it means to be born of God. This experience of the new birth must precede the witness that we are his children. This transformation is a change "from darkness to light and from the power of Satan to God." New life in Christ means both "passing from death unto life" and a resurrection from the dead. Accordingly, St. Paul wrote to the Ephesians: "You God has made alive who were dead through their trespasses and sins." He also said, "When we were dead through our trespasses, God has made us alive together with Christ and raised us up with him and seated us with him in the heavenly places in Christ Jesus."

However, what do deluded persons know about any such change as this? They are completely unfamiliar with the entire matter. These scriptures speak a language that they do not understand. They tell you that they have *always* been Christians. They cannot think of any time when they needed such an inner change wrought by the Holy Spirit. By their own statements, if they give themselves permission to think, they may know that they are not born of the Spirit. They can understand from this admission that they have never yet known God, but rather they have mistaken the word of the unconverted mind for the word of God.

6. Let us set aside the consideration of whatever the unconverted have or have not experienced in the past. By the *present* marks in people's lives, we may easily distinguish the children of God from presumptuous self-deceivers. The scriptures describe that joy in the Lord which accompanies the witness of his Spirit. It is a humble joy that brings one down to the dust and causes a pardoned sinner to exclaim:

I am of small account!
I am no better than my ancestors.
Now my eye sees you; therefore I despise myself, and repent in dust and ashes.

And wherever humility is present, there follows gentleness, patience, and kindness. There is a pliable, yielding spirit and gentleness, sweetness, and tenderness of soul that words cannot express.

Do you find this spiritual fruit in a presumptuous person who claims the witness of the Holy Spirit? It is just the reverse. The more self-confident one is of God's favor, the prouder he or she becomes. The more they exalt themselves, the more arrogant and presumptuous they behave in everything. The stronger the witness they imagine themselves to have, the more disdainful they become toward everyone around them. They grow increasingly incapable of receiving any reprimand and they become more and more impatient with corrections. Instead of being more kind, gentle, and teachable, and more "swift to hear, and slow to speak," they are slower to hear and quicker to speak. They are more unwilling to learn from anyone; they are more hot-tempered and zealous in their attitudes and more eager to express their own opinions. Indeed, there will sometimes appear a kind of ferocity in their demeanor, conversation, and actions. It is as though they are determined to wrest matters out of God's hands and take it upon themselves to "consume the adversaries."

7. Once again, the scriptures say, "The love of God is this, that we obey his commandments." And our Lord himself said, "They who have my commandments and keep them are those who love me." Love delights to obey the Lord in every detail and to do whatever is pleasing to him. One who truly loves God moves swiftly to do his will on earth as it is done in heaven.

179

Do humility and obedience describe the attitude of presumptuous persons who pretend to love God? Not at all. Rather, their supposed love for God only gives them the liberty to disobey and break his commandments—not to keep them. Perhaps when they lived in fear of the wrath of God they did strive to do his will. Now, however, they see themselves as no longer "under the law." They think that now they are not obligated to observe God's commands. They are less enthusiastic to do good works, less careful to abstain from evil, less watchful over their own hearts, and less watchful over their tongues. They are less eager to deny themselves and daily to take up their crosses. In a word, because they imagine themselves to be at liberty, the whole style of their lives has changed.

They are no longer training themselves in godliness; they are not "struggling against the enemies of blood and flesh and against the authorities and cosmic powers," nor are they "suffering like good soldiers of Christ Jesus," "enduring hardships," and "striving to enter through the narrow door." No, they have found an easier way to heaven. It is a broad, smooth, flowery path, on which they can say to themselves, "Soul, you have ample goods laid up for many years; relax, eat, drink, be merry. With undeniable evidence, it follows that they do not have the authentic witness of their own spirits. They cannot be conscious of having those marks which they do not actually possess—namely, the marks of humility, submission, and obedience. The Holy Spirit of truth cannot bear witness to a lie or testify that pretenders are children of God when all the while they are visibly children of the devil.

8. You poor self-deceiver, discover your true condition! You who are confident of being a child of God, you who say, "I have the Holy Spirit's witness in myself"—you resist all your critics. You have been weighed on the scales of scripture and found lacking. The word of the Lord has examined your soul and found you to be "rejected silver." You are not humble; this fact proves that you have not yet received the Spirit of Jesus. You are not gentle and meek; therefore, your joy is worthless. It is not joy in the Lord. You do not keep his commandments, so you do not love him. Neither do you share in the Holy Spirit. Consequently, it is as certain and as evident as the Bible can make it—the Holy Spirit does not bear witness with your spirit that you are a child of God.

O, plead with the Lord that the scales might fall from your eyes. Pray that you will know fully, even as you are fully known. Receive the sentence of death in yourself, until you hear the voice that raises the dead, saying, "Take heart, your sins are forgiven; your faith has made you well."

9. Someone may ask, "But how can those who have the authentic witness in themselves distinguish it from presumption?" I respond by asking how you tell day from night. How do you distinguish light from darkness; or the light of a star or a burning candle from the light of the noonday sun? Is there not an inherent, obvious, essential difference between the one and the other? Provided your senses are working properly, do you not immediately and directly perceive the difference? In like manner, there is an innate, essential difference between spiritual light and spiritual darkness—between the light with which the Sun of righteousness shines upon our heart and that glimmering light that arises only from " the brands that you have kindled." If your spiritual senses are rightly inclined, this distinction is also immediately and directly perceived.

10. To require a more detailed and philosophical account of the way we distinguish these differences and of the measures or essential marks by which we know the voice of God is to make a demand that can never be satisfied. Even the one who has the deepest knowledge of God cannot satisfy it. Suppose that when St. Paul pleaded before Agrippa, he (Agrippa) would have said, "You talk of hearing the voice of the Son of God. How do you know that it was his voice? By what measures or essential marks do you know the voice of God? Explain to me the manner of distinguishing his voice from a human or angelic voice." Can you believe that the Apostle Paul would have even attempted to answer such an impossible question? Nevertheless, without doubt, the moment that St. Paul heard God speak to him, he *knew* that it was the voice of God. But who is able to explain *how* he knew this? Perhaps neither human beings nor angels.

11. To come still closer to our point, suppose God were now to speak to any person, "Your sins are forgiven." God must will that the person would know his voice, or else God would have spoken in vain. God is able to cause us to hear, because whatever he wills he can do. God *does* enable us to hear his voice. The soul is utterly assured that it is the voice of God.

Yet, the one who has the inner witness of the Holy Spirit cannot explain it to those who do not have this witness. Nor indeed ought we to expect that one could do so. If there were any human way to prove, or any natural way to explain God's truth to uninitiated people, unspiritual persons might be able to discern and understand the things of the Spirit of God. However, this possibility is completely contrary to the assertion of the Apostle Paul. He said, "They are unable to understand

181

them because they are spiritually discerned." The natural man does not have the spiritual senses with which to understand spiritual reality.

12. One might raise the question, "But how can I know that my spiritual senses are rightly inclined?" This question is also one of great importance, because if we are mistaken at this point, we might continue in endless error and delusion. One might ask, "And how can I be assured that I am not deluded and that I do not confuse the voice of the Holy Spirit?"

I answer that we can be certain by the testimony of our own spirits, by "an appeal to God for a good conscience." You can have certainty of a good conscience by the fruit that God has produced in your life. In this way you will know the witness of the Spirit of God. By these means you know that you are not under any illusion and that you have not deceived your own soul. The immediate fruit of the Spirit ruling in the heart consists of "love, joy, peace, patience, kindness, generosity, faithfulness, gentleness, and self-control." And the outward fruit of the Spirit consists of doing good to everyone, doing no evil to anyone, and walking in the light with an earnest and consistent obedience to all the commandments of God.

13. By this same means you can distinguish the voice of God from any delusion of the devil. The devil's arrogant spirit cannot humble you before God. He neither can nor will soften your heart and melt it into an earnest yearning after God, which leads to a filial love for him. It is not the Adversary of God and humankind who enables you to love your neighbor or to put on humility, gentleness, patience, self control, and the whole armor of God. Satan is not divided against himself, nor is he a destroyer of sin, which is his own work. No, the witness of the Holy Spirit comes from the Son of God who came "to destroy the works of the devil." As surely as holiness comes from God and sin is the work of the devil, so surely the witness of the Holy Spirit to you is not from Satan. It comes from God.

14. With every good reason, you can say, "Thanks be to God for his indescribable gift!" Thanks be to God who allows me to say, "I know the one in whom I have put my trust." He "has sent the Spirit of his Son into our hearts, crying, 'Abba! Father!'" Even now, the Holy Spirit "bears witness with our spirits that we are children of God." Also, observe that not only your lips will proclaim his praise, but your life as well. God has sealed you for himself. Glorify him in your body and in your spirit, which are his.

Beloved, if you have this hope in you, purify yourselves as he is pure. "See what love the Father has given us, that we should be called children of God;" "cleanse yourselves from every defilement of body and of spirit, making holiness perfect in the fear of God." Let all your thoughts, words, and deeds become a living sacrifice, holy and acceptable to God, through Christ Jesus!

Notes

1. Curnock, *Wesley's Journal*, 1:467-68.
2. Ibid., 1:475.
3. Ibid., 5:424-25.
4. Jackson, *Wesley's Works*, 12:61.
5. Telford, *Wesley's Letters*, March 28, 1768, 5:358.
6. *Book of Common Prayer*, Morning Prayer.
7. *Book of Common Prayer*, Communion Liturgy.
8. *Book of Common Prayer*, Confession.

THE WITNESS OF THE SPIRIT, DISCOURSE 2

The previous sermon was published in 1746, and Wesley followed it twenty years later with this second sermon on the same subject. The two written discourses belong together, and in Wesley's 1771 collection of his Works he pointed out their connection. We saw in the Introduction to Sermon #10 that John Wesley taught that the witness of the Holy Spirit is a privilege, not a requirement. He wrote to a friend, Melville Horne:

> When fifty years ago my brother Charles and I, in the simplicity of our hearts, told the good people of England, that unless they *knew* their sins were forgiven, they were under the wrath and curse of God, I marvel, Melville, they did not stone us! The Methodists, I hope, know better now: we preach assurance as we always did, as a common privilege of the children of God; but we do not enforce it, under the pain of damnation, denounced on all who enjoy it not.[1]

In a letter to Thomas Rutherforth, onetime Regius Professor of Divinity at Cambridge and Archdeacon of Essex, Wesley wrote, "I have not for many years thought a consciousness of acceptance to be essential to justifying faith."[2]

Nonetheless, Wesley believed that the witness of the Spirit was an important aspect of Christian experience and the immeasurable privilege of believers. He considered this reality to have such significance that he devoted three sermons to its explication. Wesley's sermons about the witness of the Holy Spirit emphasize that all believers can expect to enjoy this blessing.

Methodist theology holds that we can resist God's grace and turn aside from him, thereby grieving the Holy Spirit. Wesley insisted that we must respond obediently to God for him to justify and sanctify us. Our position in Christ is not predetermined or unconditional. Initially, and throughout our lives, we must respond to the initiative of the Holy Spirit, who enables us to turn to Christ and receive the fullness of his blessings. These sermons on the witness of the Holy Spirit teach personal account ability and the New Testament requirement to "endure to the end to be saved." God favors us, but he does not force us.

Wesley was convinced that God does not want his children to live without the confident assurance that they have a right relationship with him. He contended that without the witness of the Holy Spirit to their present and final salvation, Christians could easily plunge into fear, uncertainty, and depression. As early as 1725 he wrote to his mother, "If we can never have any certainty of our being in a state of salvation, good reason it is, that every moment should be spent, not in joy, but in fear and trembling; and then undoubtedly, in this life, we are of all men most miserable. God deliver us from such a fearful expectation as this!"[3] He contended, "I believe a consciousness of being in the favour of God . . . is the common privilege of Christians, fearing God and working righteousness."[4]

Wesley taught, "There is in every believer, both the testimony of God's Spirit, and the testimony of his own, that he is a child of God."[5] The witness of the Spirit means that a *general belief* that Christ died for the sins of the world becomes also a *personal conviction* that Christ died for me. As Wesley stated in the previous sermon, "The fact is clear that we know that the Spirit of God gives believers such a witness of their adoption. While that witness is present within the soul, one can no more doubt the reality of being God's child than one can doubt that the sun shines while we stand in the full brilliance of its beams."

Sermon 11

THE WITNESS OF THE SPIRIT, DISCOURSE 2

It is that very Spirit bearing witness with our spirit that we are children of God. *(Romans 8:16)*

I. The importance of the doctrine of the witness of the Holy Spirit

1 No one who believes that the scriptures are the word of God can doubt the importance of such a truth as the witness of the Holy Spirit. This truth is revealed in the Bible not just once, nor dimly, nor in passing. Scripture discloses this truth frequently, clearly, and forthrightly for the purpose of showing that the Holy Spirit's witness to Christians is one of the special privileges of God's children.

2. It is especially necessary to explain and defend this doctrine because it is in danger on the right hand and on the left hand. If we deny this truth, there is danger that Christianity may degenerate into mere formality. On the one hand, we must avoid the pitfall of "holding to the outward form of godliness but denying its power." If we fail to recognize when we are allowing our religion to become a mere outward appearance without power, we are in danger of running into an inadequate formalism.

On the other hand, if we acknowledge the power of religion without understanding it, we run the danger of unrestrained fanaticism. With utmost urgency, therefore, we need to protect Christian believers from both these dangers—formalism and fanaticism. In explaining and confirming the momentous doctrine of the witness of the Spirit, it is important that we use both scripture and reason.

3. This undertaking is all the more needful because so little clear teaching has been written on this subject. And much of what has been written has been so erroneous that it amounts to explaining away this doctrine. It cannot be doubted that these false teachings are clumsy, unscriptural, irrational explanations of those who knew neither "what they were saying nor the things about which they made assertions."

4. It is especially important for Methodists clearly to understand, explain, and defend this doctrine, because it is an important part of the testimony that God has given them to convey to the world. God's special blessing has rested upon the Methodists as they have searched the scriptures and experienced this blessing. God has helped them recover this great evangelical truth, which for many years had been almost lost and forgotten.

II. Defining the witness of the Holy Spirit

1. What is the witness of the Spirit? The original word can be rendered either "witness" (as it is in several places), or less ambiguously, "testimony" or "record." The "testimony" of God is the record of what God reveals in the Bible. This testimony is that "God gave us eternal life, and this life is in his Son." The Holy Spirit of God gives this testimony that we are now considering. The Spirit witnesses to and with the human spirit. The Holy Spirit is the one who witnesses to us that "we are children of God."

The personal result of this testimony is "the fruit of the Spirit"—namely, "love, joy, peace, patience, kindness, generosity, faithfulness, gentleness, and self-control." Without these marks the witness itself cannot continue. The commission of any outward sin, the omission of known duty, or giving way to any inward sin inevitably destroys it. In a word, we destroy this inner witness by whatever grieves the Holy Spirit of God.

2. Many years ago,[6] I wrote:

It is hard to find human words to explain "the depth of God." Indeed, there are no earthly languages that will adequately express what the

187

children of God experience. (I desire any that have been taught by God to correct, soften, or strengthen my explanation which follows.) Perhaps one might say that the testimony of the Spirit is an inward impression on the soul whereby the Spirit of God directly witnesses to my spirit that I am a child of God—that Jesus Christ loves me and gave himself for me, that all my sins are blotted out, and that even I have been reconciled to God.

3. After twenty years of further consideration, I do not see any reason to retract any part of this explanation. Neither do I see how to alter any of these expressions to make them easier to understand. I can only add that if any of God's children will point out any other expressions that are clearer or more true to the Bible, I will readily set mine aside.

4. Meanwhile, I do not mean that the Holy Spirit witnesses through an audible voice. Nor does the Spirit always witness by an inner voice, although sometimes he may do so. Neither do I believe that the Holy Spirit always applies one or more scripture texts to the heart, although he often does. I mean that the Holy Spirit works upon the soul by his personal influence through a strong but unexplainable operation. This work of God calms the stormy wind, and troubled waves subside, bringing a sweet calm to the soul. One senses that he or she is resting in the arms of Jesus. Sinners become completely satisfied that they have been reconciled to God. They know that all "iniquities are forgiven, and their sins are covered."

5. What is the substance of the controversy concerning the witness of the Spirit? It is not whether there *is* a witness or testimony of the Spirit. It is not whether the Spirit testifies with our spirit that we are God's children. No one can deny this reality without directly contradicting the scriptures and accusing the God of truth of lying. It is clear, therefore, that everyone acknowledges that there is a direct witness of the Holy Spirit.

6. Furthermore, no one questions that there is an indirect witness or testimony that we are the children of God. This witness is almost, if not entirely, the same as the testimony of a good conscience towards God. This good conscience is the result of reason or of reflecting on what we personally experience in our own souls. Strictly speaking, a good conscience is a conclusion that we draw partly from the word of God and partly from our own experiences.

The word of God states that every one who has the fruit of the Spirit is a child of God. Experience or inward awareness tells me if I have the fruit of the Spirit in my life. From these considerations I rationally conclude, "Therefore I am a child of God." Everyone acknowledges this way

188

of reasoning, and so the reality of the witness of the Spirit is not a matter of controversy.

7. We do not contend that there can be any true witness of the Spirit without the fruit of the Spirit. On the contrary, we maintain that the fruit of the Spirit directly springs from this witness. To be sure, the fruit of the Spirit is not always present in the same degree—either when the testimony is first given or else much later. Joy, peace, and love are not always at the same level, and their testimonies are not always equally strong and clear.

8. However, the point in question here is whether there exists any *direct* witness of the Spirit apart from the testimony that arises from one's personal awareness of the Spirit's fruit.

III. Support for the direct witness of the Holy Spirit

1. I believe that there is support for the *direct* witness of the Holy Spirit. This witness is upheld by the obvious and natural meaning of the text, "It is that very Spirit bearing witness with our spirit that we are children of God." It is obvious that this passage mentions two witnesses—the witness of God's Spirit and the witness of the human spirit. They witness to the same thing.

The late Bishop of London,[7] preaching on Romans 8:16, seemed astonished that anyone doubted this truth, because the words of the text are clear and unmistakable. The bishop said, "The testimony of our own spirit is the consciousness of our own *sincerity*." To express the same thing a little more precisely, it is our consciousness of the fruit of the Spirit in our lives. When our spirit is aware of the presence of love, joy, peace, patience, gentleness, and goodness, our spirit easily infers from their presence in our lives that we are the children of God.

2. It is also true that the eminent bishop assumed the other witness to be "the consciousness of our own *good works*." He affirmed that this consciousness is our awareness of God's Spirit. According to the common meaning of the word, this awareness is included in the testimony and sincerity of our own spirits. Thus, St. Paul wrote, "This is our boast, the testimony of our conscience: we have behaved in the world with holiness and godly sincerity." It is clear that the apostle was referring to our words and actions at least as much as he was referring to our inward dispositions. This witness is not some other witness; it is the same witness that he mentioned earlier. It is the consciousness of our good works, which are only one part of our consciousness of our sincerity. It is still

only one witness, although the text speaks of two witnesses. The text speaks of the witness of the Holy Spirit and the witness of the human spirit. The witness of the human spirit is the consciousness of our good works and sincerity.

3. What then is the direct witness of the Holy Spirit to us? Even if the text were not perfectly clear, from the preceding verse we could easily learn the meaning of the Spirit's witness. "You did not receive a spirit of slavery to fall back into fear, but you have received a spirit of adoption when you cry, 'Abba! Father!'" Next we read, "It is that very Spirit bearing witness with our spirit that we are children of God."

4. The witness of the Holy Spirit is further confirmed by a parallel text in Galatians: "Because you are children, God has sent the Spirit of his Son into our hearts, crying, 'Abba! Father!'" Is this witness not something immediate and direct from God, and not the result of human reflection or deduction? Is it not the Spirit who says, "Abba, Father" in our hearts the moment he comes to us? This inner witness is given before we reflect on our own sincerity—indeed, before any reasoning whatsoever. Is this meaning not the clear and natural sense of the words that strike everyone as soon as they hear them? These texts in their most obvious meaning describe a direct witness of the Holy Spirit to the children of God.

5. In the very nature of things, the testimony of the Spirit of God must precede the testimony of our own spirit. Consider the following point. We must be holy in heart and life before we can be conscious that we are. We must love God before we can be in any way holy, because God's love is the root of all holiness. And we cannot love God until we know about his love: "We love God because he first loved us." And we cannot know his love for us until his Spirit witnesses his love to our spirit. Until he does, we cannot believe it and say, "The life I now live in the flesh I live by faith in the Son of God, who loved me and gave himself for me."

> Then, only then we feel
> Our interest in his blood,
> And cry with joy unspeakable,
> Thou art my Lord, my God![8]

Considering, therefore, that the witness of the Holy Spirit must precede the love of God and all holiness, it follows that his witness to us must precede our consciousness of it.

6. To confirm this scriptural doctrine, it is proper here to refer to the experience of the children of God. I am not speaking of the experience of two or three, or several, but of a great multitude that no one can number. This doctrine has been confirmed in this age and in every age by "a great cloud of witnesses," both living and dead.

Your experience and mine confirm it. The Spirit himself bore witness to my spirit that I was a child of God, and I immediately cried, "Abba! Father!" This reality was my experience (and yours). It came before we reflected on, or became conscious of, any fruit of the Spirit. It was from this received testimony from the Holy Spirit that love, joy, peace, and all the fruit of the Spirit then proceeded. First, I heard

> Thy sins are forgiven!
> Accepted thou art!
> They listen, and heaven
> Springs up in their heart.[9]

7. This doctrine is confirmed not only by the experience of the children of God. Thousands can declare that they never knew themselves to be in God's favor until he directly gave them the witness of his Spirit. The doctrine is also confirmed by all who are convicted of sin and feel themselves enduring God's anger. These convicted sinners cannot be satisfied with anything less than a direct witness from the Holy Spirit that God is "merciful toward their iniquities, and remembers their sins no more."

Say to any of these people, "You can know that you are God's children by reflecting on what he has done in you. Consider your love, joy, and peace." They will immediately reply, "By reflecting on the state of my soul, I know only that I am a child of the devil. I have no more love for God than the devil has. My mind is set on the flesh and hostile to God. I have no joy in the Holy Spirit, and I am deeply grieved, even to death. The wicked are like the tossing sea that cannot keep still."

How can one possibly comfort these people, other than by a divine witness that God "justifies the ungodly?" None are justified because they are good, sincere, or conformed to scripture in heart and life. Through faith, God justifies those who are ungodly, void of all real holiness, and lacking in good works. They do nothing good until they are conscious that God accepts them.

We are not accepted because of "any works of righteousness that we have done." Rather, God accepts us by his sheer, free mercy, entirely because of what the Son of God has done and suffered for us. How can it be otherwise, if one "is justified by faith apart from works prescribed by the law?" If this statement is true, what inner or outer righteousness can we have prior to justification? Is it not that we have nothing to pay? Is it not that we become conscious that "nothing good dwells within us?" Neither inward nor outward goodness is essential or indispensably necessary before we "are justified by his grace as a gift, through the redemption which is in Christ Jesus." There has never been anyone justified, nor can anyone ever be justified, until he or she is brought to the point of saying,

> I give up every plea beside,
> "Lord, I am damn'd, but Thou hast died!"[10]

8. Therefore, all who deny the existence of such a testimony in effect deny justification by faith. It follows either that those without this witness of God's Spirit never experienced justification or that they have forgotten it. As St. Peter said, "Such a one is forgetful of the cleansing of past sins." These people have forgotten the experience that God wrought in their souls when their former sins were blotted out.

9. Even the experience of the children of the world confirms the experience of the children of God. Many of those that do not know God have a desire to please him, and some of them labor hard to do so. But do not all of them regard it the highest absurdity to talk about knowing that their sins are forgiven? Who among them ever pretends such a thing? Many of them are conscious of their sincere desire to please God. To some degree, many of them undoubtedly have the testimony of their own spirit, a consciousness that they do hold to a good moral standard.

However, this testimony brings them no consciousness that they are forgiven; they have no knowledge that they are God's children. Yes, the more sincere they are, the more uneasy they generally become. Their lack of assurance clearly shows that they cannot satisfactorily know God by the mere witness of their own spirits. First, God must directly witness that we are his children.

IV. Answers to objections to the doctrine of the witness of the Holy Spirit

Many objections have been made to the doctrine of the witness of the Holy Spirit, and we will consider the major ones.

1. First, some object, "Experience is not sufficient to establish a doctrine that is not founded on Scripture." This statement is undoubtedly true, and it highlights an important principle. However, the objection does not affect the present question, because I have shown that this doctrine *is* founded on scripture. It is proper to look to experience not to *establish* a doctrine, but to *confirm* a doctrine founded on the Bible.

2. Some may object, "But lunatics, extremist French prophets, and fanatics of every kind have imagined that they experienced the witness of the Spirit." That observation is true. Perhaps several of them *did* receive this blessing, although they did not retain it long. But even if they did not receive the genuine witness of the Spirit, that fact does not at all prove that others have not experienced it. If an insane person imagines himself to be a king, it does not prove that there are no real kings.

Others may say, "But many who pleaded strongly for this doctrine have utterly discredited the authority of the Bible." Perhaps they have, but their doing so was not a necessary consequence of affirming the witness of the Spirit. Thousands of people who hold the highest esteem for the Bible pray for this blessing.

It may be said, "Yes, but many have disastrously deceived themselves that they have the witness of the Spirit, leading to the loss of any conviction of sin." I answer that a scriptural doctrine is not invalid just because some abuse it to their own destruction.

3. Some might object, "But I hold it to be an indisputable truth that the presence of the fruit of the Spirit constitutes the witness of the Spirit." I do not deny that fact, even though thousands doubt it, or even deny it. But let us set that matter aside.

Others might say, "If the evidence of spiritual fruit is present, there is no need for any other witness." I respond by saying that the only time in which there is a *complete absence* of the fruit of the Spirit is when God gives an initial and immediate witness to *new* Christians. Someone might say that we could have the witness of the Spirit without *perceiving* the Spirit's witness. I answer that to contend for this view is to argue for one's being in God's favor without knowing it. The direct witness of the Spirit may shine clearly, even while the indirect witness is under a cloud.

4. Second, it is sometimes stated that the purpose of the witness of the Spirit about which we argue is to prove that the profession we make is genuine, but it constitutes no real proof. I answer that it is not the purpose of the witness of the Spirit to verify our profession of faith. The Spirit's witness precedes our making any profession at all. The only profession we make is that we are lost, condemned, guilty, helpless sinners. The purpose of the witness of the Spirit is to assure those to whom it is

given that they are the children of God—that "they are justified by his grace as a gift, through the redemption which is in Christ Jesus."

This assurance does not assume that one's former thoughts, words, and actions conformed to the rule of scripture. It assumes quite the reverse—namely, that one is a complete sinner, both in heart and life. If it were otherwise, God would approve only those who earned justification through their own works, which would be counted to them for righteousness. I cannot help suspecting that the assumption that good works justify us lies at the root of all the objections to the doctrine of the witness of the Spirit. I say that this is so because whoever sincerely believes that God imputes righteousness without works to all that are justified will find no difficulty in acknowledging that the witness of his Spirit precedes the fruit it produces.

5. Third, people sometimes give the following objection to the witness of the Spirit: "On the one hand, one Evangelist says, 'Your heavenly Father will give the Holy Spirit to them who ask him.' On the other hand, the other Evangelist speaks of 'good things' (not the Holy Spirit), amply demonstrating that the Spirit's way of bearing witness is by giving good gifts." I answer that this assumption is in no way correct. There is nothing at all about the Spirit "bearing witness" in *either* of these texts. Therefore, until this claim is better demonstrated, I will let the matter stand as it is.

6. Fourth, some may object, "The Scripture says, 'The tree is known by its fruit.' 'Test everything.' 'Test the spirits.' 'Examine yourselves.'"

I answer that these things are absolutely true. Therefore, let all who think that they "have the witness in themselves" test whether it is of God. If fruit follows, the witness is of God; if fruit does not follow, the Spirit's witness is not of God. Assuredly, "the tree is known by its fruit." By the fruit of the Spirit, we verify whether the witness is from God.

Another person might object, "But the direct witness is never referred to in the Book of God." I answer that it does not appear *alone* as a single witness. The witness of the Holy Spirit does appear, however, as connected with the witness of the human spirit—giving a *shared* testimony of the Holy Spirit witnessing to our spirit that we are children of God. Who is able to prove that this truth is not clearly verified in the very meaning of the following text? "Examine yourselves, to see whether you are holding to your faith. Test yourselves. Do you not realize that Jesus Christ is in you?" It is by no means clear that those to whom St. Paul wrote did not know the inner presence of Christ by a direct witness of the Spirit, as well as by the secondary witness of the Spirit's fruit in their lives. How could anyone prove that those Christians did not know the witness of the spirit, first, by an inward awareness; and then, by the presence of love, joy, and peace in their lives?

7. Does the witness of the Spirit that arises from an internal and external change appear regularly in the Bible? It does indeed. And we constantly refer to scripture to authenticate the witness of the Spirit. Do all the marks that I have given to distinguish the operations of God's Spirit from delusion refer to the spiritual change that God works in us and upon us? Yes, this fact is assuredly true.

8. Fifthly, it is objected, "The direct witness of the Spirit does not protect us from the greatest delusion. Can we trust a witness that cannot be depended on in its own right—that is, one that is forced to flee to something else to prove what it asserts?" I answer that in order to protect us from all delusion God gives us *two* witnesses that we are his children. These two witnesses—the witness of God's spirit and the witness of our spirits—testify in harmony with each other. Therefore, "what God has joined together, let no one put asunder." As long as the two witnesses remain together, we cannot be deluded. We can depend on their joint testimony. They qualify to be trusted in the highest degree, and they need nothing else to prove what they assert.

Someone may object, "No, the direct witness only asserts, but does not prove anything." I answer that two witnesses will establish every word. And when the Holy Spirit witnesses with our spirit as God intends, it fully verifies that we are children of God.

9. Sixthly, it is objected, "You acknowledge that the change produced within us is a sufficient witness, except in the case of severe trials, such as that of our Savior upon the cross. However, none of us can be tried in that manner." I answer that you or I might be tried in such a manner, and so might any other child of God. In such cases it will be impossible for us to keep our filial confidence in God without the direct witness of his Spirit.

10. Finally, someone may object, "Among the most vigorous defenders of this doctrine are some of the proudest and most uncharitable of people." I answer that perhaps some of the most extravagant contenders for this doctrine *are* both proud and uncharitable. At the same time, many of the firmest contenders for this doctrine are notably meek and humble in heart. Indeed, in many other ways, as well, they are

> True followers of their lamb-like Lord.[11]

The preceding objections are the most significant that I have heard, and I believe that they contain the force of the case against the witness of the Holy Spirit. Nevertheless, I believe that whoever calmly and impartially considers these objections and the answers together will easily see that they do not destroy or weaken the evidence for this great truth. The Spirit of God does directly and indirectly witness that we are God's children.

V. Practical inferences from the doctrine of the witness of the Holy Spirit

1. Here is the sum of everything that I have said. The witness of the Spirit is an inward impression on the souls of believers, by which the Spirit of God directly witnesses to their spirits that they are children of God. The issue is not whether there is a witness of the Spirit. Rather, the issue is whether there is any *direct* witness. That is, whether there is any witness other than the testimony that arises from one's awareness of the fruit of the Spirit.

We believe that there *is* such a direct witness of the Spirit. This conviction is based on the obvious, fundamental meaning of the text for this sermon, illustrated both by the preceding verse (Rom. 8:15) and the parallel passage in Galatians. In the nature of things, the witness of the Spirit must precede the fruit that springs from it. As well, this clear meaning of the Bible is confirmed by the experience of innumerable children of God. Indeed, it is confirmed by the experience of all who are convinced of sin and cannot rest until they have a direct witness from God. Finally, many now do testify that the Holy Spirit witnesses to their spirits that they are children of God. This fact is verified among the children of the world who formerly had no witness of God's Spirit in themselves and among those who once declared that none of us can know that our sins are forgiven.

2. I will summarize the objections to the doctrine of the witness of the Spirit. (1) Scripture does not support this doctrine. (2) Lunatics and fanatics of all sorts have imagined that they possess such a witness. (3) The intent of this witness is to prove that our profession is genuine, and it does not do so. (4) The Bible says, "The tree is known by its fruit." "Examine yourselves; test yourselves." Scripture does not refer to a *direct* witness of the Spirit. (5) This doctrine does not protect us from the greatest of delusions. (6) The change wrought in us is a sufficient testimony, unless we find ourselves in the sorts of trials that only Christ suffered.

We answered these objections in this way: (1) Experience is adequate to confirm a doctrine if it is grounded in scripture. (2) Although many people may imagine that they experience what they do not experience, that fact does not undermine genuine experience. (3) The purpose of the witness of the Spirit is to assure us that we are children of God, and it satisfies this purpose. (4) The authentic witness of the Spirit is verified by the Spirit's fruit—love, peace, and joy. This fruit does not precede the witness of the spirit, but follows it. (5) It cannot be disproved that the direct and indirect witness of the Spirit is referred to in the text, "Do you not realize that Jesus Christ is in you?" (6) The Spirit of God witnessing with our spirits protects us from all delusion. (7) We are all subject to trials in which the testimony only of our own spirits is not enough. In those cases, nothing less than the direct witness of God's Spirit can assure us that we are his children.

3. Two inferences may be drawn from the whole of our discussion. First, let no one ever presume to rest in any supposed witness of the Spirit that is separate from the fruit of the Spirit. If the Spirit of God really does testify that we are the children of God, the immediate consequence will be the fruit of the Spirit—love, joy, peace, patience, kindness, generosity, faithfulness, gentleness, and self-control. During the time of strong testing when Satan sifts one as wheat, for a period this fruit may be eclipsed so that it does not seem visible to the person in the midst of temptation or trial. Nevertheless, the essential part of it remains, even under the heaviest cloud. It is true that during the hour of trial our joy in the Holy Spirit may be distant, yes, the soul may become "greatly distressed," while "the hour and power of darkness" continues. However, even this time of distress is usually overcome with an increase of the knowledge of God. And we grow until we "rejoice with an indescribable and glorious joy."

4. The second inference we draw from this discussion is that no one should rest in any supposed fruit of the Spirit without the witness of the Spirit. There may be foretastes of joy, peace, and love that are not delusions—they really are from God. And they are evident long before we have the Spirit's witness in ourselves. This fruit may be antecedent to the moment when the Spirit of God witnesses with our spirits that "we have redemption through his blood, the forgiveness of our trespasses." Yes, there may be a degree of patience, kindness, faithfulness, gentleness, and self-control before we are accepted in the Beloved One. This fruit is not just fanciful. By prevenient grace it is authentic fruit appearing prior to our receiving the Spirit's testimony of our acceptance before God. However, it is not by any means advisable to rest here. We endanger our

souls if we do. If we are wise, we will continually pray, until the Holy Spirit speaks in our hearts, "Abba! Father."

The witness of the Spirit is the privilege of all the children of God, and without it we can never be assured that we are his children. Unless the Spirit witnesses to our spirits, we cannot maintain a continuous peace or avoid perplexing doubts and fears. But when we have once received the "Spirit of adoption," this "peace which surpasses all understanding" and which expels all agonizing doubt and fear, will "guard our hearts and minds in Christ Jesus."

And when this experience has brought forth its genuine fruit (inward and outward holiness), it is undoubtedly the will of God who calls us to continue always to give us more of what God has already given. There is never any more need for us ever to be deprived of the witness of God's Spirit or the witness of our own spirits, the awareness of our walking in true righteousness and holiness.

NEWRY, April 4, 1767

Notes

1. Robert Southey, *The Life of Wesley; and the Rise and Progress of Methodism,* 1:295.
2. Telford, *Wesley's Letters,* 5:359.
3. Ibid., June 18, 1725, 1:20.
4. Ibid., 5:358.
5. Outler, *Wesley's Sermons,* 1:271.
6. *The Witness of the Spirit,* Discourse 1, I, §7.
7. Wesley is referring to Bishop Thomas Sherlock.
8. Charles Wesley, "Spirit of Faith Come Down," stanza 2, *Poet. Wks.,* 5:187.
9. Charles Wesley, "After Preaching to the Newcastle Colliers," Hymn I, stanza 9, *Poet. Wks.,* 5:116.
10. Charles Wesley, Hymn on Galatians 3:22, stanza 12, *Poet. Wks.,* 1:85.
11. Charles Wesley, *Hymns on the Lord's Supper* (1745), #146, stanza 1.

THE WITNESS OF OUR
OWN SPIRIT

The previous two sermons explain the objective basis for Christian assurance. People are Christians not because they think or assume so, but because of *God's* work within them. These sermons on assurance, of course, champion the conviction that an important component of God's work in Christians is the witness of the Holy Spirit that they are God's children. In a court of law, when a judge "justifies" prisoners and declares that they are not guilty, it is fitting for their judge to notify them that their guilt has been forgiven. Freedom from condemnation does not fully benefit prisoners until they become aware of having been pardoned. By comparison, the witness of the Holy Spirit is God's testimony to believers that they now stand in a justified relationship with God our judge.

Wesley's text for the first two sermons on the witness of the Spirit (Sermons #10 and #11) comes from a familiar passage in Romans: "For you did not receive a spirit of slavery to fall back into fear, but you have received a spirit of adoption. When we cry, 'Abba! Father!' it is that very Spirit bearing witness with our spirit that we are children of God, and if children, then heirs, heirs of God and joint heirs with Christ" (Rom. 8:15, 16). The present sermon, a logical sequel to the two previous sermons, is based on 2 Corinthians 1:12, which speaks about "the testimony of our conscience." This discourse deals with the human spirit's response to the witness of the Holy Spirit, who testifies to believers that they are children of God.

In Wesley's day, some teachers derived the assurance of salvation from the twin doctrines of unchanging predestination rooted in God's "eternal decrees" and the unconditional perseverance of the elect. For two reasons, John and Charles Wesley did not base their doctrine of assurance on these teachings.

First, the question of identifying the elect and the nonelect becomes problematic. On the one hand, Wesley observed that some people too hastily presumed that God had elected them. They took for granted that they were chosen for salvation, although they had not repented or made any serious effort to abandon their sins. The following passage sums up Wesley's estimation of such teaching: "Your supposition of God's ordaining from eternity whatsoever should be done to the end of the world; as well as that of God's acting irresistibly in the elect, and Satan's acting irresistibly in the reprobates; utterly overthrows the Scripture doctrine of rewards and punishments, as well as of a judgment to come."[1]

On the other hand, Wesley met many people who believed that they had no hope for their salvation. They felt such an intense burden of guilt and unworthiness that they could not imagine that God had elected them to salvation. Wesley described this problem:

> Take one of those who are supposed not to be elected; one whom God hath not chosen unto life and salvation. Can this man be saved from sin and hell? You answer, "No." Why not? "Because he is not elected. Because God hath unchangeably decreed to save so many souls, and no more; and he is not of that number. Him God hath decreed to pass by; to leave him to everlasting destruction; in consequence of which irresistible decree, the man perishes everlastingly."[2]

Part of Wesley's methodology was accurately and concisely to state the subject under consideration. Doing so, he believed, was necessary to clarify the issues, properly frame the question, and relate it to the Bible.

Wesley was determined to warn those who presumptuously claimed election (even if they tolerated sin in their lives). He also encouraged those who had no hope of being among God's chosen (despite their earnest prayers of repentance). Charles Wesley's hymns often echo the truths contained in John Wesley's sermons. The message that God calls everyone to know him and enjoy the assurance of his divine favor is expressed in this hymn:

> Thy sovereign grace to all extends,
> Immense and unconfined!

> From age to age it never ends;
> It reaches all mankind.[3]

Second, Wesley did not accept the doctrines of unconditional election and the assured perseverance of the saints. He opposed those who taught that God would never count present and future sins against the elect. As stated, some even refused to abandon their sins, claiming that they were clothed in "the righteousness of Christ." Wesley insisted that willful, persistent sin separates saints from God after justification, just as it separates sinners from God before justification. These three sermons on assurance underscore the biblical teaching that true faith must show itself in an inward and outward change, resulting in holiness of heart and life.

Wesley preached about the witness of the Spirit because he believed that it is entirely unacceptable and foolish to wait until after death to learn whether we are saved. During his years as a student at the University of Oxford, he struggled to find assurance of salvation, and in his mature years, he never forgot the spiritual agonies that he once suffered when he lacked the witness of the Spirit. In this sermon, Wesley affirms that believers can have the witness of the Holy Spirit who assures them that they stand in God's favor. Without assurance, people will probably live in a state of uncertainty or fear. With the witness of God's Spirit, Christians can experience the fullness of joy and peace.

This sermon also deals with Wesley's understanding of the conscience. He explains that the conscience is not mere consciousness—that is, an awareness that one exists. Conscience is the human ability to discern between right and wrong, and to render inner approval or disapproval. God, who especially uses the Bible to instruct and impress us regarding moral issues, also informs the conscience by the Holy Spirit. According to Wesley, a good conscience includes an understanding of our inner intentions and outward conduct, helping us to live a life that conforms to God's commands. He points out that one's conscience must be instructed and perfected by scripture before it can be counted as reliable.

Always, Wesley links the objective legal and ethical aspects of Christian doctrine to the subjective and personal aspects of Christian experience. God's part is to give us the assurance of his favor and to enable us to live in holiness. Our part is to trust God, remain obedient, and "fight the good fight of faith." Of course, Christians do not overcome the world, the flesh, and the devil by their own wisdom or strength. They become victorious through the power of the Holy Spirit freely given in Christ—and their human spirits witness with God's Holy Spirit that they are God's children.

THE WITNESS OF OUR OWN SPIRIT

This is our boast, the testimony of our conscience: we have behaved in the world with frankness and godly sincerity, not by earthly wisdom but by the grace of God.

(2 Corinthians 1:12)

1 This scripture echoes the voice of all true believers in Christ, who abide in faith and love. Our Lord said, "Whoever follows me will never walk in darkness." And those who have the light of Christ rejoice in that light. Believers "have received Christ Jesus the Lord, and they continue to live their lives in him." As they walk with Christ day after day, St. Paul's encouragement takes effect in their lives: "Rejoice in the Lord always; again I will say, rejoice."

2. I want us to avoid building our houses upon the sand. Rather, we must heed the warning of Christ to those who do so: "The rain fell, and the floods came, and the winds blew and beat against that house, and it fell—and great was its fall!" In this sermon, I intend to explain the nature and foundation of Christian joy. In general, we understand that joy is a contented peace and a calm and satisfied spirit, which springs from what the Apostle Paul described as the witness of a "good conscience." However, in order to understand this joy more completely, it is

necessary to ponder all of St. Paul's words. From this study it will easily
come into view what the conscience is and what is the witness of one's
conscience. Also, we will see how one who has the witness of a good conscience rejoices everlastingly.

3. First, what is the meaning of the word *conscience?* How should we
understand this term which everyone uses so often? When we consider
how many large volumes have been written on this subject, we might
conclude that the conscience is an extraordinarily difficult thing to
understand. People have vigorously searched all the treasures of ancient
and modern learning in order to understand the conscience. I fear, however, that all these elaborate inquiries have not shed much light on the
conscience. Instead, have not most of those writers confused the inquiry,
"darkening counsel by words without knowledge?" Have they not confused a subject that is clear in itself and easily understood? Set aside the
difficult terms, and everyone who has an honest heart will quickly understand the matter.

4. God made us as thinking beings who are capable of perceiving the
present and contemplating the past. We are especially able to sense
whatever transpires in our own hearts or lives, and we know what we
feel or do. We can understand these things, whether they are in the present or in the past. This is what we mean when we say that we are conscious beings. We have an awareness (or inner recognition) of present
and past things pertaining to our moods, our actions, and ourselves. But
what we usually term *conscience* implies something more than this.
Conscience is not just the knowledge of our present or the remembrance
of our life in the past. Being aware of past or present things is only one
aspect of conscience—indeed, its least function. The main purpose of
the conscience is to excuse or accuse, to approve or disapprove, to pardon or condemn.

5. Some recent writers have given a new name to this function of the
conscience. They have chosen to call it "a moral sense." However, the
traditional word *conscience* seems preferable to the new term. If for no
other reason, this term is more common and familiar to us, and therefore
we understand it more easily. For Christians, the term *conscience* is certainly preferable for another reason: It is a biblical word, which God in
his wisdom has chosen to use in the inspired scriptures.[4]

According to the general meaning of conscience as used in the Bible,
especially in the Epistles of St. Paul, we may understand it as a capacity
or power that God has implanted in every soul that comes into the
world. Conscience is the ability to perceive what is right or wrong in
one's own heart or life, in one's attitudes, thoughts, words, and deeds.

6. But what is the measure by which we are to determine right and wrong? By what are our consciences to be guided? The Apostle Paul stated the rule of non-Christians: "What the law requires is written on their hearts." St. Paul wrote,

> The Gentiles who do not possess the outward law . . . are a law to themselves. They show the work of the law—that which the outward law prescribes, written in their hearts by the finger of God. Their consciences also bearing witness, whether they walk by this rule or not, and their thoughts the meanwhile accusing, or even excusing, acquitting, and defending them. (Rom. 2:14, 15)

The Christian standard of right and wrong, however, is the word of God, which consists of the writings of the Old and New Testament. The prophets and "men and women moved by the Holy Spirit" penned all these writings. All scripture is inspired by God and is useful for teaching the entire will of God, for reproof of what is contrary to God's will, for correcting errors, and for training in righteousness.

The Bible is a lamp to Christians' feet and a light to all their paths. Christians receive the Bible alone as their standard for right or wrong and for whatever is truly good or evil. The Christian esteems nothing good except what the Bible prescribes, either directly or by obvious inference. The Christian accounts nothing to be evil other than what the Bible forbids, either in certain terms or by obvious deduction. Whatever things the scriptures neither forbid nor command, either directly or by clear inference, the Christian believes to be of an indifferent nature. In themselves, these things are neither good nor evil. In such matters the entire and only rule is one's conscience.

7. If one's main beliefs are guided in this way, then one has "an appeal to God for a good conscience." A good conscience is what St. Paul termed a clear conscience toward God and all people. That apostle said, "Up to this day I have lived my life with a clear conscience before God." In another place he said, "I do my best always to have a clear conscience toward God and all people." In order for St. Paul to make this claim, the first absolute requirement is a correct understanding of the word of God. The Bible reveals what is God's "good and acceptable and perfect" will concerning us. It is impossible for us to obey a rule if we do not understand what it is and what it means.

Second, a good conscience (which so few have attained!) requires an honest comprehension of ourselves. We need a knowledge of our hearts and lives—that is, our inner attitudes and outward conduct. If we do not know these things, it is not possible for us to compare ourselves with God's standard.

Third, a good conscience requires harmony between our hearts and lives and the written word of God. Everything must agree with scripture—our dispositions and conduct, and our thoughts, words, and deeds. Unless conformed to the Bible, if we have any conscience at all, we can only have an evil one.

Fourth, a good conscience requires an inward discernment that we are conforming to our standard, the Bible. Only this continuing awareness is properly a good conscience or, in a phrase of St. Paul, "a clear conscience toward God and all people."

8. Let everyone who desires to have a clear conscience toward God and all people give attention to laying the proper foundation. Remember, "no one can lay any foundation other than the one that has been laid, which is Jesus Christ." And let everyone also keep in mind that no one builds on Christ except by a living faith in him. We cannot partake of Christ until we can clearly testify, "The life I now live in the flesh I live by faith in the Son of God." Let us testify that "Christ who loved me and gave himself for me" is revealed in the heart. Faith alone is the evidence, assurance, and proof of things invisible.

Faith opens the eyes of our understanding and allows divine light to pour into us. Faith enables us to "behold wondrous things in God's law." We see the excellence and purity of his revelation—the breadth and length and height and depth of every commandment contained in it. It is by faith that we behold "the light of the knowledge of the glory of God in the face of Jesus Christ" and perceive, as in a mirror, everything that is within us—yes, the inmost stirrings of our souls. Only by faith can the blessed love of God be "poured into our hearts," enabling us to love one another as Christ loved us.

By the presence of Christ within us, the Lord fulfills the gracious promise given to all the Israel of God: "I will put my laws in their minds, and write them on their hearts." This relationship with Christ produces in our souls a complete harmony with God's holy and perfect law, while "bringing every thought captive to obey Christ."

As an evil tree cannot bring forth good fruit, so a good tree cannot bring forth evil fruit. In the same way, as the hearts of believers completely and consciously conform to the standard of God's commandments, they can give glory to God for a clear conscience. With the Apostle Paul, they are able to say, "This is our boast, the testimony of our conscience: we have behaved in the world with sincerity (or holiness) and godly sincerity, not by earthly wisdom but by the grace of God."

9. In the original Greek, for the phrase, *we have behaved*, St. Paul uses a single word. The meaning of this term is very broad. *We have behaved* includes our entire manner of living, indeed, all inner and outer circumstances pertaining to soul and body. The term includes every stirring of our heart, voice, hands, and physical members of our bodies. It extends to all our relationships with God and others. It touches all our actions and words, powers and abilities, and every talent that we have received.

10. The phrase *we have behaved in the world* includes even the world of the ungodly. The phrase refers not only to how we live among the children of God (comparatively, that is a small thing) but also how we live among "the children of the devil," those who "lie under the power of the evil one." What a world we live in! How thoroughly it is saturated with the spirit of evil that it continually breathes! As our God is righteous and does only good, so the god of this world and all his children are wicked, and (to the extent that God allows) they do evil to all the children of God. Like their father the Devil, they are always lying in wait or "prowling around, looking for someone to devour." They use deception or force. They employ covert devices or open violence to destroy those who will not conform to the world. By old or new weapons and through every kind of scheme, they continually war against the souls of Christians, working to draw them back onto the broad road that leads into the snare of the devil and into destruction.

11. First, Christians are to live in such a world with sincerity. When Jesus talked about having a healthy eye (a single or clear eye) he said, "The eye is the lamp of the body. So, if your eye is healthy, your whole body will be full of light." The meaning of this verse is that what the *eye* is to the body, *intention* is to every word and deed. If therefore the eye of your soul is properly focused, all your actions and manner of life will be "full of light"—the light of heaven, love, peace, and joy in the Holy Spirit.

Also, Christians are to be sincere in their hearts. The eyes of their minds are to be fixed entirely on God. In time and eternity, we aim at God alone as our Lord, portion, strength, happiness, very great reward, and our all. This attitude constitutes the single eye, the healthy eye, the holy eye. To have a healthy eye is to have a fixed intent and a sole intention to promote God's glory. A desire to do and suffer God's blessed will runs through our whole soul, fills all our heart, and is the constant spring of our every thought, desire, and purpose.

12. Second, Christians behave in the world with godly sincerity. The difference between simplicity and sincerity seems to be chiefly that sim-

plicity pertains to the intention itself, and sincerity is our fulfilling it. Sincerity has to do not merely with what we say, but with our entire manner of living. In our text, St. Paul does not use the word *sincerity* (as he sometimes does) in the narrower sense of speaking the truth and abstaining from deception, cunning, and dishonesty. In this text he uses the word in its more extensive meaning, which is fulfilling the goal for which we aim through our simplicity. Here, in fact, simplicity implies that we speak and do everything to the glory of God—that all our words and deeds flow in a steady stream. They are to be uniformly subservient to the great goal of God's glory. In our lives, we are to move constantly toward God, walking steadily on the highway of holiness, in the paths of justice, mercy, and truth.

13. St. Paul calls this earnestness a *godly* sincerity, or simplicity. This state of being is the sincerity of God, in order to prevent our mistaking it for, or confusing it with, the sincerity of non-Christians. (They do have a kind of sincerity, or single-minded simplicity, among those whom they hold in high respect.) *Godly* sincerity, however, signifies seeking the object and goal of *God* and of every Christian virtue. Whatever does not ultimately lead to God falls among the "destitute elemental spirits." By using the term *the sincerity of God*, St. Paul also points out its source, the "Father of lights, from whom every perfect gift comes." This truth is still more clearly declared in the following words, "we have behaved in the world . . . with holiness and godly sincerity, not by earthly wisdom but by the grace of God."

14. By his use of the phrase *not with earthly wisdom*, it is as though St. Paul said that we cannot live in the world by any natural strength of understanding or naturally acquired knowledge or wisdom. He was saying that we cannot gain this simplicity or live it out in the world by relying on common sense, good character, or good breeding. This way of living rises above all our natural courage and resolution, as well as all our principles of philosophy. The power of tradition is not strong enough to bring us up to this level, nor are the most refined disciplines of human education. St. Paul might have said, "Neither could I, Paul, ever arrive at this goal, even with all the advantages I enjoyed, as long as I was in the flesh, in my natural state, and pursuing it by fleshly, natural wisdom alone."

Yet, surely, if any person could have achieved godly sincerity through natural wisdom, St. Paul might have been the one to do so. We can hardly conceive of anyone who was more highly favored with all the gifts of nature and education. In addition to his natural abilities (probably not inferior to those of any person then upon the earth), he had all the benefits of schooling. He had studied at the University of Tarsus, and afterwards Gamaliel, a person who at that time had the highest reputation for knowledge and integrity in the entire Jewish nation, tutored him. St. Paul also had all the possible advantages of religious education. He was a Pharisee, the son of a Pharisee, trained up in the very strictest sect and vocation. He stood above all others, by showing an even greater strictness than they demonstrated. In his work, he had advanced in Judaism beyond many Jews of the same age. More than all others, he was far more zealous for the traditions of his ancestors in whatever he thought would please God. "As to righteousness under the law, he was blameless."

However, through his natural abilities and professional advantages, he could never have attained Christian simplicity and godly sincerity. All his human efforts to please God were wasted labor. At last, in a deep, penetrating sense of what he really was, he cried out, "Whatever gains I had, these I have come to regard as loss because of Christ. More than that, I regard everything as loss for Christ. For his sake I have suffered the loss of all things, and I regard them as rubbish, in order that I may gain Christ."

15. Through human means, St. Paul could never reach his goal. He succeeded only through "the surpassing value of knowing Christ Jesus as Lord," or by "the grace of God," which is another expression that means the same thing. The phrase *the grace of God* is sometimes understood as that freely given love and unmerited mercy by which sinners, through the merits of Christ, are reconciled to God. However, in this instance "the grace of God" means God's power through the Holy Spirit "at work in us, enabling us to will and to work for his good pleasure."

As soon as the grace of God in his pardoning love is manifested to our souls, the grace of God in the power of his Spirit begins his work within our lives. In this way, through God, we can perform what was impossible for us in our natural state. The Holy Spirit enables us to amend our conduct. All the things that we could never achieve through human wisdom, we can do through Christ who strengthens us. Now, through simplicity and godly sincerity, we conduct ourselves in the world.

16. This work of God is rightly the foundation of Christian joy. We can now easily understand how those who have this inner witness of the spirit rejoice always. They can say, "My soul magnifies the Lord, and my spirit rejoices in God my Savior." I rejoice in him, who, of his own unmerited love and free and tender mercy, has called me into this state of salvation. In God's grace and through his power, I now stand. I rejoice because his Spirit bears witness with my spirit that I am bought with the

blood of the Lamb. Trusting in him, I am a member of Christ, a child of God, and an heir of the kingdom of heaven. I rejoice because by the Holy Spirit the understanding of God's love to me has brought me to love him. And for his sake, I love every child of Adam, every soul that God has created. I rejoice because he enables me to perceive in myself "the mind that was in Christ."

This mind is one of simplicity, which is a single eye to God in every stirring of the heart. Singleness of mind is a power always to fix the loving eye of one's soul on him who loved us and gave himself for us. Having the mind of Christ is only to aim for him and his glorious will in everything we think, speak, or do. It is purity that desires nothing more than God. This purity means "crucifying the flesh with its passions and desires," and "setting our minds on things that are above, not on things that are on earth."

Having the mind of Christ is holiness, a recovery of the image of God. It is a renewal of the soul "after his likeness," a "godly sincerity," directing all our words and deeds to advance God's glory. Yes, we also rejoice and continue to rejoice because our consciences bear us witness in the Holy Spirit, by the light that he continually gives us. He enables us to "lead a life worthy of the calling to which we have been called." We "abstain from every form of evil," "fleeing from sin as from a snake."

As we have opportunity, we do every kind of good we can to all people. We follow our Lord in all our steps and do what is pleasing in his sight. We rejoice because, through the inspiration of God's Holy Spirit, we both understand and sense that he enables all our works. Yes, it is God within us who makes possible our good works. We rejoice in seeing, by the light of God that shines in our hearts, that we have the power to walk in his ways. And through his grace we do not turn aside to the right or the left.

17. I have explained the foundation and nature of that joy in which a mature Christian continually celebrates. From this explanation we may easily conclude several things: First, this joy does not come from any human source or natural cause. It does not come from any sudden burst of emotion. Such an occurrence may produce an onset of joy that is temporary, but the Christian rejoices continually. Christian joy cannot depend on physical health, comfort, strength, or a sound body. The contentment that God gives remains equally strong in sickness and in pain. Indeed, perhaps joy is far stronger in discomfort than in good health and easy circumstances. Many Christians have never experienced any joy to be compared with the joy that filled their souls when their bodies were almost worn out with pain, or exhausted with grievous sickness.

Least of all, can true joy be attributed to material prosperity, the favor of others, or the abundance of worldly things. When the faith of Christians is tried as by fire and by all kinds of outward afflictions, they rejoice in God, whom, although unseen, they love with an indescribable and glorious joy. Surely, never have people rejoiced like those who were treated as "rubbish of the world, the dregs of all things." These children of God wandered from place to place, needing every material thing. They endured hunger, cold, nakedness, trials, "cruel derision," and "even chains and imprisonment." Yes, they finally "counted not their lives valuable, in order to finish their courses with joy."

18. Second, from the preceding considerations we may conclude that the joy of a Christian does not arise from having a blind conscience or from not being able to discern good from evil. Far from it! Christians were complete strangers to the joy of the Lord until God opened their eyes of understanding. They did not know true joy until their spiritual senses were enlivened to discern spiritual good and evil. The eyes of their souls did not grow dim (never before had they been clear-sighted). The Christians' quick perceptions of even the smallest things are a source of amazement to those that do not know God.

As a speck is visible in the light of a sunbeam, so it is that every trace of sin becomes visible to the Christian who is walking in the light of the eternal Son of God. Christians no longer close the eyes of conscience. Blind sleep is now a thing of the past. Their souls are always wide awake—no more slumber or folding of the hands to rest. Christians are always standing on the watchtower and listening to what their Lord will say. Always, Christians rejoice in this one thing—"seeing him who is invisible."

19. Third, neither does the joy of a Christian arise from any form of spiritual ignorance or coldness of conscience. It is true that those whose "senseless minds are darkened," whose hearts are hardened, unfeeling, apathetic, and therefore without spiritual understanding, may experience a kind of joy. They may even delight in committing sin, which they will probably call "liberty!" This "freedom," however, is only a simple stupor of the soul, a fatal dullness of the spirit and the ignorant blindness of a seared conscience. By contrast, Christians have an acute sensibility to God, a sensibility which previously they could never have imagined possible. Since the love of God began to reign in their hearts, Christians have received sensitive consciences never before known to them. Now, their privilege and joy is that God hears their daily prayer:

> O that my tender soul might fly
> The first abhorr'd approach of ill,

> Quick as the apple of an eye,
> The slightest touch of sin to feel.[5]

20. I conclude by saying that Christian joy delights to obey God; it is gladness in loving God and in keeping his commandments. Yet, keeping the commandments of God is not for the purpose of fulfilling the conditions of the covenant of works. It is not through any works of righteousness that we have done that we obtain pardon and acceptance with God. Not at all! God has already pardoned and accepted Christians through his mercy in Christ Jesus. It is not by our own obedience that we can obtain life and become free from the death of sin. Christians already have life through the grace of God. God has made alive those who "were dead through trespasses and sins." Now we are "alive to God, through Jesus Christ our Lord."

In holy love and happy obedience, Christians rejoice to walk according to the covenant of grace. They exult in knowing that "being justified through his grace," we have "not accepted the grace of God in vain." God has freely reconciled us to himself—not because of our determination or labors, but through the blood of the Lamb. So, we keep God's commandments in the strength that he has given us.

God has "girded us with strength for the battle," and we joyfully "fight the good fight of the faith." Through him who lives in our hearts by faith, we rejoice to "take hold of eternal life." This gift is our cause for rejoicing. Our "Father is still working;" therefore, we also perform the works of God—although not in our own strength or wisdom, but through the power of God's Spirit freely given in Christ Jesus. May God work in us that which is pleasing in his sight! To God belongs the glory and the power forever and ever.

Note: This sermon describes the experience of those who are strong in faith. It may discourage those who are weak in faith, but the next sermon may be helpful to them. —John Wesley

Notes

1. Jackson, *Wesley's Works*, 10:220.
2. Ibid., 10:208..
3. Franz Hildebrandt and Oliver A. Beckerlegge, *The Works of John Wesley,* Bicentennial Ed. (Nashville: Abingdon Press, 1983), *A Collection of Hymns for the Use of the People Called Methodists*, Hymn #207, stanza 3, 7:338.
4. The KJV, which Wesley used, employs the word *conscience* 31 times.
5. Charles Wesley, "Watch in All Things," stanza 10, *Poet. Wks.*, 2:273.

ON SIN IN BELIEVERS

In Wesley's day, certain zealots claimed to be free from the power of sin and "the very being of sin." Moreover, they claimed that believers became entirely sinless at the moment they were converted to Christ. Many of these people were followers of Count Nikolaus Ludwig von Zinzendorf, the leader of the Moravian Christians. Count Zinzendorf was a generous and charitable man, but he lacked theological understanding. Indeed, he belittled theological study. The following conversation took place between Wesley and Zinzendorf:

> **Wesley:** Does not every believer, while he increases in love, increase equally in holiness?
>
> **Zinzendorf:** Not at all. In the moment he is justified, he is sanctified wholly. From that time he is neither more nor less holy, even unto death.
>
> **Wesley:** Is not therefore a father in Christ holier than a newborn babe?
>
> **Zinzendorf:** No. Our whole justification and sanctification are in the same instant, and he receives neither more nor less.
>
> **Wesley:** Does not a true believer increase in love to God daily? Is he perfected in love when he is justified?
>
> **Zinzendorf:** He is. He never can increase in the love of God. He loves altogether in that moment, as he is sanctified wholly.

Wesley was exasperated by Zinzendorf's confused interpretation of Scripture and his lack of understanding of the Christian experience. In the sermon's conclusion Wesley said that denying the presence of sin in believers "leads to the most fatal of consequences. It cuts off all our need to guard against our evil nature, against Samson's 'Delilah.'" Wesley saw the evils to which this innovative notion led, and this sermon brilliantly speaks to the issue.

Wesley's study, personal experience, and observation confirmed the truth of the church's teaching about sin in believers. The Thirty-nine Articles state, "This infection of nature [sin] doth remain, yea in them that are regenerated."[1] Wesley's sermon explains that throughout Christian history Protestants and Roman Catholics alike recognize that sin remains in believers. With regard to Christian discipleship, the implications of this reality are enormous. For example, if new Christians are without sin, in what sense do they need to discipline themselves in their spiritual warfare against the world, the flesh, and the devil? Indeed, all the churches' ministries of spiritual formation are predicated on the fact that there is sin in believers. Only the Moravian Christians taught that there is no sin in new Christians. Wesley pointed out that this innovative doctrine cannot be reconciled with the Bible, church doctrine, or common experience. For him, if a doctrine is new, it is not true; and if it is true, it is not new.

Wesley contends in this sermon that, although justification marks a momentous change in one's life, the new birth does not remove all traces of sin in believers. Toward the end of this discourse, Wesley states, "The doctrine that there is no sin in believers tears away the defense of weak believers, deprives them of their need to trust, and therefore leaves them exposed to all the assaults of the world, the flesh, and the devil."

This sermon recognizes that there are two opposing tendencies existing within new Christians. These contrary tendencies are nature and grace, flesh and spirit, love for self and love for God. New Christians are indeed initially sanctified, but they are not entirely sanctified. They are, at the same time, both spiritual and carnal. God calls them to a journey that leads to holiness, entire sanctification, and fruitful service. This sermon shows the way.

ON SIN IN BELIEVERS

If anyone is in Christ, that person is created anew.
(2 Corinthians 5:17)

I. The question of sin in Christian believers

1 Do those who are in Christ have sin remaining within them? Is there any sin in those that are born of God, or do they have complete deliverance from it? Let no one imagine that this question is one of simple curiosity or that the answer makes little difference one way or the other. Most certainly, this question is one of utmost importance for every serious Christian. Resolving this matter very greatly concerns both one's present and eternal happiness.

2. Yet, I do not know that the question was ever argued in the ancient Church. Indeed, there was no room for debating this matter, because all Christians agreed on the subject. Furthermore, as far as I have observed, the entire company of ancient Christians who left us anything in writing stated their views with one voice. They believed that even believers in Christ, until they are "strong in the Lord and in the strength of his power," need to struggle against "enemies of flesh and blood" as well as against "cosmic powers."

3. In this matter (as in most points), our own church exactly duplicates the view of the ancient church. Our church teaches:

Original sin is the corruption of the nature of every man, whereby man is in his own nature inclined to evil, so that the flesh lusts against the Spirit. And this infection of nature does remain, indeed, in them that are regenerated; whereby the lust of the flesh is not subject to the law of God. And although there is no condemnation for them that believe, yet this lust has of itself the nature of sin.[2]

4. The same testimony is given by all other Christian Churches—not only by the Greek and Roman Churches, but by every Protestant Church in Europe, of whatever denomination. Indeed, some of these churches seem to carry the matter too far. They describe the corruption of heart in believers in a way that scarcely allows that they can ever have victory over sin. Because these churches place such a strong emphasis on sin in believers, Christians are said to be in perpetual bondage to sin. These churches barely allow any distinction between believers and unbelievers.

5. To avoid this extreme position, many well-meaning people, particularly those under the teaching of the late Count Zinzendorf, ran to another extreme. They affirmed that "all true believers are not only saved from the dominion of sin, but from the being of inward and outward sin, so that sin no longer remains in them." And about twenty years ago, many of our countrymen absorbed this opinion from them—namely, the view that those who believe in Christ have no sinful nature corrupting them.

6. It is true that when the German Moravians were prodded about this subject many of them soon admitted that "sin did still remain in the flesh, but not in the heart of a believer." After a time, when the absurdity of this view was shown, they rightly gave up the point, admitting that sin did still remain in the one that is born of God, although it does not reign.

7. However, the English Moravians that had received this doctrine from them (some of them received it directly from Mr. Zinzendorf, and some of them received it second or third hand) were not so easily persuaded to part with a favorite opinion. Even when most of them were convinced that this teaching was utterly indefensible, a few could not be persuaded to give it up. Even to this day, they continue to maintain this opinion.

II. Victory over sin is available to Christian believers

1. For the sake of those Christians who really do reverence God and want to know "the truth as it is in Jesus," is it not appropriate to con-

sider the matter calmly and impartially? In doing so, I will use synonymously the words, *regenerate, justified*, and *believers*, even though these terms do not have precisely the same meaning. (*Regenerate* refers to an inward, actual change; *justify* refers to a relative change; and *believers* implies the means by which the other two take place.) Still, these terms essentially mean the same thing, because every person who believes is both justified and born of God.

2. By the term *sin*, here I am referring to inward sin. I mean any sinful disposition, emotion, or affection, such as pride, self-will, and any kind of love of the world—for example, lust, anger, or any inclination contrary to the mind that was in Christ.

3. The question we are discussing is not about outward sin or about whether a child of God commits overt sins. We all agree and solemnly affirm that "Everyone who continues in the practice of sin is a child of the devil." We also agree that "those who have been born of God do not continue to sin." Neither are we investigating whether inward sin will always remain in the children of God—that is, whether sin will continue in the soul as long as it continues in the body. Furthermore, we are not investigating whether a justified person can slip back into either inward or outward sin. We are simply asking, "Are justified or regenerate persons freed from all sinful tendencies as soon as they are justified?" We are asking, "Is there after justification no sin in one's heart then or ever, unless one falls from grace?"

4. We acknowledge that the state of justified persons is inexpressibly great and glorious. Believers are born again, "not of blood or of the will of the flesh or of the will of man, but of God." They are children of God, members of Christ, and heirs of the kingdom of heaven. "The peace of God, which surpasses all understanding, guards their hearts and minds in Christ Jesus." The Christian's very body is a "temple of the Holy Spirit," and a "dwelling place for God" through the Holy Spirit. Christians are "created anew" in Christ Jesus; they are washed and sanctified. Their hearts are purified by faith and cleansed from the corruption that is in the world. "God's love has been poured into their hearts through the Holy Spirit."

As long as they "live in love" (which one may always do), they worship God in spirit and in truth. They "obey God's commandments and do what pleases him," doing their best "always to have a clear conscience toward God and all people." And from the moment people are justified, they have authority over both outward and inward sin.

III. The sin that remains in Christian believers

1. Some may object, "But are not new believers freed from all sin, so that no corruption remains in their hearts?" I cannot say this. I cannot believe it. St. Paul speaks to the contrary. He is addressing believers and describing their state when he says, "What the flesh desires is opposed to the Spirit, and what the Spirit desires is opposed to the flesh; for these are opposed to each other." Nothing can be more explicit. Here, the apostle directly affirms that the flesh, or evil nature, exists even in believers. And the flesh opposes the Spirit. He states that two principles still remain in regenerate people and that these principles are "opposed to each other."

2. Elsewhere, St. Paul writes to the believers at Corinth as those who were sanctified in Christ Jesus. He says, "I could not speak to you as spiritual people, but rather as people of the flesh, as infants in Christ. For as long as there is jealousy and quarreling among you, are you not of the flesh, and behaving according to human inclinations?" Here, the apostle speaks to those who were undoubtedly Christian believers. In the same breath, he refers to them both as brothers and sisters and also as still being, in a measure, "people of the flesh," or carnal. He affirmed that there was jealousy (an evil disposition) and quarreling among them.

Yet he does not in the least suggest that they had lost their faith. Indeed, he clearly declared they had not done so, because he called them infants *in Christ*. And, what is most noteworthy of all, he speaks of being carnally minded and being infants in Christ as both being true at the same time. In this way, St. Paul clearly explains that while Christians are infants in Christ, to some degree they are carnal.

3. Certainly, this important point runs through all the epistles of the Apostle Paul. Indeed, it runs through all the Holy Scriptures. There are two contrary principles in believers—nature and grace, the flesh and the Spirit. Almost all the biblical admonitions and encouragements to Christians are based on this assumption. Counsel is aimed at wrong dispositions or practices in those who the inspired writers acknowledge as believers. And the apostles always encouraged Christians to fight with and conquer these flaws by the power of faith that was in them.

4. We cannot doubt that there was faith in the church at Ephesus. Our Lord said to the people, "I know your works, your toil and your patient endurance. You are enduring patiently and bearing up for the sake of my name, and you have not grown weary." Yet, at the same time, was there no sin in the Ephesian church? There was indeed, or else Christ would not have added, "I have this against you, that you have abandoned the love you had at first." This cooling of love for Christ was real sin that

God saw in the church—the sin for which the church was admonished to repent. We have no authority to say that the Ephesian Church had no authentic faith.

5. The church at Pergamum was also encouraged to repent. This admonition implies that sin was present. At the same time, our Lord explicitly says, "You did not deny your faith in me." And to the church in Sardis, Christ said, "Strengthen what remains and is at the point of death." The good that remained was ready to die, but it was not actually dead. We conclude that there was still a spark of faith in the church, to which, accordingly, the church at Sardis was admonished to hold fast.

6. Once again, when St. Paul encouraged believers to "cleanse themselves from every defilement of body and of spirit," he clearly taught that those believers were not yet fully cleansed. Will you respond by saying, "The one that abstains from every form of evil, by the very nature of the case, cleanses himself from all filthiness?" That supposition is not at all true. For instance, if someone vilifies me I may feel bitterness, which is uncleanness in my spirit. If I do not respond to that person outwardly and if I "abstain from every form of evil," my lack of an outward response does not cleanse me from the bitter spirit I feel, to my distress.

7. The view that "there is no sin in believers, no carnal mind, no inclination to backslide" is contrary to the word of God. It is also contrary to the experience of God's sons and daughters. Christian believers constantly feel their hearts disposed to backslide. They have a natural tendency toward evil, a proneness to depart from God and cling to the things of earth. Daily, they are aware that iniquity remains in their hearts. Pride, self-will, unbelief, and sin cling to everything they say and do—even to their highest behavior and holiest obligations.

At the same time, they "know that they are God's children." They cannot doubt it for an instant. They sense God's Spirit clearly "bearing witness with their spirits that they are children of God." "They even boast in God through our Lord Jesus Christ, through whom we have now received reconciliation." Thus, they are equally assured both that sin is in them and also that "Christ is in them, the hope of glory."

8. Someone may ask, "Can Christ be in the same heart where sin is?" I answer that without a doubt he can, otherwise the heart would not need to be cleansed from sin. Where sickness is, there is the physician.

> Never will He thence depart,
> Inmate of an humble heart;
> Carrying on His work within,
> Striving till He cast out sin.[3]

Christ cannot reign where sin reigns. Neither will he dwell where any sin is allowed. However, he dwells in the hearts of believers who fight against every sin—even if they are not yet cleansed "in accordance with the sanctuary's rules of cleanness."

9. I have already observed that the opposing doctrine—that there is no sin in believers—is quite new in the church of Christ. It was never heard of for seventeen hundred years, not until Count Zinzendorf invented the notion. I do not remember ever seeing the least hint of this opinion either in any ancient or modern writer, unless perhaps in the writings of some of the unconstrained, raving Antinomians. These teachers at the same time affirmed and denied this doctrine, allowing that there was sin in their flesh, but not in their hearts. Whatever doctrine is newly invented must also be false, because the apostolic religion is the only true one. No doctrine can be right unless it accords with the same doctrine that was "from the beginning."

10. We may state one more argument against this new and unscriptural doctrine—the doctrine's destructive consequences. Suppose someone says, "I felt angry today." I must reply, "If Christians have no sin and you have anger, then you are not a Christian." Another might say, "I know that what you are saying is correct, but my will is quite opposed to it." I must tell him, "If Christians have no sin, then you are not a Christian because you have sin and you are under the wrath of God."

What will be the normal consequence of these exchanges? If one believes what I say, his or her soul will be grieved and wounded, and perhaps completely destroyed because he or she will "abandon that confidence which brings a great reward." And having abandoned one's shield, how can one "quench all the flaming arrows of the evil one?" How will one conquer the world—seeing that "the victory that conquers the world is our faith?" That one stands disarmed in the midst of his enemies, open to all their assaults. It is little wonder, then, if such people are completely defeated and enemies capture them at will. Is it any surprise that people will plunge from one wickedness to another, and never any more receive good? Therefore, by no means can I accept the notion that, starting from the moment they are justified, there is no sin in believers.

First, the doctrine is contrary to the entire tone of Scripture. Second, the doctrine is contrary to the experience of the children of God. Third, the doctrine is utterly new, and until yesterday it was never heard of in the world. Finally, the doctrine naturally leads to the most fatal consequences. This teaching not only harms those that God has not harmed, but it may drag them into everlasting damnation.

IV. Answers to objections

1. Let us now give a fair hearing to the chief arguments of those who try to support the doctrine that there is no sin in believers. First, they attempt to prove their idea from the Bible. They argue, "The scripture says that every believer who is born of God is clean, holy, sanctified, and pure in heart. The believer's heart is a temple of the Holy Spirit." They say, "Now, as what is born of the flesh is flesh and altogether evil, so what is born of the Spirit is spirit and is altogether good." They continue, "Christians cannot be clean, sanctified, and holy, while at the same time be unclean, unsanctified, and unholy. They cannot at once be pure and impure, nor have a new and an old heart at the same time. Neither can their souls be unholy, while they are 'temples of the Holy Spirit.'" I have represented this objection as strongly as possible, so that its full weight will come into view. Let us now examine it, part by part.

(i) Let us look at the claim, "What is born of the Spirit is spirit, and altogether good." I acknowledge the actual scripture verse, but not the added comment about it. The biblical text affirms only that every person who is "born of the Spirit" has become a spiritual person. That is true, but I contend that one may be a spiritual person, and yet not be *thoroughly* spiritual. The Christians at Corinth were spiritual people; otherwise, they would not have been Christians at all. Still, they were not altogether spiritual. In part, they were still carnally minded. Someone might object, "But they had fallen away from grace." St. Paul says, "No." Even in their immature state, the Corinthian Christians were still infants in Christ.

(ii) How should one reply to the claim, "One cannot be clean, sanctified, and holy, while at the same time be unclean, unsanctified, and unholy?" I answer that one may indeed be both at the same time. The Corinthian Christians were in this condition. "You were washed," says the apostle, "you were sanctified," that is, cleansed from "fornication, idolatry, drunkenness" and all other outward sin. Yet, at the same time, in another sense of the word they were unsanctified; they were not washed. They were not inwardly cleansed from envy, evil suspicion, and prejudice.

Objectors might say, "But surely, they did not have a new heart and an old heart at the same time." I answer that it is most certain they did have two natures. They were Christians, and their hearts were truly renewed, but not entirely renewed. Their carnal minds were nailed to the cross; yet their carnality was not totally destroyed. One might object, "But could they be unholy while they were at the same time 'temples of the Holy Spirit?'" I reply that it is certain that they were temples of the Holy Spirit, yet it is equally certain that in some degree they were carnal, that is, unholy.

2. The objector might say, "There is one more scripture that will resolve the question: 'If anyone is in Christ, there is a new creation: everything old has passed away; see, everything has become new.' Certainly one cannot be a new creation and an old creation at the same time." To this objection, I answer, "Yes, one most certainly can." One may be *partially* renewed, which was the case with those at Corinth. Undoubtedly, they were "renewed in the spirit of their minds." Otherwise, they could not have been "infants in Christ." Still, their entire minds were not renewed. This fact is evident, because they envied one another.

The objector might say, "But the scripture explicitly says, 'everything old has passed away; everything has become new.' And we must not interpret the apostle's words so as to make him contradict himself. If we will allow him to be consistent with himself, the obvious meaning of the words leads us to conclude that the believer's old understanding of justification, holiness, happiness, indeed everything about God in general has now passed away, including his former desires, plans, affections, dispositions, and conduct."

I answer that all these areas of a believer's life do undeniably become new, greatly changed from what they once were. And yet, although they are new, they are not *completely* new. To their sorrow and shame, new believers still feel the remains of the earlier self. Carnal believers sense the presence of the obvious imperfections of their former disposition and affections. However, believers do not need to come under sin's mastery so long as they discipline themselves in prayer.

3. The sum of the entire position that there is no sin in believers is as follows: "If one is clean, then he is completely clean; if he is holy, he is entirely holy." (It is easy to compile twenty more expressions of the same sort.) However, this way of arguing is really no better than a play on words. The fallacy in this argument is that of moving from the particular to the general; it is drawing a universal conclusion from a particular assumption. Pose the argument in its entirety, and it runs this way: "If one is holy in any degree, then he is completely holy." That conclusion is not a valid one. Infants in Christ are holy, and yet they are not entirely holy. They are to a degree free from sin; yet not fully free. Sin remains in new believers, although it does not reign within them.

If you conjecture that sin does not remain in newborn Christians (whatever may be the case with mature Christians), you certainly have not considered the height, and depth, and length, and breadth of the law of God. I am speaking of the law of love, as given by St. Paul in the thirteenth chapter of 1 Corinthians. Nor have you adequately considered that every failure to conform to the law is sin. Is there no lack of compliance to this law in the heart or life of an infant in Christ? (Whatever may be the case with a mature Christian, that is another question.) One must be a stranger to human nature if one remotely imagines that every immature Christian fully complies with the law of love as it is stated in 1 Corinthians 13!

4. Again, the disputant may posit another objection: "But believers walk 'according to the Spirit.' Because the Spirit of God dwells in them, consequently believers are delivered from the guilt and power of sin—in a word, from the existence of sin."

I answer this assertion by pointing out that the argument unites the presence of the Holy Spirit and the absence of sin as if they are the same things. But they are *not* the same thing. The *guilt* of sin is one thing, the *power* of sin is another, and the *existence* of sin is still another. I acknowledge that believers are delivered from the guilt and power of sin, but I deny that they are delivered from the *existence* of sin. Furthermore, none of the biblical texts proves otherwise. Christians may have the Spirit of God dwelling in them and "walk according to the Spirit," while at the same time they still feel "the flesh opposing the Spirit."

5. The objector may say, "But the church is the body of Christ. This fact implies that the members of the church are washed from all filthiness. Otherwise it will follow that Christ and Belial are joined with each other."

I answer, "No. The conclusion does not follow from the premise." Those who constitute the mystical body of Christ still feel the flesh opposing the Spirit. Christ has no fellowship with the devil or with sin; indeed, Christ enables Christians to resist the devil and to overcome sin.

6. Again, someone may object, "But have not Christians come to the 'heavenly Jerusalem' where 'nothing unclean can enter?'" I answer, "Yes, and they belong to 'an innumerable company of angels, and take their place among the spirits of the righteous made perfect.'"

> Him let earth and heaven proclaim,
> Earth and heaven record His name,
> Let us both in this agree,
> Both His one great family.[4]

As the company of angels and saints, believers are likewise holy and undefiled, so long as they "walk according to the Spirit." However, they are aware that there is another principle in them—the flesh. And the flesh and the spirit "are opposed to each other."

7. The objector may say, "But Christians are reconciled to God. This could not be true if any carnal disposition remained in them, for 'the carnal mind is hostile to God.' Consequently, there cannot be any reconciliation with God, except by the destruction of the mind that is set upon the flesh."

I answer that we are reconciled to God through the blood of the cross. In that instant, the mind of the flesh, the corruption of nature, which is enmity with God, is put under our feet. Although the flesh has no more dominion over the Christian, it continues to exist, and in its nature it is still hostile to God, warring against his Spirit.

8. The objector may contend, "But those who belong to Christ Jesus have crucified the flesh with its passions and desires." I reply that Christians have indeed nailed the flesh to the cross, but the flesh still remains in them, and it often struggles to come down from the cross.

Someone might counter, "No. Christians have 'stripped off the old self with its practices.'" I agree that they have and that "everything old has passed away; see, everything has become new." A hundred texts may be cited to the same effect; and they all yield the same answer. To say everything in a word, "Christ gave himself for the Church, that it might be without a spot or wrinkle." And in the end God's plan shall be completed. However, from the beginning until now, this plan yet awaits complete fulfillment.

9. Someone may argue, "But let experience speak. At the moment of justification, everyone finds that they become completely free from all sin." I reply that I doubt that they do. If they are completely free from all sin, do they afterward continue in this state? If you say, "If they do not, it is their fault," I say that your theory remains yet to be demonstrated.

10. Perhaps someone might contend, "In the very nature of things, can one have inner pride without it inescapably expressing itself in haughty behavior? Can one have any anger in him without it unavoidably leading to enraged actions?"

I answer that people may have pride in their hearts, and in some areas of their lives they may regard themselves more highly than they should. Therefore, in that detail they behave haughtily. Yet, they may not be proud persons in their overall character. They may have a degree of anger in their hearts, even strong inclinations toward wrath. Yet, it is not necessary for them to give in to the anger they feel. You might object, "Can anger and pride reside in a heart where there is *nothing else* but modesty and humility?" I answer, "Of course not. However, pride and anger may be in the heart where there is *much* modesty and humility."

You may object, "It does no good to say that these dispositions may be present in the heart, but that they do not *reign* in the heart. Sin cannot exist in any form or degree where it does not reign, because guilt and power are essential characteristics of sin. Therefore where *any* sin exists in the heart, *everything* in the life must be sinful."

I respond that this is strange reasoning indeed! Are you really saying that sin cannot exist in any degree, where it does not totally reign? Such a notion is absolutely contrary to the experience of everyone; it is contrary to the sum total of scripture and all common sense. For instance, resentment in response to an insult is sinful and incompatible with the law of love. This attitude has existed in me a thousand times. Yet it did not reign in me, nor does it now.

You may insist, "But guilt and power are necessary components of sin; therefore, where one is present the entire life is sinful." I reply, "Not at all. In the example before us, if I do not for an instant yield to the resentment I feel, there is no guilt. And God does not condemn me for what I only *feel*." In this case, sin has no power. Even though what I feel is opposed to the Spirit, it cannot prevail. Therefore, in this example as in ten thousand other instances, there is the presence of sin's influence, without either its guilt or power.

11. Again, you may object, "But the assumption that there is sin in a believer contains the seeds of everything that is fearful and discouraging. It implies that we must contend with a force that governs us and takes control of our hearts, working in defiance of our Redeemer."

My response is that I do not accept this argument. The acknowledgment that there is sin in believers does not mean that it must govern them, any more than saying that one who is crucified has control over those that are crucifying him. Still less does the presence of sin in believers imply that sin controls their hearts. Satan, the intruder, still remains where he once reigned, but now he lives in chains. In some sense, Satan does war against the Redeemer, but he grows weaker and weaker. At the same time, the believer continues from strength to strength, conquering and yet to conquer.

12. Still, you may further object, "I am not satisfied yet. Those who have sin in them are slaves to sin. Therefore, you presume that people are justified while they are slaves to sin. Mr. Wesley, you say that Christians may be justified while they have pride, anger, or unbelief in them. If

you maintain that these sins (at least for a time) are in all who are justified, is it any wonder that we have so many proud, angry, unbelieving believers?"

I respond by saying that I do not suggest that all who are justified are also slaves to sin. However, I do think that sin remains (at least for a time) in everyone who is justified.

Someone may protest, "But, if sin remains in believers, they are sinful people. For instance, if pride is in Christians, then they are proud; if self-will is in Christians, then they are obstinate. If unbelief is in them, then they are skeptics—consequently, they are not even Christian believers. How do they differ from unbelievers, from unregenerate people?"

I reply that this train of thought is only a mere play on words. It means no more than if there is sin, pride, or self-will in certain Christians, these things are present. In that sense, no one can deny that they are proud or self-willed. But they are not proud or self-willed in the same sense as unbelievers who are *governed* by pride or self-will. Christians differ from unregenerate people who willingly obey sin. Christians do not. Fleshly impulses are present in both believers and unbelievers, yet unregenerate people "walk according to the flesh," while Christians "walk according to the Spirit."

You may object, "But how can unbelief be in believers?" I answer that the word *unbelief* has two meanings. It can mean *no faith*, or it can mean *weak faith*. The word can mean the *absence* of faith or the *frailty* of faith. In the first sense, unbelief is not in a believer; in the second sense, frail faith is in every infant in Christ. The faith of immature believers is commonly mixed with doubt or fear; it is *weak* faith. Jesus asked, "Why are you afraid, you of little faith?" Speaking to his disciple Peter, Jesus shows us that Peter, a believer, had fragile faith and much disbelief.

13. Once again, the objector may counter, "But the doctrine that sin remains in Christian believers implies that they may be in God's favor while sin still remains in their hearts." I reply that if we understand the doctrine correctly, no such consequence necessarily follows. Christians may be in God's favor even if they *feel* sin, but not if they *yield* to sin. Believers that have sin still in them do not forfeit their favor with God; however, giving way to sin does indeed lead to God's disfavor. Although your flesh opposes the Spirit, you may still be a child of God. But if you "walk according to the flesh," you are a child of the devil. The doctrine of sin in believers does not encourage us to obey sin, but to resist it with all our might.

V. The nature of flesh and spirit

1. The sum of all we have been saying about sin in believers is as follows: In all Christians, even after they are justified, there are two contrary principles—human nature and divine grace. St. Paul calls these principles *flesh* and *Spirit*. Consequently, even though infants in Christ are sanctified, they are only partially sanctified. To a degree, according to the measure of their faith, they are spiritual. Yet, to a degree they are also still carnally minded. Accordingly, scripture repeatedly encourages believers to guard against the flesh as well as the world and the devil. The consistent experience of the children of God confirms this reality. While they sense the witness of the Spirit in themselves, they also sense a carnal propensity that has not completely yielded to the will of God. They know that they are in Christ; and yet they find that their hearts are inclined to depart from him. In many instances, they sense within themselves a tendency toward evil and a reluctance to do what is good.

The strange doctrine that there is no sin in believers is a completely new one. It has never been heard of in the church of Christ, from the time of his coming into the world until the time of Count Zinzendorf. That view leads to the most fatal of consequences. It cuts off all our need to guard against our evil nature, against Samson's "Delilah." We are told that she is gone, although she is still lying at our bosom. The doctrine that there is no sin in believers tears away the defense of weak believers, deprives them of their need to trust, and therefore this doctrine leaves them exposed to all the assaults of the world, the flesh, and the devil.

2. Let us, therefore, hold fast to the sound doctrine "that was once and for all entrusted to the saints." The saints have transmitted this faith through the written word to all succeeding generations. This faith is that, although we are renewed, cleansed, purified, and sanctified the instant we truly believe in Christ, yet at that point we are not *completely* renewed, cleansed, and purified. The flesh, the evil nature, still remains (although it is subdued) and the flesh still wars against the Spirit.

For that reason, let us use all diligence in "fighting the good fight of the faith." So much the more, let us earnestly "stay awake and pray" against the enemy within. All the more carefully, let us take ourselves in hand and "put on the whole armor of God." Although "we struggle against flesh and blood" and "against the rulers, against the authorities, against the cosmic powers of this present darkness," we are able "to withstand on that evil day, and having done everything, to stand firm."

Notes

1. Thirty-nine Articles, Art. 9.
2. Thirty-nine Articles, Art. 9.
3. Charles Wesley, "Hymn for Whitsunday," stanza 4, *Poet. Wks.* I:188.
4. Charles Wesley, "The Communion of the Saints," part VI, stanza 1, *Poet. Wks.*, I, 364.

Introduction to Sermon 14

THE REPENTANCE OF BELIEVERS

The *Repentance of Believers* logically follows the previous sermon, *On Sin in Believers*. Concerning repentance, John Wesley taught, "Repentance is of two sorts; that which is termed legal, and that which is styled evangelical repentance. The former . . . is a thorough conviction of sin. The latter is a change of heart (and consequently of life) from all sin to all holiness."[1] He preached that the first kind of repentance is necessary to become a Christian, and the second kind of repentance is necessary to *grow* as a Christian.

Wesley states in this sermon that the repentance of believers is "full as necessary, in order to our continuance and growth in grace, as the former faith and repentance were in order to our entering into the kingdom of God." The repentance of *unbelievers* is the repentance that precedes justification, and scripture terms it "the repentance that leads to life." Wesley describes this repentance as "a conviction of our utter sinfulness and guiltiness and helplessness, and which precedes our receiving [the] kingdom of God."[2] On the other hand, the repentance of *believers* is the repentance that leads to growth, sanctification, and holiness.

In *The Principles of a Methodist Farther Explained*, Wesley said,

> I have again and again, with all the plainness I could, declared what our constant doctrines are; whereby we are distinguished only from Heathens, or nominal Christians; not from any that worship God in spirit and in truth. Our main doctrines, which include all the rest, are three, — that of repentance, of faith, and of holiness. The first of these we account, as it were, the porch of religion; the next, the door; the third, religion itself.[3]

228

The repentance of believers moves them toward holiness, and this repentance takes place recurrently throughout one's Christian life.

This sermon contains three divisions: (1) The believers' convictions of the sin that remains in their hearts. This malady includes sins of omission and commission. These lapses include sloth, pride, self will, love of the world, covetousness, and inclinations contrary to love. (2) The believers' convictions of their personal flaws, failings, unworthiness, and continuing necessity of the atoning blood of Jesus Christ. (3) The believers' convictions of their utter helplessness and dependence on God's mercy and help in every area of their lives.

The repentance of believers moves them toward full sanctification. We have seen that Wesley did not believe that Christian conversion lifts one immediately into a state of sinless perfection. The flesh continues to war against the spirit; nature resists grace; self-will struggles against God's will. Honest Christians are forced to face the presence of lingering attitudes that are contrary to holiness of heart and life. Jealousy, resentment, covetousness, envy, willfulness, and imbalance do not disappear when one comes to faith in Christ. The lure of the world continues to beckon. In this sermon Wesley states, "Self-will and pride are types of idolatry, and both are directly contrary to the love of God. The same analysis can be made concerning the love of the world. True believers are likewise inclined to sense in themselves a love for the present age. More or less, sooner or later, in one area or another, every believer recognizes it."

Wesley highlights the truth that Christian believers have an advocate with God the Father. Furthermore, there is no condemnation for those who are in Christ. Yet self-aware believers cannot deny their sins of commission and omission. Clearly, therefore, the repentance of believers has an important place in the Christian life. Here, Wesley points out that a Christian's conviction of lingering sin constitutes an essential component of God's process of full redemption.

In addition to helping believers grow toward Christian maturity, this sermon can also serve to restore backsliders. If Wesley believed that Christians could fall from grace, he also believed that backslidden Christians could be restored. Elsewhere he wrote, "If it be asked, 'Do any real apostates find mercy from God?' Do any that have 'made shipwreck of faith and a good conscience,' recover what they have lost? Do you know, have you seen, any instance of persons who found redemption in the blood of Jesus, and afterwards fell away, and yet were restored, — renewed again to repentance? Yea, verily; and not one, or an hundred only, but I am persuaded, several thousands."[4] This sermon offers hope both to Christians, who are struggling with sin in their lives, and to backsliders who earnestly desire to return to Christ. Wesley closes this sermon with an echo of St. Paul's encouraging words: "His almighty grace will abolish every proud obstacle raised up against the knowledge of God, and we take every thought captive to obey Christ."

Many of Charles Wesley's hymns reinforce the theme of this sermon. For instance, worshipers pray the following words of Charles Wesley as they sing them:

1   O for a heart to praise my God,
A heart from sin set free!
A heart that always feels thy blood,
So freely spilt for me!

2   A heart resigned, submissive, meek,
My great Redeemer's throne,
Where only Christ is heard to speak,
Where Jesus reigns alone.

3   O for a lowly, contrite heart,
Believing, true, and clean,
Which neither life nor death can part
From him that dwells within!

4   A heart in every thought renewed,
And full of love divine,
Perfect, and right, and pure, and good—
A copy, Lord, of thine!

8   Thy nature, gracious Lord, impart;
Come quickly from above;
Write thy new name upon my heart,
Thy new, best name of love![5]

Sermon 14

THE REPENTANCE OF BELIEVERS

Repent, and believe in the good news. (Mark 1:15)

1 Many people commonly assume that repentance and faith pertain entirely to the beginning of the Christian life. They suppose that repentance and faith are necessary only at the point of our setting out on the journey in the kingdom of God. This outlook may seem to be confirmed by the great Apostle Paul when he admonished the Hebrew Christians to "go on to perfection." In that passage, he instructed them to "leave behind the basic teaching about Christ, and not lay again the foundation of repentance from dead works and faith toward God." At the least, this instruction means that the Hebrew Christians to whom this letter was addressed should move beyond repentance and faith, which at the beginning of their Christian walk occupied almost all their thoughts. To Christians who had already begun the Christian life, St. Paul said, "Press on toward the goal for the prize of the heavenly call of God in Christ Jesus."

2. It is undoubtedly true that repentance and faith are absolutely necessary at the beginning of the Christian life. Repentance includes a conviction of our total sinfulness, guilt, and helplessness. This repentance precedes our entering the kingdom of God, which our Lord stated is "within us." Of equal importance is faith, by which we receive the kingdom of God, consisting of "righteousness, and peace, and joy in the Holy Spirit."

231

3. As necessary as repentance and faith are *before* we become Christians, they are also necessary *after* we have believed the good news of the kingdom. We understand repentance and faith in another sense, which is not quite the same and yet not entirely different from references to conversion. Indeed, we need repentance and faith in every subsequent stage of our Christian journey, and without both of them, we cannot "run the race that is set before us." Repentance and faith are fully as necessary to continuing and growing in grace as they are to entering the kingdom of God.

In what sense are we to repent and believe *after* we are justified? This question is an important one, which is worthy of considering with the utmost attention. First, we will discuss in what sense believers need to repent.

I. The nature of repentance in believers

1. Repentance frequently means an inward change of heart from sin to holiness. Here, however, we are speaking of repentance in a quite different sense. We are speaking of repentance as a form of self-knowledge. Repentance in believers includes their understanding that they are sinners. Yes, even though we know that we are children of God, we are still guilty, helpless sinners.

2. When we first find redemption in the blood of Jesus, God pours his love into our hearts. And when his kingdom begins within us, it is natural for us initially to suppose that we are no longer sinners because all our sins are covered and demolished. At that point, we no longer feel any evil in our hearts, and we easily suppose that none is there. In fact, some well-meaning people have imagined that after justification they were completely free from sin. They assume that when they were justified they were also entirely sanctified. They have indeed adopted that theology, despite contrary evidence in scripture, reason, and experience. These people sincerely believe and earnestly contend that all sin is destroyed when we are justified and that there is no sin in the heart of a believer. They hold that Christians are free of sin from the instant they are justified.

We readily acknowledge that those who "trust in Christ are born of God" and that "those who have been born of God do not continue sinning." However, we cannot agree with the notion that they do not feel any sin within them. Although sin does not *reign* over new Christians, it does *remain* in them. The conviction of Christian believers that sin lingers in their hearts is an important aspect of the repentance about which I am now speaking.

3. It is seldom very long before those who imagined that all sin was removed at justification sense that pride remains in their hearts. Although new Christians understand that they have God's favor, they are soon convicted that in many respects they have thought of themselves more highly than they ought to think. They have taken credit for something that was purely a gift, and they have delighted in it as though they had not received it freely. Christians cannot, and they should not, abandon their confidence in Christ as redeemer. The Holy Spirit bears witness with their spirits that they are children of God.

4. Soon, however, Christians sense self-will in their hearts; they experience desires that are contrary to God's will. Obviously, as long as we have any understanding at all, we retain a will. The will is a fundamental part of human nature; it is a necessary component of every intelligent being. In his human form among us, our blessed Lord himself had a will. Otherwise he would not have taken on human form. However, his human will was always unfailingly subject to the will of his Father. At all times, on all occasions, and even in the deepest affliction, he could say to his Father, "Not what I want but what you want."

However, not even authentic believers in Christ have that depth of obedience to God the Father. To some extent, believers set their own wills against the will of God. They decide in favor of something because it is pleasing to their natural desires, even if it does not please God. And they reject some things because they are painful to human nature, although they are God's will for them. If they remain faithful to God, with all their might they fight against self-will, whose very force proves that it exists and that Christians are aware of its presence within them.

5. Self-will and pride are types of idolatry, and both are directly contrary to the love of God. The same statement can be made concerning the love of the world. Christian believers are inclined to sense in themselves a love for the present age. Every believer recognizes it more or less, sooner or later, in one area or another. It is true that when Christians first "pass from death unto life" they desire nothing more than God. True believers can sincerely say, "All my longing is known to you; your name and renown are my soul's desire." New believers exclaim, "Whom have I in heaven but you? There is nothing on earth that I desire other than you."

However, this new zeal does not continue unabated. In the process of time, even if only for a few moments, the Christian will again feel either "the desire of the flesh, the desire of the eyes, or pride in riches." If believers do not continually watch and pray they may find evil desires reviving within them. Indeed, these impulses press relentlessly, threatening the Christians' downfall and draining almost all their strength. They may feel the assaults of excessive passions—yes, a strong inclination to "love the creature rather than the Creator." In God's place, perhaps one might be tempted to put a child, a parent, a husband, wife, or "one's most intimate friend." In a thousand different ways, Christians may feel desires for earthly things or pleasures. In the same proportion, they are also tempted to forget God, not looking for happiness in him. Christians can tend to "love pleasure rather than love God."

6. If Christians do not guard themselves every moment, they will again feel the desire of the eye, the lust to gratify the imagination with something large, beautiful, or rare. In how many ways does this desire assail the soul? Perhaps with regard to the smallest trifles, such as dress or furniture—things never designed to satisfy the appetite of an immortal spirit. Still, even after we have "tasted of the powers of the age to come," how natural is it for us to sink again into these foolish, base desires for things that perish with the using! Even for those who "know the one in whom they have put their trust," how difficult it is to conquer even one aspect of the desire of the eye—curiosity. How hard it is constantly to trample curiosity under foot and not to desire something just because it is new!

7. And how arduous it is even for God's children wholly to conquer the pride of life! St. John seems to liken pride to what the world terms "the feeling of importance." This hunger is nothing other than a desire for, and a delight in, "the glory that comes from others." The hunger and love for applause is always joined proportionately to the fear of being ignored.

Closely allied with the desire for human praise is being ashamed of what we ought to glorify. The craving for praise is seldom separated from the fear of people, and this failing brings a thousand snares to the soul. Even among those who seem strong in the faith, where is the person who does not find some of these evil inclinations within? Because evil roots remain in the heart, becoming free from these lusts is only a part of what it means to be "crucified to the world."

8. Do we not also feel other attitudes that are as contrary to the love of our neighbor as those we have mentioned which are contrary to the love of God? Loving one's neighbor means not being "irritable or resentful." Do we find this quality among Christians? Do we never find among Christians any jealousies, cravings for controversy, and groundless or

unreasonable suspicions? Let the one that is innocent in these particulars cast the first stone at his neighbor.

Who are they that do not sometimes feel other inclinations or inward stirrings which they know to be contrary to brotherly love? If you do not feel hostility, hatred, or bitterness toward others, then have you no trace of envy? Especially do you envy those who enjoy some real or supposed good that you desire but cannot have? Do we never find within us any degree of resentment when we are injured or slighted, especially by those we dearly love and try our best to help or accommodate? Does injustice or ingratitude never arouse in us any desire for revenge? Have we no wish to repay evil with evil instead of "overcoming evil with good"? This survey of common flaws shows us how much remains in our hearts that is contrary to love for neighbor.

9. Covetousness of every sort and degree is certainly as contrary to the love of neighbor as it is to the love of God. Greed can take the form of the love of money, which is much too frequently "the root of all kinds of evils." Covetousness can also take the form of desiring more money or material goods. Even among the genuine children of God, how few are entirely free from the love of worldly riches and the desire for material things!

A great man, Martin Luther, used to say that he "never had any covetousness in him," not only in his converted state, but "ever since he was born." If that were the case, I would not hesitate to say that he was the only man ever born (except Jesus Christ) who from birth never coveted. No, I believe that there has never been anyone who became a Christian who lived very long after justification who did not feel more or less envious, especially of material things. We may therefore establish as an indisputable truth that covetousness, pride, self-will, and anger remain even in the hearts of justified Christians.

10. Because Christians experience covetousness, many thoughtful persons believe that the latter part of the seventh chapter of Romans is addressed not to those under the law (which was surely the meaning of St. Paul), but to those under grace. They understand the last half of Romans chapter 6 to refer to those who are "justified by God's grace as a gift, through the redemption that is in Christ Jesus." And, indeed, it is entirely certain that even in those who are justified there remains a mind that in some measure is set on the flesh.

The Apostle Paul wrote to the believers at Corinth, "You are still of the flesh." That is, they had hearts inclined to backsliding; they were too quick to "turn away from the living God." The Corinthian Christians had a propensity toward pride, self-will, anger, revenge, and the love of the world and every evil. Indeed, they harbored "a root of bitterness," which, if restraint were taken away for a moment, would instantly spring up within them. Yes, these Christians still had within them such a depth of corruption that we cannot possibly comprehend it without clear light from God. Now, an awareness of this corruption remaining in the heart forms the basis of the repentance of believers.

11. We should also understand that, even as sin remains in our hearts, so it also clings to all our words and actions. Indeed, it is to be feared that many of our words are more than just mingled with sin—they are entirely sinful. This charge is true of all unkind conversation that does not arise from brotherly love. Such is the case with all talk that does not conform to that golden rule, "In everything do to others as you would have them do to you."

Included in this kind of conversation are slander, gossip, rumors, and evil speaking. This kind of sin involves repeating the faults of absent persons (for no one wants others to recite his faults when he is not present). How few are there, even among Christians, who are not in any way guilty of evil conversation? How many observe the virtuous rule of antiquity,

> Of the dead and the absent,
> Speak nothing but good![6]

Suppose there are some that observe this rule. Do they likewise abstain from frivolous conversation? All such trivial conversation is sinful, and it "grieves the Holy Spirit of God." Indeed, "On the Day of Judgment you will have to give an account of every careless word you utter."

12. Suppose one is continually diligent to "watch and pray" and does "not enter into the temptation" of evil speaking. Suppose one constantly "sets a guard over his mouth and keeps watch over the door of his lips." Suppose Christians discipline themselves in their conversation and their "speech is always gracious and seasoned with salt" and it is "useful for building up and gives grace to those who hear." Yet, do they not daily slip into worthless discourse, despite their concern not to engage in evil speaking? Even when they attempt to speak for God, are their words pure and free from unholy contamination? Do they find no wrong in their intentions? Do they speak only to please God, and not partly to please themselves? Is their speaking unconditionally to do the will of God, and not their own wills also? Even if they begin with a single eye to please God, do they continue "looking to Jesus" and communing with him all the time that they are talking with their neighbor? When they are

reproving sin, do they feel no anger or unkindness toward the sinner? When they are instructing the ignorant, are they free from pride and self-seeking? When they are comforting the afflicted, or encouraging one another to love and to good deeds, do they never perceive any inward self congratulation?

Do they applaud themselves while thinking, "Now, you have certainly spoken well?" Do they have any conceit or any desire that others would think well of them and esteem them for their work? In some or all of these respects, how much sin clings to the best conversation of Christian believers! The conviction of these sins is another part of the repentance that belongs to justified Christians.

13. If their consciences are completely awake, how much sin can Christians find clinging to their actions as well! Are there not many Christians whose lives are not condemned by the world, but who still cannot be acclaimed or excused if we judge them by the word of God? Do not many of their actions, of which they are aware, fail to promote the glory of God? Are not many of their deeds (through which they did not even intend to glorify God) done without an eye fixed on him? And concerning those deeds done with an eye to God (of which there are not many), were their eyes *entirely* fixed on God? In many of their actions, are they not doing their own will at least as much as God's will? Are they seeking to please themselves as much as or as more than to please God? And while they aim at doing good to their neighbor, do they not feel various kinds of wrong attitudes? Consequently, their so-called good deeds are far from being altogether good, because they are polluted with such a mixture of evil. Such are their works of mercy.

Furthermore, is there not the same mixture in their deeds of piety? While they are listening to the word that can save their souls, do they not frequently find that God's word causes them to fear condemnation, rather than leading them to hope for salvation? Is it not often this way while they are praying, either in public or in private? While they are engaged in the most solemn service of the holy sacrament, what kinds of thoughts arise within them? Are their hearts not sometimes wandering to the ends of the earth and filled with such imaginations as to make them fear that their participation in communion is an abomination to the Lord? Thus, their motives are so mixed that they are now more ashamed of their best service than once they were of their worst sins.

14. Of how many sins of omission are Christians guilty! We understand the words of the Apostle James: "Whoever knows the right thing to do and fails to do it, commits sin." Are Christians not aware of a thousand instances when they might have done good to the bodies and

souls of enemies, strangers, and fellow Christians, but they failed to do so? And in their duty toward God, of how many omissions have they been guilty? How many opportunities to take Holy Communion, hear God's word, and attend public or private prayers they have neglected! With good reason that holy man, Archbishop Usher, after all his labors for God, cried out almost with his dying breath, "Lord, forgive me my sins of omission!"

15. Beside outward omissions, do not Christians find inward defects without number within themselves? There are flaws of every kind. They fail to have the love, reverence, and confidence toward God they should have. They do not show the love that is appropriately due to their neighbors and to every human soul. No, they even lack the love that is due to their sisters and brothers, to every one of God's children, whether at a distance from them or near them. They do not have a righteous temperament to the degree that they should. They are deficient in everything. In the deep awareness of themselves, with Monsignor De Renty they are prepared to cry out, "I am a ground all overrun with thorns." Or, with Job, they can confess, "I am vile; I despise myself, and repent as in dust and ashes."

16. Another aspect of the repentance that properly belongs to believers is a conviction of guilt. However, it is important that we exercise caution so as properly to understand the particular sense in which believers are guilty. It is certain that "there is therefore now no condemnation for those who are in Christ Jesus," who maintain faith in him, and who in the strength of that faith "walk not according to the flesh but according to the Spirit." Even so, believers cannot hold up under the strict justice of God any more than they could before they trusted in Christ. This failure to meet the demands of the law means that in all their ledgers they are still worthy of death. And, if it were not for the atoning blood of Christ, the law would absolutely condemn them to death. Consequently, believers completely understand that they still deserve punishment, although through Jesus Christ it has been canceled.

In this area of guilt, there are extremes in two directions. Few steer clear of the pitfalls. Most people come down on one extreme or the other, (i) either believing that they are condemned when they are not, or (ii) believing that they deserve to be acquitted from all guilt, although they have not repented. The truth lies between these extremes. Strictly speaking, believers still deserve only the damnation of hell. But the condemnation they deserve does not come upon them because they "have an Advocate with the Father." Christ's life, death, and intercession continue to stand between them and condemnation.

17. Another aspect of the repentance of believers is the conviction of their utter helplessness. Here, I refer to two things. (i) In themselves, believers are now no more able than they were before they were justified to think a single good thought, form any good desire, speak a good word, or do any kind of good work. Believers still have no kind of ability or degree of strength within themselves. They possess no power to do good, resist evil, overcome sin, or withstand the world, the devil, and their own evil natures. It is true that believers can do all things, but not through their own strength. They have power to overcome all spiritual enemies, because "sin has no dominion over them." In whole or in part, the victory of believers does not come from human nature; it is the sheer gift of God. Believers do not receive God's complete power, as though they have a supply laid up for many years. They receive God's strength moment by moment.

18. (ii) The helplessness of believers means their complete inability to deliver themselves from the guilt that deserves just punishment, of which they are still conscious. Believers are helpless to remove pride, self-will, love of the world, anger, and the general inclination to stray from God. They cannot free themselves even through the grace they have received (to say nothing of their natural powers). Through experience, we know that, despite all our efforts, these evils remain in the hearts of regenerated people, and cling to all their words and actions. In addition, believers are utterly powerless to elude uncharitable and unprofitable conversation completely. In themselves, they are unable to avoid sins of omission or to remedy the numberless defects of which they are aware— especially their insufficiency of love and their lack of right of attitudes toward God and others.

19. If any are not convinced of what I say, and if any believe that those who are justified are able to remove these sins out of their hearts and lives, let them try an experiment. By the grace that they have already received, let them attempt to expel pride, self-will, or inbred sin. Let them see if they can cleanse their words and actions from all taints of evil and uncharitable and unprofitable conversation. Let them see if they can rid themselves of all sins of omission. Finally, let them try to provide a remedy for the numberless defects that they still find in themselves. Let them not stop with one or two experiments, but repeat the trial again and again. The longer they try, the more deeply they will be convinced of their utter helplessness in all respects.

20. Indeed, the helplessness of believers is an obvious truth. It is so apparent that almost all the widely scattered children of God, however they differ in other points, will concur on this point. They will agree that

only "by the Spirit we can put to death the deeds of the body" and resist and conquer both outward and inward sin. Christians generally agree that although day by day we may weaken our enemies, we are powerless to eliminate them. By all the grace that comes to us at justification we cannot abolish our spiritual enemies. Even as we watch and pray ever so much, we are unable wholly to cleanse our hearts or hands.

Most assuredly, we cannot become entirely holy until the second time it pleases our Lord to speak to our hearts, "Be clean." Only then is the leprosy cleansed. Only then, the evil root (the mind that is set on the flesh) is destroyed, and inbred sin exists no more. If there is no such second change, no instantaneous deliverance after justification and nothing but a gradual work of God (that there is a gradual work no one denies), then we must be content, as well as we can, to remain full of sin until death. If God does not work in our hearts, we must remain guilty until death, constantly deserving punishment. As long as all this sin remains in our hearts and clings to our words and actions, it is impossible for us to become free from guilt or deserved punishment. In fact, in the light of God's exacting justice, everything we think, speak, and do continually increases guilt and deserved punishment.

II. The nature of faith in believers

1. All the facts that I have been talking about call for the repentance of believers. And until we do repent we cannot make any further spiritual progress. We must first become aware of our disease before we can find a cure. If God calls us to repent, he also calls us to "believe the good news."

2. The faith of believers should be understood in a particular sense: it is different from the faith that leads to justification. The faith of Christian believers is belief in the good news of salvation that God has prepared for all people. Saving faith is trust that the one who is the reflection of God's glory and the exact imprint of God's very being is able for all time to save those who approach God through him. Jesus Christ is able to save you from all the sin that remains in your heart. He is able to rescue you from all the sin that clings to each one of your words and actions. He is able to save you from sins of omission, and to supply whatever is lacking in you. Of course, this deliverance is impossible for mortals, but with the God-Man, Jesus Christ, all things are possible. What is too difficult for him who has "all authority in heaven and in earth?"

240

To be sure, the LORD's manifest *ability* to transform us is not a suffi-cient foundation for our believing that he *wills* to do so. It is necessary for him to reveal his promise that he desires to exercise his power in our behalf. And he has done just that very thing. Over and over and in the strongest terms, he has promised to deliver us. In both the Old and New Testaments, Christ has given us his "precious and very great promises." We read of these promises in the law, which is the most ancient part of God's divine word. The law says, "The Lord your God will circumcise your heart and the heart of your descendants, so that you will love the Lord your God with all your heart and with all your soul." In the Psalms we read, "He will redeem the Israel of God from all its iniquities." Likewise, in the Prophet Ezekiel we find the promise, "I will sprinkle clean water upon you, and you shall be clean from all your uncleanness-es, and from all your idols I will cleanse you. . . . I will put my spirit with-in you, and make you follow my statutes and be careful to observe my ordinances. . . . I will save you from all your uncleannesses."

Also, in the New Testament we read, "Blessed be the Lord God of Israel, for he has looked favorably on his people and redeemed them. He has raised up a mighty savior for us. . . . He has remembered his holy covenant, the oath that he swore to our ancestor Abraham, to grant us that we, being rescued from the hands of our enemies, might serve him without fear, in holiness and righteousness before him all our days."

3. You have, therefore, every good reason to believe that God is both able and willing to cleanse you from every defilement of body and spirit and to "save you from all your uncleannesses." As a believer, this cleans-ing is what you now long for. The faith that you now mainly need is to believe that the Great Physician, the lover of our souls, is willing to make you clean.

But is he willing to do this for you tomorrow or today? Allow him to answer for himself: "Today, if you hear his voice, do not harden your hearts." If you put it off until tomorrow, you "harden your hearts" and "refuse to hear his voice." Therefore, believe that Christ is willing to save you today. He is willing to rescue you immediately. "See, now is the acceptable time." This moment, Christ says, "Now, be made clean!" Only believe, and you will instantly find that "all things can be done for the one who believes."

4. Continue to trust in Christ "who loved you and gave himself for you," "bore your sins in his body on the cross," and saves you from all condemnation by his blood continually applied in your behalf. It is in this way that we continue in a justified state. And when we advance "through faith for faith," when we have the faith to be cleansed from

241

indwelling sin and to be saved from all our uncleannesses, we are saved from all the guilt and deserved punishment that once we felt. Then, in the full assurance of faith we can move from

> Every moment, Lord, I *want*
> The merit of thy death

to the greater affirmation,

> Every moment, Lord, *I have*
> The merit of thy death![7]

By faith in Christ's life, death, and intercession for us, renewed from moment to moment, we become completely clean. The Lord purifies our hearts and lives, and there is now no condemnation or deserved punishment for us.

5. By this same faith, every moment we feel the power of Christ resting upon us. Through Christ alone we are enabled to continue in this life of the Spirit, without which, despite all our present holiness, we would become devilish the next moment. As long as we retain our faith in him, however, "with joy we will draw water from the wells of salvation." We lean on our beloved Christ, "the hope of glory" who is in us, living in our hearts by faith and ever interceding for us at the right hand of God. From him we receive help to think, speak, and do what is acceptable in his sight.

In the words of our *Book of Common Prayer*, in all their actions, "Christ goes ahead of those that believe and supports them with his continual help." All their plans, conversations, and actions are begun, continued, and ended in him. Christ "cleanses the thoughts of their hearts, by the inspiration of his Holy Spirit, that they may perfectly love him, and worthily magnify his holy name."

6. In the children of God, therefore, repentance and faith perfectly harmonize with each other. In repentance we sense the sin remaining in our hearts and clinging to our words and actions. Through faith we receive the power of God in Christ that purifies our hearts and cleanses our hands. In repentance we are still aware that we deserve punishment for all our attitudes, words, and actions. Through faith, we are conscious that our Advocate with the Father is continually interceding for us and that he is ever turning condemnation and punishment away from us all. In repentance we have the continuing conviction that we are completely helpless. Through faith, we "receive mercy and find grace to help in time of need."

Repentance disclaims all possibility of any help other than from Christ. Faith accepts all the support we need from him who has all authority in heaven and earth. Repentance says, "Without him I can do nothing." Faith says, "I can do all things through him who strengthens me." Through Christ, I can both overcome and expel all the enemies of my soul. Through him, I can 'love the Lord my God with all my heart, and with all my soul, and with all my mind, and with all my strength.' Yes, and I can serve him 'in holiness and righteousness all my days.'"

III. Lessons and applications

1. From what has been said, we may easily learn how harmful is the opinion that we are wholly sanctified when we are justified. At justification, our hearts are not yet completely cleansed from all sin. It is true, as I have said, that at justification we are delivered from the dominion of outward sin. Also, at justification the power of inward sin is broken so that we need no longer follow sin or be subject to it.

However, it is by no means true that at justification inward sin is totally destroyed or that the root of pride, self-will, anger, and the love of the world is then taken out of the heart. Nor is it true that the mind that is set on the flesh and inclined toward backsliding is entirely exterminated. It is not merely an innocent, harmless mistake to assume the contrary, as some may think. Not at all. This teaching does immense harm. It completely obstructs the way to any further change, because it is obvious that "those who are well have no need of a physician, but those who are sick." If, therefore, we think that we are already made whole, there is no need to seek any additional healing. Given this presumption, it is absurd to expect a further deliverance from sin, whether gradual or instantaneous.

2. On the contrary, the need for a greater change in our lives rests on our deep conviction that we are not yet whole, that our hearts are not fully purified; that there is yet in us a "mind set on the flesh" and "hostile to God." In justified persons, sin is indeed weakened, but it is not destroyed. And the presence of sin in believers shows beyond doubt the absolute necessity of a further change in their lives. We acknowledge that we are born again at the very moment of justification. In that moment, we experience an inward change "out of darkness into God's marvelous light." We are transformed from the image of a savage and the devil into the image of God. We exchange the "earthly, sensual, devilish mind" for the same mind that was in Christ Jesus.

However, at that point are we totally changed? At the time of conversion, are we completely transformed into the image of him who created us? Far from it! We still retain a depth of sin. And it is the awareness of this sin that compels us to cry to Christ who is "mighty to save" and who is able to deliver us fully. Consequently, those believers who have so little concern about entire sanctification are the ones who are not convinced of the deep corruption of their hearts, or else they are only slightly or theoretically convinced.

Some people may possibly hold the opinion that full sanctification can come either at death or at some unspecified future time. However, they have no great inner concern because they lack a sense of need; they have no great hunger or thirst for sanctification. And they cannot desire righteousness until they better understand themselves. They cannot long for entire sanctification until they repent in the way that I have described. Only then will God unveil the inbred monster's face and show them the real state of their souls. Only then, when they feel the burden of their inbred sin, will they pray for deliverance from their sinful state. Not until they repent will they cry out, in the agony of their soul,

> Break off the yoke of inbred sin,
> And fully set my spirit free;
> I cannot rest till pure within,
> Till I am wholly lost in thee.[8]

3. Second, from what we have considered we may learn that a deep conviction of our defects (or guilt) after we are justified is absolutely necessary for us fully to appreciate the true value of Christ's atoning blood. Believers need to understand their condition if they are to see that they need Christ as much after they have been justified as they did before they were justified. Without a conviction of our true condition, we will account the blood of the covenant as a common thing, something we do not greatly need because all our sins are already wiped away.

If both our hearts and lives are still unclean, there is a sort of guilt that we are incurring every moment. We would be constantly liable to new condemnation, if it were not that

> He ever lives above
> For us to intercede,
> His all-redeeming love,
> His precious blood, to plead.[9]

It is this kind of repentance and the faith so closely connected with it that are expressed in these powerful lines,

> I sin in every breath I draw,
> Nor do Thy will, nor keep Thy law
> On earth, as angels do above;
> But still the Fountain open stands,
> Washes my feet, and head, and hands,
> Till I am perfected in love.[10]

4. Third, a deep conviction of our utter helplessness, total inability to retain anything we have received, and powerlessness to deliver ourselves from the world of iniquity remaining in our hearts and lives will teach us truly by faith to depend upon Christ as our priest and king. In this way, we come to magnify him to the praise of his glorious grace, to make him our fully adequate savior, and sincerely to "place the crown upon his head." These excellent words have frequently been misused and therefore lose their force. However, they are fulfilled in a powerful and deep sense when we move out of ourselves in order to be swallowed up in Christ.

The repentance of believers means that we must sink into nothing, so that the Lord may become all in all for us. Then, his almighty grace will abolish "every proud obstacle raised up against the knowledge of God, and we take every thought captive to obey Christ."

LONDONDERRY, April 24, 1767.

Notes

1. *Explanatory Notes Upon the New Testament*, Matt. 3:8.
2. Outler, *Wesley's Sermons*, 1:335.
3. Telford, *Wesley's Letters*, Letter to Thomas Church, June 17, 1746, 2: 267.
4. Outler, *Wesley's Sermons*, 3:224.
5. *Hymns and Sacred Poems*, 1742, pp. 30, 31. Also, George Osborn, *The Poetical Works of John and Charles Wesley*, 13 vols. (London: Wesleyan-Methodist Conference Office, 1868), 2:77, 78; Hildebrandt and Beckerlegge, *Hymns*, Bicentennial ed., Hymn #334, 7:490; and *The United Methodist Hymnal*, 1989, Hymn #417.
6. Sextus Propertius [born c. 55 B.C.], *Elegies*, II, xix, 32.
7. Charles Wesley, Hymn on Isaiah 53:2, "And a Man Shall Be as a Hiding Place," *Poet. Wks.*, 2:207.
8. Charles Wesley, Hymn on Matthew 11:28, "Come Unto Me," stanza 3, *Poet. Wks.*, 2:145.
9. Charles Wesley, "Behold the Man," stanza 2, *Poet. Wks.*, 2:323.
10. Charles Wesley, "A Thanksgiving," stanza 16, *Poet. Wks.*, 2:234.

THE GREAT ASSIZE

The word *assize* means "assembly." In the eighteenth century, *assize* took on a special connotation, which pertained to the periodic sessions of the judges, jurists, and legal professionals of the English superior courts. These assizes (court sessions) tried cases, adjudicated civil and criminal litigation, and acquitted or passed sentences on the accused. Thus, in time the term assize came to refer to a judgment. "The Great Assize" and "the Last Assize" were common eighteenth-century terms used to refer to God's final judgment.

During these eighteenth-century English court sessions, it was customary for the officials to arrange a religious service in the local parish church of the town where the assize was being held. The judges, wearing apparel of scarlet and ermine, solemnly assembled in the sanctuary to hear a sermon. On these formal occasions they were accompanied by court officials, trumpeters, and uniformed guards with javelins. Ordinarily, the High Sheriff of the county arranged for a clergyman to preach the sermon on these magisterial occasions. In Wesley's day, the High Sheriff of Bedfordshire was a Methodist, William Cole, Wesley's friend and supporter. In 1758, Cole invited Wesley to preach the sermon at the assize in Bedford. The service was held in St. Paul's Anglican Church.

Wesley preached this sermon on Friday, March 10. To prepare the message, Wesley had again "retired for a few days to Lewisham," to the home of Ebenezer Blackwell, his friend and benefactor.[1] Wesley was ill at the time. Nevertheless, he finished writing the sermon and set off for Bedford. His journal describes his trip:

I took horse [March 6] about seven o'clock. The wind being east, I was pleasing myself that we should have it on our back: But in a quarter of an hour it shifted to the north-west, and blew the rain full in our face: And both increased, so that when we came to Finchley-Common, it was hard work to sit our horses. The rain continued all the way to Dunstable, where we exchanged the main road for the fields; which, having been just ploughed, were throughly   Thursday, the 9th, I rode to Bedford, and found the sermon was not to be preached till Friday.[2] Had I known this in time, I should never have thought of preaching it; having engaged to be at Epworth on Saturday.[3]

As soon as Wesley finished preaching the sermon, he began a hurried journey to Epworth, located 120 miles from Bedford.

This discourse is the only one that Wesley is known to have preached before a civil court, and it differs somewhat in style from his other sermons. Ordinarily, he used a "plain style" to address the crowds, which often contained uneducated people. However, Wesley wrote this sermon in a different mode. Wesley's use of scripture is copious. He also quotes from Virgil, Ovid, and Edward Young (1683–1765), a currently popular poet and dramatist. The sermon, especially in its introduction and conclusion, contains more florid oratory than Wesley ordinarily used.

The large congregation in Bedford that day listened carefully and respectfully to Wesley's message. By this time, he had become legendary throughout England as an evangelist and leader of the Methodists. Wesley recorded his assessment of the occasion:

The congregation at St. Paul's was very large and very attentive. The Judge, immediately after sermon, sent me an invitation to dine with him. But having no time, I was obliged to send my excuse, and set out between one and two. The north-east wind was piercing cold, and, blowing exactly in our face, soon brought an heavy shower of snow, then of sleet, and afterwards of hail. However, we reached Stilton at seven, about thirty miles from Bedford.[4]

As noted, Wesley was scheduled to preach the next evening at Epworth. He reached his destination on Saturday at 10:00 P.M. That day, in seventeen hours he traveled 90 miles in wind, snow, sleet, and hail, riding part way on a lame horse and part way in a post chaise. He was 55 years old, and he reported that at the end of his journey he was nearly as fresh as he had been when he began this trip.[5]

The Great Assize compares the present earthly courts with the coming day when God will pass his final verdict on all humankind. Wesley

247

emphasizes that God's eternal judgment will be far more awesome than that of any earthly judge or court. In that great day, all our motives, thoughts, and attitudes will come under God's intense scrutiny, and with perfect judgment he will pronounce final rewards and punishments. God will assess our stewardship of decisions, words, opportunities, and possessions. Because Jesus Christ shared our human experience, he understands our temptations, sins, sorrows, and frailties. Therefore, the last judgment will be just. At the final judgment, God will permanently separate the saved and the unsaved. The wicked who ignore or reject God's grace will be judged and condemned; the righteous will enter God's eternal bliss and receive heaven's rewards.

Sermon 15

THE GREAT ASSIZE

We will all stand before the judgment seat of God.
(Romans 14:10)

This sermon was preached at the Court Session held before the Honorable Sir Edward Clive, Knight, one of the Judges of His Majesty's Court of Common Pleas, in St. Paul's Church, Bedford, on Friday, March 10, 1758; published at the request of William Cole, Esq., High Sheriff of the county, and others.

1. Many circumstances contribute to the awesome solemnity of today's gathering. The representative crowd of people of every age, gender, rank, and condition of life assembled here, whether willingly or unwillingly convened in this place, has come from near and distant places. Called together are criminals that will promptly be brought in (with no way to escape) and officers waiting at their various posts to execute the orders that will be given by the representatives of our gracious king whom we so greatly respect and honor.

The purpose of this assembly also adds its measure of seriousness to this occasion. Its objective is to hear and decide all kinds of cases. Some of them are of the most important nature; certain cases even concern issues of life or death (the death that uncovers the face of eternity!). Undoubtedly, to add to the seriousness of these gatherings (not only in the minds of the unrefined members of society) our wise forebears did not hesitate to establish several details related to this solemn assembly. The ceremonies of this gathering make use of the eye and ear to affect more deeply the heart. When seen in this light, the trumpets, poles, and raiment are no longer trifling or insignificant. Rather, in their own way they promote the most important interests of society.

2. But as awesome as this solemn occasion may be, one far more exalted is near at hand. In a short time, "we will all stand before the judgment seat of God. 'As I live, says the Lord, every knee shall bow to me, and every tongue shall acknowledge God.'" And in that day of final reckoning, "each of us will be accountable to God."

3. If all people had a deep sense of this coming judgment, how effectively it would guarantee the interests of society! Who can conceive a more compelling motive as a basis for the practice of genuine morality, the steadfast pursuit of solid virtue, and the consistent practice of justice, mercy, and truth? What could strengthen us in everything that is good and discourage us from all evil like a strong conviction that "the Judge is standing at the doors" and that shortly we all shall stand before him?

4. Therefore, in light of the coming Great Assize it may not be inappropriate or untimely to consider several things: (1) the main circumstances leading to our appearance before the judgment seat of Christ, (2) the nature of the judgment of Christ, (3) the circumstances that follow the judgment of Christ, and (4) an application of this truth to those hearing the sermon.

I. The main circumstances leading to our appearance before the judgment seat of Christ

In the first place, let us consider the main circumstances that will precede our standing before the judgment seat of Christ.

1. First, God will show "signs on the earth below." Specifically, the Lord will "arise to shake terribly the earth." "The earth will stagger like a drunkard, it will sway like a hut." On the earth there shall be earthquakes in all places in every part of the habitable world (not just in several different places). This upheaval will be "such as have not occurred since people were upon the earth, so violent will be that earthquake." In one of these disturbances on the earth, "every island will flee away, and no mountains will be found." Meanwhile, all the waters of the globe will feel the violence of the shaking. "The roaring of the sea and waves" will churn with such disturbance as never before known since the time when "the great deep burst forth" to destroy the earth, which then "was formed out of water and by means of water." The air will fill with cyclones and violent storms, which will be packed with dark clouds and

columns of smoke resounding with thunder from pole to pole, and ripped with ten thousand lightning bolts.

Furthermore, these disturbances will not stop with our atmosphere. "The powers of the heavens will be shaken. There will be signs in the sun, the moon, and the stars"—those that are fixed and those that revolve around them. "The sun shall be turned to darkness, and the moon to blood, before the great and terrible day of the Lord comes." The stars will cease to sparkle; yes, and "fall from heaven, being cast out of their orbits."

Then the people will hear a universal shout from all the companies of heaven, followed by the "voice of the archangel" proclaiming the approach of Jesus Christ. "The sound of God's trumpet" will call to all that sleep in the dust of the earth. In response to the summons of the trumpet, all the graves will open and the bodies of the dead will arise. Also, "the sea will give up the dead that are in it." Each person will rise with his or her own material substance, although changed in its properties in ways that we cannot now conceive. "This perishable body must put on imperishability, and this mortal body must put on immortality." Yes, Death and Hades, the invisible world, will deliver up the dead that are in them. Everyone who ever lived and died since God created humankind will be raised imperishable and immortal.

2. At the same time, the Son of Man will send out his angels, "and they will gather his elect from the four winds, from one end of heaven to the other." And the Lord himself will come on the clouds of heaven in his glory and the glory of the Father, with ten thousands of his holy ones, and he will sit on the throne of his glory. "All the nations will be gathered before him, and he will separate people one from another as a shepherd separates the sheep from the goats, and he will put the sheep at his right hand and the goats at the left."

The beloved disciple, John, wrote about this general Judgment Day: "And I saw the dead, great and small, standing before the throne, and books were opened (a figurative expression, simply referring to the Lord's going from person to person). Also another book was opened, the book of life. And the dead were judged according to their works, as recorded in the books."

II. The nature of the judgment of Christ

I have given a scriptural account of the circumstances that will take place before the coming great judgment. Now, secondly, to the extent that it has pleased God to reveal it, we will consider the judgment itself.

1. The person by whom God will judge the world is his only begotten Son. His "origin is from of old, from ancient days," and he is "over all, God blessed forever." "He is the reflection of God's glory and the exact imprint of God's very being." "The Father has given all judgment to him because he is the Son of Man." "Though he was in the form of God, he did not regard equality with God as something to be exploited, but emptied himself, taking the form of a slave, being born in human likeness." And being found in human form, he humbled himself and became obedient to the point of death—even death on a cross. Therefore God also highly exalted him, in his human nature, and appointed him, as representative man, to try the children of men—that is, to judge the living and the dead. Christ will judge those who will be found alive at his coming and those who will have already been gathered to their ancestors.

2. The Prophet Joel referred to this coming judgment as "the great and the terrible day." In general, scripture speaks of the Day of Judgment as "the day of the Lord." The period from the creation of the first man and woman to the end of all things is the day of humankind. The time in which we are now living is properly our day. But when this day has ended, the day of the Lord will begin.

Who can say how long our day will continue? "With the Lord one day is like a thousand years, and a thousand years are like one day." From this expression, some of the ancient Church Fathers drew the inference that what we commonly call the Day of Judgment would be precisely a thousand years. It appears that they did not exceed the truth; no, probably they did not come up to it. If we consider the number of persons who are to be judged and the actions to be examined, it does not seem that a thousand years will be enough time for the transactions of that Day of Judgment. It may not be improbable to say that the coming judgment may take several thousand years. However, God will reveal this matter at the proper time.

3. With regard to the *place* where humankind will be judged, we have no explicit account in Scripture. An eminent writer believes that the judgment will be on earth. (He is not alone in this view; many have held the same opinion.) Our works are done on the earth, and they may be judged here. In the coming judgment God will employ his mighty angels

> To smooth and lengthen out the boundless space,
> And spread an area for all human race.[6]

Perhaps, however, it is more in line with the Lord's own account of his coming in the clouds to assume that the judgment will take place above the earth—perhaps "twice a planetary height." This assumption seems favored in St. Paul's letter to the Thessalonians: "The dead in Christ will rise first. Then we who are alive, who are left, will be caught up in the clouds together with them to meet the Lord in the air; and so we will be with the Lord forever." Thus, it seems most probable that God's great white throne will be highly exalted above the earth.

1. Who can count the number of persons to be judged, any more than one can count the drops of rain or the sands of the sea? St. John said, "I looked, and there was a great multitude that no one could count, from every nation, from all tribes and peoples and languages, standing before the throne and before the Lamb, robed in white, with palm branches in their hands." How immense must be the total multitude of nations, tribes, peoples, and languages. The Great Judgment will include all those that have descended from the loins of Adam, since the world began until it will be no more! Let us take for granted the common supposition, which seems in no way absurd, that the earth bears at any one time no less than four hundred millions of living souls. What a vast assembled gathering must all those generations make that have succeeded each other for seven thousand years!

> Great Xerxes' world in arms, proud Cannae's host,
> They all are here, and here they all are lost.
> Their numbers swell to be discern'd in vain;
> Lost as a drop in the unbounded main.[7]

Every man, woman, and infant that lived only a few days, everyone who ever breathed the life-giving air will then hear the voice of the Son of God. They will spring to life and appear before the Lord. This picture seems to be the natural meaning of the expression "the dead, great and small." This phrase includes everyone without exception—those of every age, gender, or rank. It refers to all who ever lived, died, or underwent any change equivalent to death. Long before the great Day of Judgment, the illusory specter of human greatness ceases and sinks into nothing. At the moment of death, human greatness vanishes away. Who in the grave is rich or great?

3. In the Day of the Lord every person will "give an accounting of his own works." Yes, we will be required to give a full and true explanation of everything we ever did while in the body, whether good or evil. O what a scene will then be disclosed in our sight and in the sight of angels! Ruling over all will not be the fabled Rhadamanthus; it will be the Lord God Almighty, who knows everything in heaven and in earth.

253

O're these drear realms stern Rhadamanthus reigns,
Detects each artful villain, and constrains
To own the crimes, long veiled from human sight:
In vain! Now all stand forth in hated light.[8]

Not only will the actions of every human soul then be brought into the open, but also all the words that have ever been spoken. Jesus said, "I tell you, in the Day of Judgment you will have to give an account for every careless word you utter; for by your words you will be justified, and by your words you will be condemned." In that day, will God not also bring to light all circumstances that have accompanied every word or action that lessened or increased their goodness or evil? How easy it is for God to judge perfectly, seeing that he "searches out our paths and our lying down, and he is acquainted with all our ways." We know that "the darkness is not darkness to him," but "the night is as bright as the day."

6. Yes, God "will bring to light the things now hidden in darkness and will disclose the purposes of the heart." This revelation is no marvel for God, for he "is able to judge the thoughts and intentions of the heart." All things "are naked and laid bare to the eyes of the one to whom we must render an account." "Hell and destruction lie open before the Lord, and how much more are human hearts."

7. The great day of God will reveal all the inner workings of every human soul. His judgments will uncover every appetite, emotion, preference, and inclination—all in their various combinations. God will make known all moods and dispositions which constitute the full and complex character of every individual. It will be clearly and infallibly seen who were righteous and who were unrighteous, and to what degree every action, person, and character was either good or evil.

8. "Then the king will say to those at his right hand, 'Come, you that are blessed by my Father, inherit the kingdom prepared for you from the foundation of the world; for I was hungry and you gave me food, I was thirsty and you gave me something to drink, I was a stranger and you welcomed me, I was naked and you gave me clothing, I was sick and you took care of me, I was in prison and you visited me.'" In like manner, all the good they did upon earth will be declared before humankind and angels—whatever, either in word or deed, they have done in the name, or for the sake, of the Lord Jesus. In that day, all their good desires, intentions, thoughts, and holy endowments will also come to light. Although these works were unknown or forgotten in human society, God has transcribed them in his book. Likewise, all sufferings for the

name of Jesus and for the appeal of a good conscience will be revealed and praised by God the righteous Judge. Before the saints and angels, God will show their nobleness and eternal weight of glory beyond all measure.

9. If we review the entire life of everyone, there is not a person on earth who does not sin. Will our evil deeds also be remembered and disclosed before the great gathering at the final judgment? Many believe that their sins will not be remembered. They ask, "Would not a judgment for sins mean that death does not end our sufferings, because we would still have to endure sorrow, shame, and confusion?" They further inquire, "How can a judgment for sins be harmonized with Ezekiel's speaking for God: 'If the wicked turn away from all their sins that they have committed and keep all my statutes and do what is lawful and right, they shall surely live; they shall not die. None of the transgressions that they have committed shall be remembered against them.' How can a judgment for sin be made consistent with the promise that God has made to all who accept the gospel covenant—'I will forgive their iniquity, and remember their sin no more?' An apostle wrote, 'I will be merciful toward their iniquities, and I will remember their sins no more.'"

10. I offer the following answer: For the full exposition of the glory of God, and for the clear and perfect manifestation of his wisdom, justice, power, and mercy toward those who are to inherit salvation, it is obviously and utterly necessary that all the circumstances of their lives be seen openly. Along with the circumstances of our lives, the Great Judge will reveal all the dispositions, desires, thoughts, and intents of our hearts. Otherwise, how would we understand from what a depth of sin and misery the grace of God has delivered us? Indeed, if the complete lives of all people were not clearly seen, we would not understand the entire amazing composition of divine providence. We would not be able to see the thousand instances that justify the ways of God with us.

Without the utmost fulfillment of our Lord's words (without restrictions or limitations) the profusion of God's dispensations throughout history would make no sense to us at all. "Nothing is covered up that will not be uncovered, and nothing secret that will not become known." Only when God has brought to light all "the things now hidden in darkness" (and whoever was involved in them) will we then see that his ways were wise and good. We will see that God saw through the thick cloud and governed all things by the wise counsel of his own will. At the Great Judgment we will understand that nothing was left to chance or to the caprice of human beings. Rather, powerfully and graciously, God arranged all circumstances and shaped everything into one unbroken chain of justice, mercy, and truth.

11. In the discovery of the divine perfections, the righteous will rejoice with unspeakable joy. They will be far from feeling any painful sorrow or shame for any of their past transgressions that have been long since swept away as a cloud and cleansed by the blood of the Lamb. It will be generously comfortable for the redeemed that all their transgressions will not once be spoken of to their disadvantage. Their sins, transgressions, and iniquities will be remembered no more to their condemnation. This is the plain meaning of the promise, and to their eternal consolation, God's children will find it true.

12. After the righteous are judged, God will turn to those at his left hand, and they will be judged according to what they have done. God will judge their outward works and all the wicked words they have ever spoken. Indeed, God will judge all the evil desires, affections, and dispositions that have, or have had, a place in their souls. The Great Judge will bring to light all the evil plans they ever cherished in their hearts.

The joyful decree of acquittal will then be proclaimed to those upon God's right hand, and the horrifying sentence of condemnation will be passed upon those on his left hand. Both judgments must forever remain as unchanging and permanent as the very throne of God.

III. The events that follow the judgment of Christ

1. In the third place, we may consider a few of the events that will transpire after the general judgment. First will be the implementation of the sentence pronounced on the evil and on the good. Jesus said that the unrighteous "will go away into eternal punishment, but the righteous into eternal life." It should be observed that the very same word, *eternal,* is used for both the first and the second clauses.

Therefore, it follows that if the punishment were to end, so would the reward. But that prospect cannot be, unless God himself could come to an end, or unless his mercy and truth could fail. "Then the righteous will shine like the sun in the kingdom of their Father," and "in God's presence there is fullness of joy; at his right hand are pleasures forevermore." Here, all descriptions fall short, and all human language fails! Only the one who was caught up into the third heaven could have a proper conception of it. But even then, he could not describe what he had seen. These things "no mortal is permitted to repeat."

In the meantime, the wicked—all the people that forget God—shall be turned into hell. They "will suffer the punishment of eternal destruction, separated from the presence of the Lord and from the glory of his might." They will be "thrown alive into the lake of fire that burns with sulfur," originally "prepared for the devil and his angels." There, they will "gnaw their tongues in agony;" they will look upward and curse God There, the dogs of hell pride, hatred, revenge, rage, terror, despair—continually devour them. In hell "there is no rest day or night, and the smoke of their torment goes up forever and ever." "Their worm does not die, and the fire is not quenched."

2. Then, "the sky will vanish like a scroll rolling itself up," and "the heavens will pass away with a loud noise." The wicked will flee "from God's presence, and no place will be found for them." The Apostle Peter disclosed the actual manner of this dissolution: "In the coming of the day of God, the heavens will be set ablaze and dissolved, and the elements will melt with fire."

The furious fire will destroy the beautiful fabric of the entire natural order, the connection of all its parts will be demolished, and every atom will be separated from the others. By this same fire "the elements will be dissolved, and the earth and everything that is done on it will be consumed." The enormous works of nature, the everlasting hills and mountains that have defied the ravages of time and stood unmoved so many thousands of years, will melt in fiery ruin. How much less will the works of art, even of the most durable kind, and the utmost efforts of human industry be able to withstand the flaming conqueror! Tombs, pillars, triumphal arches, castles, and pyramids will incinerate. Everything will die, perish, and vanish away like a dream disappears when one awakens!

3. Some great and good men have assumed that it requires the same almighty power to annihilate things as to create them—that is, to speak existence into nonexistence, or to speak something into being out of nothing. On this assumption, they conclude that no part of the universe will be totally or finally destroyed—not even a single atom. Rather, they say that the final effect of fire that we have yet been able to observe is to reduce into glass what had reduced to ashes by a lesser heat. Thus, they conclude that in the coming Day of Judgment the whole earth, if not the material heavens also, will undergo this same kind of change. Then, fire can have no farther power over the elements. This theory they believe is suggested by the expression found in the Revelation made to St. John: "In front of the throne there is something like a sea of glass, like crystal." In the present, we cannot affirm or deny this theory. However, we shall know hereafter.

4. First, scoffers and amateur philosophers ask, "How can these things be? From what source would come such an immense quantity of fire that could consume the heavens and the entire globe of earth and water?" We may remind them, first, that this problem is not unique to the Christian system of thought. Unbiased pagans almost universally held the same view. Thus, one of those celebrated freethinkers echoed this opinion, which was commonly held by his peers:

> He remembered also that it was in fate that a time would come when sea and land, the unignited palace of the sky, and the besieged structures of the universe, will be destroyed by fire.[9]

Second, the question about the source of fire is easy to answer, even from our slight and superficial acquaintance with the natural order. There are abundant storehouses of fire already prepared and stored up against the coming Day of the Lord. How quickly could the Lord order a comet to come down from the most distant parts of the universe! In its return from the sun, if it were to strike the earth when it is some thousand times hotter than a red-hot cannon ball, who does not understand the immediate consequence? We need not look as far away as the celestial heavens. Might not the same lightnings that the Lord of nature commands to "light up the world" also bring ruin and utter destruction?

Or to go no farther than the globe itself, who knows from age to age what huge reservoirs of liquid fire are contained in the bowels of the earth? Mount Etna, Mount Hecla, Mount Vesuvius, and all the other volcanoes that belch out flames and coals of fire are so many proofs of God's power. Are not the mouths of those fiery furnaces so many evidences that God has in readiness what he needs to fulfill his word?

Yes, when we look no further than the surface of the earth and the things that surround us on every side, it is most certain (as a thousand experiments prove, beyond all possibility of denial) that we ourselves, our entire bodies, are full of fire, as well as every thing around us.[10] Is it not easy to make this ethereal fire visible even to the naked eye? Can we not produce the very same effects on combustible matter that are produced by cooking fires? Is there need for anything more than for God to loosen that secret chain that now holds back this irresistible agent that lies quietly in every particle of matter? How quickly such fire would cleave the world into pieces, and bring common ruin to us all!

5. There is one more circumstance that will unfold after the final judgment that deserves our serious consideration. The Apostle Peter said, "We wait for new heavens and a new earth, where righteousness is at

home." This same promise appears in the prophecy of Isaiah: "I am about to create new heavens and a new earth; the former things shall not be remembered or come to mind." How great will be the glory of the new earth! St. John beheld this wonder in his visions of God: "I saw a new heaven and a new earth; for the first heaven and the first earth had passed away."

In the apostle's vision, only righteousness resided in the new heaven and the new earth. He added, "I heard a loud voice from the throne saying, 'See, the home of God is among mortals. He will dwell with them as their God.'" Therefore, of necessity, they will all be happy. "God will wipe every tear from their eyes. Death will be no more; mourning and crying and pain will be no more." "Nothing accursed will be found there any more, and his servants will see his face."

The redeemed will have the nearest access to God and the closest resemblance to him. Using the strongest idiom in the language of scripture to denote the most perfect happiness, St. John recorded, "And his name will be on their foreheads." God will unreservedly acknowledge the redeemed as his own property, and his glorious nature will most visibly shine forth through them. "And there will be no more night; they need no light of lamp or sun, for the Lord God will be their light, and they will reign forever and ever."

IV. An application of the truth of the coming judgment

It remains now only for us to apply the preceding considerations to all those today who are present here before God in his place of judgment. Are we not directly led to make an application? The seriousness of the present court where we are assembled today naturally points us to that coming day when the Lord will judge the world in righteousness. By reminding us of the awesome time that is to come, this truth can furnish us with many lessons for our instruction. I will touch on a few of these lessons. May God write them on all our hearts!

1. First, how beautiful are the feet of those that the wise and gracious providence of God sends to render justice on earth, to defend the injured, and punish the wrongdoers! Are not the officers of this court "God's servants for our good?" Are they not the principal supporters of the public peace, advocates of innocence and virtue, and the important protection of all our temporal blessings? And does not every one of these officers of the court represent both an earthly ruler and the Judge of the earth—him on whose "robe and thigh he has a name inscribed, 'King of kings and

Lord of lords?'" O, that all these court officers, these sons of the right hand of the Most High, may be holy as God is holy! May they be wise with "the wisdom that sits by God's throne." May these officers be like Christ who is the eternal Wisdom of the Father!

May they show no partiality, as God has none; may they "repay all according to their deeds." Like God, may they be steadfastly and undeniably just, while "compassionate and merciful." In so doing, they are God's servants who do not carry the sword in vain, and they will be ominous indeed to those that do evil. In this way, the laws of our land will have their full use and due respect, and the king's throne "will be established in righteousness."

2. You truly honorable men (in a lower degree than God), God and the king have commissioned you to administer justice. May we not justly compare you to those ministering spirits who will attend the Heavenly Judge coming in the clouds? May you, like them, burn with love for God and humankind! May you love righteousness and hate wickedness. May you all minister in your different areas (such an honor God has given you) "for the sake of those who are to inherit salvation" and to the honor of your great sovereign king. May you remain the keepers of peace, the blessing and adornment of your country, the protectors of a needy land, and the guardian angels of all those who are around you!

3. As a charge from God, before whom you stand, your office is to administer what is given to you. How closely you are called to resemble those who stand before the face of the Son of Man, those servants of his who heed his words and do what pleases him. Does it not highly concern you to be as upright as the angels? Is it not important for you to confirm yourselves as servants of God? Has not God called you to do justice, love kindness, and "in everything do to others as you would have them do to you?" In that Great Day, that wonderful Judge, under whose eye you continually stand, will say to you also, "Well done, good and trustworthy servants; enter into the joy of your master."

4. Allow me to add a few words to all the rest of you who on this day are present before the Lord. Should you not keep it in your minds all the day long that a more exalted day is coming? Here today, we have a large assembly! But what is it to compare with the coming day when every eye will look at the general gathering of everyone who has ever lived on the face of the earth?

In today's assembly a few people will stand at the judgment seat to be judged concerning that with which they are charged. They are now restrained in prison, perhaps in chains, until they are brought in to be tried and sentenced. However, all of us (I myself and those who hear my voice) will "stand at the judgment-seat of Christ." We are now restrained on this earth (which is not our final home) in prisons of flesh and blood. Perhaps many of us are also in chains of darkness until we are ordered to be brought forth for the final judgment. Here in this court, one is questioned about one or two deeds that he is charged with committing. There in the Great Assize we will each give an account of every one of our works, from the cradle to the grave. We will be called to account for every one of our words, desires, attitudes, and each of the thoughts and intents of our hearts. Up unto the time that God says, "Give me an accounting of your management, because you cannot be my manager any longer," we must answer for the use we have made of our various talents, whether of mind, body, or fortune.

In this court, it is possible that some who are guilty may escape for a lack of evidence; but there will be no lack of evidence in that final court. Everyone with whom you had the most secret dealings, who were privately aware of all your plans and actions, will be ready to testify about you. So also will all the spirits of darkness that inspired your evil plans and assisted in their implementation. As well, all the angels of God will be ready to testify—those eyes of the Lord that range through the whole earth, who watch over your soul, and worked for your good, so far as you would permit.

Your own conscience will also testify as a thousand witnesses in one, now no longer capable of being blinded or silenced. Your conscience will be compelled to know and to speak the naked truth about all your thoughts, words, and deeds. And is your conscience as a thousand witnesses? Yes, but God is as a *thousand* consciences! O, who can stand before the face of the great God, our Savior Jesus Christ?

Look! Look! The Lord is coming! He makes the clouds his chariots! He rides upon the wings of the wind! A devouring fire goes before him and after him follows the flame of a devouring fire! Look! He sits upon his throne, clothed with light as with a garment, clothed with majesty and honor! Observe that his eyes are like a flame of fire, and his voice is like the sound of many waters!

How will you escape? Will you call to the mountains to fall on you, the rocks to cover you? What a terror! The mountains themselves, the rocks, the earth, the heavens, are themselves just ready to come to nothing! Can you avert the sentence? With what? With all the objects of your house? With thousands of pieces of gold and silver? Blind miserable creature! You came naked from your mother's womb, and you will go naked into eternity.

Hear the words of the Lord, your Judge: "Come, you that are blessed by my Father, inherit the kingdom prepared for you from the foundation of the world. What a joyful sound! How greatly different from the words that echo through the expanse of heaven: "You that are accursed, depart from me into the eternal fire prepared for the devil and his angels." Who is the one that can prevent or delay the full implementation of either sentence? Human hope is in vain! Look, hell has yawned from beneath to receive those who are prepared for destruction! Let the everlasting doors lift up their heads, that the heirs of glory may come in!

5. "What sort of persons ought you to be in leading lives of holiness and godliness." We know it cannot be long before the Lord will descend with the archangel's call, and the sound of God's trumpet, when all of us will appear before him, and give an accounting of our own works. "Wherefore, beloved, seeing you are waiting for these things," seeing you know that "he will come and will not delay," "strive to be found by him at peace, without spot or blemish."

Why should you not be ready? Why should one of you be found on God's left hand, when he appears? He does "not want any to perish, but all to come to repentance." Repentance leads to trust in a bleeding Lord. It leads to faith moving toward spotless love and the full image of God renewed in the heart, producing holiness in all our conduct. Can you doubt this promise, when you remember that the Judge of all is also the Savior of all? Has he not bought you with his own blood so that you will not perish, but have everlasting life?

O, receive his mercy, rather than his justice; receive his love, rather than the thunder of his power! He is not far from each one of us; and he has come, not to condemn, but to save the world. He stands in our midst! Sinner, even now does he not knock at the door of your heart! O, in this your day, may you know "the things that make for your peace." O, in humble faith, and in holy, active, patient love, give yourselves now to him who gave himself for you! Then you will rejoice with overwhelming joy in his day when he comes in the clouds of heaven.

Notes

1. Ward and Heitzenrater, *Wesley's Journal and Diaries*, Feb. 27, 1758, 21:136.
2. Probably a heavy court agenda required rescheduling the sermon for the next day.
3. Ward and Heitzenrater, *Wesley's Journal and Diaries*, March 6, 1758, 21:136.
4. Ibid., March 10, 1758, 21:137.
5. Ibid.

6. Edward Young, *Last Day*, ii. 19, 20, in John Wesley's *Collection of Moral and Sacred Poems*, 1744, 2:76.

7. Ibid., 189-94, in John Wesley's *Collection of Moral and Sacred Poems*, 2:80.

8. Virgil's *Aeneid*, vi. 567-569.

9. Ovid, *Metamorphoses*, i. 256-58.

10. In the eighteenth century, the new discovery of electricity was of continuing interest for Wesley. Here, he refers to electricity as a form of fire.

THE MEANS OF GRACE

John Wesley preached and published this sermon for the benefit of people seeking to become Christians and for Christians who wanted to grow in Christ. Here, Wesley robustly encourages the use of the "means of grace," a theme he tirelessly advocated throughout his ministry. The phrase—*means of grace*—was familiar in eighteenth-century England. It appears to have come from the 1662 Anglican Prayer Book, which gives thanks for "the means of grace and for the hope of Glory." The term is also found in the church's *Catechism:*

Q. What meanest thou by this word Sacrament?

A. I mean an outward and visible sign of an inward and spiritual grace given unto us, ordained by Christ himself, as a means.

In this sermon, Wesley offers a definition: "By the 'means of grace' I refer to the outward symbols, words, and actions that God ordained to be the ordinary channels through which he might convey to us his prevenient, justifying, and sanctifying grace." Elsewhere, Wesley further amplified his views on the means of grace:

> It is generally supposed that "the means of grace" and "the ordinances of God" are equivalent terms. We usually mean by that expression those that are usually termed "works of piety," namely, hearing and reading the Scripture, receiving the Lord's Supper, public and private prayer, and fasting. And it is certain these are the ordinary channels which convey the grace of God to the souls of men.[1]

Vigorous controversy raged in eighteenth-century England over the value of the means of grace. Wesley's personal involvement in this controversy came immediately after his evangelical conversion. In London, certain Moravian Christians of the Fetter Land Society completely opposed using the means of grace. In his journal, Wesley gave the following account:

> About September, 1739, while my brother and I were absent, certain men crept in among them unawares, greatly troubling and subverting their souls; telling them, they were in a delusion, that they had deceived themselves, and had no true faith at all. "For," said they, "none . . . will . . . ever have [a clean heart], till you leave off using the means of grace; (so called;) till you leave off running to church and sacrament, and praying, and singing, and reading either the Bible, or any other book; for you cannot use these things without trusting in them. Therefore, till you leave them off, you can never have true faith."[2]

Wesley sharply disagreed with this position taken by the Moravian Christians. His conflict with them became so strong that in 1739 he broke fellowship with the Fetter Lane Society and formed his own society, which began to meet in London in an abandoned foundery.

The Moravians contended that we should not use any of the means of grace to seek God because we are saved by faith alone. They argued that all religious activities were mere human attempts at "works righteousness." They also preached that such practices contradicted the gospel of grace. Because the Moravians waited quietly in "stillness" for God to save their souls, they gained the name "Quietists." Debate over the stand taken by the Moravian Christians was called the "stillness controversy."

During the mid-1740s, some of Wesley's converts came under the influence of the Quietist doctrine of stillness. These maverick Methodists had received profound experiences of God's grace, which for them were of infinitely greater value than routine participation in the church's sacramental services. In reaction to religious "formalism," some of these converts began to disparage all "outward observances." Influenced by the Quietists, some of the Methodists regarded the means of grace as unnecessary, unhelpful, or even harmful. These sincere people contended that because they had feasted on the living bread of Christ, they had no need for Holy Communion. Those that had been influenced by Quietist teaching felt that because the Spirit of Christ had baptized them, they did not need the sacrament of baptism with water. They preferred lively worship in a Methodist chapel to sitting in the parish church reciting the liturgy and receiving sacraments in religious services that seemed to them to lack spiritual power. Some even waited for the Holy Spirit to speak directly to them, and they neglected the Bible. This present sermon, therefore, was originally written for those Methodists who had been influenced either to disparage or to neglect the means of grace.

Wesley, of course, believed that God by the Holy Spirit sometimes directly gives his grace, apart from the use of any means. However, he believed that scripture instructs us to use the means of grace when they are available to us. Accordingly, we read in Wesley's journal such passages as the following: "In the afternoon I exhorted four or five thousand people . . . neither to neglect nor rest in the means of grace."[3] Wesley explained his reason for promoting their use:

> There are "means of grace," i.e., outward ordinances, whereby the inward grace of God is ordinarily conveyed to man, whereby the faith that brings salvation is conveyed to them who before had it not. . . . He who has not this faith ought to wait for it in the use both of [the Lord's Supper] and of the other means which God hath ordained.[4]

In this sermon, Wesley stresses (1) *God's* work in bringing about conversion and giving Christian assurance and (2) *our* faithful and disciplined use of all the means of grace that God has ordained. Albert Outler observed, "The result [of combining the two] is a sort of 'high-church' evangelicalism—a rare combination, then and since."[5] Because the means of grace are of great value in the Christian life, the present sermon is as relevant today as it was in the eighteenth century.

THE MEANS OF GRACE

You have turned aside from my statutes and have not kept them.   *(Malachi 3:7)*

I. The place of ordinances in the Christian Church

1 Now that "life and immortality have been brought to light through the gospel," is there any longer a place in the church for ordinances? Under the Christian dispensation, has God ordained any "means" as regular channels of his grace? This question would never have been proposed in the apostolic church, unless by one who openly embraced heathenism. The entire body of early Christians agreed that Christ had ordained certain outward means for conveying inner grace into our souls. The constant use of these means was beyond all dispute, for as long as "all who believed were together and had all things in common" and "devoted themselves to the apostles' teaching and fellowship, to the breaking of bread and the prayers."

2. In the course of time, however, "the love of many grew cold." Some Christians began to mistake the *means* for the *end*. They understood religion as consisting of outward works, rather than as a heart renewed after the image of God. They forgot that "the aim" of every commandment is "love that comes from a pure heart and sincere faith." They lost sight of Christ's instruction, "You shall love the Lord your God with all your heart, and with all your soul, and with all your mind." They forgot

267

that real religion is being purified from pride, anger, and evil desire, "through faith in the power of God."

Others in the church seemed to think that, although religion did not principally consist of outward means, yet there was something in their use that pleased God. They thought that the use of the outward means would make them acceptable in God's sight—even if they were not faithful in the weightier matters of the law, such as justice, mercy, and the love of God.

3. Among those who abused the means of grace, it is evident that their use did not move them along toward the goal that God intended. Rather, the things that should have worked for their spiritual health became for them an occasion for stumbling. They were so far from receiving any blessing from using the means of grace that these ordinances only brought down a curse upon their heads. They were so far from growing more heavenly in heart and life that they became twice as much the children of hell as they were before they became Christians.

Others clearly saw that using the means did not convey the grace of God to those children of the devil. Therefore, from these particular instances, they drew the sweeping conclusion that the means of grace did not convey the grace of God.

4. The number of those who abused the means of grace was far greater than the number of those who ignored them. Eventually, there arose certain people of great intelligence (sometimes joined with considerable learning) who also were people of love. They were experientially familiar with true, inward religion. Some of them were burning and shining lamps, persons "famous in their generations." As such, they were worthy examples within the church of Christ—persons who stood in the gap against the swelling tide of ungodliness.

We cannot assume that, at first, these holy and venerable Christians intended anything other than showing that, apart from the religion of the heart, outward religion is worth nothing. They wanted to demonstrate that "God is spirit, and those who worship him must worship in spirit and truth." They wished to show that, without a heart devoted to God, external worship is lost labor. They understood that the outward ordinances of God are of much profit when they advance inward holiness. However, they also knew that if the ordinances do not lead to holiness, they are futile, worthless, and "lighter than a breath." Indeed, if ordinances are used to substitute for a life of holiness, they become utterly "abhorrent to the Lord."

5. Some of these Christians became strongly persuaded that the appalling misuse of the ordinances of God that had spread over the

whole church had almost driven true religion out of the world. It is not strange that some of these Christians, in their fervent zeal for the glory of God and the recovery of souls from fatal delusion, spoke as if outward religious forms were absolutely nothing. They talked as though the means of grace had no place in the religion of Christ. It is not at all surprising that they did not always express themselves with sufficient caution. Therefore, careless hearers might believe that these fervent Christians condemned all outward means as completely unprofitable. Congregations came to believe that God had never intended for the means of grace to serve as the ordinary channels for conveying his grace into our souls.

Again, it is not impossible that, in time, some of these holy Christians actually fell into this way of thinking. Particularly, this outlook was true of those who, not by choice but by the providence of God, were cut off from all these ordinances. Some of them wandered about; having no secure place to live, some lived in hiding places and caves of the earth. These Christians experienced the grace of God within themselves, although they were deprived of all outward means. They might easily have concluded that God would give the same grace to those who deliberately refrained from using the means of grace.

6. Experience teaches us how easily this notion spreads and insinuates itself into people's minds. It is especially true for those who have been completely awakened out of the sleep of spiritual death and have begun to feel the weight of their sins as a burden too heavy to bear. These people are usually restless in their awakened state. Trying in every way to escape from their sins, they are always ready to grasp at any new thing, any additional proposal that promises them relief or happiness. They most likely try nearly all of the outward means of grace, only to find no comfort in them. It may be that they experience increasing remorse, fear, sorrow, and condemnation.

It is easy, therefore, to persuade these people that it is best for them to dispense with the means of grace. They are already weary of striving in vain (as it seems to them). Seeking to quench the inner fire, they feel that they "labor only to feed the flames." Therefore, they are happy for any pretext to set aside what gives no contentment to their souls. They are ready to abandon their painful strife and to sink into languid inactivity.

II. The means of grace explained

1. Next, I propose to examine the general question of whether there *are* any means of grace.

By the "means of grace" I mean *the outward symbols, words, and actions that God ordained to be the ordinary channels through which he might convey to us his prevenient, justifying, and sanctifying grace.* I use the expression "means of grace" because I know of no better one. Also, for many ages the expression has been widely used in the Christian Church, particularly in our own Church of England. The church instructs us to bless God both for "the means of grace and the hope of glory."[6] We are taught in our Catechism that a sacrament is "an outward sign of inward grace, and a means whereby we receive the same."

The chief of these means of grace are *prayer* (whether in secret or with the large congregation), *searching the Scriptures* (which implies reading, hearing, and meditating on the Bible), and *receiving the Lord's supper* (eating bread and drinking wine in remembrance of Christ). We believe that these means are ordained by God to be the ordinary channels of conveying his grace to our souls.

2. We acknowledge that the entire value of the means of grace depends on their actual service to religion's *aim*. We also believe that all these means, when separated from their goal, are "less than nothing and emptiness." If the means do not actually promote the knowledge and love of God, they are not acceptable in his sight. Indeed, they are instead an abomination to God, a stench in his nostrils, and he is furious against them. Above all, if we use the means of grace as a kind of substitute for the religion they were designed to serve, it is not easy to find words to describe the enormous absurdity and wickedness of turning God's means against himself. In this way, we banish Christianity *from* the heart by the very means that God ordained for bringing it into the heart.

3. We also acknowledge that every outward means of any kind, if separated from the Spirit of God, cannot profit us at all. In themselves, the means cannot in any degree advance us toward the knowledge and love of God. Without debating this matter, we can agree that any help that we receive on the earth comes from God himself. It is God alone, by his own almighty power, who works in us what pleases him. And unless God works in and through all outward things, they are only weak and impoverished foundations. Therefore, those are wrong who suppose that there is any inherent power whatsoever in the means of grace; "they know neither the scriptures nor the power of God."

We know that there is no innate authority in the *words* that are spoken in prayer, in the *letter* of scripture we read or the *sound* of its public recitation, or the *bread and wine* we receive in the Lord's supper. God alone is the giver of every good gift and the Author of all grace. The entire power comes from him, by whom all the means of grace convey blessing to our souls. We also know that God is able to give the same grace without any of these means being present on the face of the earth. In this sense, we may assert that, with regard to God, there is no such thing as means. With means or without means, he is equally able to work whatever pleases him.

4. We further acknowledge that the use of every one of the means of grace will never atone for a single sin. It is the blood of Christ alone by which any sinner can be reconciled to God. There is no other propitiation for our sins, no other "fountain for sin and impurity." All believers in Christ are deeply convinced that our only merit is in him and that there is no saving value in any of our own good works. There is no credit in verbalizing a prayer, studying scripture, listening to the word of God, or partaking of the sacramental bread and cup. No one who knows the grace of God would deny that the phrase that some use—"Christ is the only means of grace"—denotes only that Christ is the sole meritorious *cause* of grace.

5. Once again, we acknowledge the sad truth that to this day a large percentage of those who are called Christians abuse the means of grace to the ruin of their souls. This charge is doubtless the case with all those who are content with "holding to the outward form of godliness while denying its power." On the one hand, they may naively presume that they are already Christians because they do this and that good work, although Christ has not yet been revealed to them. Nor has God's love been "poured into their hearts."

On the other hand, they may assume that they are certainly Christians, specifically because they use the means of grace. They foolishly dream (although they may be hardly aware they are doing so) that there is some kind of power in the means by which sooner or later they will certainly become holy (they do not know when). Or, they may think that there is a sort of merit in using the means of grace which will surely influence God to give them holiness or accept them without it.

6. These people scarcely understand the great foundation of the whole Christian structure: "By grace you have been saved." Only through the merits of God's well-beloved Son are we saved from our sins, and from sin's guilt and power, and restored to the favor and image of God. We are not justified by any power, wisdom, or strength that we possess, or by the merit of any other human being. We are saved simply through the grace and power of the Holy Spirit who activates grace in everyone.

7. The main issue still remains, and we can state it this way: We know this salvation is the gift and work of God, but how can people find salvation when they are convinced that they are not saved? If you say,

"Believe, and you will be saved," some will answer, "Yes, but how shall I believe?" You reply, "Wait upon God." They answer, "That is well and good, but how am I to wait? Shall I use the means of grace, or wait on God without them? Am I to wait for the grace of God that brings salvation by using these means or by setting them aside?"

8. It is not possible to imagine that the word of God would fail to give direction regarding this important point. We cannot believe that the Son of God, who came down from heaven for us mortals and for our redemption, should have left us confused with regard to a question so closely connected to our salvation. In fact, he has *not* left us confused; he has shown us the pathway we should take. We have only to turn to the scriptures and examine what is written there. If we simply accept their teaching, we need have no further doubt about the matter.

III. Scriptural encouragement to use the means of grace

1. According to the teaching of the Bible, all who desire the grace of God are instructed to wait for it by using the means that he has ordained. We are to use these ordinances and not set them aside.

First, all who desire the grace of God are to wait for it by the use of prayer. Our Lord himself gave us this explicit direction. In his Sermon on the Mount, he begins by explaining the overall nature of true religion and describing its main aspects. Then, he adds, "Ask, and it will be given you; seek, and you will find; knock, and the door will be opened for you. For everyone who asks receives, and everyone who seeks finds, and for everyone who knocks, the door will be opened." Here, in the clearest way, Christ instructed us to ask in order to receive. He instructed us to seek in order to find the grace of God, the pearl of great price. If we want to enter into the kingdom of God, Christ commands us to knock at the door and to continue asking and seeking.

2. So that there would be no doubt about his instruction, our Lord underscores this point in a more particular manner. He appeals to everyone's heart:

> Is there anyone among you who, if your child asks for bread, will give a stone? Or if the child asks for a fish, will give a snake? If you then, who are evil, know how to give good gifts to your children, how much more will your Father in heaven give good things to those who ask him?

On another occasion, Jesus included all "good things" in a single gift—"How much more will the heavenly Father give the Holy Spirit to those who ask him!" It should particularly be noticed that the persons directed to ask had not yet received the Holy Spirit. Nevertheless, our Lord instructed them to use prayer as a means of receiving the Holy Spirit. He promised that prayer would be effective. As we ask, we will receive the Holy Spirit from him whose "compassion is over all that he has made."

3. If we would receive any gift from God, the absolute necessity of using the means of prayer further appears in the remarkable passage that immediately precedes the words we have been discussing:

> Suppose one of you has a friend, and you go to him at midnight and say to him, "Friend, lend me three loaves of bread." And he answers from within, "Do not bother me. I cannot get up and give you anything." I tell you, even though he will not get up and give him anything, because he is his friend, at least because of his persistence, he will get up and give him whatever he needs. So I say to you, Ask, and it will be given you; search and you will find; knock, and the door will be opened for you. Even though he will not get up and give him anything, because he is his friend, at least because of his persistence, he will get up and give him whatever he needs.

How could our blessed Lord be any more clear? By the means of prayer and by persistently asking, we may receive from God what otherwise we would not receive.

4. Elsewhere, Jesus told them a parable about their need always to pray and not to lose heart. He told his disciples that through the means of prayer they would receive from God whatever petition they asked of him. Jesus said,

> In a certain city there was a judge who neither feared God nor had respect for people. In that city there was a widow who kept coming to him and saying, "Grant me justice against my opponent." For a while he refused; but later he said to himself, "Though I have no fear of God and no respect for anyone, yet because this widow keeps bothering me, I will grant her justice, so that she may not wear me out by continually coming." (Luke 18:2-5)[7]

Our Lord himself made the application of this parable. "Hear what the unjust judge said. And will God not avenge His own elect who cry out day and night to Him, though He bears long with them? I tell you that He will avenge them speedily—if they pray and do not lose heart."

5. In another place, Jesus gave us more familiar words about praying. They contain equally full and explicit instruction to wait for the blessings of God in private prayer. The command is linked with a positive promise that by the means of prayer we will obtain our request. Those familiar words are, "When you pray, go into your room, and when you have shut your door, pray to your Father who is in the secret place; and your Father who sees in secret will reward you openly."

6. If it is possible for any instruction regarding prayer to be clearer, it is the one that God gave us through the Apostle James. It concerns all kinds of prayer, public or private; and a blessing is attached to it: "If any of you lacks wisdom, let him ask of God, who gives to all liberally and without reproach, and it will be given to him." Notice that St. James says *if* they ask. Otherwise, "You do not have because you do not ask."

Someone may object, "But this verse provides no direction for unbelievers, those that do not know the pardoning grace of God. The apostle adds, 'But ask in faith,' otherwise one 'must not expect to receive anything from the Lord.'" I answer that in this context the meaning of the word "faith" is established by the apostle himself, as if he purposely wanted to anticipate this objection. In the words immediately following, St. James instructed us to ask in faith, never doubting that God hears our prayers, and God will fulfill the desires of our hearts.

The flagrant, blasphemous absurdity of assuming that this passage is talking about faith in its full Christian meaning is based on flawed logic. Such an interpretation would require us to understand that St. James first says in this passage that the Holy Spirit guides one who knows that he does not have Christian faith (here called wisdom) to ask God for it. The verses contain a positive promise that "it will be given to the seeker." Then, the verse immediately adds that it will *not* be given to him unless the seeker has faith before he asks for it! Who can accept such reasoning? From this scripture, as well as the other scriptures already cited, we must conclude that all who desire the grace of God are to wait for it by the means of prayer.

7. *Second, All who desire the grace of God are to wait for it by searching the Scriptures.*

From the instruction of our Lord, it is also simple and clear that the Bible is a means of grace. Christ said to the unbelieving Jews, "Search the scriptures" because they "testify on my behalf." For the very purpose of revealing who he was, Jesus directed the Jews to examine the scriptures. It is a shamelessly false assertion to say, "This is not a command, but only an assertion that they did search the scriptures." I desire those who contend for this view to tell us how a command can be more clearly expressed than in the literal directive, "Search the scriptures." In the original Greek language, these words are an imperative *command*. Christ's directive is as clear as words can make it.

What a great blessing from God accompanies the use of scripture! This blessing appears in what is recorded concerning the Bereans. After hearing the preaching of St. Paul, they "examined the scriptures every day to see whether these things were so. Many of them therefore believed." It is indeed probable that in some of those who welcomed the message very eagerly, "faith came from what was heard" as St. Paul preached. It was later confirmed by reading the scriptures. As I stated earlier, "searching the scriptures" generally includes hearing, reading, and meditating.

8. Scripture is also a means by which God reveals, confirms, and enlarges true wisdom. Paul wrote to Timothy, "From childhood you have known the sacred writings that can instruct you for salvation through faith in Christ Jesus." In the fullest manner that we can conceive, the next verse confirms the truth that scripture is the chief means which God ordained for conveying his various graces to us. "All scripture is inspired by God and is useful for teaching, for reproof, for correction, and for training in righteousness, so that everyone who belongs to God may be proficient, equipped for every good work."

9. It should be noticed that these words primarily and directly pertain to the scriptures that Timothy had known from childhood. St. Paul was referring to the Old Testament, for the New Testament was not yet written. He was "not in the least inferior to the chief apostles," nor, I think, inferior to any man now upon the earth—and he was far from making light of the Old Testament! Observe this, you who give such little importance to one-half of the Bible, for fear that one day you will "be amazed and perish." The portion of scripture that you neglect, the Holy Spirit explicitly declares "useful" as a God-ordained means for "teaching, for reproof, for correction, and for training in righteousness" so that "everyone who belongs to God may be proficient, equipped for every good work."

10. Scripture not only has value for the people of God who already walk in "the light of his countenance." Scripture is also useful for those who yet live in darkness, seeking him whom they do not know. The Apostle Peter wrote, "We have the prophetic message more fully confirmed"—literally, "and we have the prophetic word more sure." The Old Testament prophetic word has been confirmed by our being "eyewitnesses of his majesty," and "hearing the voice of the Majestic Glory, saying, 'This is my Son, my Beloved, with whom I am well pleased.'"

St. Peter said, "We have the prophetic message (a term he used for the scriptures) more fully confirmed. You will do well to be attentive to this as to a lamp shining in a dark place, until the day dawns and the morning star rises in your hearts."

11. *Third, all who desire an increase of the grace of God are to wait for it by partaking of the Lord's supper.* The Lord himself has given this instruction:

> On the night when he was betrayed he took a loaf of bread, and broke it and said, "This is my body that is for you (that is, a sacred symbol of my body). Do this in remembrance of me." In the same way he took the cup also, after supper, saying, "This cup is the new covenant in my blood (the sacred symbol of that covenant). Do this ... in remembrance of me." For as often as you eat this bread and drink the cup, you proclaim the Lord's death until he comes. (1 Cor. 11:23-26)

Before God, and angels, and people, by these visible signs you also openly demonstrate the same faith and express your solemn remembrance of his death, until he comes in the clouds of heaven.

Take care that you "examine yourselves," whether you understand the meaning and plan of this holy institution and whether you really yearn to be made conformable to the death of Christ. Only then, without doubting, you may "eat of the bread and drink of the cup."

St. Paul explicitly repeats the instruction first given by our Lord: "eat" and "drink." In the Greek language, both verbs are in the imperative mood. These words do not imply a mere permission only. They are an explicit command to all those who are already filled with peace and joy in believing. They can truly say, "The remembrance of our sins is grievous unto us, the burden of them is intolerable."

12. From the words of St. Paul it is evident that Holy Communion is a standard, stated means of receiving the grace of God. In the preceding chapter, the apostle wrote, "The cup of blessing that we bless, is it not a sharing in the blood of Christ? The bread that we break, is it not a sharing in the body of Christ?" Is not the eating of this bread and the drinking of this cup the outward, visible means through which God conveys grace to our souls? Is it not all of the spiritual grace, righteousness, peace, and joy in the Holy Spirit that were purchased by the body of Christ once broken, and the blood of Christ once shed for us? Therefore, let everyone who truly desires the grace of God eat of that bread and drink of that cup.

IV. Objections considered

1. God has clearly shown us the means by which we are to seek after him. Yet, people who are wise in their own estimation have offered innumerable objections to God's revealed truth. It seems necessary to consider a few of these objections to using the means of grace. I deal with these objections not because they have any merit, but because people so often raise them. Especially, in recent times, these protests have led unstable people away from the true way. Also, the words of deceitful teachers have harassed and undermined those who were running well in the Christian way. They present themselves as apostles of Christ, just as Satan disguises himself as "an angel of light."

The first and main objection is stated this way: "You cannot use these means of grace without trusting in them for your salvation." I implore you, where is your assumption found in the Bible? I expect you to show me clear scripture for your assertion. If you cannot ground your view in the Bible, I refuse to risk accepting what you say, because I do not believe that you are wiser than God.

If what you say is true, certainly Christ would have known it. And if he had known it, he would surely have warned us; he would have addressed this matter long ago. Because Christ gave no warning against using the means of grace, there is not a word supporting your view in the entire revelation of Jesus Christ. I am as fully assured that your assertion is false as I am certain that the revelation concerning the means of grace comes from God.

However, critics might say, "Just stop using the means of grace for a short time to see whether you trusted in them or not." You are asking me to disobey God in order to know whether I believe in obeying him! Do you really advocate such advice? Do you deliberately teach others to "do evil, that good may come?" O, tremble at the sentence of God against such teachers! Truly, their "condemnation is deserved."

The objector may reply, "No, if you are troubled when you quit using the means of grace, it is clear that you trusted in them." By no means is this statement true! If I am troubled when I willfully disobey God, it is clear that his Spirit is still striving with me. But, if I am not troubled over willful sin, then it is apparent that I am given over to a debased mind.

What do you mean by my "trusting in them?" Are you asking if I am looking for the blessing of God in their use? Are you asking me whether I believe that if I use the means of grace I will gain what otherwise I could not gain? Yes, I do use the means of grace. God being my helper, I will continue to do so, even to my life's end. By the grace of God, in this way

I will trust in the means of grace until the day of my death. That is, I will believe that whatever God has promised he is also faithful to carry out. Seeing that God has promised to bless me through these means, I trust it will be according to his word.

2. Second, some people have objected, "Using the means of grace is seeking salvation by works." I respond by asking whether you know the meaning of the expression you use. What is "seeking salvation by works?" In the writings of St. Paul, it means seeking to be saved by observing the ritual works of the Mosaic law or expecting salvation for the sake of our own good deeds, through the merit of our own righteousness. How is either of these dangers implied by my waiting on God by the means he has ordained and expecting that he will meet me there because he has promised to do so?

I do expect that God will fulfill his word and that he will meet and bless me as I use the means of grace. Yet God gives his favor not for the sake of any works that I have done or for the merit of my righteousness. God blesses us only through the merits, sufferings, and love of his Son, in whom he is always well pleased.

3. Third, it has been zealously contended that "the only means of grace is Christ." I answer that this remark is a mere playing on words. Examine your statement, and the objection vanishes away. When we say, "Prayer is a means of grace," we understand that prayer is a channel through which the grace of God is conveyed to us. When you say "Christ is the only means of grace," you mean that he is the sole payment and procurer of grace—that "no one comes to the Father except through him." Who denies it? But this truth is completely irrelevant to the present question.

4. Fourth, some object, "Do the scriptures not instruct us to *wait* for salvation? Does not David say, 'For God alone my soul waits in silence; from him comes my salvation?' And does not Isaiah teach us the same thing: 'O Lord . . . we wait for you.'" Yes, these verses cannot be denied. Because salvation is the gift of God, we are undoubtedly to wait on him for it. But *how* shall we wait on God? If God himself has appointed a way to wait on him, can you find a better way? God has given us a way, and this way has been comprehensively and clearly revealed to us.

The very words of the prophet Isaiah that I just cited lay the question to rest. The entire sentence reads this way: "In the path of your judgments (meaning "statutes," "law," or "commandments"), O Lord, we wait for you." David also waited for God in the same way, as his own words clearly witness: "I hope for your salvation, O Lord, and I fulfill your commandments." "Teach me, O Lord, the way of your statutes, and I will observe it to the end."

5. Some reply, "Yes, but God has appointed another way to wait on him: 'stand firm, and see the deliverance that the LORD will accomplish for you today.'" Let us examine the scriptures to which you refer. The first of them, with the context, reads this way: "As Pharaoh drew near, the Israelites looked back, and they were in great fear. . . . They said to Moses, 'Was it because there were no graves in Egypt that you have taken us away to die in the wilderness?' . . . And Moses said to the people, 'Do not be afraid, stand firm, and see the deliverance of the Lord.' . . . Then the LORD said to Moses, 'Tell the Israelites to go forward. But you lift up your staff, and stretch out your hand over the sea and divide it, that the Israelites may go into the sea on dry ground.'" This was the salvation of God that the people of Israel stood firm to see—by marching forward with all their might!

The other passage where this expression occurs I will quote at length:

> Messengers came and told Jehoshaphat, "A great multitude is coming against you from . . . beyond the sea." . . . Jehoshaphat was afraid; he set himself to seek the LORD, and proclaimed a fast throughout all Judah. Judah assembled to seek help from the LORD; from all the towns of Judah they came to seek the LORD. Jehoshaphat stood in the assembly of Judah and Jerusalem, in the house of the LORD. . . . Then the spirit of the LORD came upon Jahaziel. . . . He said . . . "Do not fear or be dismayed at this great multitude. . . . Tomorrow go down against them. . . . This battle is not for you to fight; take your position, stand still, and see the victory of the LORD." . . . They rose early in the morning and went out. . . . As they began to sing and praise, the LORD set an ambush against the Ammonites, Moab, and Mount Seir . . . and they all helped to destroy one another.

Such was the salvation that the children of Judah saw. But how does all this prove that we should wait for the grace of God without using the means that he has ordained?

6. I will mention only one more objection, which indeed does not properly belong in this section of the sermon. Nevertheless, because this objection has been so frequently pressed, I will not completely ignore it. The objector complains, "Does not St. Paul say, 'If with Christ you died . . . why do you submit to regulations?' Therefore a Christian, one who is dead with Christ, does not any more need to use the ordinances."

You are saying, "Since I am a Christian, I am not subject to the ordinances of Christ!" Surely, by the absurdity of this statement, at first glance, you must see that the ordinances mentioned here cannot be the ordinances of Christ. They are clearly the Jewish ordinances, to which certainly a Christian is no longer subject. It is undeniably clear that the words that immediately follow—"Do not handle, do not taste, do not touch"—evidently refer to the ancient ordinances of the Jewish law. This protest is the weakest one of all. So, despite the objections to the contrary, the important truth must stand unshaken—all who desire the grace of God are to wait for it in the means which God has ordained.

V. Using the means of grace

1. We have established that all who desire the grace of God are to wait for it by the means he has ordained. Now, we need to inquire into *how* these means should be used, both as to the order and the manner of using them.

With regard to the order of their use, we may observe that there is a sequence that God is generally pleased to use to bring sinners to salvation. Foolish, insensible people are continuing in their own way, not having God in their thoughts, when God comes upon them in unexpected prevenient grace. Perhaps without any outward means at all, God may move through an arresting sermon or conversation, some terrible providence, or by a direct impulse of his convicting Spirit. The sinner is awakened to a desire to "flee from the wrath to come."

Then, awakened sinners intentionally seek out how they can avoid God's wrath. If they find a preacher who really speaks to the heart, they are astonished and begin searching the scriptures to find whether these things are so. The more they hear and read, the more convicted they become, and day and night the more they meditate on biblical truth. Perhaps they find some other book that explains and reinforces what they have heard and read in scripture. And by all these means the arrows of conviction sink deeper into their souls.

They begin also to talk about the things of God that are constantly uppermost in their thoughts. Yes, they also talk with God in prayer—although because of fear and shame they hardly know what to say. Whether or not they can speak, they cannot help but pray, even if only with "sighs too deep for words." Yet, they are in doubt whether "the high and lofty one who inhabits eternity" will pay heed to such sinners as they are. They want to pray in the great congregation with the faithful ones who know God. There, they see others go to the table of the Lord. One thinks, "Christ has said, 'Do this!' Why is it that I do not partake of Holy Communion? I am too great a sinner. I am not qualified. I am not worthy." After that person struggles with these scruples awhile, he or she at last makes a decision. That one continues in God's way by using the means of grace. Such seekers persist in hearing, reading, meditating, praying, and partaking of the Lord's supper. At last, in the manner that pleases him, God says to their hearts, "Your faith has saved you; go in peace."

2. By complying with God's stated ways of seeking him, we can learn what means of grace to recommend to others. If any of these means will reach an ignorant and careless sinner, it is probably through hearing or discussion. Therefore, to the sinner that never gives any thought to salvation, we might recommend using these means of grace. To those who begin to feel the weight of their sins, hearing and reading the word of God (and perhaps other serious books) may be a means of bringing deeper conviction. Will you not also advise others to meditate on what they read so that it may have its full force upon their hearts? Without reluctance, seekers should talk about salvation with those who walk in the same path. When trouble and heaviness grip them, should you not then earnestly encourage them to pour out their souls before God in prayer?

Should they not "pray always and not lose heart?" When they feel the inadequacy of their own prayers, should you not work together with God, reminding the seekers to attend the house of the Lord and pray with all those who reverence him? If they do so, they will soon remember the final word of the Lord to his disciples—"do this in remembrance of me." This is a clear exhortation that this is the time to cooperate with the stirring of the blessed Spirit. In this way, we can lead others, step by step, through all the means of grace that God has ordained. We encourage seekers not according to our own will, but just as divine guidance and the Spirit of God lead and open the way.

3. Even as we find no command in scripture regarding any particular sequence to be observed in using the means of grace, neither do God's divine intervention and the Spirit of God hold to an unvarying pattern in seeking us. The means by which God leads different people to find his blessing are varied, mixed, and combined together in a thousand different ways. Yet common sense tells us to follow the leading of God's providence and Spirit. Partly by providence, God guides us individually as to the means we should use to seek his grace. Sometimes God gives us the opportunity to use one means, and sometimes another. Partly, God uses our experiences, through which his free Spirit is most pleased to work in our hearts. In the meantime, the certain and ordinary rule for all who yearn for the salvation of God is to use all the means of grace that he has ordained whenever opportunities occur. Who knows which means God will use to give to you the grace that brings salvation?

4. As to the manner of using the means of grace, if they are to convey any grace at all to those who use them, we must remember several things. First, always retain a keen sense that God is above all the means we may use to seek him. Take caution, therefore, not to limit the Almighty. He works whatever and whenever he chooses. He can convey his grace either with or without any of the means that he has appointed. Perhaps he will work in one way or perhaps in another.

> For who has known the mind of the Lord?
> Or who has been his counselor? (Rom. 11:34)

Every moment, then, look for God's appearance! It may be during the hour that you are engaged in his ordinances; or it may be before or after that hour, or even when you are impeded from using the means of grace. God is not hindered—he is always ready, always able, always willing to save. "It is the Lord; let him do what seems good to him."

Second, before you use any of the means of grace, let it be deeply impressed on your soul that they have no inherent power in themselves. A means is, in itself, a poor, dead, empty thing. A means is separate from God; it is a dry leaf, a shadow. Neither is there any merit in using a means of grace. Nothing we do is intrinsically pleasing to God. I can do nothing for which I deserve any favor from his hands, not even a drop of water to cool my tongue. But because God invites, I respond. Because he directs me to use means to wait on him, I will use them and wait for his free mercy, from which comes my salvation.

Settle this in your heart that the mere work done profits us nothing. There is no power to save in the deed itself; the only power is in the Spirit of God. There is no merit except in the blood of Christ. Therefore, the means that God himself ordained convey no grace to the soul unless one trusts in Christ alone. Yet, the one that does truly trust in him cannot fall short of the grace of God—even if one were to be cut off from every outward ordinance and shut up in the center of the earth.

Third, in using all the means of grace, seek God alone. In and through every outward thing, look only to the power of his Spirit and the merits of his Son. Beware that you do not remain in the work itself; to do so is to lose all your labor. Nothing short of God himself can satisfy your soul. Therefore, in everything fix your eye on him who is "above all and through all and in all."

Remember also to use all the means of grace only as helps. Use them as God has ordained. Do not use them for their own sake, but in order to renew your soul in true righteousness and holiness. If the means actually lead to this end, well and good. But if not, they are filth and dross.

Finally, after you have used any of the means of grace, be careful how you evaluate yourself. Do you congratulate yourself as having done some great thing? This attitude turns everything into poison. Remember, if God is not present, what does my work avail? Consider whether you have been adding sin to sin. How long must I wait? O Lord, save me, or I perish. Lord, do not hold this sin against me. If God were there and if his love flowed into your heart, you will quickly forget the outward ordinance. You see, you know, and you feel that God is all in all. Humble yourself. Kneel down before him. Give him all your praise. "May God be glorified in all things through Jesus Christ." Let all your bones cry out, "I will sing of your steadfast love, O Lord, forever; with my mouth I will proclaim your faithfulness to all generations."

Notes

1. Outler, *Wesley's Sermons*, 3:385.
2. Curnock, *Wesley's Journal*, 1:430.
3. Ward and Heitzenrater, *Wesley's Journal and Diaries,* November 15, 1739, 19:122.
4. Ibid., Nov. 7, 1739, 121.
5. Outler, *Wesley's Sermons*, Introductory commentary on Sermon #16, 1:377.
6. *Book of Common Prayer,* "A General Thanksgiving."

THE CIRCUMCISION OF
THE HEART

John Wesley first preached *The Circumcision of the Heart* at Oxford in St. Mary's Church on New Year's Day, 1733. This day was the occasion of the Feast of the Circumcision of Christ. The Collect for the day was,

> Almighty God, who madest thy blessed Son to be circumcised, and obedient to the law for man; Grant us the true circumcision of the spirit; that, our hearts, and all our members, being mortified from all worldly and carnal lusts, we may in all things obey thy blessed will; through the same thy Son Jesus Christ our Lord. Amen.

Drawing inspiration from the liturgy, Wesley spoke on the circumcision of the heart. The sermon's text is from Romans: "Real circumcision is a matter of the heart—it is spiritual and not literal" (Rom. 2:29). It will be remembered that the book of Deuteronomy states, "The LORD your God will circumcise your heart and the heart of your descendants, so that you will love the Lord your God with all your heart and with all your soul, in order that you may live" (Deut. 30:6). In this sermon about heart circumcision, we see the concrete realities of obedience and fruit joined with the subjective experience of assurance. This assurance comes through the witness of our spirits that we belong to God.

284

In 1738, after Wesley's experience of an evangelical conversion, he revised this sermon, and eventually he included it in the second volume of his Sermons on Several Occasions (1748). Thereafter, he continued to preach this message without further revision. In 1778, thirty years after he published *The Circumcision of the Heart*, Wesley wrote,

> I was musing here on what I heard a good man say long since, "Once in seven years I burn all my sermons; for it is a shame if I cannot write better sermons now than I could seven years ago." Whatever others can do, I really cannot. . . . I know not that I can write a better on the Circumcision of the Heart, than I did five-and-forty years ago. Perhaps, indeed I may have read five or six hundred books more than I had then, and may know a little more History, or Natural Philosophy, than I did; but I am not sensible that this has made any essential addition to my knowledge in Divinity. Forty years ago I knew and preached every Christian doctrine which I preach now."[1]

In 1765 in a letter to John Newton, Wesley reflected on this sermon: "January 1, 1733, I preached the sermon on the Circumcision of the Heart; which contains all that I now teach concerning salvation from all sin, and loving God with an undivided heart. In the same year I printed, (the first time I ventured to print any thing,) for the use of my pupils, *A Collection of Forms of Prayer*; and in this I spoke explicitly of giving '*the whole heart and the whole life to God.*' This was then, as it is now, my idea of Perfection."[2]

Although this sermon was first written in 1733, it ranks among Wesley's clearest statements about holiness of heart and life. He explains that the circumcision of the heart is a complete surrender of the soul to God, by which every thought, word, disposition, and deed are devoted to him. The circumcised heart exclusively seeks those things that bring honor and glory to God. The only good things are those that are properly attuned to the One who is eternally good. This way of life transcends the circumcision of the flesh. It is the circumcision of the heart.

THE CIRCUMCISION OF
THE HEART

*Preached at St. Mary's, Oxford, before the University on
January 1, 1733.*

*Real circumcision is a matter of the heart—it is spiritual
and not literal.*   *(Romans 2:29)*

1   It is the thoughtful assertion of an excellent man[3] that one who
now preaches the most essential duties of Christianity runs the danger of being judged by a great part of his hearers as "an innovator of new doctrines." Most people have moved away from the substance of Christianity, even while continuing to profess that religion. No sooner are any of Christianity's truths proposed which contrast the Spirit of Christ with the spirit of the world, than they cry out, "You are bringing strange things to our ears. We would like to know what it means." All the while, the preacher is only teaching them about "Jesus and the resurrection," with its necessary outcome—If Christ is risen, then you ought to die to the world and to live wholly for God.

2. Unconverted people, who are alive to the world and dead to God, are annoyed with the exhortation to die to this world. Such people will not readily accept this preaching as being God's truth, unless it is so lim-

ited in its interpretation as to have no practical use or significance. They do not receive the words of God's Spirit, taken in their clear and obvious meaning. God's truths are foolishness to them. Indeed, they are unable to understand them because they are spiritually discerned. The truths of God are discernible only by a spiritual sense, which has not yet awakened within them. Because they lack spiritual discernment, they reject the wisdom and power of God as trivial human fantasies.

3. One of those important truths that can only be spiritually discerned is that real circumcision is a matter of the heart. It is spiritual, not physical. The circumcision of the heart is the distinguishing mark of a true follower of Christ, one who is in a state of being accepted by God. It is not circumcision of the flesh, or baptism, or any other outward ritual. It is a right state of the soul, a mind and spirit renewed after the image of him who created it. The Apostle Paul himself attests to God's approval of this right state of one's spiritual being: "Such a person receives praise not from others but from God."

It is as though St. Paul said, "Whoever you are that follow your great Master, do not expect the praise of those who do not follow him. They will not say to you, 'Well done, good and trustworthy servant!'" Understand that the world considers the circumcision of the heart, which is the seal of the true Christian calling, to be foolishness. Be content to wait for your applause until the day of your Lord's appearing. In that hour, in the great assembly of men and angels, you will have praise from God.

In this sermon, (1) I plan to inquire especially into the nature of the circumcision of the heart, and (2) I will offer some reflections that naturally arise from such an inquiry.

I. The nature of the circumcision of the heart

1. First, I will discuss the kind of circumcision of the heart that receives God's approval. In general, we may say that the circumcision of the heart is the habitual inclination of soul toward what scripture terms *holiness*. The circumcision of the heart involves being cleansed from sin, that is, "from every defilement of body and of spirit." This cleansing results in being endued with those virtues that were also in Christ Jesus. The circumcision of the heart is being "renewed in the spirit of our mind," so as to be "perfect as our heavenly Father is perfect."

2. To be more specific, the circumcision of heart implies *humility, faith, hope,* and *love.* Humility is a correct judgment of ourselves. It

cleanses our minds from pride concerning our own goodness. Humility frees us from an unwarranted opinion of our own abilities and attainments, which are really the true fruit of a corrupted nature. Humility cuts away the self-centered thought, "I am rich, I have prospered, and I need nothing" and convinces us that we are by nature "wretched, pitiable, poor, blind, and naked." Humility convinces us that, even at our best, we are only sin and vanity. Humility helps us comprehend the truth that confusion, ignorance, and error dominate our minds. We come to see that unreasonable, worldly, sensual, devilish passions lay hold of our wills. In a word, humility shows us that there is not a healthy component in our soul and that all the foundations of our nature are unstable.

3. At the same time, humility leads us to perceive that in ourselves we are not adequate to help ourselves. Without the Spirit of God, we can do nothing but add more sin to the sin we already have. We come to recognize that it is God alone "who is at work in us" by his almighty power "enabling us both to will and to work for his good pleasure." Without the supernatural assistance of God's Spirit, it is as impossible for us to think a good thought as it is for us to create ourselves or to renew our whole souls in righteousness and true holiness.

4. A sure result of our having formed a correct judgment of our sinfulness and helplessness is our indifference to the "glory that comes from others" for some supposed attribute we may have. Those who understand themselves do not desire or value the applause which they know that they do not deserve. It is therefore "a very small thing to be judged by any human court." By comparing what is said in their favor or what has been said against them with what they sense in their own hearts, truly humble people have every reason to think that the world and the god of this world have been "liars from the beginning."

According to God's will, one would want those who are not attached to this world to look upon themselves as faithful stewards of the Lord's belongings. Possibly, gaining the high regard of others might be a means to enable one to be of greater use to one's fellow servants. Even if a desire to serve is the aim for hoping for the approval of others, one is in no way dependent on this approval. Humble persons are certain that whatever God wills, he never lacks the people to do it, because even from stones God is able to lift up servants to accomplish his plans.

5. This, then, is the kind of humility that those who follow Christ's example and walk in his steps learn from him. Furthermore, the knowledge of their spiritual disease leads more and more to their being cleansed from pride and vanity. This cleansing prepares them, with a willing mind, to embrace the second thing implied in circumcision of the

heart—faith. Faith alone can make us whole; it is the only medicine given under heaven to heal our spiritual disorders.

6. *Faith* is the best guide to the blind, the clearest light to those who are in darkness, and the most perfect instructor of the foolish. True faith is "mighty through God, to destroy strongholds." It overthrows all the prejudices of corrupt reason, all the false maxims cherished among the masses, all evil customs and habits, and all the "wisdom of the world which is foolishness with God." Faith destroys fantasies, arguments, and "every proud obstacle raised up against the knowledge of God." Faith "takes every thought captive to obey Christ."

7. All things can be done for the one who believes. With the eyes of the heart enlightened, people of faith may know what is the hope to which they have been called. In body and in spirit, our calling is to glorify God who bought us with so high a price. We are God's possession, by both creation and redemption. Those who are circumcised in heart know "the immeasurable greatness of God's power." God resurrected Christ from the dead, and he is able to enliven us who are dead in sin "through his Spirit that dwells in us." "And this is the victory that conquers the world, our faith."

Such faith is a steadfast agreement with everything that God has revealed in scripture. Particularly, faith affirms the following important truths:

- Christ Jesus came into the world to save sinners.
- He himself bore our sins in his body on the cross.
- He is the atoning sacrifice for our sins, and not for ours only but also for the sins of the whole world.

Faith also affirms the revelation of Christ in our hearts with a divine assurance of his free, unmerited love for us as sinners.

The Holy Spirit forms within us a sure confidence of God's pardoning mercy. This confidence enables every true believer to declare, "I know that my Redeemer lives." We know that we have an "advocate with the Father" and that "Jesus Christ the righteous" is our Lord and "the atoning sacrifice for our sins." True believers testify, "I know that Christ loved me and gave himself up for me. Christ has reconciled me to God and I have 'redemption through his blood, even the forgiveness of sins.'"

8. This kind of faith cannot fail to give evidence of the power of God who inspires it. For God's children, this evidence includes being delivered from the yoke of sin. God purifies the believers' consciences from dead works, by so strengthening them that they no longer are constrained to

obey the desires of sin. Instead of "yielding their bodies as instruments of sin and wickedness," they now "yield themselves entirely to God, as those who have been brought from death to life."

9. Those who are born of God by faith also have a strong encouragement through *hope*. The next thing implied by the circumcision of the heart is the witness of human spirits with the Holy Spirit, who witnesses in their hearts that they are the children of God. Indeed, the Holy Spirit works in them a clear and living confidence that their hearts are right toward God. They possess the solid assurance that, through God's grace, they now do those things that are acceptable in his sight. They know that now they are on the path that leads to life and that, by God's mercy, they will continue on that path to the end.

God gives them a living hope of receiving all good things from his hand. Those who trust have a joyful expectation of a crown of glory reserved in heaven for them. This anchor keeps Christians steady in the midst of the storms of this difficult world, and hope preserves them from striking upon those fatal rocks of pride and despair. Christians are not discouraged by the supposed "harshness" of Christ, and they do not "despise the riches of his goodness."

Christians whose hearts are circumcised do not perceive the difficulties of the race set before them to be greater than they have the strength to surmount. Nor do Christians expect obstacles to be so small that they can overcome them without exerting all their strength. Past experiences of victory assure Christians that "in the Lord their labor is not in vain," if "whatever their hands find to do," they "do it with all their might." Experience teaches us not to harbor the futile notion that we can gain any advantage, demonstrate any virtue, or attain any commendation by faint hearts or feeble hands. We gain victory as we follow the same course as the great Apostle to the Gentiles. He said, "I do not run aimlessly, nor do I box as though beating the air; but I punish my body and subjugate it, so that after proclaiming to others I myself should not be disqualified."

10. Through discipline, all good soldiers of Christ fortify themselves to endure hardships. Confirmed and strengthened by discipline, the follower of Christ will be able to renounce the works of darkness—every appetite and inclination that does not submit to God's law. St. John said, "All who have this hope in them purify themselves, just as God is pure." By God's grace in Christ and through the blood of the covenant, the Christian's daily responsibility is to purify the innermost recesses of the self from the lusts that formerly possessed and defiled the soul.

Genuine Christians turn away from all impurity, envy, hatred, anger, lusts, and inclinations that belong to the flesh. These things spring from natural depravity, and our fallen natures cherish and cling to them. Christians know well that the body is the temple of God, and they will not allow anything into it that is profane or unclean. "Holiness befits God's temple forevermore." Our bodies are the temples where the Spirit of holiness promises to dwell.

11. Whoever you are that have added a living hope and a steadfast faith to your deep humility, to a good extent you have cleansed your heart from its inbred corruption. Yet you lack one more thing. If you would be perfect, add to all these *love*. Affix love, and you have the circumcision of the heart. "Love is the fulfilling of the law" and the aim of all God's instruction. Very excellent things are spoken about love: love is the basic attribute, spirit, and life of every virtue.

Love is the first and greatest commandment, and love combines all the commandments into one. "Whatever is true, whatever is honorable, whatever is just, whatever is pure, whatever is pleasing, whatever is commendable, if there is any excellence and if there is anything worthy of praise," they are all contained in this one word—love. Perfection, honor, and happiness are found in love. The royal law of heaven and earth is this: "You shall love the Lord your God with all your heart, and with all your soul, and with all your mind, and with all your strength."

12. This commandment does not forbid us from loving anything other than God. The commandment also includes loving our sisters and brothers. Nor does the command to love forbid us from taking pleasure in anything other than God, as some have strangely imagined. To believe this notion is to assume that God, the fountain of holiness, is the creator of sin. He has inseparably connected pleasure to the use of those things that are necessary to sustain the life that he has given us. Therefore, avoiding all pleasures cannot be a part of God's command to love him completely.

Both our blessed Lord and his Apostles too frequently and plainly tell us the real significance of this command for us to misunderstand its meaning. With one voice, they all agree that the true meaning of the command to love is that our single ultimate end will be the worship of the one true God: "The Lord is our God, the Lord alone. Do not follow other gods." "You shall love the Lord your God with all your heart, and with all your soul, and with all your mind, and with all your strength." "To him you shall hold fast." "His name and his renown are the soul's desire." Again, the meaning of the great commandment to love is that the one perfect God shall be your ultimate end. One thing you are to desire for its own sake—the attainment of him who is all in all. One happiness shall you intend for your soul—union with him who made you. Your highest aim should be to have "fellowship with the Father and with his Son Jesus Christ" and to be "united with the Lord in one Spirit." This one intention you are to pursue to the end of time—the enjoyment of God now and forever.

Desire other things only so far as they move you toward this end. Love the created thing only as it leads to the Creator. Let every step you take move you toward this goal. Let every inclination, thought, word, and deed become subordinate to your love for God. Whatever you desire or fear, whatever you seek or shun, whatever you think, speak, or do, let it lead to your happiness in God, the sole Source and End of your being.

13. Have no ultimate goal in view other than God. Our Lord has taught that there is need of only this one thing. And if your eye is individually fixed on this single end, "your whole body will be full of light." St. Paul said, "This one thing I do: I press on toward the goal for the prize of the heavenly call of God in Christ Jesus." St. James echoes the same thought: "Cleanse your hands, you sinners, and purify your hearts, you double-minded." In like manner, St. John wrote, "Do not love the world or the things in the world. The love of the Father is not in those who love the world; for all that is in the world—the desire of the flesh, the desire of the eyes, the pride in riches—comes not from the Father but from the world." These things are not from the Father of Spirits. They do not come from him, nor does he approve them. Rather, they are from the world. These things include, first, seeking happiness in the things that gratify the desire of the flesh by their pleasing impressions on the physical senses.

The second thing that comes from the world is the desire of the eye, or fantasizing about things to be desired for their novelty, fame, or beauty.

Third, coming from the world is the pride of life, whether it expresses itself by pomp, prominence, power, or the usual consequences of them, which is worldly applause and admiration. These things that do not please the Father are the characteristic marks of those who will not allow God to reign over them.

II. How we can know we possess the blessing of the circumcision of the heart

1. I have spoken particularly about the nature of the circumcision of the heart, which will bring praise from God. Now, in the second place, I

will reflect on the natural question that follows. What is the clear measure by which all people can judge for themselves whether they belong to the world or to God?

First, it is clear from what has been said that no one has a claim on God's approval unless his or her heart is circumcised by humility. In your own eyes, you must see yourself as weak, wretched, and sinful. We must become deeply convicted of the inbred "corruption of our nature, by which we are very far gone from original righteousness."[4] We must see ourselves as we really are—prone to every evil, disinclined to do good, corrupt, and abominable. A repentant person confesses having a "mind that is set on the flesh that is hostile to God; it does not submit to God's law—indeed it cannot."

We cannot have God's approval unless we continually feel in our inmost souls that without the presence of the Spirit of God, we cannot think, desire, speak, or do any good thing or live in a way that is well-pleasing in God's sight. I am saying that we have no claim to God's praise until we feel our lack of him. First, we must "seek the glory that comes from the one who alone is God. Genuine Christians do not seek the honor that comes from people, unless it leads toward the glory of God.

2. Another truth that naturally follows is that none of us will obtain the honor that comes from God unless our hearts are circumcised by faith. This faith is a trust in the power of God. We cannot receive God's approval unless we refuse to be led any longer by our senses, appetites, and passions. We must renounce these blind leaders of the blind, so esteemed by the world and natural reason. We must live and walk by faith, and order every step as "seeing him who is invisible." Those who have God's approval do not look at what can be seen. "What can be seen is temporary, but what cannot be seen is eternal." The Christian governs all desires, plans, thoughts, actions, and behavior as one who has entered the holy place behind the curtain, where Jesus sits at the right hand of God.

3. I wish that those who employ much of their time and efforts laying "another foundation" were better acquainted with true faith. I wish that those who ground their religion in the perpetual adequacy of material things and their value, virtue, and beauty would stop to contemplate their true worth. I wish that they would consider the "reasons" (as they refer to them) lying behind good and evil, and the relationships of people to one another. Their explanations of the foundations of "Christian duty" either coincide with the scripture, or they do not.

If they do coincide with the Bible, why are well-meaning people confused and drawn away from the weightier matters of the law by a myriad of terms, while they explain away the easiest Christian truths into obscurity? If their explanations do not accord with scripture, they are obligated to consider who really is the author of their new doctrines. Does their doctrine likely come from an "angel from heaven," who preaches a gospel contrary to the gospel of Christ Jesus? If this is the case, God (not us) has pronounced his sentence: "Let them be accursed."

4. Our gospel knows no other foundation of good works except faith in Christ. The gospel clearly informs us that we are not his disciples so long as we deny him to be the Author, or his Spirit to be the Inspirer and Perfecter, of both our faith and our works. "Anyone who does not have the Spirit of Christ does not belong to him." Christ alone can bring to life those who are dead to God. He can breathe into them the very breath of Christian life. He precedes, accompanies, and supports them with his grace in order to bring their good desires to a righteous conclusion. "All who are led by the Spirit of God are children of God." This statement is God's short and clear explanation of true religion and virtue. "For no one can lay any foundation other than the one that has been laid; that foundation is Jesus Christ."

5. Thirdly, from what has been said, we may learn that we are not truly "led by the Spirit" unless the "Spirit bears witness with our spirits that we are children of God" (Rom. 8:16). Those who are led by the Spirit see the prize and the crown before them, and they rejoice in "the hope of sharing the glory of God."

Those teachers err greatly who say that in serving God we should have no concern about our own happiness! Indeed, God specifically teaches us to "look ahead to the reward." We are to compare our present toil with the "joy set before us," and to weigh these "momentary afflictions" in comparison with the "eternal weight of glory beyond all measure." God "by his great mercy" must first "give us a new birth into a living hope" for "an inheritance that is imperishable, undefiled, and unfading." Until Christ brings us to a new birth, we are "aliens from the commonwealth" of promise; we are "without God in the world."

6. If these things are so, it is none too soon for unbelievers to deal realistically with their own souls. They are far from fulfilling the terms of God's covenant and obtaining his promises. They do not have this joyful assurance within themselves. Instead, they quarrel with the covenant and revile its conditions. They complain that God's requirements are too severe, and that no one ever has lived or ever could live up to them. What is this attitude but a reproach to God—as though he is a hard master, requiring of his servants more than he enables them to perform? These unbelievers speak as though God ridicules the helpless

people he created, tying them to impossible duties that are beyond their abilities or God's grace.

7. Blasphemers might try to convince others to believe that they are blameless because they think that they can fulfill God's commands without taking any pains to do so. What an empty hope it is to think that anyone could ever expect to see the kingdom of God without first striving and agonizing "to enter in at the narrow door." It is folly for those who were "conceived and born in sin" and whose "hearts are destruction" even once to entertain the notion of being "purified just as the Lord is pure." First, it is necessary for them to walk in his steps, and to "take up their cross daily." For the sake of Christ, one must be willing to "cut off the right hand," and "tear out the right eye and throw it away." Without a constant and continued course of general self-denial, we should never dream of shaking off our old doctrines, desires, and inclinations and of being "sanctified entirely in spirit, soul, and body."

8. Can we conclude anything less than this from the previously cited words of St. Paul? He lived "with weaknesses, insults, hardships, persecutions, and calamities for the sake of Christ." He also performed "signs and wonders and mighty works" and was "caught up to the third heaven." Yet, as a recent author strongly expressed it, "All of Paul's virtues would have been uncertain, and even his salvation would have been in danger, without his constant self-denial."[5] Paul said, "I do not run aimlessly, nor do I box as though beating the air." By these words he clearly teaches us that the one who does not also exercise strong discipline and daily deny self runs the race unpredictably, and boxes with as little purpose as the one who "beats against the air."

9. Finally, from what we have said, we may conclude that if our hearts are not circumcised by love we speak vainly of "fighting the good fight of faith." Without discipline, it is futile to hope to attain an imperishable crown. In engaging their entire selves in the zealous pursuit of love, which is the one thing necessary for God's children, it is absolutely essential for them to become free from the desire of the flesh, the desire of the eyes, and the pride in riches. Without love, whoever is alive is to be reckoned as dead before God. "If I speak in the tongues of mortals and of angels, but do not have love, I am a noisy gong or a clanging cymbal. And if I have prophetic powers, understand all mysteries and knowledge, and have all faith so as to remove mountains, but do not have love, I am nothing." Even if "I give away all my possessions, and if I hand over my body so that I may boast, but do not have love, I gain nothing."

10. Love, therefore, is the sum of the perfect law; it is the true circumcision of the heart. Perhaps some would summarize the entire affair

this way: "Let the spirit return to God who gave it, with the whole train of its affections. Let the spirit go to the source of all rivers, from which they flow again." The only sacrifice that God will receive from us is the living sacrifice of the heart he has chosen. Let the heart be continually offered up to God through Christ, in flames of holy love. And let nothing be allowed other than him, for he is a jealous God. God will not share his throne with any other, and he will reign without a rival. Entertain no plans or aspirations except those that have God as their ultimate object. The children of God who once walked with him but who are now dead continue to speak to us about the way we should walk. These ancient Christians said:

> Desire to live only as you praise his name. Let all your thoughts, words, and deeds move toward God's glory. Set your heart firmly on him and on other things only as they are found in him and come from him. Let your soul be filled with such a complete love for God that you can love nothing else except for his sake. Let the intent of your heart be pure, with an unchanging regard for his glory in everything you do. Fasten your eyes upon the blessed hope of your calling, and cause all the things of the world to minister to that end.[6]

Only as we live in the way that those now glorified saints admonished do we have "the same mind that was in Christ Jesus." The circumcision of the heart means that in every motion of our heart, in every word of our tongue, in every work of our hands, we pursue nothing except as it relates to God and is in subordination to him, working in the service of his desires. The circumcision of the heart means that we do not think, speak, or act to satisfy our own wills, but the will of him that sent us. "So, whether we eat or drink, or whatever we do, we do everything for the glory of God."

Notes

1. Ward and Heitzenrater, *Wesley's Journal and Diaries*, Sept. 1, 1778, 23:104-05.
2. Telford, *Wesley's Letters*, May 14, 1765, 4:299.
3. Wesley is referring to William Law.
4. Thirty-nine Articles, Art. 9, "Of Original or Birth Sin."
5. William Law, *Works*, 3:117.
6. This uncertain source, from which Wesley quotes or paraphrases, is probably from a sixteenth or seventeenth-century Puritan writer.

THE MARKS OF THE NEW BIRTH

I n Wesley's previous sermons on foundations of the Christian faith he explains that the new birth initiates a new relationship with God through justification, adoption, and the witness of the Spirit. He also points out that the experience of being reconciled with God results in the infusion of new life through regeneration and initial sanctification. The new birth brings freedom from the *guilt* of sin and the promise of deliverance from the *power* of sin. Now, in this sermon Wesley explains that the new birth also imparts to Christians a new set of affections and motives.

Wesley rejected physical or emotional manifestations as the certain marks of the new birth. In a letter to Thomas Hartley, Wesley complained about the teaching of a prominent preacher:

> In several parts of his Journals, [he] lay down some marks of the new birth, not only doubtful, but exceptionable; as, particularly, where persons appeared agitated or convulsed under the ministry; which might be owing to other causes, rather than any regenerating work of God's Spirit. . . . They may be from God; they may be from nature; they may be from the devil.[1]

For Wesley, emotional or physical signs cannot be accounted as the essential marks of the new birth. Rather, moral transformation is the primary evidence of Christianity. In this sermon Wesley develops three "genuine" marks of the new birth—*faith, hope,* and *love.*

Faith, the first mark of the new birth, is both an intellectual assent to revealed truth and a personal trust in Christ. In this discourse, Wesley contends, "An immediate and constant fruit of this faith through which we are born of God is power over sin. This fruit cannot in any way be separated from faith, even for an hour. I am speaking of power over every kind of outward sin, over every evil word and work." Wesley concedes that Christians make mistakes and commit errors of judgment, but the new birth enables them to conquer a pattern of willful disobedience to God's will, so far as they are able to understand it. Faith does not make it impossible for Christians to sin, but it does make it possible for them not to sin willfully.

Hope is the second mark of the new birth. Christian hope is the inner witness of the Holy Spirit to the human spirit that one has become a child of God. Also, this assurance involves belief in the trustworthiness of God's promises revealed in the Bible. Hope confidently believes in God for all things needful in the present life and the life to come. This hope brings inexpressible joy to the believer. Wesley declares, "Indescribable indeed! It is not for the human tongue to describe this joy in the Holy Spirit. It is 'the hidden manna' which no one knows, except those who receive it. But this much we know: it not only remains, but it overflows even in the depth of affliction." Christian hope sustains the Christian in all phases of life, whether they are pleasant or difficult.

The third mark of the new birth is love. Through the Holy Spirit, God pours his love into the hearts of those who have justifying faith. This love enables them to serve both friend and enemy, placing the needs of others above the needs of self. Concerning those who have these marks of love, Wesley declared, "They delight in God. He is the joy of their hearts; their 'shield,' and their 'very great reward.' The desire of their souls is toward him; it is their 'food to do his will.' Their 'souls are satisfied as with a rich feast, and their mouths praise him with joyful lips.'"

This sermon calls readers to sincere self-examination as to whether they truly evidence the marks of the new birth. By the marks of faith, hope, and love, we can know that we are responding positively to God's gracious work in our lives. Wesley insists that Christians must not rely solely on having been baptized as proof that they are Christians. He writes, "Do not say in your heart, 'I was once baptized, so therefore I am now a child of God.' I truly regret that this outcome will by no means automatically continue in your life. How many are the baptized gluttons, drunkards, liars and common swearers, abusive critics, and gossips, whoremongers, thieves, and extortioners? What do you think? Are these people now the children of God?"

This sermon presents a compelling case for faith, hope, and love as the biblical signs that God has worked and continues to work through his grace in the lives of Christian believers.

Sermon 18

THE MARKS OF THE NEW BIRTH

So it is with everyone who is born of the Spirit. (John 3:8)

1 In what way are those who are "born of the Spirit" born of God? In other words, what does it mean to be born again, born of God, born of the Spirit? What is implicit in becoming a child of God or receiving "the Spirit of adoption?" We know that these privileges, by the free mercy of God, are usually attached to baptism, which our Lord calls being "born of water and of the Spirit." We want to inquire into what these privileges are. What, then, is the new birth?

2. Perhaps it is not necessary to give a definition of this experience, because scripture does not give one. However, the question is of the deepest concern to every human being, because "no one can see the kingdom of God without being born again." Therefore, in the clearest manner, I propose to point out the marks of the new birth, just as I find them stated in scripture.

I. Faith as a mark of the new birth

1. *Faith* is the first mark of the new birth, and it is the foundation of all the rest. St. Paul confirms that faith is a necessary essential: "In Christ Jesus you are all children of God through faith." Also, St. John wrote, "But to all who received him, who believed in his name, he gave power (perhaps best translated *right or privilege*) to become children of God."

Those who believe on his name are "born, not of blood or of the will of the flesh or of the will of man, but of God." Again, St. John wrote in his General Epistle, "Everyone who believes that Jesus is the Christ has been born of God."

2. The apostles, however, were not speaking of merely a theoretical or speculative faith. Saving faith is not a mere agreement with the proposition that Jesus is the Christ. Faith is not a simple intellectual concurrence with the affirmations contained in our creed or in the Old and New Testaments. Faith is not merely an assent to any or all of these scriptural affirmations.

If intellectual consent were saving faith, the demons would be born of God, because they have this kind of intellectual faith. They "believe—and shudder." They have no doubt that Jesus is the Christ and that all scripture is true as God is true, because it has been given by the inspiration of God. Faith is not merely an intellectual belief in the divine truth of scripture that has been confirmed by miracles. The demons heard the words of Jesus and they knew that he was a faithful and authentic witness. They could not keep from admitting the truth of the testimony of Jesus about himself and about the Father who sent him. They also saw the mighty deeds that Jesus did, and they believed accordingly that he "came from God." Yet, despite their cognitive understanding, they are still "kept in eternal chains in deepest darkness for the judgment of the great day."

3. This kind of intellectual faith is no more than empty belief. True and living Christian faith, by which we are born of God, is more than mental assent and cognitive understanding. True faith is a disposition that God forms in the heart. It is a certain trust and confidence in God, that, through the merits of Christ, our sins are forgiven and we are reconciled to God's favor. This kind of faith means that we must first renounce ourselves in order to be "found in Christ." For us to be accepted through Christ, we need totally to reject all "confidence in the flesh." We must see that we "have nothing to pay." Having no trust in our own good works or any kind of human righteousness, we must come to God as lost, miserable, self-destroyed, self-condemned, ruined, helpless sinners. Our mouths are completely silenced, and we are altogether "held accountable before God."

Those who make judgments about things that they do not understand commonly refer to this conviction of sin as "worry" or "anxiety." But the sense of sin must combine with an abundant conviction (such as no words can express) that both the desire for salvation and salvation itself come only from Jesus Christ. These two things—conviction of sin and belief in the full sufficiency of Christ—must come first. Then follows an active faith and trust in Christ, who (in the words of the homily) "for them paid our ransom by his death and fulfilled the law in his life."[2] Then, by this kind of faith we are born of God. This truth is "not only a belief of all the articles of our faith, but also a true confidence in the mercy of God, through our Lord Jesus Christ."[3]

4. An immediate and constant fruit of this faith through which we are born of God is power over sin. Even for an hour we cannot in any way separate this fruit from faith. I am speaking of power over every kind of outward sin, over every evil word and work. Wherever the blood of Christ is applied, it "purifies our conscience from dead works" and inward sin. The blood of Christ cleanses the heart from every unholy desire and disposition.

St. Paul, in the sixth chapter of his Epistle to the Romans, has thoroughly described this fruit of faith: "How can we who died to sin go on living in it? Our old self was crucified with him so that the body of sin might be destroyed, and we might no longer be enslaved to sin. So, you also must consider yourselves dead to sin and alive to God in Christ Jesus. Therefore, do not let sin exercise dominion in your mortal bodies. Do not permit sin to reign in your mortal bodies. Present yourselves to God as those who have been brought from death to life. For sin will have no dominion over you. Thanks be to God that you, having once been slaves of sin, have been set free." St. Paul concludes, "Having been set free from sin, you have become slaves of righteousness."

5. The Apostle John just as firmly asserts this priceless privilege of the children of God, especially with regard to power over outward sin. As one who was overwhelmed by the depth of the riches of the goodness of God, St. John acclaimed, "See what love the Father has given us, that we should be called children of God. . . . Beloved, we are God's children now; what we will be has not yet been revealed. What we do know is this: when he is revealed, we will be like him, for we will see him as he is." St. John adds, "Those who have been born of God do not sin, because God's seed abides in them; they cannot sin, because they have been born of God."

However, some people will say, "That is true. Whoever is born of God does not *habitually* commit sin." I reply, "*Habitually*? From which source do you derive that interpretation? I do not read it in St. John's epistle." God clearly says, "He does not commit sin," and you add *habitually*! Who are you to amend the word of God and add words to this book? Beware, I beg you, that God does not add to you all the plagues that are written in the book of Revelation! The qualification that you wish to add invalidates the text. By this cunning method of deceiving, the precious promise is utterly lost. This deception and disdain of others renders the word of God of no effect. Beware, that by taking away from the words of this book, you do not take away their entire meaning and spirit. For fear that God will take away your name out of the book of life, do not amend God's word and leave only what we may call a dead letter!

6. Let us allow the Apostle John to interpret his own words, by the entire substance of his discourse. In 1 John 3:5 he said, "You know that he was revealed to take away sins, and in him there is no sin." What conclusion does St. John draw from this statement? He declared, "No one who abides in him sins; no one who sins has either seen him or known him."

To emphasize this important truth, St. John delivered an especially necessary warning: "Little children, let no one deceive you"—because many will attempt to do so in order to persuade you that you can be unrighteous and continue to commit sin while still remaining God's children! St. John continues, "Everyone who commits sin is a child of the devil; for the devil has been sinning from the beginning." Then, he adds, "Those who have been born of God do not sin, because God's seed abides in them; they cannot sin, because they have been born of God. The children of God and the children of the devil are revealed in this way." They are revealed by whether they do, or do not, commit sin. St. John makes the same point in the fifth chapter of his first epistle: "We know that those who are born of God do not sin, but the one who was born of God (Jesus Christ) protects them, and the evil one does not touch them."

7. Another fruit of living faith is *peace*. "Since we are justified by faith," having every sin blotted out, "we have peace with God through our Lord Jesus Christ." Indeed, the night before his death, our Lord himself solemnly bequeathed his peace to all his followers. He said, "You who believe in God, believe also in me." To those who believed in him, he said, "Peace I leave with you; my peace I give to you. I do not give to you as the world gives. Do not let your hearts be troubled, and do not let them be afraid." And Jesus repeated his promise: "I have said this to you, so that in me you may have peace." This peace is "the peace of God, which surpasses all understanding."

It has not entered into the hearts of unconverted people to fathom this serenity of soul, and not even spiritual people can find words to express this peace. All the powers of earth and hell are unable to take away this peace that comes from God. Waves and storms beat upon it, but they cannot move it because it is founded upon a rock. It keeps the hearts and minds of the children of God—at all times and in all places. Whether they are in comfort or in pain, in sickness or health, in plenty or need, God's children are happy in his peace. They have learned to be content under every condition and in all circumstances. They give thanks to God through Christ Jesus, because they are well assured that "whatsoever is, is best;" it is God's will concerning them. In all the unpredictable changes of life, "their hearts are firm, secure in the Lord."

II. Hope as a mark of the new birth

1. A second scriptural mark of those who are born of God is *hope*. Addressing all the children of God who were then scattered widely, St. Peter said, "Blessed be the God and Father of our Lord Jesus Christ! By his great mercy he has given us a new birth into a living hope." St. Peter said, "a *living* hope," because there is also a *dead* hope (as well as a dead faith), a hope that does not come from God. This dead hope is an enemy of God and people, as it is clearly known by its fruits. Dead hope is the offspring of pride, and it is the parent of every evil word and work. On the contrary, everyone who possesses this *living* hope is "holy as he that calls him is holy." All those who have this hope can truly say to their sisters and brothers in Christ, "Beloved, we are God's children now, and we will see him as he is. And all who have this hope in them purify themselves, just as he is pure."

2. In the Epistle to the Hebrews, this hope is called the "full assurance of faith" and the "full assurance of hope." These expressions are the best that our English language can convey, even if they are weaker than the original language of scripture. First of all, this hope entails the testimony of our own spirit, or conscience, that we are walking "with holiness and godly sincerity." Second, and most importantly, hope includes "the Holy Spirit bearing witness with our spirits that we are children of God, and if children, then heirs—heirs of God and joint heirs with Christ."

3. Here, let us carefully observe what God himself is teaching us regarding this glorious privilege of his children. In this scripture, who is it that bears witness? It is not only our spirit, but also another spirit—precisely the Spirit of God. It is he who "bears witness with our spirits." To what does the Holy Spirit bear witness? The Spirit witnesses "that we are children of God, and if children, then heirs of God and joint heirs with Christ—if, in fact, we suffer with him so that we may also be glorified with him."

Having this blessing, we are to deny ourselves, daily take up our crosses, and cheerfully endure persecution or reproach for the sake of Christ. In this way, we may also be "glorified with him." In whom does the Spirit of God bear this witness? The Spirit bears witness in all who are God's children. In the preceding verses, the apostle refers to this witness as verification that we are sons and daughters of God. St. Paul said, "For all who are led by the Spirit of God are children of God. For you did not receive a spirit of slavery to fall back into fear, but you have received a spirit of adoption." When we cry, "Abba! Father!" it follows that "it is that very Spirit bearing witness with our spirits that we are children of God."

4. The variation of this phrase in Romans 8:15 deserves our attention. I will paraphrase the passage: You did not receive a spirit of slavery to fall back into fear, but you have received a spirit of adoption, by which we cry, "Abba! Father!" You, as many as are children of God, in virtue of your filial relationship with God, have received the same spirit of adoption as we apostles, prophets, and teachers, we through whom you have believed (we, the "servants of Christ and stewards of God's mysteries"). *We* and *you* have the same Lord, so we also have the same Spirit. And as we have the same faith, we have the same hope. *You* and *we* are marked with the seal of the promised Holy Spirit and sealed with the same "Spirit of promise," who is the guarantee of our inheritance toward redemption as God's own people.

5. This blessing fulfills the scripture that promises, "Blessed are those who mourn, for they will be comforted." It is easy to believe that sorrow may precede this witness of God's Spirit with our spirits. Indeed, to some degree, we must "mourn" while we agonize under the fear of God and a sense of his wrath towards us. However, as soon as anyone feels this anguish, his or her "pain will turn into joy." Whatever the anguish may have been, as soon as our hour has come, the anguish is turned into joy that we are children of God.

The pain is remembered no more. It may be that many of you now have sorrow, because you are "aliens from the commonwealth of Israel, and strangers to the covenants of promise, having no hope and without God in the world. But when the Holy Spirit has come, "then your hearts will rejoice." Yes, "your joy will be full," and "no one will take your joy from you." You will say, "We boast in God through our Lord Jesus Christ, through whom we have now received reconciliation." "We have obtained access to this grace in which we stand; and we boast in our hope of sharing the glory of God."

St. Peter said:

> Blessed be the God and Father of our Lord Jesus Christ! By his great mercy he has given us a new birth into a living hope through the resurrection of Jesus Christ from the dead, and into an inheritance that is imperishable, undefiled, and unfading, kept in heaven for you, who are being protected by the power of God through faith for a salvation ready to be revealed in the last time. In this you rejoice, even if now for a little while you have had to suffer various trials, so that the genuineness of your faith—being more precious than gold that, though perishable, is tested by fire—may be found to result in praise and glory and honor when Jesus Christ is revealed. Although you have not seen him, you love him; and even though you do not see him now, you believe in him and rejoice with an indescribable and glorious joy. (1 Peter 1:3-8)[4]

These blessings are inexpressible indeed! It is not for the human tongue to describe this joy in the Holy Spirit. It is "the hidden manna" which no one knows, except those who receive it. But this much we know: it not only abides, but it overflows even in the depths of affliction.

When all earthly comforts fail for God's children, "Are the consolations of God too small?" Not at all! When sufferings abound the most, the consolations of God's Spirit much more abound. Through hope, the children of God "laugh at destruction when it comes." God's children laugh at pain, hell, and the grave, because they know him who "has the keys of Death and Hades." God will soon throw death and the grave into the abyss. Christian hope hears even now a loud voice from heaven saying,

> See, the home of God is among mortals.
> He will dwell with them as their God;
> they will be his peoples,
> and God himself will be with them;
> he will wipe every tear from their eyes.
> Death will be no more;
> mourning and crying and pain will be no more,
> for the first things have passed away. (Rev. 21:3, 4)

III. Love as a mark of the new birth

1. *Love* is a third scriptural mark of those that are born of God, and the greatest of all. This mark of the new birth is "God's love poured into our hearts through the Holy Spirit that has been given to us." "Because we are children, God has sent the Spirit of his Son into our hearts, crying, 'Abba! Father!'" Through the Holy Spirit, God's children continually look up to God as their loving Father who is reconciled.

They cry to him for their daily bread—for everything that they need, whether for their souls or their bodies. They continually pour out their hearts before God, knowing that they "have obtained the requests made of him." They delight in him. He is the joy of their hearts, their "shield," and their "very great reward." The desire of their souls is toward him; it is their "food to do his will." Their "souls are satisfied as with a rich feast, and their mouths praise him with joyful lips."

2. "Everyone who believes that Jesus is the Christ has been born of God, and everyone who loves the parent loves the child." The child of God rejoices in God as a personal Savior. Christians "love the Lord Jesus Christ with an undying love." They are so "united to the Lord" as to "become one spirit with him." Believers' souls cling to the Lord and prefer him as altogether radiant and "distinguished among ten thousand." Love knows and feels the force of Solomon's words, "My Beloved is mine, and I am his." "You are the most admirable of all; grace is poured upon your lips; therefore God has blessed you forever."

3. The necessary fruit of this love for God is love for our neighbors and for every soul that God has created, including our enemies and those that even now persecute us. Christians love everyone, even as they love their own souls. Our Lord has expressed it still more strongly by teaching us, "Love one another, just as I have loved you." Accordingly, the commandment written in the hearts of all those who love God is no less than the command of Jesus to "love one another as I have loved you."

The Apostle John said, "We know love by this, that he laid down his life for us." Then St. John properly concludes, "We ought to lay down our lives for one another." If we feel that we are willing to love in this way, then we truly *do* love our neighbors. "We know that we have passed from death to life because we love one another." "By this we know that we abide in him and he in us, because he has given us of his Spirit." "Love is from God, and everyone who loves is born of God and knows God."

4. Possibly, some may ask, "Does the apostle not say, 'The love of God is this, that we obey his commandments?'" That is true. And obeying God's commandments includes loving one's neighbor, even as one loves God. But what would you infer from this statement? Would you conclude that keeping the outward commandments is all that is implied in loving God with all your heart, with all your mind, and soul, and strength, and in loving your neighbor as yourself? Would you conclude that love for God is only outward service, but not an affection of the soul? Would you conclude that love for neighbor is not a disposition of heart, but only a pattern of outward works?

Just to state such a foolish interpretation of the apostle's words is enough to defeat the argument. The obvious and certain meaning of the text is that keeping the first and greatest commandment is the sign or proof of our love for God. To keep the first and greatest commandment is to keep all the rest. If genuine love is poured into our hearts, it will constrain us to keep this commandment. Those who love God with all their hearts will serve him with all their strength.

5. *Universal obedience* to God and compliance with his will certainly constitute a second fruit of our love for him. We cannot separate love for God from obedience to God. Genuine love for God is marked by the observance of all his commands, internal and external. Our love shows itself in the obedience of heart and life, in every attitude and circumstance. One of the dispositions most obviously implied here is being "zealous of good deeds." Obedience to God includes hungering and thirsting to do all kinds of good to all people, rejoicing to "spend and be spent" for every human being. And genuine obedience means that we do not look for any repayment in this world, but only in the resurrection of the righteous.

IV. An application and encouragement

1. I have clearly given those marks of the new birth that I find laid down in Scripture. To the important question, "What does it mean to be born of God?" God himself gives the answer. If we appeal to scripture, we find a description of everyone who is born of the Spirit. The following statement represents the teaching of the Spirit of God concerning what it means to be a child of God: A Christian believes in God, through Christ, so as "not to commit sin." At all times and in all places, he or she enjoys "the peace of God, which surpasses all understanding." To be born of the spirit is to hope in God through his beloved son so as to have the "testimony of a good conscience." The Spirit of God "bears witness with your spirits, that you are God's children."

Having these blessings, you cannot help rejoicing in him, through whom you have received reconciliation. A mark of the new birth is to love God who has loved you as you never did love any other living thing. This love constrains you to love all people as you love yourself, with a love burning constantly in your heart and blazing out in all your actions and conversations. Your entire life becomes a "labor of love." Your life is a single continued obedience to God's commands: "Be merciful, just as your Father is merciful;" "you shall be holy, for I am holy;" "be perfect, therefore, as your heavenly Father is perfect."

2. Who are you, then, that are born of God in this way? If you are truly born of God you "understand the gifts bestowed on you by God." You know well that you are God's children, and you can "reassure your hearts before him." And every one of you that has observed these words cannot help feeling and knowing with certainty whether at this hour you are a child of God or not. Answer only to God, and not to others! The question is not what you were made in baptism (do not evade the question), but, what are you *now*?

Is the Spirit of adoption now in your heart? Search your own self. I am not asking whether you were born of water and of the Spirit. Rather, I am asking if your body is a temple of the Holy Spirit within you. I acknowledge that you were circumcised with "the circumcision of Christ," as St. Paul purposely termed baptism. I am asking if the Spirit of Christ and of glory rests upon you at *present*. If not, "your circumcision has become uncircumcision"—that is, your baptism has become of no account.

3. Do not say in your heart, "I was once baptized, so therefore I am now a child of God." I truly regret that the work done in your baptism will by no means automatically continue throughout your life. How many baptized gluttons, drunkards, liars and common swearers, abusive critics, and gossips, whoremongers, thieves, and extortioners are there? What do *you* think? Are these people now the children of God? Indeed, whoever you are, if you are one of these people, I say to you, "You are from your father the devil, and you choose to do your father's desires." In the name of him who you crucify afresh, I call out to you. In the very words that Jesus spoke to your circumcised predecessors, I declare, "You snakes, you brood of vipers! How can you escape being sentenced to hell?"

4. How indeed can you escape unless you are born again! For you are now dead in trespasses and sins. Therefore, do not say that you cannot be born again because the only new birth is in baptism. Such an attitude will seal you all under damnation and dispatch you to hell, without help or hope.

Perhaps some people will agree that this condemnation is fair and just. In their zeal for the Lord of hosts, they may say, "Utterly destroy the sinners, the Amalekites. Let these Gibeonites be utterly destroyed. They deserve no less!" No, you and I deserve hell just as much as the Amalekites and the Gibeonites. It is by free and undeserved mercy that at the present we are not all in the unquenchable fire.

You may say, "But we are baptized; we were born again by water and by the Spirit." So were they. This fact does not prevent us from becoming like them. Do you not know that "what is prized by human beings is an abomination in the sight of God"? Stand up, you "worldly saints," you who have the esteem of others. Who will cast the first stone at the miserable creatures not fit to live upon the earth—these common harlots, adulterers, and murderers? First, however, learn the meaning of the verse, "All who hate a brother or sister are murderers." "Everyone who looks at a woman with lust has already committed adultery with her in his heart." "Adulterers, do you not know that friendship with the world is enmity with God?"

5. "Very truly, I tell you, no one can see the kingdom of God without being born from above." Lean no more on that broken reed of a staff that you were born again in baptism. Who denies that you once were made children of God, and heirs of the kingdom of heaven? But, nonetheless, you are now children of the devil. Therefore, you must be born again.

And do not allow Satan to put it into your heart to quibble about words, when the matter is so clear. You have heard what the marks are that distinguish the children of God. All you that do not have these marks of the new birth on souls (whether you are baptized or not baptized) need to receive these marks in your lives. Without them, you will certainly perish everlastingly. If you have been baptized, you have only one hope. Those who were made children of God by baptism, but are now the children of the devil, may yet again receive "power to become children of God." They may receive again what they have lost—the Spirit of adoption, crying in their hearts, "Abba! Father!"

Amen, Lord Jesus! May all who prepare their hearts yet again to seek your face, receive again that Spirit of adoption, and cry out, "Abba! Father!" May they again receive the power to believe in your name and to become God's children. May they know and feel that they have "redemption in your blood, the forgiveness of sins" and that "they cannot sin, because they have been born of God." Let them receive a "new birth into a living hope" and "purify themselves, just as he is pure." And because they are your children, let the Spirit of love and of glory rest upon them. Cleanse them "from every defilement of body and of spirit," and teach them to "make holiness perfect in the fear of God."

Notes

1. Telford, *Wesley's Letters*, March 27, 1764, 4:234.
2. *Homilies*, "Of Salvation," Part 1.
3. *Homilies*, "Of Salvation," Part 3.

THE GREAT PRIVILEGE OF THOSE THAT ARE BORN OF GOD

I n this sermon John Wesley explains that a new spiritual birth is to the human soul what a physical birth is to the body. He compares the birth of a new Christian to the birth of a baby. The senses of unborn infants exist, but they are not yet functional and responsive to the world. In their mothers' wombs, developing children have eyes and ears, but they cannot see or hear. The unborn child does not know the mother, although she provides the child with life and nourishment. In like manner, those who are not Christians are not yet spiritually alive to God, although God nourishes their existence. They are "dead in their trespasses and sins." Unregenerate people subsist by the grace of God in whom they "live and move and have their being." Yet, they live without the knowledge of God. They do not hear his voice, sense his presence, or know him personally. The new birth enables people's spiritual eyes and ears to see and hear divine reality. In sum, only those who are born of God can experience a conscious awareness of God.

This sermon explains that life in Christ is marked by both objective and subjective changes. Objectively, newborn Christians benefit from justification and adoption. Justification pertains to pardon, and adoption means that one has become a member of the family of God.

311

Subjectively, newly born Christians benefit from regeneration and initial sanctification. Regeneration means that God imparts spiritual life to the soul and one becomes a new creation in Christ. In initial sanctification, God begins the work of making us holy, as Christ is holy.

For Wesley, justification and adoption are things that God does for us by giving us a new relationship with him. Wesley refers to these blessings as a *relative* change. Regeneration and sanctification are things that God does *in* us. Wesley refers to this experience as a *real* change. The new birth can never be earned or deserved. It is God's gift to humankind, made possible by the death and resurrection of Christ, and personally appropriated by us through repentance and faith.

This sermon deals with "the great privilege of those that are born of God," which is receiving the grace to become free from willful sin. The text for this sermon is from the First Epistle of John: "Those who have been born of God do not continue in sin" (1 John 3:9). As stated in the introduction to this volume, Wesley's understanding of the Christian life is *relational,* and he defines sin in interpersonal terms: "Sin is a voluntary transgression of the revealed, written law of God. Sin is a deliberate violation of any commandment of God, acknowledged to be such at the time that it is broken." The great privilege of those that are born of God is the freedom not to sin willfully against God or neighbor. This benefit is the distinctive gift of holiness that God gives to his children.

With this privilege comes responsibility. It is possible to overcome temptation, but it is not inevitable that Christians will do so. God gives believers the grace to overcome sin. Yet, he does not guarantee that they will not fall into its snare. In their temptations, God gives his children grace to resist sin, but they are responsible for obeying him. There are numerous biblical accounts of believers who failed to use this grace. Through disobedience and sin, they turned away from their Creator.

Wesley points out that either overcoming sin or falling into sin hinges on one's use or misuse of human freedom. Christians sin not because they must do so, but because they *choose* to do so. This sermon outlines the ways in which believers can fall into sin, and shows how they can avoid it.

The religion espoused by John Wesley is an ethical one, in which holiness is central. Thus, moral uprightness lies at the heart of his preaching, and holiness is necessarily linked with human freedom and responsibility. This sermon stresses God's call to Christians to remain vigilant, so as to avoid sin. God calls them to embrace the way of holiness, which is the great privilege of those that are born of God.

THE GREAT PRIVILEGE OF THOSE THAT ARE BORN OF GOD

Those who have been born of God do not sin. (1 John 3:9)

1 It has been frequently assumed that being born of God and being justified are identical and that "the new birth" and "justification" are only different terms for the same experience. On the one hand, this belief assumes that those who are justified are also born of God. On the other hand, this belief considers that whoever is born of God is also justified. Many people believe that God bestows both justification and the new birth at the same moment, because they refer to the same thing. They think that in a single point of time, one's sins are blotted out and one is born again.

2. Certainly, we acknowledge that, in point of time, justification and the new birth are inseparable from each other. Yet, they are easily distinguished from each other because their natures differ widely. Justification signifies only a *relative* change, while the new birth is a *real* change. In justifying us, God does something *for* us. In giving us spiritual life through the new birth, God works *in* us.

Justification changes our outward relationship to God so that we are no longer enemies of God, but his children. By the new birth our inmost souls are transformed, so that we are no longer sinners, but saints. Justification restores us to God's *favor*; the new birth restores us to his *image*. Justification removes the *guilt* of sin, and the new birth takes away the *power* of sin. Therefore, while the two gifts of God take place concurrently, they are of an entirely different character.

3. The failure to discern the wide difference between being justified and being born again has given rise to extremely serious theological confusion in many who have dealt with this subject. This confusion becomes especially notable when they have attempted to explain the great privilege of the children of God—namely, "those who have been born of God do not sin."

4. In order clearly to comprehend this privilege of believers, first it will be necessary to consider the correct meaning of the expression, "those who have been born of God." And, secondly, we need to examine in what sense they "do not sin."

I. The meaning of the new birth

1. First, we will consider the precise meaning of the expression, "those who have been born of God." Overall, we find a clear meaning in those scripture passages that use the expression, "born of God." We learn from these verses that being born of God does not mean just being baptized. Nor does it mean that we make some outward changes in our lives. To be more precise, being born of God means a vast inner change that God works in the soul by the administration of the Holy Spirit. This transformation involves our entire existence. From the instant we are born of God, we live in a completely different way than we did before our new birth. As it were, we are brought into another world.

2. The basis and rationale for the expression "born of God" is easily understood. When we experience this great change, we may say fittingly that we are born again. There is such a close parallel between the natural and the spiritual birth that an examination of the natural birth is the easiest way to understand the spiritual birth.

3. The child that is not yet born certainly depends on oxygen, as does everything that has life. However, the unborn child is not aware of this dependence (unless in a very feeble and inadequate way). The unborn baby hears little, if anything; the ears are still closed up. The child cannot see because its eyes are firmly shut and it is surrounded with total darkness. It may be that there are some faint beginnings of animation as the time for its birth draws near. The unborn child has certain actions

that distinguish it from a sheer mass of matter, but the developing baby has no understanding of the world. Before birth, the avenues to the mind are closed. Consequently, the child has almost no exchange with the visible earth. He or she has no knowledge, understanding, mental conception, or thought of things that happen in the world.

4. The reason the unborn child is a complete stranger to the visible world is not that it is physically separated from it. The world is very near to the baby, and it surrounds the child on every side. But the child's senses are not sufficiently developed; they are not yet in contact with its surroundings. It is possible to communicate with the material world only through an active mind, and a thick shroud keeps the unborn baby's mind from comprehending anything.

5. However, as soon as the baby is born into the world, the child begins to live in a completely different way. The infant now feels the surrounding air coming into the lungs, as he or she inhales and exhales to sustain life. And life produces a continuing growth of strength, motion, and sensation. All the physical senses are now awakened and connected with the appropriate things.

The newborn child's eyes are opened to see the light silently flowing into it's being. It discovers both itself and an infinite variety of things with which it was completely unacquainted. The ears are opened, and endless varieties of sound rush in. The physical senses are engaged with their relevant objects. In this way, the newborn infant engages the visible world and acquires more and more knowledge of all the material things under the sun.

6. It is much the same with the one that is born of God. Before that great change of the new birth takes place, we exist by God in whom "we live and move and have our being." Yet, we are not aware of him. We do not experience God or have an inward consciousness of his presence. Until we are born of God, we do not understand the divine breath of life, without which we cannot live for an instant. Nor are we aware of any of the things of God. They make no impression upon the soul. From on high, God is continually calling to us, but we do not hear him. Our spiritual ears are closed, so that the "voice of the charmer" is lost to us, although the Lord "charms ever so wisely." The eyes of the heart are closed, and we do not see the things of the Spirit of God. Complete and utter darkness covers our souls and surrounds us.

It is true that we may have some faint dawning of life or some small starts of spiritual stirring. However, we have no capacity to discern spiritual things. As a result, we do not "receive the gifts of God's Spirit, for they are foolishness to us, and we are unable to understand them because they are spiritually discerned."

7. For that reason, we have hardly any knowledge of the invisible world and scarcely any interchange with it. Not that the spiritual world is far away. Not at all. We are in the midst of it, and it surrounds us completely. The "other world," as we usually call it, is not far from every one of us. It is above, beneath, and all around us. However, unconverted people do not discern it, partly because they have no spiritual senses, which are the only means by which we can discern the things of God. Also, a thick veil surrounds us and we do not know how to penetrate it.

8. But when we are born of God (born of the Spirit) how completely the nature of our existence changes! The entire soul is now conscious of God. By indisputable experience, we can say, "You search out my path and my lying down, and are acquainted with all my ways." We are enabled to say, "You hem me in, behind and before, and lay your hand upon me."

The Spirit (or breath) of God is directly breathed into the newborn soul. And the same breath that comes from God also returns to God. As we continually receive the Spirit by faith, we constantly commune with God by love, prayer, praise, and thanksgiving. These things—love, praise, and prayer—are the breath of every soul that is truly born of God. By this new kind of spiritual breathing, our spiritual life is daily sustained and increased. In addition, one partakes of spiritual strength, action, and feeling. All the capacities of the soul are now awake and able "to distinguish good from evil."

9. "The eyes of the heart are enlightened," and we "see him who is invisible." We perceive "what is the immeasurable greatness of God's power" and his love toward those who believe. New believers understand that God is merciful to sinners and that they have been reconciled to God through his beloved son. They clearly apprehend both God's pardoning love and all "his precious and very great promises." "God who said, 'Let light shine out of darkness,' has shone (and continues to shine) in our hearts to give the light of the knowledge of the glory of God in the face of Jesus Christ." All the darkness has passed away, and those who are born of God now live in the light of God's countenance.

10. One's ears are now opened, and the voice of God no longer calls in vain. The person that is born of God hears and obeys the heavenly calling and knows the voice of the Shepherd. All the spiritual senses are now awakened, and one has a distinct relationship with the invisible world. Now, one knows more and more of the things that, prior to the new birth, "no eye has seen, nor ear heard, nor the human heart con-

ceived." One now experiences the peace of God, joy in the Holy Spirit, and the love of God, which he pours into the hearts of those who believe in him through Christ Jesus. Consequently, the veil is removed that once blocked out the light and voice of God. As well, Christians have the knowledge and love of God. The ones who are born of the Spirit live in love. "Those who abide in love abide in God, and God abides in them."

II. How Christians have victory over sin

1. We have considered the meaning of the expression, "those who have been born of God." Now, in the second place, it remains for us to consider in what way those who are born of God "do not sin."

As we have already pointed out, new Christians receive into their souls both the breath of life from God and the gracious influence of his Spirit. They continually commune with God through the Spirit. By faith, those who believe and love in this way discern the continual action of God upon their spirits, and by a kind of spiritual response they return the grace received by giving to God continuous love, praise, and prayer. Therefore, those who are born of God do not sin. Jesus Christ protects them, and as long as "God's seed abides in them, they cannot sin, because they have been born of God."

2. By sin, here I am speaking of outward sin, according to the clear, common meaning of the word. Sin is a voluntary transgression of the revealed, written law of God. Sin is a deliberate violation of any commandment of God, acknowledged to be such at the time that it is broken. As long as they abide in faith, love, and the spirit of prayer and thanksgiving, those who have been born of God do not and cannot sin. For as long as we trust in God through Christ, love him, and pour out our hearts before him, we cannot voluntarily transgress any of his commands. We cannot speak or act in ways that he has forbidden. As long as that seed remains in us (a loving, praying, thankful faith), it induces us to refrain from whatever we know to be abhorrent to God.

3. But here a difficulty will immediately occur. And to many, it seems insurmountable. The difficulty has caused them to deny the clear assertion of the apostle that those who have been born of God do not sin. In doing so, they forfeit this great privilege of those that are born of God. It is clear, in fact, that those we cannot deny to have been truly born of God, nevertheless, not only *could*, but also *have* committed sin, even flagrant, outward sin. (The Spirit of God has given us this reliable

testimony about them in his word.) They transgressed God's clearly revealed laws by saying or doing what they knew was forbidden.

4. David was unquestionably born of God before he was anointed king over Israel. He knew the one in whom he had put his trust; "he was strong in his faith as he gave glory to God." He prayed,

> The Lord is my shepherd, I shall not want.
> He makes me lie down in green pastures;
> he leads me beside still waters;
> Even though I walk through the darkest valley,
> I fear no evil;
> for you are with me. (Ps. 23:1-4)

David was filled with such love for God that it often compelled him to cry out, "I love you, O Lord, my strength. The Lord is my rock, my fortress, and my deliverer, my God, my rock in whom I take refuge." David was a man of prayer; he poured out his soul before God in all circumstances of life. He was profuse in praises and thanksgiving. He declared,

> I will bless the Lord at all times.
> You are my God, and I will give thanks to you;
> you are my God, I will extol you.

Nevertheless, such a child of God as David could and did sin. Indeed, he committed the terrible sins of adultery and murder.

5. Even after the Holy Spirit was given more fully, and after Jesus Christ "brought life and immortality to light through the gospel," we do not lack the same kind of tragic examples. Undoubtedly, the Bible recorded these cases for our instruction. We have another example in Barnabas. Probably because of his selling all that he had and bringing the money for the relief of his poor sisters and brothers, the apostles surnamed him Barnabas, which means "the son of consolation." He was so respected in Antioch that the Christians selected him from among all the disciples, along with Saul, to carry material relief to the Christians in Judea. On his return from Judea, by the particular direction of the Holy Spirit, Barnabas was solemnly "set apart for the work to which God called him." God summoned Barnabas to accompany the great Apostle Paul in ministry among the Gentiles and to be his fellow laborer in every place.

Nevertheless, the disagreement between Barnabas and Paul became so severe that they parted company. Because John Mark "had deserted them in Pamphylia and had not accompanied them in the work," Paul did not think that it was good to take him on the second journey to visit the sisters and brothers. For that reason, "Barnabas took Mark with him and sailed away to Cyprus," forsaking Paul to whom he had been so closely joined in the Holy Spirit.

6. A case more unexpected than both these examples is given by St. Paul in his Epistle to the Galatians. I refer to the Apostle Peter, the mature, zealous, and foremost apostle, who was one of the three most highly favored of the Lord's disciples. St. Paul said, "When Peter came to Antioch, I opposed him to his face, because he stood self-condemned; for until certain people came from James, he used to eat with the Gentiles"—those unbelievers who were converts to Christianity. Peter had been especially instructed by God that he "should not call anyone profane or unclean." St. Paul wrote about the state of affairs:

> Until certain people came from James, he, Peter, used to eat with the Gentiles. But after they came, he drew back and kept himself separate for fear of the faction that demanded circumcision for all new believers. And the other Jews joined him in this hypocrisy, so that even Barnabas was led astray by their hypocrisy. But when I saw that they were not acting consistently with the truth of the gospel, I said to Peter before them all, "If you, though a Jew, live like a Gentile and not like a Jew, how can you compel the Gentiles to live like Jews?" (Gal. 2:12-14)

Here is a further example of one who was undoubtedly born of God, yet he committed plain, undeniable sin. How can this sin be reconciled with the assertion of St. John (if taken in the obvious literal meaning) that "those who have been born of God do not sin?"

7. I call attention to what has already been stated. As long as "the one who was born of God (namely, Jesus Christ) protects them, the evil one does not touch them." But if Christians do not protect themselves, and if they fail to abide in the faith, they may commit sin just as any other person.

It is easy, therefore, to understand how children of God might be drawn away from their steadfastness, even though the great truth of God declared by the apostle remains constant and unshaken. Those who strayed did not "protect themselves" by the grace of God, which was sufficient for them. Step by step, they fell into sin.

First, they slipped into negative thoughts and inward sin by failing "to rekindle the gift of God that was within them." They failed to discipline themselves in prayer, and they ceased "pressing on toward the goal for the prize of the heavenly call." Next, they fell into positive inward sin, inclining to wickedness in their hearts and yielding to some evil desire or attitude. Finally, their faith failed. They lost sight of the pardoning God, and they forsook their love for him. Becoming weak, and the same as any other person without faith, they were capable of committing outward sin.

8. A particular example will clarify this failure. David was born of God, and by faith he saw God. He sincerely loved God. He could truly say, "Whom have I in heaven but you? And there is nothing on earth (no person or thing) that I desire other than you." But natural corruption remained in his heart; and this bent to sin is the seed of all evil.

David was walking about on the roof of his house, probably praising the God whom his soul loved. Then, he looked down and saw Bathsheba. He felt a temptation, a thought inclined to evil. The Spirit of God did not fail to convince him of the evil of his desire. He doubtless heard and understood God's warning voice. Nevertheless, in some measure he yielded to the thought and the temptation began to prevail over him. This temptation defiled his spirit. He still saw God, but now more dimly. He still loved God, but not to the same degree—not with the same strength and fervency of affection.

God restrained him again. God's Spirit was grieved, and his voice, although fainter and fainter, still whispered to David, "Sin is lurking at the door;" "turn to me and be saved." But David did not listen to God. He looked again, not to God, but to the forbidden object. He continued looking at Bathsheba until nature became stronger than grace, and David's natural desires ignited lust in his soul. The eye of his mind was now closed again, and God vanished out of his sight. The love of God, faith, and divine supernatural communion with God together ceased. David rushed onward as "a horse plunging headlong into battle." After that, he knowingly committed the outward sin.

9. You can observe the undeniable progress from grace toward sin. Step by step, sin develops in the following way: (1) The divine seed of loving, conquering faith remains in the one that is born of God. "He protects himself," and by the grace of God, "he cannot sin." (2) A temptation arises; it does not matter whether it is from the world, the flesh, or the devil. (3) The Spirit of God gives warning that sin is near, and he bids us more strongly to stay awake and pray. (4) The temptation causes us somewhat to heed the temptation, and it begins to grow pleasurable to us. (5) The Holy Spirit is grieved because our faith has weakened and our love for God is growing cold. (6) The Holy Spirit reproves us more sharply, saying "This is the way; walk in it" (Isa. 30.21). (7) We turn

away from the disturbing voice of God and listen to the pleasing voice of the tempter. (8) Evil desire begins in the soul and spreads until faith and love disappear. Because the power of the Lord has departed from us, we are then capable of committing outward sin.

10. I will explain this progression into sin by yet another example. The Apostle Peter was full of faith and the Holy Spirit, and by protecting himself, he had a clear conscience toward God and all people. "Until certain people came from James," he walked in holiness and godly sincerity; he ate with the Gentiles, knowing that what God declared to be clean was not profane or impure. However, certain people of the "circumcision faction" visited him. These guests were Jewish converts to Christianity who were zealous for retaining circumcision and the other rites of the Mosaic Law. Their presence caused a temptation to arise in Peter's heart. He feared those of the "circumcision faction" and coveted their esteem, favor, and praise more than he wanted God's approval.

The Holy Spirit warned him that sin was near. Nonetheless, to some degree he yielded to the sinful fear of human opinion. St. Peter's faith and love were proportionately weakened. Again, God rebuked him for yielding to the devil. Yet St. Peter would not listen to the voice of his Shepherd. Rather, he gave in to slavish fear and quenched the Spirit in doing so. Then God withdrew, and faith and love were quenched. Then, St. Peter committed the outward sin. He did not walk virtuously; he did "not act consistently with the truth of the gospel." He kept himself separate from his Christian brothers and sisters, and by his immoral example (if not also his advice) he "compelled the Gentiles to live like Jews" and "to submit again to a yoke of slavery," from which "Christ had set them free."

It is indisputably true that those who are born of God, while protecting themselves, do not and cannot sin. Yet, if they do not protect themselves, they may selfishly commit all manner of sin.

III. Lessons and applications

1. From the preceding considerations, first, we may learn a clear and unequivocal answer to a question that has frequently perplexed many people with sincere hearts. The question is, "Does sin precede or follow the loss of faith? Does a child of God first commit sin, and therefore lose faith? Or, does one first lose faith before committing sin?"

I answer that, at the least, some sins of omission must necessarily precede the loss of faith. There is some inward sin involved. However, the loss of faith must precede outward sin. The more believers examine their hearts, the more they will become convinced of the truth that faith working by love expels both inward and outward sin from those who discipline themselves in prayer. Even so, we are always liable to temptation, particularly to the sin that clings so closely. If the loving eye of the soul is steadily fixed on God, the temptation soon vanishes away. If not, we are drawn away, or as the Apostle James says, "drawn out" from God by our own desire. We are caught by the bait of present or promised pleasure. Desire is conceived in us and it leads to sin. This inward sin destroys our faith and casts us headlong into the snare of the devil, so that we are capable of committing any kind of outward sin.

2. Second, from what has been said, we may understand the life of God in the soul of a believer. We comprehend its precise nature and what is directly and necessarily implied in these considerations. Exactly and essentially, the life of God in the soul involves the continuing inspiration of God's Holy Spirit. It is God's breathing into the soul, and the soul's breathing back what it first receives from God. This exchange is a continual action of God upon the believers' souls and a response of the believers' souls to God. The Life of God in our souls is his unceasing presence as a loving, pardoning God, who is revealed to our hearts and received by faith. This life requires our unceasing return of love, praise, and prayer. We offer up to him all the thoughts of our hearts, words of our mouths, and works of our hands. Our entire bodies, souls, and spirits become holy sacrifices, acceptable to God in Christ Jesus.

3. Third, we see the absolute necessity of this response of the soul (or whatever we may call it) to God, in order to nourish the divine life within. It clearly appears that God does not continue to act upon the soul unless the soul constantly responds to him. God anticipates our responses with the blessings of his goodness. He first loves us, and manifests himself to us. While we are yet afar off he calls us to himself and shines upon our hearts. But if we do not then love him who first loved us, and if we will not listen to his voice, and if we turn our eye away from him, refusing to follow the light which he pours in upon us, his Spirit will not always work with us. God will gradually withdraw from us and leave us to the darkness of our own hearts. He will not continue to breathe into our souls unless our souls breathe toward him in return. We must give back to God our love, prayer, and thanksgiving, as a sacrifice with which he is well pleased.

4. Finally, let us learn to follow the instruction of the great Apostle Paul: "Do not become proud, but stand in awe." Let us fear sin more than death or hell. Let us have a watchful (but not agonizing) fear, so as

not to trust our own deceitful hearts. "If you think you are standing, watch out that you do not fall." Even the one who stands fast in the grace of God and in the faith that overcomes the world may nevertheless fall into inward sin and "suffer shipwreck in the faith." How easily, then, will outward sin regain its dominion over the one who falls!

Therefore, you, O child of God, stay awake constantly so that you can always hear the voice of God! Be faithful to pray without ceasing. At all times and in all places, pour out your heart before God! Doing so, you will always believe, always love, and never fall into sin.

THE LORD OUR RIGHTEOUSNESS

In 1765, John Wesley wrote in his journal: "I preached on those words in the Lesson for the day, 'The Lord our righteousness.' I said not one thing which I have not said, at least, fifty times within this twelve-month: Yet it appeared to many entirely new, who much importuned me to print my sermon, supposing it would stop the mouths of all gainsayers. Alas, for their simplicity! In spite of all I can print, say, or do, will not those who seek occasion of offence find occasion?"[1] From these words, it is clear that Wesley had been forced to takes sides in a theological controversy. This dispute, to which Wesley referred from time to time, continues to resurface in the church, even today.

The theological debate in question was about the nature of the atonement of Christ. As formulated in Wesley's day, the issue at stake was whether Christ's atoning death is justification's *formal* cause or its *meritorious* cause. Those who understood Christ's death as the formal cause of justification inseparably linked the atonement with the doctrines of election and irresistible grace. They contended that all those for whom Christ died would be saved unconditionally. However, they added that Christ did not die for everyone, but only for the elect. These teachers argued that Christ did not die for the non-elect, who could not and would not be saved. This view posits a *limited atonement*.

On the other side of the debate were those who regarded Christ's atonement as the *meritorious* cause of justification. This view also holds that the death and resurrection of Christ constitute the only basis for salvation. Christ's atonement, however, does not benefit us unless we respond to the grace he gives to us. Wesley took this view. He sought common ground with other Christians, where possible. He agreed that the sole basis for justification is the atonement of Christ. He further agreed with his theological detractors that good works gain us no merit before God. However, Wesley pointed out that scripture speaks often about the need for human response and moral accountability. According to Wesley, Christ's atonement is a substitute for the *punishment* due us because of our sins, but the atonement is not a substitute for the obedience and faithfulness that we owe to him.

Furthermore, Wesley disagreed with the "Predestinarians." He contended that Christ died for *everyone* and that *whoever* believes in him will be saved. In the course of this debate, he wrote:

> Show me the scriptures wherein God declares in equally express terms [that] (1.) "Christ did not die for all, but for some only." (2.) "Christ is not the propitiation for the sins of the whole world;" and, (3.) "He did not die for all, at least, not with that intent, that they should live unto him who died for them." Show me, I say, the scriptures that affirm these three things in equally express terms. You know there are none.[2]

John Wesley insisted that Christ died for all, even if some people fail to respond to his grace and are forever lost. He opposed the formula: "The elect will be saved, do what they will; the non-elect will be damned, do what they can."

Due to Wesley's affirmation that we are responsible to respond to God's grace, his critics accused him of teaching the "heresy" that we are justified through works. This sermon answers their charge. In Wesley's day, some even claimed that because Christ's righteousness was imputed to them irresistibly, they were excused from the need to repent, amend their lives, and obey the moral law. Wesley asks, "If God imputes all of Christ's righteousness to Christians, why should they engage in good works?" Wesley championed the view that although good works are not the *root* of salvation, they are the *fruit* of salvation. Furthermore, he insisted that God does not impart Christ's righteousness to those who do not trust him to do so. He believed that grace is resistible. Indeed, for over fifty years, he traveled throughout Great Britain entreating people not to turn aside from the grace that God offers to every person.

In most instances, Wesley's handling of theological conflict remains a model for today. He left us an example of integrity, good will, courtesy, and respect for those who differed from him and even libeled him. Concerning the debate that forms the background of this sermon, Wesley penned a letter that further reveals the way he dealt with controversy. He wrote to the Countess of Huntingdon:

> Their general cry has been, "He [Wesley] is unsound in the faith; he preaches another Gospel!" I answer, Whether it be the same which they preach or not, it is the same which I have preached for above thirty years. This may easily appear from what I have published during that whole term. . . . But it is said, "O but you printed ten lines in August last, which contradict all your other writings!" Be not so sure of this. It is probable, at least, that I understand my own meaning as well as you do; and that meaning I have yet again declared in the sermon last referred to [*The Lord Our Righteousness*]. By that [sermon] interpret those ten lines, and you will understand them better: Although I should think that any one might see, even without this help, that the lines in question do not refer to the condition of obtaining, but of continuing in, the favour of God. But whether the sentiment contained in those lines be right or wrong, and whether it be well or ill expressed, the Gospel which I now preach, God does still confirm by new witnesses in every place; perhaps never so much in this kingdom as within these last three months. Now, I argue from obvious and undeniable fact that God cannot bear witness to a lie. The Gospel therefore which he confirms, must be true in substance. There may be opinions maintained at the same time which are not exactly true; and who can be secure from these? Perhaps I thought myself so once: When I was much younger than I am now, I thought myself almost infallible; but, I bless God, I know myself better now. To be short: Such as I am, I love you well. You have one of the first places in my esteem and affection. And you once had some regard for me. But it cannot continue, if it depends upon my seeing with your eyes, or on my being in no mistake. . . . My dear friend, you seem not to have well learned yet the meaning of those words, which I desire to have continually written on my heart, "Whosoever doeth the will of my Father which is in heaven, the same is my brother, and sister, and mother."[3]

Despite Wesley's engagement in theological controversy, he persistently worked for Christian unity. In *The Character of a Methodist*, he declared:

> I beseech you, brethren, by the mercies of God, that we be in no wise divided among ourselves. Is thy heart right, as my heart is with thine? I ask

no farther question. If it be, give me thy hand. For opinions, or terms, let us not destroy the work of God. Dost thou love and serve God? It is enough. I give thee the right hand of fellowship . . . Let us strive together for the faith of the Gospel; walking worthy of the vocation wherewith we are called; with all lowliness and meekness, with long-suffering, forbearing one another in love, endeavouring to keep the unity of the Spirit in the bond of peace; remembering, there is one body, and one Spirit, even as we are called with one hope of our calling; "one Lord, one faith, one baptism; one God and Father of all, who is above all, and through all, and in you all."[4]

While showing a spirit of good will, Wesley never compromised the truth concerning matters of theological substance. He did not arrive at his theological views offhandedly, and he did not abandon his doctrinal opinions because some took offense at them. He based his religious beliefs on scripture, the centuries-long consensus of Christian tradition, his own experience, logic, and interviews with thousands of genuine believers.

In theological debate, Wesley usually remained charitable and courteous, while holding firm to gospel essentials. He spoke disapprovingly of a certain writer of his day "who seriously believed himself the most knowing man in the kingdom, and despised all that contradicted him...as the mire in the streets." Wesley continued, "It strikes at the root of charity, inspiring into its strictest votaries [devotees] deep censoriousness toward the world in general, and an inexpressible bitterness toward all who do not receive their new apostle."[5]

Although Wesley was self-confident, he was also humble and willing to stand corrected when shown by scripture to be in error. When possible, he sought agreement, fellowship, and cooperation with other Christians.[6] He wrote in the Preface to these Standard Sermons, "Are you convinced that you see more clearly than I do? It is not improbable that you may. If so, treat me as you would want to be treated yourself under the same circumstances. Lead me to a better way than I have yet known."

This sermon reiterates a prominent theme in Wesley's preaching. Christ saves us from both the guilt of sin and the power of sin. God's plan for Christians, many times repeated in the Bible, is that they may be holy, as Christ is holy.[7] Wesley closes this sermon with a plea for Christian charity and mutual love: "We have 'one Lord, one faith, one hope of our calling.' Let us all strengthen each other's hands in God and with one heart and one mouth declare to all humankind, 'The Lord is our righteousness.'"

Sermon 20

THE LORD OUR RIGHTEOUSNESS

*Preached at the chapel in West-Street, Seven-Dials On
Sunday, November 24, 1765*

*This is the name by which he will be called: "The Lord
is our righteousness."*   *(Jeremiah 23:6)*

1   How shameful and how countless are the conflicts that have arisen
over religion! These controversies have appeared not only among
the children of this world who do not know what true religion is.
Religious conflicts also appear among the children of God who have
experienced "the kingdom of God within them" and have tasted of
"righteousness, and peace, and joy in the Holy Spirit." In all eras, very
many Christians have turned their weapons against each other, instead
of joining together against the common enemy. These Christians not only
have dissipated their precious time, but they have wounded each other's
spirits, weakened each other's hands, and severely hindered the great
work of their common Master! Many fragile people have been wounded
by these religious controversies! How many of the "lame have been put
out of joint!" How many are the sinners that have been confirmed in
their disregard of all religion and in their contempt for those who pro-

fess it! And how many of "the holy ones in the land" have been constrained to "weep in secret!"

2. To what lengths would everyone who loves God and neighbor be
willing to go (and even suffer) to remedy this painful evil? Would they
not do all they could to remove controversy from among the children of
God and to restore or preserve peace among them? Other than maintaining a good conscience, what would a sincere Christian consider too
costly to part with in order to promote peace and unity among God's
children?

Perhaps we cannot make these wars cease to the end of the earth or
reconcile all the children of God with each other.
Nevertheless, let all Christians do what they can. If it is only two small
copper coins, let each one contribute what he or she can toward
Christian unity. Happy are those who are able, to any degree, to promote
"peace among those whom God favors." Especially, let there be harmony among good people, those who are enrolled under the banner of "the
Prince of Peace." Let Christians be particularly committed "so far as it
depends on them to live peaceably with all."

3. It would be a considerable step toward this glorious goal if we
could help good people to understand one another. Many religious disputes arise simply from the lack of understanding and from mere confusion. Frequently, neither of the contending parties understands what
their opponents mean. Consequently, each party violently attacks the
other party, although there is no substantive difference between them.
And yet it is not always an easy matter to convince people of this fact,
particularly when their emotions are aroused. Under these circumstances, understanding encounters the greatest of difficulties.

However, understanding is possible—especially when we make an
effort. We can gain comprehension not by trusting in ourselves, but by
depending entirely on God with whom all things are possible. When we
rely on God, how quickly he is able to disperse the cloud and to shine
upon our hearts. He can enable people of different parties to understand
each other and the truth as it is in Jesus!

4. One very important aspect of this certainty is contained in the
words cited in the text of this sermon: "This is the name by which he will
be called: 'The Lord is our righteousness.'" This truth penetrates deeply
into the core of Christianity. In a way, it supports Christianity's entire
framework. Without doubt, we may affirm this truth in the words that
Martin Luther used to maintain another fact closely connected to it. The
confession that Christ is our righteousness is "the doctrine on which the
church stands or falls." This truth is certainly the "pillar and ground" of

the Christian faith, the only source of salvation. This doctrine of the catholic and universal faith is found among all the children of God. In the words of the Athanasian Creed, unless one keeps this truth—the Lord is our righteousness—entire and undefiled, "without doubt he shall perish everlastingly."[8]

5. Therefore, might one not reasonably anticipate that however Christians differ in other respects, everyone who names the name of Christ should agree on this point? Nonetheless, agreement is far from being the case! There is scarcely any other doctrine about which Christians are so little agreed. All those that profess to follow Christ seem widely and irreconcilably mired in disagreement. I say *seem*, because I am thoroughly convinced that many Christians only *appear* to differ. The disagreement lies more in words than in substance. Christians are much more nearly agreed in understanding than in language. To be sure, there are wide differences in words, not only between Protestants and Roman Catholics, but between Protestants and Protestants. Indeed, there is disagreement even between those who agree on justification by faith and every other fundamental doctrine of the gospel.

6. If the difference lies more in opinion than real experience and more in wording than in opinion, how can it be that even the children of God should so vehemently dispute with each other about the matter? We may find several reasons for the disagreement. The main problem is that Christians fail to understand one another. They are too keenly attached to their opinions, and particularly to their *way of expressing* their views about the Lord who is our righteousness.

In order to remove this barrier to understanding each other on this subject, by the help of God, at least in some measure, I will attempt to clarify (1) the righteousness of Christ and (2) when and in what sense his righteousness is imputed to us. I will conclude (3) with a brief and clear application.

I. The righteousness of Christ

With regard to the question, "What is the righteousness of Christ?" I answer that it is twofold. It is both divine and human righteousness.

1. Christ's divine righteousness belongs to his divine nature, because he is the "*I am.*" Jesus Christ exists "over all, God blessed forever." In the words of the Athanasian Creed, he is the Supreme One, the Eternal One, "equal with the Father, as touching his Godhead, though inferior to the Father as touching his manhood."[9] Christ's holiness is eternal, fun-

damental, and unchanging. He is infinite justice, mercy, and truth—and in everything Christ and the Father are one.

However, in the present question before us I do not perceive that the divine righteousness of Christ is of immediate concern. I believe that there are few people, if any, who now argue for the imputation of Christ's divine righteousness to us. Whoever believes the doctrine of imputation understands it mainly, if not entirely, as the *human* righteousness of Christ.

2. The human righteousness of Christ belongs to him in his human nature, inasmuch as he is the one mediator between God and humankind, Christ Jesus, himself human. Christ's human righteousness is both internal and external. His internal righteousness is the image of God stamped on every endowment and aspect of his soul. It is a copy of God's divine righteousness, so far as it can be imparted to a human spirit. It is a reflection of God's divine purity, justice, mercy, and truth. It includes love, adoration, and submission to his Father. This righteousness is humility, meekness, kindness, love for lost humankind, and every other holy and heavenly disposition. Christ possesses these virtues in the highest degree, without any defect or mixture with the profane.

3. The least part of his external righteousness was that he did nothing wrong. He knew no outward sin of any kind, and "no deceit was found in his mouth." He never spoke an improper word or did an unworthy deed. So far, I have only spoken about his *negative* righteousness, although other than in Jesus Christ this righteousness has never belonged to any human being, and it never will.

Additionally, Christ's outward righteousness was also *positive*. "He has done everything well." In every word of his mouth and work of his hands, Jesus did precisely the "will of him that sent him." In the entire course of his life he did the will of God on earth, as the angels do it in heaven. Everything that he did and said was exactly right in every aspect and circumstance. The whole and the parts of his obedience were complete. "He fulfilled all righteousness."

4. Christ's obedience involved even more than all these things. It involved both doing and suffering. He did the entire will of God, from the time he came into the world, until "he himself bore our sins in his body on the cross." He continued obedient by making a full atonement for our sins and then "bowed his head and gave up his spirit." This suffering obedience is usually termed the "passive righteousness of Christ." We usually refer to his perfect words and deeds as his "active righteousness." The active and passive righteousness of Christ were never, in fact, separated from each other. And we, also, should not separate them,

either in speaking or thinking. It is with regard to both these passive and active aspects that Jesus is called "the Lord our righteousness."

II. The imputation of Christ's righteousness to us

But when can any of us actually say, "The Lord our righteousness?" In other words, when and in what sense is the righteousness of Christ imputed to us?

1. Search through the entire world: all the people in it are either believers or unbelievers. The first thing, therefore, that produces no dispute among reasonable people is that the righteousness of Christ is imputed to believers, and it is not imputed to unbelievers.

But *when* is it imputed? The righteousness of Christ is imputed when people truly believe in him. In that instant the righteousness of Christ becomes theirs. It is imputed to all who believe, as soon as they believe. The righteousness of Christ is inseparable from faith. For if one believes according to scripture, that person trusts in the righteousness of Christ. There is no true faith (that is, justifying faith) that does not have the righteousness of Christ as its object.

2. It is true that believers may not all speak alike; they may not all use the same language. And we should not expect that they should. We cannot reasonably require uniform language of every Christian. A thousand different circumstances may cause people's modes of expression to vary from those of others. But a difference of expression does not necessarily imply a divergence of opinion. Different persons may use various expressions, and yet mean the same thing. Nothing is more common than this fact. However, we seldom make sufficient allowance for it. Indeed, it is not easy for us, when speaking of something after the passing of a good amount of time, to employ exactly the same wording we used originally, although the thought remains the same. How then can we stubbornly require others to use precisely the same expressions that we use?

3. We may go a step further still. People may differ from us in their opinions and their expressions, and nevertheless be partakers with us of the same precious faith. It is possible that they may not have a precise understanding of the very blessing that they enjoy. Their ideas may not be as distinct as ours, and yet their experience may be just as sound. There is a wide difference between the natural endowments of people, especially in their understanding. Furthermore, our differences are greatly magnified due to the nature of our education. Indeed, education alone may give rise to unimaginable variations in people's differing opinions.

Why would this truth not apply to our present discussion as well as to any other subject? Although people's opinions and ways of expression may be confused and inaccurate, their hearts may cling to God through his beloved son. They may have a genuine share in his righteousness.

4. Therefore, let us make all the allowances for others that we would wish for ourselves if we were in their places. Who is unaware of the amazing power of education (to touch again only on that factor)? And who that understands the situation can expect, let us say, a member of the Church of Rome to think or speak clearly on the subject of the righteousness of Christ? When he was dying, Cardinal Robert Bellarmine was asked, "Unto which of the saints will you turn?" He cried out, "It is safest to trust in the merits of Christ." If we had heard him, would we have affirmed that he had no share in Christ's righteousness (notwithstanding his mistaken theological opinions)?

5. In what sense is the righteousness of Christ imputed to believers? In this sense: all believers are forgiven and accepted, not for the sake of anything in them or of anything that ever was, is, or ever can be done by them. They are forgiven and accepted completely and entirely for the sake of what Christ has done and suffered for them. I repeat this truth again: They are forgiven and accepted not for the sake of anything residing in them or done by them, not because of their own righteousness or works.

Christ saves us not because of the works of righteousness that we have done, but because of his own mercy. "For by grace you have been saved through faith, and this is not your own doing; it is the gift of God, not the result of works, so that no one may boast." We are saved entirely and solely because of what Christ has done and suffered for us. We are "justified by his grace as a gift, through the redemption that is in Christ Jesus." And Christ is both the means of our obtaining the favor of God and of our continuing in his favor. It is through Christ's merit that we first come to God and through which we ever after remain in him. Until our spirits return to God, Christians walk in this incomparably new and living way.

6. I have constantly believed and taught this doctrine for nearly twenty-eight years. I first published this sermon to the entire world in the year 1738 and ten or twelve times since. To the same purpose, I have used the following words and many others extracted from the homilies of our church:

> These things must go together in our justification: Upon God's part, his
> great mercy and grace; upon Christ's part, the satisfaction of God's justice,

by the offering his body, and shedding his blood; and upon our part, true and living faith in the merits of Jesus Christ. So that in our justification there is not only God's mercy and grace, but his justice also. And so the grace of God does not shut out the righteousness of God in our justification; but only shuts out the righteousness of man, that is, the righteousness of our works.

That we are justified by faith alone, is clearly spoken to take away all merit of our works and wholly to ascribe the merit and deserving of our justification to Christ only. Our justification comes freely from the mere mercy of God. For whereas all the world was not able to pay any part toward our ransom, it pleased Him, without any of our deserving, to prepare for us Christ's body and blood, whereby our ransom might be paid, and his justice satisfied. Christ, therefore, is now the righteousness of all them that truly believe in him.[10]

7. A year or two after 1738, I published the hymns, and since then I have republished them several times (a clear testimony that my judgment was still the same). All these hymns speak to the same purpose. To cite all the passages on this theme would require me to transcribe a great part of the volumes of hymns. One example illustrates them all. This hymn was reprinted seven years ago, five years ago, two years ago, and some months afterward:

> Jesu, thy blood and righteousness
> My beauty are, my glorious dress:
> 'Midst flaming worlds, in these array'd,
> With joy shall I lift up my head.[11]

From beginning to the end, the entire hymn expresses the same sentiment.

8. In my sermon "Justification by Faith," published nineteen years ago and again seven or eight years ago, I expressed the same concept in these words:

Because the Son of God has "tasted death for everyone," God has "reconciled the world to himself, not counting our sins against us." "Therefore just as one man's trespass led to condemnation for all, so one man's act of righteousness leads to justification and life for all." Now, for the sake of his well-beloved son, God takes into account what he has done and suffered for us. On only one condition, which God enables us to meet, God guarantees to remit the punishment due to our sins and to bring us back into his favor. As the pledge of eternal life, God restores our dead souls to spiritual life.[12]

9. This concept is more thoroughly and precisely expressed in the Treatise on Justification, which last year I abridged from John Goodwin's *Imputatio Fide*. In part, that treatise said:

> We may understand the phrase "imputing Christ's righteousness" to mean bestowing on us the righteousness of Christ, including his passive and active obedience. We receive the privileges, blessings, and benefits purchased by Christ. Thus, a believer may be said to be justified by Christ's imputed righteousness. This gift means that God justifies the believer for the sake of Christ's righteousness, and not for any righteousness of his own. John Calvin said, "Christ, by his obedience, procured and merited for us grace and favor with God the Father." He also said, "Through his obedience, Christ obtained or purchased righteousness for us."[13] All such expressions mean that we are justified only by the grace of God and that Christ is our righteousness. That God procured this righteousness for us by the death and resurrection of Christ means the same thing—the righteousness of Christ, both his active and passive righteousness, is the meritorious cause of our justification by God's hand. On our believing in Christ, God will account us righteous.

10. Perhaps some people will object, "But you affirm that *faith* (not the righteousness of Christ) is "reckoned to us as righteousness." St. Paul affirms this doctrine again and again. Accordingly, I affirm it also. For every believer, faith is imputed for righteousness. I am speaking of our placing faith in the righteousness of Christ. This avowal is exactly the same thing that I said earlier. By that expression I mean nothing more than that we are justified by faith in the work of Christ, not by faith in our works (or placing faith in our faith). Every believer is forgiven and accepted, only for the sake of what Christ has done and suffered.

11. Someone may ask, "Is not a believer invested or clothed with the righteousness of Christ?" I answer that this statement is undoubtedly true. Accordingly, the words cited above are the language of every believing heart:

> Jesu, thy blood and righteousness
> My beauty are, my glorious dress.[14]

That is, for the sake of Christ's active and passive righteousness, I am forgiven and accepted by God.

Someone may ask, "Must we not put off the filthy rags of our own righteous deeds before we can put on the spotless righteousness of Christ?" I answer that certainly we must do so. In simple terms, we must repent before we can believe the gospel. Before we can truly rely on Christ, we must be separated from dependence upon ourselves. We must cast away all confidence in our own righteousness, or we cannot have a true confidence in the righteousness of Christ. Until we are delivered from trusting in anything that we do, we cannot thoroughly trust in what Christ has done and suffered for us. First, we receive the sentence of death in ourselves. Then, we trust in him who lived and died for us.

12. Someone may ask, "But do you not believe in *inherent* righteousness?" I answer, "Yes, in its proper place." However, inherent righteousness is not the *ground* of our acceptance with God. It is the *fruit* of salvation. Inherent righteousness is not a substitute for imputed righteousness; it is a *result* of imputed righteousness. I believe that God implants actual righteousness in every one to whom he has imputed it. I believe that Jesus Christ "became for us wisdom from God, and righteousness and sanctification and redemption." I mean that God sanctifies as well as justifies all who believe in him. Those to whom the righteousness of Christ is imputed are made righteous by the Spirit of Christ. They are renewed in the image of God, "created according to the likeness of God in true righteousness and holiness."

13. Someone may object, "But do you not put faith in the place of Christ or his righteousness?" I respond, "Not at all." I take particular care to put each one of these factors in its proper place. The righteousness of Christ is the complete and only foundation for all our hope. It is by faith that the Holy Spirit enables us to build upon this foundation. God gives this faith to us. And God accepts us at the moment we trust in Christ. He accepts us not for the sake of our faith, but because of what Christ has done and suffered for us.

You see, each of these things has its proper place, and none of them clash with each other. We believe in Christ, we love him, and we strive to live "blamelessly according to all the commandments and regulations of the Lord." At the same time,

> Thus while we bestow
> Our moments below,
> Ourselves we forsake,
> And refuge in Jesus' righteousness take:
> His passion alone
> The foundation we own,
> And pardon we claim,
> And eternal redemption in Jesus' name.[15]

14. Therefore, I no more deny the righteousness of Christ than I deny the Godhead of Christ. One may just as well charge me with denying the one as the other. Neither do I deny imputed righteousness. This charge against me is another unkind and unjust accusation. I always have affirmed, as I do now, that the righteousness of Christ is imputed to every believer. Who are they that deny it? Those that reject this truth are unbelievers, whether they are baptized or unbaptized. Such people allege that the glorious gospel of our Lord Jesus Christ is a cleverly devised myth. Unbelievers include all Socinians and Arians—all who deny the supreme Godhead of the Lord who bought them. Accordingly, they deny Christ's divine righteousness; they believe that he is an ordinary human being. They disavow that his human righteousness is imputed to anyone, and they take the position that God accepts all people because of their own righteousness.

15. The Church of Rome also denies the imputation of the human righteousness of Christ as the entire and only meritorious cause of the justification of sinners before God. As well, that church's members who are true to the principles of their own church also deny the imputation of Christ's righteousness. Undoubtedly there are many among them whose experience goes beyond their doctrine. Although they are far from expressing themselves properly, they experience what they do not know how to express. Indeed, with their hearts they believe, although their conceptions of this great truth are as undeveloped as their wording. They truly rest on Christ alone for their present and eternal salvation.

16. To this group of Christians we may also add those in the Reformed Churches who are usually termed "mystics." One of the chief of these mystics in the present century (at least in England) was Mr. William Law. It is well known that he absolutely and zealously denied the imputation of the righteousness of Christ, as zealously as Robert Barclay did. Barclay did not hesitate to say, "Imputed righteousness—imputed nonsense!" The body of the people known by the name of Quakers espouses the same opinion.

Indeed, the majority of those who affirm that they are members of the Church of England either know nothing about imputed righteousness, or else they deny both the imputed righteousness of Christ and justification by faith. They allege that these doctrines nullify the need for good works. To these people we may add a considerable number of those commonly called Anabaptists, as well as thousands of Presbyterians and Independents, lately instructed by the writings of Dr. John Taylor.

Concerning Taylor, I am not called to pass judgment. I leave such people to God who judges them. But will any one dare to affirm that all mystics (such as Mr. Law in particular) Quakers, Presbyterians, Independents, and all members of the Church of England who are not clear in their opinions or expressions are empty of all Christian experience? Dare we conclude that they are all in a state of damnation, "having no hope and without God in the world?" However confused their ideas and incorrect their language may be, do not many of them have hearts that are right toward God? Do not many of them effectively know "the Lord who is our righteousness?"

17. Blessed be God, we are not among those that are so untutored in their conceptions and expressions. We Methodists no more deny the wording than the blessing, but we are unwilling to impose our terminology on other people. Let others use either this wording or similar expressions, which they consider to be more exactly scriptural. Only let their hearts rest on what Christ has suffered and accomplished for their pardon, grace, and glory.

I cannot express myself better than in the words of Mr. James Hervey, whose thoughts are worthy to be written in letters of gold: "We are not solicitous as to any particular set of phrases. Only let men be humbled as repenting criminals at Christ's feet, let them rely as devoted dependents on his merits, and they are undoubtedly in the way leading to a blessed immortality."[16]

18. Is there any need or possibility of saying more? Only let us live by this declaration, and all the contention about this or that particular phrase is pulled up by the roots. Keep to this fourth-century guideline:

> Humbled as repenting criminals at Christ's feet, let them rely as devoted dependents on his merits and they are undoubtedly in the way leading to a blessed immortality.[17]

What further room is there for argument? Who denies this principle? Can we not all meet on this ground? What then are we to squabble about?

As a man of peace, I am here proposing terms of reconciliation to all the contending parties. We desire no better way. We accept the terms and subscribe to them with heart and hand. Whoever refuses so to do, mark that person! He or she is an enemy of peace, "a troubler of Israel," a disturber of the Church of God.

19. In the meantime, when they become a covering for one's unrighteousness, we are afraid of the improper use of the phrases, "the righteousness of Christ," or "the righteousness of Christ is imputed to me". We have seen this done a thousand times. Suppose someone has been

reproved for drunkenness. The person replies, "O, I pretend to no righteousness of my own; Christ is my righteousness." Suppose that another person has been told, that "the thieves and the unjust will not inherit the kingdom of God." That person confidently replies, "I am unjust in myself, but I have a spotless righteousness in Christ." So, there are those who claim to have "the righteousness of Christ," even though they are far from the practices and attitudes of a Christian. They do not have "the same mind in them that was in Christ Jesus," nor in any respect do they "walk just as he walked." Yet these people claim a shield that is impervious to all reprimands. In their sin, they profess to have "the righteousness of Christ."

20. Seeing so many deplorable instances of this kind makes us cautious in using these expressions. I cannot refrain from calling on all of you who frequently use these terms. I plead with you in the name of God our Savior, to whom you belong and whom you worship. Solemnly safeguard all who hear you against all pernicious abuse of this biblical language. Warn others (it may be they will hear your voice). Caution them against "continuing in sin in order that grace may abound." Warn them against making "Christ the servant of sin."

Admonish them against an empty imagination that they are accounted holy in Christ, if their profession of faith voids the solemn decree of God, "without holiness no one will see the Lord!" Caution them that if they remain unrighteous, the righteousness of Christ will profit them nothing! Cry aloud—is there not just cause? The righteousness of Christ is imputed to us for the very purpose that "the just requirement of the law might be fulfilled in us." God calls us "to live lives that are self-controlled, upright, and godly."

III. An application

It remains only to make a short and clear application. First, I address myself to you who violently oppose these expressions, "the righteousness of Christ" and "imputed righteousness." I refer to those who are swift to condemn as "Antinomians" all that use these expressions. Is this stance not bending the branch too much the other way? Why should you condemn all those who do not speak exactly as you do? Why should you quarrel with them for using the phrases they like, any more than they should quarrel with you for taking the same liberty? If others do quarrel with you about your terminology, do not imitate the bigotry for which you blame them. At the least, allow them the liberty that they ought to allow you. Why should you be angry about a way of expressing something?

You may reply, "O, the expression has been abused!" I answer, "And what expression has not been abused?" However, we may remove the abuse and continue the use. Above all, be sure to retain the important significance that is concealed in the saying. All the blessings I enjoy and all I hope for in time and eternity are given wholly and solely for the sake of what Christ has done and suffered for me.

Second, I would append a few words to you who are fond of the expressions, "the righteousness of Christ" and "imputed righteousness." Permit me to ask, "Do I not give enough liberty to you?" What more can any reasonable person desire? I acknowledge the entire meaning for which you contend—namely, that we have every blessing through the righteousness of God our Savior. A thousand times over, I consent to your using whatever wording you choose. Only guard your language against frightful abuse, which you are as deeply concerned to prevent as I am.

I myself frequently use the expression in question—"imputed righteousness." I often put this expression and similar ones into the mouth of an entire congregation. Allow me liberty of conscience in using these expressions; permit me the right of private judgment. Allow me to use an expression just as often as I consider it preferable to some other phrase. Do not become angry with me if I cannot deem it proper to repeat any particular expression every two minutes! You may do so if you please, but do not condemn me because I do not. Because of my particular choice of wording, do not depict me as a "Papist" or "an enemy to the righteousness of Christ." Be patient with me, as I am with you. How else can we "fulfill the law of Christ?" Do not create an uproar, as though I were "subverting the very foundations of Christianity." Whoever makes these charges does me much wrong. "Lord, do not hold this sin against him."

For many years, I have laid the very same gospel foundation as you have put down. Indeed, "no one can lay any foundation other than the one that has been laid; that foundation is Jesus Christ." On the foundation of Christ, by faith, I build inward and outward holiness, even as you do. Therefore, do not allow any dislike, unkindness, reserve, or coldness in your heart.

If we have a difference of opinion, where is our religion if we cannot think and let think? What impedes your forgiving me as easily as I forgive you, especially when we are only talking about a difference of wording? No, our differences are scarcely even as much as that. The controversy is only whether a particular mode of expression should be used more or less frequently. Surely, we would need to have an earnest desire to dispute with one another before we could make mere wording a bone of contention!

For such small trifles as these, let us no longer give our common enemies room to scorn the Lord! Instead, let us conclusively remove the opportunity from those who seek an opportunity to do so! Let us finally join hearts and hands in the service of our great Master (O why was it not done before?). We have "one Lord, one faith, one hope of our calling." Let us all strengthen each other's hands in God and with one heart and one mouth declare to all humankind, "The Lord is our righteousness."

Notes

1. Ward and Heitzenrater, *Wesley's Journal and Diaries*, November 24, 1765, 22:25.

2. Jackson, *Wesley's Works, Predestination Calmly Considered*, §39, 10:225.

3. Telford, *Wesley's Letters*, June 19, 1771, 5:259-60.

4. Davies, *The Methodist Societies: History, Nature, and Design*, 9:42.

5. Jackson, *Wesley's Works*, 9:513.

6. Allan Coppedge, *John Wesley in Theological Debate* (Wilmore, Ky.: Wesley Heritage Press, 1987), p. 270.

7. Thomas Oden, *John Wesley's Scriptural Christianity: A Plain Exposition of His Teaching on Christian Doctrine* (Grand Rapids: Zondervan Publishing House, 1994), pp. 206-12.

8. Athanasian Creed, § 2.

9. Athanasian Creed, § 33.

10. *Homilies*, "The Doctrine of Salvation, Faith, and Good Works," I, 7.

11. John Wesley, "The Believer's Triumph," translated from a German hymn by Zinzendorf, stanza 1, *Poet. Wks.*, I, 346.

12. *Justification by Faith*, I, § 8.

13. John Calvin, *Institutes*, I. 2, 17.

14. John Wesley, "The Believer's Triumph," translated from a German hymn by Zinzendorf, stanza 1, *Poet. Wks.*, I, 346. Also in Wesley's *Hymns and Sacred Poems*, (1740), p. 177.

15. Charles Wesley, "Hymns for Christian Friends," Hymn 14, stanza 4, *Poet. Wks.* V, 424.

16. James Hervey, *Theron and Aspasio*, 1761, Dialogue II, 1, 55.

17. Wesley's paraphrase of the Council of Antioch, A.D. 341.

Index

Abraham, 26, 32, 101, 115, 116, 241
Acton, Lord John, 9
Ad populum, 22
Adam and Eve, 62, 64, 98-100, 107, 110, 112-15, 117-19, 121, 130, 144, 209, 253
Adoption, 24, 40, 80, 104, 136, 143, 152-54, 162, 164, 165, 167, 172, 174, 176, 185, 190, 198, 199, 297, 300, 305, 309, 310, 311, 312
Agrippa, 47, 181
Aldersgate, 33, 34, 95
"Almost Christian, The," 47-60
Amalekites. 309
Ammonites, 279
Anabaptists, 10, 337
Anglican Church. *See* Church of England
Antichrist, 70
Antinomians, 219, 339
Antioch, 318, 319
Antioch, Council of, 341
Apostles, 10, 39, 82, 83, 164, 217, 267, 275, 277, 301, 305, 318
Aquinas, Thomas, 10
Arians, 337
Armor of God, 182, 226
Articles of Religion, Thirty-nine, 95, 108, 125, 136
Athanasian Creed. *See* Creeds
Atonement, 19, 37, 39, 40, 41, 101, 104, 107, 111, 116, 121, 138, 143, 324, 325, 331
Augustine, 168

Bacon, Francis, 23, 27
Baptism, 63, 265, 287, 300, 309, 310, 327

Barclay, Robert, 337
Barnabas, 318, 319
Bathsheba, 320
Bedford, 246, 247, 249
Bedfordshire, 246
Bellarmine, Cardinal Robert, 333
Bereans, the, 275
Bible, 10, 14, 18, 19, 30, 38, 49, 50, 51, 53, 70, 95, 100, 129, 131, 135, 169, 173, 177, 180, 186-88, 193, 195, 196, 200, 201, 203-05, 213, 220, 265, 266, 270, 272, 274, 275, 277, 293, 298, 318, 327
Blackstone, William, 75
Blackwell, Ebenezer, 246
Blood of Christ, 34, 39, 42, 143, 145, 238, 271, 276, 282, 302
Book of life, the, 251, 303

Calvin, John, 10, 335, 341
Cambridge, university of, 25, 184
Christ, 15, 19, 23, 24, 30, 34, 35, 38-46, 48, 49, 52, 54-57, 59, 60, 62, 64-70, 72, 75, 77, 79-85, 89-91, 94-96, 99-107, 111-13, 115-17, 121-23, 125-32, 135, 136, 138-45, 147-50, 152, 155-58, 162-68, 173, 175, 178, 180, 183, 185, 188, 192, 194, 196-99, 201, 202, 205, 208, 209, 211, 212, 214-23, 225, 226, 229-33, 235, 238-45, 248, 250-53, 256, 260, 261, 264, 265, 267-72, 274-80, 282-84, 286-90, 292, 294-96, 298, 300-5, 307-09, 311, 312, 316-19, 321, 322, 324, 325, 327, 329-40
Christian, 9, 10, 19, 20, 23-25, 27, 29, 34, 39-41, 43, 45, 47-56, 60, 64, 66,